james halliday

classic

wines

of australia
and new zealand

THIRD EDITION

james halliday

classic
wines

of australia and new zealand

THIRD EDITION

HarperCollinsPublishers

HarperCollins*Publishers*

This edition published in 2002
First published in Australia in 1997
by HarperCollins*Publishers* Pty Ltd
ABN 36 009 913 517
A member of the HarperCollins*Publishers* (Australia) Pty Limited Group
www.harpercollins.com.au

HarperCollins*Publishers*
25 Ryde Road, Pymble, Sydney NSW 2073, Australia
31 View Road, Glenfield, Auckland 10, New Zealand
77–85 Fulham Palace Road, London W6 8JB, United Kingdom
Hazelton Lanes, 55 Avenue Road, Suite 2900, Toronto, Ontario, M5R 3L2
and 1995 Markham Road, Scarborough, Ontario, M1B 5M8, Canada
10 East 53rd Street, New York NY 10022, USA

National Library of Australia Cataloguing-in-publication data:

Halliday, James, 1938–.
Classic wines of Australia and New Zealand.
3rd ed.
ISBN 0 7322 6515 0
1. Wine and wine making – Australia – Directories. 2. Wine and
wine making – New Zealand – Directories. I. Title.
641.220994

Cover photograph by Kevin Judd
Typeset by HarperCollins Design Studio in Bembo 10/12
Printed and bound in Australia by Griffin Press on 80gsm Econoprint

9 8 7 6 5 4 3 2 1
05 04 03 02

about the author

James Halliday is Australia's most respected wine writer. Over the past 30 years he has worn many hats: lawyer, winemaker and grape grower, wine judge, wine consultant, journalist and author. He has now discarded his legal hat, but actively continues his other roles, incessantly travelling, researching and tasting wines in all the major wine-producing countries. He is past Chairman of Judges at the National Wine Show, Canberra, the Royal Adelaide Wine Show and the Sydney International Wine Competition.

James Halliday has written or contributed to more than 40 books on wine and calculates he has also penned (he is still to master a computer) more than two million words for his weekly wine columns (since 1983 for the *Weekend Australian*) and magazine articles. Various of his books have been translated into Japanese, French, German, Danish and Icelandic, and have been published in the United Kingdom and the United States as well as Australia.

His most recent works include the second edition of *Wine Atlas of Australia and New Zealand*, *Collecting Wine, You and Your Cellar* and a comprehensive annual guide to individual wineries and wines, entitled *James Halliday's Australian Wine Companion*.

australia

contents

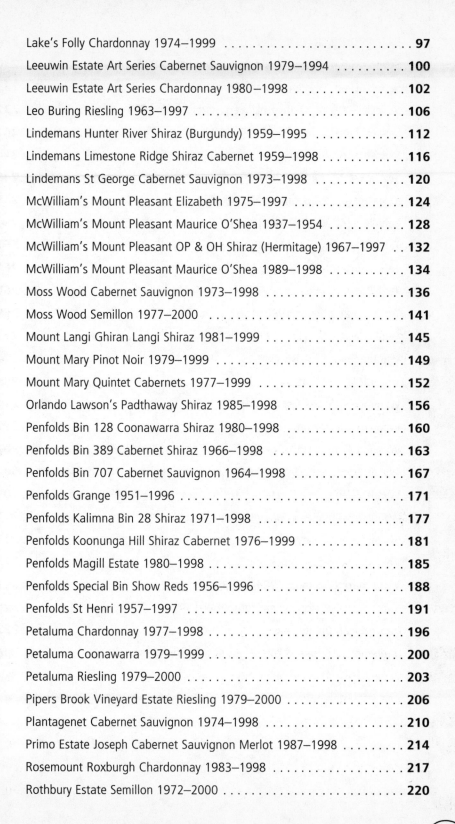

contents

key to symbols

NOT READY; leave it in the cellar

STILL EVOLVING, but drinking well

PRIME OF ITS LIFE; gloriously mature

DRINK SOON; the end is in sight

YOU MISSED THE BOAT—and the wine

★★★★★ A perfect expression of the marque

★★★★☆ Close to perfection

★★★★ A very good wine by any standard

★★★☆ What a mortal winemaker might expect

★★★ Fractionally short of the standard

★★☆ No longer deserves the label

★★ A decayed relic, probably never very good

NR No rating

introduction

the most frequently asked question of wine writers and judges are 'How can you tell whether or not this wine will be great when it is mature?' and 'When should I drink this wine?' For the uninitiated, reading the future of a wine seems even more difficult than accurately predicting the stock market or exchange rates five or ten years hence.

Historians are quick to point to that the future can be better foretold from the past than the present. The wonderful thing about wine is that it coalesces past and present in the framework of a vertical tasting — a tasting in which you open many different vintages of the same wine and taste them on the one occasion, your tongue rippling up and down the scales of time like the fingers of a pianist on the piano. To achieve this you must have a glass for each vintage, and all must be on the table at the one time — unless there are more than (say) 20 wines, in which case the tasting may be divided into sections, known technically as flights. This enables you to go backwards and forwards, smelling and tasting from young to old, old to young. (There is indeed a strong argument that the primary evaluation should progress from the oldest wine to the youngest, but that decision depends on the particular characteristics of the style of the wine and, to a degree, on the length of the span of vintages involved.)

Any wine more than a few years old will evolve as it breathes in the glass. So this alone will provide additional insights. But, more importantly, you can see ever so clearly the often magical changes which occur as a wine ages, moving from raw, perhaps slightly aggressive or abrasive adolescence to the many-splendoured perfection of maturity and then the gentle decline to fragile, almost luminous, old age.

Wine is truly a living thing and, as with life, there will be some unexpected twists along the way — some exciting, some disappointing. All are there before you in a vertical tasting; the greater the wine and the longer the timeframe, the more fascinating and rewarding is the tasting.

During the past 30 years I have been privileged to participate in many such remarkable tastings and dinners. In the early 1970s, Len Evans — then presiding over his restaurant and wine shop complex at Bulletin Place in Sydney — staged a series of vertical tasting dinners which are unlikely ever to be repeated, in this country at least. It is hard to say whether 20 vintages of Chateau Petrus, including the fabulous run of 1945, '47, '48, '49 and '53 (which made the '61 look slightly pedestrian) was better than a vertical of all the great vintages of Chateau Lafite made between 1928 and 1966. What is certain is that the most awe-inspiring were a tasting of 51 vintages of Chateau d'Yquem held in Brisbane in March 1985, spanning 1899 to 1981 and including all the famous years, and most recently (in 2001) a tasting of every vintage of Chateau Latour from 1920 to 1998.

The opportunities to stage similar tastings with Australian wines are, of course, limited. But I have been extraordinarily lucky to be in the right place at the right time on many occasions over the past 30 years. It was the realisation of this that led me to the idea of writing this book, which incorporates notes from several of the more recent of those tasting dinners, but for which I have also methodically arranged or participated in vertical tastings over the past few years.

In some instances the wines came from my own cellar, but, in even more cases, others have generously provided some or all of the wines. To thank all would be impossible, just as it would be to re-stage every tasting for each new edition of this book. So a simple thank you to all those who have helped me, and a word of warning to those who read this book. The older tasting notes and ratings must be read within the context of the tasting date, rather than today.

australia

classic wines

bannockburn pinot noir 1981-1999

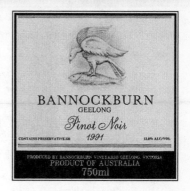

If ever the spirit of Burgundy was to breathe on an Australian winery, it would be at Bannockburn. Winemaker Gary Farr has made annual pilgrimages to Domaine Dujac in Burgundy's Morey St Denis since 1983, and became an indispensable part of owner Jacques Seysses's vintage team. But as with all Flying Winemakers, Gary Farr has received as much as he has given, and since 1984 (the first Australian vintage following his baptism at Domaine Dujac) radically changed both the viticulture and the winemaking practices at Bannockburn.

The uncompromisingly cool climate of Geelong has been recognised as ideally suited to pinot noir for over a century, the black loam over limestone soils likewise. But with the addition of a very high density planting of pinot noir (9000 vines per hectare as opposed to the Australian traditional 2000 vines) and the no-holds-barred adoption of the fermentation and maturation techniques of Domaine Dujac, Farr has added a whole new dimension to the concept of Pinot Noir in Australia.

The fermentation of 100 per cent whole bunches was unique to Bannockburn and largely responsible for the instantly recognisable style. In the past few years Gary Farr has relented a little, and crushed a proportion of the grapes in a successful quest for a little more sweet fruit flavour even if at the expense of structure and complexity.

First tasted in September 1994, updated, and later vintages added.

1999 ★★★★☆   *April 2001*
Appealing and healthy red, with none of the grey/blue tinges which sometimes bedevil Pinot. A clean, complex bouquet has plum, cherry, strawberry and spice fruit with some savoury undertones. The palate has very good balance, structure and length; the amalgam of fruit and more savoury characters is bonded by good oak handling and fine tannins. On the very brink of five stars.

1998 ★★★☆   *April 2001*
The year of the hailstorm, and sourced from all over southeast Australia. The approach worked well with Chardonnay and Shiraz, but, almost inevitably, not nearly as well with the Pinot Noir. Medium to full red, the bouquet has ripe plum, prune and sweet chocolate aromas, the flavours of the palate tracking the bouquet. Gary Farr undoubtedly made the best of a bad job.

1997 ★★★★★   *March 2000*

Medium red–purple; the aromas are exceptionally complex, savoury/foresty/plummy/oaky, but it is the palate which lifts the wine into the highest class, intense and with the ultimate peacock's tail finish.

1995 ★★★★   *October 1997*

Medium red; an undeniably complex bouquet with a mix of briary/leafy/forest aromas attesting to the high percentage of whole bunches (and hence stalks) in the fermenter. The palate continues the wholly idiosyncratic style of Bannockburn with a potent mix of briary/foresty/gamey characters over the underlying plum and cherry fruit.

1994 ★★★★☆   *May 1997*

Strong red–purple; an exceedingly complex and powerful bouquet vividly attesting to the whole-bunch maceration and fermentation techniques used. Both the bouquet and palate border on the masculine — so powerful are the foresty/stemmy notes — but there is a mass of dark, brooding pinot noir fruit to support the other characters.

1993 ★★★☆   *November 1995*

Medium red; fairly light fruit with pronounced stalky/stemmy aromas and a strong carbonic maceration influence. On the palate, the carbonic maceration influence is once again all-pervasive with stemmy/briary flavours. A technique which works best when the fruit is richest, which it was not in '93.

1992 ★★★★★   *September 1994*

Fresh red–purple of medium density, with rich plum, cherry berry fruit aromas, much more direct and sweeter than the older wines in the line-up. The palate, similarly, shows much stronger fruit, with plums and spices of various kinds, finishing with well-balanced tannins.

1991 ★★★★   *September 1994*

Somewhat lighter in colour, with fragrant spicy/cherry fruit aromas in a lighter mould than one might expect from the year. The palate is complex, with spicy cherry/stemmy fruit, finishing with soft tannins.

1990 ★★★★   *September 1994*

Medium red, with some tawny/brick hues starting to appear. The bouquet is at the sweeter end of the spectrum, of light to medium intensity with plum and cherry fruit intermingling with a touch of sappier, greener carbonic maceration spice. The palate is complex, with carbonic maceration characters still evident; while not a big-bodied wine, is still developing character.

1989 ★★★★☆   *September 1994*

A particular success for what was by and large a difficult vintage. The colour is strong, the bouquet typically complex with an amalgam of briary/stemmy/plum fruit with a hint of sweet oak. The palate is concentrated and complex, with a slightly gamey finish.

1988 ★★★★★   *September 1994*

A classic example of the Bannockburn style; a firm, concentrated bouquet with a range of aromas from earthy to stemmy to plummy fruit. The palate is holding that fruit well, with spice and tobacco flavours, and a pleasingly long finish.

1987 ★★★   *September 1994*

May have been a bad bottle (Gary Farr quite likes the wine) but showing some slightly cheesy/lactic aromas; the palate has echoes of the bouquet, with slightly fading, dusty fruit.

1986 ★★★★   *September 1994*

Medium to full red; a potent, earthy/plummy bouquet still holding some primary fruit. A substantial wine in the mouth, with similar ripe plum fruit, and lingering tannins. As with all of the wines, the oak is well balanced and integrated. •D•

1985 ★★★☆   *September 1994*

Holding its colour well, with a complex, lifted fragrant bouquet showing sappy, cedary, earthy notes. The flavours track the bouquet, with the primary fruit now gone.

1984 ★★★★   *September 1994*

Medium to full red; the richest and strongest of the older wines, with real style. The palate has an obvious whole-bunch/stem component and is holding good tannin structure. A touch of volatility does not mar the wine, which is still powerfully impressive.

1983 ★★★   *September 1994*

Distinctly less complex than the younger wines, with a firm, ripe, indeed very ripe, bouquet showing red cherry and hay aromas. Full and round in the mouth; very much the product of a warm vintage.

1982 ★★★   *September 1994*

Medium red, with some tawny hues; quite ripe, with earthy/chocolatey characters on the bouquet, and on the palate similar earthy/minty/chocolate fruit flavours which are starting to fade, and are not particularly varietal.

1981 ★★☆   *September 1994*

Light to medium brick–red in colour, with a cedary/spicy/leafy bouquet lifted by a touch of volatility. On the palate holding its texture, but the fruit is starting to fade and lose varietal character. Partially redeemed by a pleasant finish.

★★★★★ Perfect   ★★★★☆ Close to perfect   ★★★★ Very good   ★★★☆ Expected
★★★ Short of standard   ★★☆ Undeserving   ★★ Decayed relic   NR No rating

bass phillip pinot noir 1984-1997

Phillip Jones is an artist, terrorist and anarchist all rolled into one. It is thus appropriate, indeed inevitable, that he should have made Pinot Noir his Holy Grail. Since 1984 he has made a succession of ever challenging and frequently dazzling Pinots from his (now) 4-hectare estate, and the chosen few who regularly buy and taste his wines have no doubt that he produces Australia's greatest Pinots.

The early vintages were made in one- or two-barrel lots, and were bottled direct from barrel, which led to considerable bottle (or batch) variation — a practice continued up to 1988. From 1989 on, as production edged up over 600 cases a year, three wines were introduced: the Pinot Blend (there are two rows of gamay vines) at the bottom, then Pinot Noir, and the Premium at the top. But to keep even his aficionados on their toes, since 1989 Phillip Jones has intermittently kept a single (best) barrel of his Premium separate, and bottled it as Reserve, replete with the smallest label in the world: a golden version of the Bass Phillip logo, half the size of a postage stamp.

The ever-present anarchist in Phillip Jones waged war with the licensing authorities in Victoria and for all too long the wines were not sold. But happily that is all behind him (and them), and since 1991 the wines have been commercially available.

That, at least, is the theory. These wines are on a par with Giaconda as the most difficult to obtain in Australia: getting your name onto the mailing list is akin to winning the lottery.

First tasted in November 1994, updated, and later vintages added.

1997 Premium ★★★★★ *March 2000*

An exceptionally deep, almost opaque purple–red; the bouquet is extremely complex, with savoury/bacony oak woven through the lusciously ripe fruit. The same velvety richness runs through the depths of the palate, where plum intersects with spice, bacony oak and tannins. An exceptional example of the impact vintage can make on terroir, for this is way outside the mainstream style of Bass Phillip, however good the wine undoubtedly is.

1996 Reserve ★★★★★ *January 1998*

Dark red–purple; an exceptionally powerful, deep yet tightly folded bouquet, with dark plum and spice leads into a power-laden, potent dark plum, forest and briar-flavoured palate. Borders on the unappealing now, so unready is it, but time will create its own magic.

Not Ready ⟍ Still evolving ▌ Prime of its life ✎ Drink soon ⛾ Missed the boat

1995 Reserve ★★★★★   *March 1997*

Medium to full red–purple; very concentrated, with similar foresty notes to the Premium, but more oak. The palate has superb structure; silky, fine, long and complex. The cherry and plum fruit builds early, but carries right through to the back palate of outstanding length.

1994 Premium ★★★★★   *February 1997*

Medium red–purple; if anything the darkest of the trio. A stylish, and again fragrant bouquet, slightly firmer and more sappy. The palate is particularly well balanced and harmonious; between May 1996 and February 1997 the sweet fruit component seemed to increase, rather than diminish, highlighting a wonderfully silky texture.

1993 Premium ★★★★☆   *November 1994*

Medium red–purple; a fragrant, earthy bouquet, vaguely reminiscent of the '85, with well-balanced and integrated oak. Round, sweet and delicious in the mouth, with fine tannins and good acid. Excellent balance and structure, but early maturing.

1992 Premium ★★★★★   *November 1994*

Medium to full red–purple; a concentrated, youthful, complex bouquet with spicy fruit and well-integrated oak. The palate is power-packed, with cherry, strawberry and spice; fine tannins, considerable length; oak still to fully integrate. 14.2 per cent alcohol. Warm summer and sunny harvest conditions.

1992 Pinot Noir ★★★★☆   *November 1994*

Incredibly deep colour; concentrated, powerful plummy fruit aromas with a hint of lift. A total contrast to the '91 in style, with big fruit, big tannins and heaps of plummy fruit. Should develop superbly; less spicy than the '91 Pinot Noir.

1991 Premium ★★★★★   *November 1994*

Rather lighter in colour than the '92, and remarkably fresh and unevolved, with fragrant cherry and strawberry aromas. The palate is luscious with sweet cherry pip fruit. There are flavours of vanilla bean, probably from the new oak into which the wine went relatively late in its life, causing it to look awkward when first bottled. 14.5 per cent alcohol. Very ripe grapes from a warm season, but without any shrivel.

1991 Reserve ★★★★★   *November 1994*

Superb red–purple colour; an exceptional wine in every respect with intense black cherry fruit and a hint of plum. Has the sweetness and that ultimate supple, velvety structure of great Pinot, with opulent red berry and plum fruit on the mid-palate, and wonderful tannins on the finish. Needs another scale of points.

1991 Pinot Noir ★★★★   *November 1994*

Light to medium red in colour, with fairly light and faintly dusty bouquet, and spice and cherry characters gradually coming up in the glass. The palate, too, initially seemed hard, then sweet cherry stone fruit evolved.

1990 Premium ★★★☆   *November 1994*

Bright, light red; the bouquet is fragrant, but has dusty, slightly vegetal overtones. The palate is long and smooth, but lacks the richness and texture of the best wines, and generally shows lower alcohol and higher than usual yields, with harvest continuing to the end of May.

classic wines

★★	★★★ Perfect	★★★★☆ Close to perfect	★★★★ Very good	★★★☆ Expected
	★★★ Short of standard	★★☆ Undeserving	★★ Decayed relic	NR No rating

1989 Reserve ★★★★★   November 1994
Medium to full red in colour, with a powerful, complex bouquet with obvious oak input. The palate is likewise very powerful, with pronounced stemmy characters which came together and merged with sweeter berry fruit. Great power and vinosity, notwithstanding the ten days of rain before harvest.

1989 Premium ★★★★☆   November 1994
Medium red; the bouquet shows a trace of volatile lift, with spice, tobacco and ripe, dark plum aromas. The palate is rich with mouthfilling spice, plum and tobacco, with tannins adding to the texture. The tobacco/stemmy characters did become more obvious as the wine sat in the glass.

1989 Pinot Noir ★★★☆   November 1994
Served ex-magnum. Light red in colour, quite Burgundian in a lighter mould, with fragrant spicy/stalky fruit on the bouquet. The palate did not quite live up to the bouquet, being stylish but very light bodied.

1988 Pinot Noir ★★★   November 1994
Decanted three and a half hours before service, others two hours, the '85 four hours. Deep red, but seemed baggy and tired on both bouquet and palate. The palate does have ripe earthy flavours but is drying out somewhat; shows the stemmy characters from 100 per cent whole bunches and foot stamping. Cellar management problems also interfered with this vintage.

1987 Pinot Noir ★★★★★   November 1994
Good colour, with a tightly-knit bouquet showing elusive smoky/bacon aromas and some earthy/stemmy fruit. A powerful wine in the mouth, long and firm, with rich plum fruit flavours echoing Pommard; held its texture and flavour. Others in the tasting were less impressed with the wine. A cold summer with harvest in wet, sleety, freezing conditions.

1986 Pinot Noir ★★★★★   November 1994
Medium red; a complex, sappy and fragrant bouquet with sweet violets and strawberry fruit still there; also hints of earth and volatility. The palate showed all the above, but is holding well, with sweeter notes coming up progressively, and ultimately some stalky tannins. A cool growing season with relatively low sugar levels, around 12° baumé.

1985 Pinot Noir ★★★★★   November 1994
Light to medium red; incredibly youthful and extremely Burgundian, with sappy, sweet, tangy slippery aromas. An astonishing wine in the mouth, very fresh, fruity and tangy with ripe flavours sustained by 13.8 per cent alcohol. Decanted four hours before service, and showed no change over the ensuing three hours.

1984 Pinot Noir ★★★★★   November 1994
The last bottle in Phillip Jones' possession — a magnum. The colour is still marvellously deep, the bouquet profoundly complex with briar, earth, berries and violets. On the palate the primary fruit has gone, to be replaced by secondary briary/tobacco characters. Despite its age, held up remarkably in the glass.

best's great western bin 0 shiraz (hermitage) 1962-1998

best's Great Western winery and vineyards are among the best kept secrets of Australia. Indeed the vineyards, with vines dating back to 1867, have secrets which may never be revealed: for example certain vines planted in the Nursery Block have defied identification and are thought to exist nowhere else in the world. The cellars, too, go back to the same era, constructed by butcher-turned-winemaker, Joseph Best, and his family.

Since 1920, the property has been owned by the Thomson family, with father Viv and sons Ben and Bart representing the fourth and fifth generations. Shiraz, or hermitage as it has traditionally been called in this part of Victoria, has always been the most important of the red varieties, although there are very old (and significant) plantings of such exotic varieties as pinot meunier and dolcetto.

Best's Shiraz is a classic example of a wine made so as to emphasise the character of the terroir and the quality of the vintage. It is made with care but without artifice, and in particular without the distracting influence of American oak. Thus the flavours change with the vintage, sometimes spicy, sometimes minty, sometimes cherry-accented, sometimes veering towards plum.

Running throughout is the supple, fine-grained, almost silky texture and structure reflecting grapes grown in a climate which ripens them slowly but surely, and soils which neither spoil nor starve the vines. The result is a wine of great harmony and elegance.

The 1962 to 1992 vintages were tasted in November 1994; subsequent vintages on release.

1998 ★★★★☆   *February 2001*
Medium red–purple; the aromatic and intense bouquet has a mix of spice, leaf and red berry fruit, the palate likewise in the cherry spectrum with sparkles of mint and spice. A typically elegant wine.

1997 ★★★★☆   *October 1999*
Medium red–purple; the bouquet is quite fragrant, with a mix of cherry, berry and mint, the palate with fresh, lively fruit, fine acid and tannin balance, and subtle oak.

1995 ★★★★   *January 1998*
Medium to full red; there are fragrant red cherry, berry and cedar aromas on the moderately intense bouquet, followed logically by sweet red cherry fruit and silky tannins on the palate. Subtle oak treatment throughout.

classic wines

★★★★★ Perfect   ★★★★☆ Close to perfect   ★★★★ Very good   ★★★☆ Expected
★★★ Short of standard   ★★☆ Undeserving   ★★ Decayed relic   NR No rating

1994 ★★★★★ *October 1996*

Medium to full red–purple; a clean and fresh bouquet which has lots of rich and concentrated black fruit through to black and red cherry aromas, a hint of mint and subtle, sweet oak. There is perfectly ripened sweet but not jammy red cherry fruit running through the palate, even into dark plums; spotlessly clean, with harmonious but subtle oak, finishing with soft, fine tannins.

1993 ★★★★☆ *November 1994*

Filled with vibrant spice and pepper aromas and spice aromas and flavours; very lively on the palate, but not lush. It will be interesting to see how the wine develops once bottled.

1992 ★★★★★ *November 1994*

Of medium to medium-full weight, with stylish, fresh cherry and berry fruit aromas leading on to a wonderfully concentrated palate, with mouthfilling dark cherry fruit and excellent structure.

1991 ★★★★☆ *November 1994*

A deeply-coloured, concentrated and ripe wine with fragrant spice, mint and cherry fruit, finishing with nicely balanced tannins.

1990 ★★★★ *November 1994*

Surprisingly firm and closed, bordering on tough at this stage. However, has classic dark berry fruit underpinning both the bouquet and the palate, with flavours of black cherry and firm tannins.

1989 ★★★☆ *November 1994*

This was a much better vintage in Central Victoria than in many other parts of Australia; the wine shows it, with ample fresh mint and cherry fruit aromas, and plenty of stuffing on the palate. Very nearly achieved an even higher rating.

1988 ★★★★☆ *November 1994*

As with all of the wines to this point, holding its youthful red–purple hues. The bouquet is clean, with distinct bubblegum/mint aromas, but good weight and ripeness. On the palate there is plenty of extract with ripe, black cherry and mint fruit flavours, nicely balanced by soft tannins.

1987 ★★★☆ *November 1994*

A distinctly idiosyncratic wine with complex liquorice and vegetal notes to the bouquet, and a similarly multiflavoured and somewhat unusual palate, suggesting less than perfect ripeness in a cool vintage. Nonetheless, it all comes together.

1986 NR *November 1994*

A wine which appeared to be slightly corked and impossible to rate. A good vintage, and theoretically should be a very good wine.

1985 ★★★★ *November 1994*

Holding its hue well; of light to medium weight, with the still-fresh fruit of the bouquet also showing a nice touch of charry oak. A pleasantly ripe palate with attractive red cherry fruit and the silky/satiny texture of the marque.

1984 ★★★☆   *November 1994*

Again, the medium to red–purple is youthful; the bouquet is firm, with a curious liniment/mint edge. The palate is of light to medium weight, with fine mint and cherry fruit, and that typical satiny/silky texture.

1983 ★★☆   *November 1994*

An abrupt transition, partly due to age and partly to the vintage. Medium brick–red colour, with some earthy/burnt toffee characters to the bouquet. The palate is ripe, quite tannic but lacks mid-palate flesh.

1982 ★★   *November 1994*

The colour is sound, but the wine is fairly light and plain, without a great deal of either fruit or character.

1981 ★★★   *November 1994*

Reddish–brick in colour; soft, clean and ripe earth and chocolate aromas which are repeated on the palate, with a touch of mint also showing. The tannins are soft, but still present.

1980 ★★   *November 1994*

A surprisingly developed wine, with dull aspects to both colour and bouquet, generally lacking the zip and sparkle one would expect. Very possibly a poor bottle, but rated as it tasted.

1978 ★★★★   *November 1994*

The youthful red–purple colour heralds a fresh and stylish wine, with lots of complexity to the bouquet, and even a hint of oak. On the palate there is hallmark satiny red cherry fruit with light but well-balanced tannins. Very elegant.

1977 ★★★★☆   *November 1994*

Quite strong, albeit developed red colour; the bouquet is starting to show secondary Shiraz characters, almost Hunter-like, but soft and very attractive. The palate is quite unexpected after the bouquet, with quite pronounced pepper and spice fruit, good intensity and perfectly balanced tannins. Overall, quite delicious.

1976 ★★★   *November 1994*

Relatively unevolved, with clean, red berry fruit and faint minty overtones to the bouquet. The palate is something of a disappointment, showing some faintly astringent/stemmy characters, but is certainly very youthful and could conceivably improve.

1970 ★★★★   *November 1994*

A classic old-style Australian Shiraz, with a smooth but very sweet, coffee-tinged bouquet which is spotlessly clean. There is rich, sweet fruit in abundance on the palate, with chocolate and coffee flavours nicely balanced by tannins and good acidity.

1968 ★★★   *November 1994*

While predominantly Shiraz, has some Malbec (locally known as Dolcetto) in the blend. Developed red colour of medium depth; aged but sweet liquorice and earth fruit aromas lead on to a palate which starts with attractive, sweet toffee-accented fruit, lightening off somewhat on the finish.

★★★★★ Perfect   ★★★★☆ Close to perfect   ★★★★ Very good   ★★★☆ Expected
★★★ Short of standard   ★★☆ Undeserving   ★★ Decayed relic   NR No rating

classic wines

11

1967 ★★★   *November 1994*

A blend of Shiraz (predominantly) and Mataro, the latter perhaps giving the slightly herbal overtones to the bouquet and adding an edge of tannin to the palate.

1964 ★★★☆   *November 1994*

Medium to full brick–red in colour; a ripe, sweet fruit bouquet with hints of chocolate leads on to a very strongly flavoured palate, still with lots of sweet fruit, and a hint of mint, and then finishing with tannins which threaten to outlive the wine. Nonetheless, very impressive.

1962 ★★★★☆   *November 1994*

A beautiful old wine, with classic earth, chocolate and liquorice aromas which are faithfully reproduced by the palate. Still in superb condition, with fine tannins, and no obvious end to its life.

brokenwood graveyard shiraz
1983-1998

brokenwood Graveyard Shiraz has rightly claimed a place for itself as one of the Hunter Valley's — indeed Australia's — best red wines, although the label was only introduced as such in 1984. Essentially similar wines were made right from the first vintage of the winery in 1973, but the first 100 per cent Graveyard vintage was 1983.

The name comes from the fact that one of the two vineyard blocks adjacent to the winery was at one time (in the nineteenth century) dedicated — but never used — as a cemetery. Here vines with limited canopy growth and very low yields produce highly-coloured and intensely-flavoured wines. Since Iain Riggs assumed winemaking responsibilities in 1983, the style has changed to a degree, principally by virtue of later picking and the introduction of more new oak. But the essential character has remained much the same: the changes that occur with age are largely a function of the way broodingly rich and dark young Hunter Shiraz gradually softens and mellows into a wine which reflects the terroir more than most.

Vintage conditions inevitably make their mark: the Hunter Valley has an unhappy habit of dumping a substantial part of its annual rainfall just as picking commences. Sometimes conditions dry out, sometimes they do not, but it almost invariably follows that the best red wine years are those unaffected by rain — vintages such as '86, '91 and '98. But, as the notes show, even the lesser vintages age remarkably well.

First tasted in November 1994, updated, and later vintages added.

1998 ★★★★★　　　　　　　　　　　　　　　　　　　　　*October 2000*
Strong purple–red, it has pristine dark cherry varietal fruit, exemplary oak, and a hint of regional smoke on the bouquet. The palate has equal proportions of power, finesse and length; just be patient.

1995 ★★★★★　　　　　　　　　　　　　　　　　　　　　*October 1996*
Strong purple–red; a complex array of aromas running through dark fruits, mint and vanilla, with the oak well balanced and integrated. A beautifully balanced and constructed wine, with intense fruit, well-integrated oak and guaranteed to evolve superbly over the decades.

classic wines

★★★★★ Perfect　　　★★★★☆ Close to perfect　　★★★★ Very good　　★★★☆ Expected
★★★ Short of standard　　★★☆ Undeserving　　★★ Decayed relic　　NR No rating

◀■ *1994* ★★★★★   *November 1994*

Vivid purple–red; lovely plum and blackberry fruit is woven throughout sweet, spicy vanillin oak. The palate is well balanced and not the least extractive, seemingly a little lighter than the '93, perhaps due to the yield approaching one tonne to the acre.

◀■ *1993* ★★★★★   *November 1994*

Youthful purple–red; complex and concentrated fruit aromas of liquorice, game and spice dominate the bouquet. The palate is absolutely delicious, with blackberry, liquorice and spice, finely balanced tannins and very well-handled oak. Yield: 2.5 tonnes from 12 acres.

◥ *1991* ★★★★★   *November 1994*

Medium to full red–purple; a concentrated, rich and faintly gamey bouquet, still closed in on itself. The palate is powerful, rich and complex with concentrated gamey/briary/liquorice/cedary characters all evident. The tannins are well balanced; a powerhouse which will live for 30 years. Yield: less than one tonne per acre.

◥ *1990* ★★★★   *November 1994*

Medium to full purple–red; a very fragrant and lively bouquet with some lift, more fruit-driven than many of the other wines. On the palate it lacks the depth of fruit of the best vintages, but is smooth, and the tannins are well balanced. Will gain complexity with time.

◥ *1989* ★★★★★   *November 1994*

Medium to full red; the bouquet shows obvious vanillin oak influence though is still fruit-driven with liquorice, blackberry and earth aromas. The palate, too, shows the first really marked American oak influence in modern and totally seductive style, complex and sweet.

▮ *1988* ★★★★☆   *November 1994*

Medium to full red–purple; the bouquet showed quite pronounced earth and spice aromas which came up progressively, softer than the '87. The palate has complex chocolate, prune, briar and earth flavours, with an echo of spice, but is slightly tough and lacks the voluptuous sweet richness of the very best wines.

▮ *1987* ★★★★★   *November 1994*

Dense red–purple; a fruit-driven bouquet, spotlessly clean, with powerful blackcurrant and blackberry fruit. The palate is powerful yet supple with generous plum and liquorice flavours, and near-perfect tannin structure woven through the wine.

◥ *1986* ★★★★★   *November 1994*

Medium to full purple–red; the bouquet is complex, with clean but powerful sweet fruit and a hint of vanillin oak. In the mouth a superb wine with lovely plum, black cherry and sweet chocolate flavours. A classic Hunter in the making; great now but will become better and better.

◥ *1985* ★★★★☆   *November 1994*

Very good purple–red; youthful, rich and complex game and liquorice aromas, with a hint of volatility. A high-toned, potent and powerful wine on the palate with the requisite balance, but many years away from being ready.

1984 ★★★☆   *November 1994*

Medium red; the bouquet is of light to medium intensity, with complex minty/ leafy/dusty aromas. In this context, a lighter, more elegant style with cedary/briary flavours.

1983 ★★★★   *November 1994*

Medium to full red, with just a touch of purple; the bouquet is concentrated and powerful with berry, earth and briar aromas, and a hint of volatility. The palate is powerful, with berry/briary notes and powerful tannins — perhaps too powerful. A heatwave vintage with very stressed, low-yielding vines.

★★★★★ Perfect   ★★★★☆ Close to perfect   ★★★★ Very good   ★★★☆ Expected
★★★ Short of standard   ★★☆ Undeserving   ★★ Decayed relic   NR No rating

brokenwood semillon 1983-2000

brokenwood Semillon is what the renowned English winewriter Oz Clarke would call a 'New Classic'. It was first made in 1983, along with a wood-matured version. Both wines were made until 1989, when Iain Riggs took the decision — bravely but correctly — to discontinue the wooded style.

Bravely, because young, unwooded Hunter Semillon, like John Donne's lover, tends to be pale and wan. The great Semillons for which the Hunter is legendary seldom reached their peak at less than ten years of age, when they acquire a honeyed, nutty richness that utterly belies their low alcohol (between 10 per cent and 11 per cent) and the absence of any oak in fermentation or maturation.

One answer is to use oak, skin contact, highly aromatic yeasts and/or residual sugar (or any combination thereof) to give character to the young wine. The problem is that this is a fly-now, pay-later approach: such wines do not prosper with age.

Brokenwood's Semillon comes up with a different answer. It accepts the vintage conditions, and likewise the low alcohol, producing a fresh crisp wine which would have once been called Chablis. Most will be consumed in the smart restaurants of Sydney within a year of its release, but (allowing for the vagaries of the often-difficult Hunter Valley climate, and for the transition phase between youth and maturity) it can develop great character with bottle age.

Reflecting that ability, the ILR Semillon, a reserve wine, has now been introduced, and is first sold when five years old.

First tasted in November 1994, updated, and later vintages added.

2000 ★★★★★   *October 2000*
From a truly great (read dry) vintage, and tailor-made to give great enjoyment when young. Has developed nicely, if briskly, since released, starting to build an overlay of honey and toast on the herb/grass/lemon flavours of youth; plenty of mouthfeel and substance, balanced by lemony acidity on the finish.

1999 ★★★★☆   *March 2000*
Light green–yellow; a fragrant bouquet with lots of lemon grass and citrus aromas is followed by a highly flavoured, lively, zesty palate with very good acidity and length.

1998 ★★★★   *October 1998*
Light to medium yellow–green; the bouquet has good weight with some sweeter fruit notes, progressively building in flavour through to the back palate and finish. Excellent acidity and length; very much the result of a benign Hunter vintage.

◄ Not Ready ❱ Still evolving ❘ Prime of its life ⬩ Drink soon ⬜ Missed the boat

1997 ★★★★★ *October 1997*

Medium yellow–green; spotlessly clean and smooth, and a great rendition of the variety on the bouquet. The palate is perfectly balanced, with fine, delicate lemony/grassy fruit, with enough character to make it thoroughly enjoyable now, but with the capacity to age and develop beautifully.

1996 ★★★★★ *October 1996*

Light green–yellow; the bouquet is firm, crisp and tight with classic varietal character in a herbaceous mould. The palate is classically restrained and built to stay, with good balance, length and acidity. These wines require a degree of faith in their youth.

1995 ★★★★★ *October 1995*

Light green–yellow; the bouquet is fragrant with quite intense lemony/grassy/toasty fruit, leading on to a crisp and long palate with excellent varietal herbaceous fruit flavours; great now, but can only get better.

1994 ★★★★★ *November 1994*

A fragrant and clean bouquet with considerable intensity and lift; both the aromas and flavours show classic herbal/citrus characters, and the wine has the structure and length to guarantee a long future, however enjoyable it may be now. A miracle considering the searing heat (and bushfires) of early summer.

1993 ★★★ *November 1994*

The colour is bright and light, showing almost no change, but perhaps the wine is starting to go through the dumb phase of transition. There seem to be slightly burnt characters evident, apparently deriving from fermentation, although some honeyed characters are starting to appear.

1992 ★★★★ *November 1994*

Again, showing relatively little colour change, with a clean, fresh and youthful bouquet leading on to a very firm palate with lime/herbaceous notes, finishing with good grip and length. A wine which once again shows that good Semillon can come from wet Hunter vintages.

1991 ★★★ *November 1994*

Very marked colour change, into full yellow. A fast developing style with hay, straw and honey aromas and flavours. Very much the product of a hot, dry vintage.

1990 ★★★☆ *November 1994*

Some bottle variation evident; an interesting, complex wine with characters outside the mainstream, and some of the bottles showing intriguing 'dirty French' characters, no doubt deriving from the botrytis which developed on the crop.

1989 ★★★★☆ *November 1994*

Medium to full yellow, marginally more developed than the '90. Classic developed Hunter bouquet, with intense honey and herb aromas. Lovely balance and mouthfeel, with some botrytis influence adding to, rather than diminishing, its appeal.

1988 NR *November 1994*

Cork problems bedevilled this vintage, and both bottles tasted were affected, although the underlying fruit and structure seemed to be good. Not possible to rate.

classic wines

★★★★★ Perfect   ★★★★☆ Close to perfect   ★★★★ Very good   ★★★☆ Expected
★★★ Short of standard   ★★☆ Undeserving   ★★ Decayed relic   NR No rating

17

1987 ★★★★☆   *November 1994*

Medium to full yellow, with clean, smooth and rich honey and nut bouquet.
A wine which is ageing gracefully, with complex honey and citrus flavours and
nice mouthfeel.

1986 ★★★★★   *November 1994*

Full yellow colour, with lifted toasty aromas and a most attractive, developed toasty
palate, finishing with good acidity and freshness. Volatility is apparent in the wine,
but in no way harms it. The product of a great vintage.

1985 ★★★★★   *November 1994*

Bright yellow, with marvellous fruit on the aroma still showing citrussy/lemony
aromas. A far more elegant wine than the surrounding vintages, crisp, light and
fresh, with a long finish, and an indefinite life in front of it. Another excellent
growing season.

1984 ★★☆   *November 1994*

Deep yellow colour; tending rather broad and blowsy on the bouquet with honey
and tobacco aromas and obvious botrytis influence, leading on to a palate in which
the phenolics are starting to break up somewhat.

1983 ★★★☆   *November 1994*

Medium to full yellow; rich honey, hay and straw aromas lead to a wine which has
lots of mid-palate weight, in part thanks to the high alcohol. Came up in the glass,
although overall it is showing some signs of drying out.

cape mentelle cabernet sauvignon 1976-1996

Successive Jimmy Watson Trophies awarded to Cape Mentelle's '82 and '83 Cabernet Sauvignons brought lasting fame to the winery and, of course, to David Hohnen. Yet, against the odds he found that these massively constructed wines, with their high levels of extract and tannins, were extremely difficult to sell. So in 1984 he made what he describes as a low pH, Croser-style red (which didn't work either), and then in the second half of the 1980s deliberately lightened off the style.

Various techniques were used, including the incorporation (since 1985) of around 5 per cent Merlot, and the installation of irrigation in 1988 — aimed not at increasing the yield, but at reducing stress, increasing fruit sweetness and reducing tannins. Both these initiatives have worked and are an important part of today's mix; one or two other experiments did not work so well, and have been discontinued.

The next significant change came in 1990 with the introduction of more new French oak (courtesy of new French money provided by newly introduced majority owner Veuve Clicquot). Someone else's money perhaps, but Hohnen is not given to extravagance, and no one could accuse the wine of being over-oaked. The fruit focus was switched back to the home vineyard, and (cautiously) the wine has been given more weight.

These changes have brought a sea change in the style and character of what was always a very good wine, but which is now more than that. Between 2000 and 2500 cases of wine are made from a 5-hectare vineyard block (now 30 years old), and the quality and consistency of the wines from the 1990s vintages is beyond reproach. Even the ever self-critical David Hohnen is prepared to say 'I think we are getting there'.

First tasted in October 1995, updated, and later vintages added.

1996 ★★★★   *October 2000*

Medium red–purple; obvious bottle development has led to secondary aromas in a sweet yet savoury mix of chocolate, berry and vanilla. The palate flows directly from the bouquet; here, too, gently sweet oak helps.

1995 ★★★★☆   *March 1999*

Medium to full red–purple; a bouquet with uncommon depth and complexity, and a range of secondary earthy/cedary/berry characters already starting to appear. A wine with similarly good structure and depth to the palate, although the flavours are tending more towards the savoury end of the spectrum than the opulently fruity.

classic wines

| ★★★★★ Perfect | ★★★★☆ Close to perfect | ★★★★ Very good | ★★★☆ Expected |
| ★★★ Short of standard | ★★☆ Undeserving | ★★ Decayed relic | NR No rating |

19

1994 ★★★★★   *February 1998*

Medium to full red–purple; the bouquet is clean, of medium intensity with perfectly blended blackberry/cassis fruit and cedary oak. The palate provides more of the same, with a harmonious blend of cassis, blackberry and cedar, finishing with soft, lingering tannins.

1993 ★★★★★   *July 1997*

Dense red–purple; the bouquet is rich and full with attractive dark chocolate and blackberry fruit aromas supported by subtle oak. A powerful and concentrated wine on the palate with briary, dark chocolate and blackberry fruit, with that touch of astringency of Cabernet Sauvignon. The tannins are persistent but fine.

1992 ★★★★☆   *October 1995*

Strong red–purple; a powerful and complex array of earthy/cedary/minty aromas with just a faint hint of greener/more gamey characters on the bouquet. A smooth, rounded wine in the mouth, with an array of flavours running through mint, redcurrant and sweet vanilla. Well weighted tannins.

1991 ★★★★★   *October 1995*

A strong, still youthful purple–red colour; the bouquet is more powerful, concentrated and even riper than the '90, with rich, dark berry/dark chocolate fruit. A concentrated and powerful palate which is a superior version of the '83. Ripe red and black berry flavours intermingle with dark chocolate, with persistent but balanced tannins giving a pleasantly chewy texture. The oak influence, too, seems more obvious than in the older wines, but not oppressively so.

1990 ★★★★★   *October 1995*

Medium to full red–purple; a clean bouquet of medium to full intensity, with perfectly ripened blackcurrant/blackberry fruit married with subtle oak. The spotlessly clean palate shows precisely ripened cabernet, almost lush; smooth, round and mouthfilling, with blackcurrant fruit surrounded by soft tannins.

1989 ★★★☆   *October 1995*

Medium to full red, with just a touch of purple; the bouquet is clean, but slightly diffuse, with red berry, vanilla and a faint hint of mint; the palate is soft and ripe, with an unusual combination of prune and mint flavours, finishing with soft tannins. Not particularly concentrated.

1988 ★★★   *October 1995*

Medium to full red, with a touch of purple; the bouquet is of light to medium intensity, elegant and cedary, though not particularly fruity. There is an array of flavours on the palate, with hints of chocolate; quite sweet overall, with soft tannins, although shows the diluting effect of rain on an otherwise ripe crop.

1987 ★★★   *October 1995*

Medium to full red–purple, quite strong; the bouquet is relatively subdued, tending astringent/barky, with gravelly notes predominating over berry fruit. A quite powerful wine on the palate with length, but again tending to be barky/earthy, and the tannins looking likely to outlive the fruit.

◄ Not Ready   ▼ Still evolving   ▮ Prime of its life   ✍ Drink soon   ▯ Missed the boat

1986 ★★★★☆   *October 1995*

Red–purple, but much less dense than the younger vintages; a compellingly complex bouquet with fragrant fruit and cedar aromas, showing perfect fruit ripeness, although now developing secondary characters. An elegant palate with near-perfect balance and structure; cedary, with hints of blackcurrant and finishing with fine tannins. The product of an excellent vintage.

1985 ★★☆   *October 1995*

Medium red; a much lighter bouquet than the older wines with herbal/minty notes. The palate shows distinctly underripe leafy/minty flavours, finishing with soft tannins. A very cold vintage in which the fruit did not reach full ripeness.

1984 ★★★☆   *October 1995*

Dark red, still retaining some purple hues; an elegant bouquet with cedary notes, and some Bordeaux-like aromas reminiscent of the '80. A firm, youthful and relatively unevolved wine compared to the others, but lacks their mouthfeel and complexity. There are red berry fruit flavours, but all in all, the wine shows the effects of an excessively low pH.

1983 ★★★★☆   *October 1995*

Dark red, still with hints of purple, surprising and impressive; the bouquet is complex, with dark chocolate and slightly stewed prune fruit characters, together with a hint of gaminess. The palate is distinctly ripe and sweet, with prune and blackberry fruits, that touch of gaminess appearing, and ample tannins. A difficult, hot vintage.

1982 ★★★★   *October 1995*

Dark red; quite fragrant fruit aromas with pronounced herbaceous/minty overtones; the palate is quite striking, with minty/piney/herbaceous fruit flavours and appropriately balanced tannins. Very much the product of an unusually cool vintage.

1981 ★★★   *October 1995*

Dark red; a concentrated bouquet, though significantly less aromatic than many of the older wines. A firm, concentrated palate with briary/woody characters and tannins which run right through the wine, threatening to overwhelm it. A tiny crop, and always tannic.

1980 ★★★   *October 1995*

Dark red tending to brick; an austere bouquet with touches of earth and gravel, together with more cedary notes, in some ways recalling Bordeaux. A fairly dry and tough wine, lacking sweet fruit on the mid-palate, and once again with tannins to the fore. A hot vintage.

1979 ★★★   *October 1995*

Dark red; a complex bouquet with faintly astringent petrol/earthy notes, perhaps a residue from sulphide. On the palate, drying out slightly, with earthy notes and abundant tannins; the flavours are of bitter chocolate, but are not excessively astringent.

classic wines

★★★★★ Perfect	★★★★☆ Close to perfect	★★★★ Very good	★★★☆ Expected
★★★ Short of standard	★★☆ Undeserving	★★ Decayed relic	NR No rating

1978 ★★★★☆   *October 1995*

Red–brown of medium depth; a much riper wine with complex, powerful fruit aromas tending to bitter chocolate on the bouquet. The palate is still very rich, with masses of ripe fruit running the gamut through cedar, dark chocolate and prune, finishing with good tannins. The first vintage utilising French oak.

1977 ★★★   *October 1995*

Quite brown; distinctly herbaceous cool-grown cabernet aromas, much less ripe than either the '76 or '78. The palate precisely tracks the bouquet with more of those herbaceous cabernet flavours balanced by tannins and a hint of sweet vanillin oak.

1976 ★★★★   *October 1995*

Quite brown in colour; the bouquet is still fragrant with hints of coffee and mint, and distinctly sweet. Holding those smooth, chocolate and mint fruit flavours on the palate, although the tannins are starting to soften right out. Matured in American oak and made by John Kosovich in the Swan Valley.

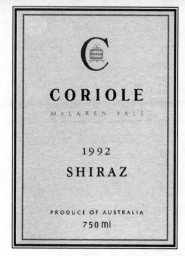

When Dr Hugh Lloyd embarked on a search for land in McLaren Vale in the mid-1960s he did so with the intention of growing almond trees, not vines. The discovery of an old, dilapidated winery called Chateau Bon Santé and 8 hectares of 60-year-old vines of various types led to a change of plan and the establishment of Coriole in 1967.

The winery has been rebuilt, and the vineyards much expanded, including one of Australia's few plantings of sangiovese. But it is Shiraz for which Coriole is best known, with the core of the wine coming from the old vines, now over 100 years old.

Both the original and the subsequent plantings of shiraz are on red loam over an ironstone or limestone subsoil, and produce some of the finest grapes to come from McLaren Vale. Up to 1989 the grapes from the 1.3 hectares of old shiraz vines were incorporated into the Shiraz made by Coriole. In that year a decision was taken to keep the material separate, and since then the 4 to 4.5 tonnes has produced the eagerly sought-after Lloyd Reserve, all 250 cases of it.

By this time the 'new' plantings were over 20 years old, so it cannot be said the standard wine has suffered in any way — as the tasting notes clearly show.

First tasted in March 1996, updated, and later vintages added.

1997 ★★★★★ October 2000
Medium to full red; the bouquet is sweet and smooth, with delicious dark berry/cherry fruit, some spice and subtle oak. An elegantly framed and built palate, with a mix of dark cherry and more savoury flavours finishes with fine-grained tannins. It carries its 14° alcohol easily.

1996 ★★★★★ March 1999
Dark, dense red–purple; the bouquet offers a quite incredible essence of McLaren Vale chocolate, utterly delicious. The palate is likewise packed with dark Swiss chocolate, dark cherry, a hint of vanilla oak and long, lingering tannins.

1995 ★★★★★ January 1998
Dark red–purple; the bouquet is powerful and concentrated, with dark berry/foresty fruits and subtle oak; the palate shows the same dark cherry and regional bitter chocolate flavours, with quite pronounced tannins and high total extract. Bred to stay.

classic wines

★★★★★ Perfect	★★★★☆ Close to perfect	★★★★ Very good	★★★☆ Expected
★★★ Short of standard	★★☆ Undeserving	★★ Decayed relic	NR No rating

1994 ★★★★★ *December 1996*

Dense red–purple; a full, deep and concentrated bouquet with dark plum fruit and subtle oak. Concentrated and rich, with dark plum and black cherry fruit; the tannins run through the palate, and together with the fruit, have literally swallowed up the oak.

1992 ★★★★★ *March 1996*

Full red–purple, with clean, rich, ripe pepper-spice-black cherry aromas. In the mouth, full-bodied, potent and powerful with lots of fruit and well-structured tannins.

1991 ★★★★☆ *March 1996*

Medium to purple–red colour, with a spotlessly clean bouquet showing most attractive sweet, ripe dark cherry and blood plum aromas. The palate is well balanced and harmonious, with the oak better handled than in the 1990 wine; beautifully ripened dark berry fruits and fine tannins.

1990 Reserve ★★★★★ *March 1996*

Bright purple–red; a clean, smooth and harmonious bouquet, less concentrated than the '89 Reserve. The palate is elegant, with dark cherry/chocolate fruit and fine tannins, with distinctly more concentration than the standard release of the year.

1990 ★★★★ *March 1996*

The colour is bright, and the bouquet firm and clean, with dark chocolate, berry and cherry fruit aromas intermingling. In the mouth there is a cunning touch of spicy American oak evident in thoroughly modern style; a fraction less assertive use of the oak might have produced an even better wine.

1989 Reserve ★★★★★ *March 1996*

Superb deep colour, with intensely concentrated briary/sweet fruit aromas and exceptionally complex multiflavoured palate. The tannins start early and run throughout, giving great structure. All the good features of the standard wine multiplied and focused.

1989 ★★★☆ *March 1996*

A strongly-coloured wine with earthy edges to the bouquet lending a touch of austerity. The palate has plenty of fruit weight with hints of dark chocolate, and well-balanced tannins.

1988 ★★★★☆ *March 1996*

Clean, firm and youthful with dark cherry and chocolate aromas, and latent earthy characters underneath. The palate is firm, elegant and fresh, with impeccable structure and very good balancing acidity on the finish.

1987 ★★★ *March 1996*

A wine which changed considerably in the glass, showing a youthful colour throughout, but with an edge of volatility and barnyard giving way to earthy, ripe fruit characters as it breathed. Errant characters reappeared on the complex palate which had plenty of structure and extract, but just a hint of bitterness. Conceivably, a slightly corked bottle.

◄ Not Ready ❭ Still evolving Ꙭ Prime of its life ◢ Drink soon ◻ Missed the boat

1986 ★★   *March 1996*

Medium to full red colour, but marred by pronounced lactic/bacterial characters on the bouquet. The flavours are more attractive, with dark chocolate fruit and good tannin balance.

1984 ★★★★★   *March 1996*

Exceptionally good colour, still retaining some purple hues. The bouquet is both positive and fresh, with lifted chocolate fruit complexed by oak. The palate is beautifully balanced with archetypal bitter chocolate fruit flavours, fine structure and fine tannins. A classic.

1983 ★★★   *March 1996*

A solid wine, somewhat closed in on itself with background hints of earth to the bouquet. In the mouth a big wine, having a rather hard shell around dark cherry fruits, and a firm finish.

1980 ★★★☆   *March 1996*

Rich, redolent of McLaren Vale chocolate overtones to warm, sweet fruit; also hints of vanilla in the bouquet. An altogether strong wine with substantial tannin impact in the mouth, and although it has a long future, will not achieve the balance of the best of the wines in the line-up.

1977 ★★★   *March 1996*

Medium red colour, with a pleasantly aged, soft, gently earthy aroma which harks directly back to the '70. The palate is likewise fully aged with earthy/bitter chocolate flavours and fine tannins.

1976 ★★★☆   *March 1996*

Strong red in colour with plenty of depth; the bouquet is very ripe, with lifted, earthy aromas. The palate shows sensitively extracted, soft, fine tannins which are the hallmark of the better wines in the line-up and which will sustain it for some years to come.

1974 ★★★★   *March 1996*

Remarkable colour density for a very poor vintage, and likewise amazing fruit to the bouquet with traces of liquorice and hints of brandysnap. Rich and complex in the mouth, with plenty of fruit weight still present, and again some of those brandysnap characters. Well-balanced tannins.

1972 ★★   *March 1996*

Light brick–red in colour, with aged, faintly gamey/lactic aromas; fading on the palate, again with suggestions of a touch of bacterial spoilage.

1971 ★★★   *March 1996*

Brick–red, and of medium weight, but with evidence of volatility running through both bouquet and palate. There are hints of earth, regional dark chocolate and the remnants of a wine which was once much better.

1970 ★★★★   *March 1996*

The colour is still bright, though tending brick; there is fragrant, gently ripe sweet fruit with pleasant hints of earth. The palate is holding its structure with soft, fine tannins, but the fruit has softened to the point where it is simply a lovely old wine, which could come from literally anywhere or be made from any grape variety.

★★★★★ Perfect   ★★★★☆ Close to perfect   ★★★★ Very good   ★★★☆ Expected
★★★ Short of standard   ★★☆ Undeserving   ★★ Decayed relic   NR No rating

classic wines

craiglee shiraz 1979-1999

Craiglee is one of the great historic wineries of the nineteenth century, established at Sunbury by J S Johnston in 1864. It was Johnston who produced the 1872 Craiglee Sunbury Hermitage, a cache of which was found buried in the winery in the late 1950s by the late Tom Seabrook. I have shared in several bottles of that wine, the best ethereal but utterly remarkable for its freshness.

It was the tasting of one of the bottles in 1972 which prompted the Carmody family (who had acquired the property from the Johnstons in 1961) to investigate the feasibility of re-establishing the vineyard, which had gone out of production in the late 1920s. It was Murray Clayton, then Victorian State Government viticulturist, who advised the Carmodys to take heed of the lessons of the nineteenth century, and to plant the then unfashionable shiraz rather than the in-vogue cabernet sauvignon.

Son Pat Carmody began his studies in wine science at the Riverina College of Advanced Education (now Charles Sturt University) in 1974, and plantings began in 1976, the first tiny vintage in 1979.

Carmody reckons the vines first started to come into balance in 1984, and it is clear the quality of the wine took a giant leap forwards from that time on — but with typical modesty, and without defensive apologies, he presented every vintage at a retrospective tasting held at the winery on 25 July 1997.

It was held in the historic two-storey bluestone winery in which Johnston made his wine, but in which (thanks to the public guardians of our health) Carmody cannot do likewise. It does, however, serve as one of the most atmospheric cellar-door sales facilities to be found anywhere in Australia — a mere 15 minutes drive north from Tullamarine Airport.

The inevitable question is whether wines such as the 1991 and 1994 will live as long as the 1872. Well, the 1872 was made from vines which were only eight years old, and from grapes picked at under 20° brix, producing a wine with only 10 degrees alcohol.

First tasted in November 1994, updated, and later vintages added.

1999 ★★★★   *May 2001*

Medium red–purple, starting to show some signs of colour shift. The bouquet has very pronounced white pepper/spice aromatics, the palate again very spicy, but with infinitely less body and extract than the 1998. Will develop quickly; this was a pretty ordinary vintage for much of southern Victoria.

◀━ Not Ready   ◥ Still evolving   ▮ Prime of its life   ✐ Drink soon   ⬙ Missed the boat

1998 ★★★★★   *May 2001*

Medium to full red–purple; the bouquet is redolent of dark plums, spice being little more than a background whisper. A luscious, round palate offering a mix of ripe plum and sweet cherry moves through to a soft tannin finish. The oak handling cannot be faulted. It's not often that Craiglee Shiraz reaches 14° alcohol, but it did in this great vintage.

1997 ★★★★★   *May 1999*

Medium to full purple–red; a clean and powerful bouquet with classic black cherry and spice aromas; a lovely wine on the palate, with black cherry fruit together with hints of spice and liquorice; fine tannins and subtle oak.

1996 ★★★★☆   *October 1998*

The colour is not nearly as deep as one might expect, and the bouquet, too, is relatively light, albeit with attractive cherry spice fruit and a hint of charry oak. All of this leaves one unprepared for the marvellous flavour of the palate, with intense spice and cherry fruit, looking for all the world like a high-quality, lighter-year Northern Rhône Valley red.

1995 ★★★☆   *July 1997*

Medium purple–red; the bouquet is light, with ever so slightly squashy berry aromas. A lighter style wine on the palate, with earthy notes, and lacking the richness and concentration of the best years.

1994 ★★★★★   *July 1997*

Strong red–purple colour; a powerful bouquet with a classic mix of spice, liquorice, black cherry and berry introduces a long and classically flavoured and constructed palate. Sweet, fine tannins are woven through strongly varietal black cherry and spice fruit.

1993 ★★★★☆   *July 1997*

Still holding primary purple–red hues; a powerful and potent bouquet, quite different from any of the wines in the line-up, with an almost resiny overtone to spicy fruit. The palate is vibrant, with a mix of peppery/spicy and cigar box flavours and textures. Trembled on the brink of top rating.

1992 ★★★★☆   *July 1997*

Strong purple–red; the bouquet is of medium intensity, with red and black cherry tinged with earth and spice aromas, starting to show the first signs of evolution. The palate has those soft sweet tannins which are the mark of Craiglee, but the alcohol is a little on the high side and arguably out of balance with the fruit, reminiscent in some ways of the '85. Nonetheless, a flavoursome mouthful.

1991 ★★★★★   *July 1997*

Medium to full purple–red; a ripe, opulent and concentrated bouquet with spice, black cherry and black fruit aromas followed by a wonderfully concentrated and ripe palate; black fruit and cherry flavours intermingle with spice and lingering tannins. Very much in the style of a top Rhône Valley red.

classic wines

★★★★★ Perfect	★★★★☆ Close to perfect	★★★★ Very good	★★★☆ Expected
★★★ Short of standard	★★☆ Undeserving	★★ Decayed relic	NR No rating

1990 ★★★★☆ *July 1997*

Still holding strong red–purple colour; the bouquet is clean, firm and fresh, with black cherry/blackberry and spice fruit. A very powerful wine on the palate, with significantly higher tannins than most in the line-up. A multiple trophy winner from an ideal vintage that in 1997 was undergoing the transition from young to mature wine.

1989 ★★★★ *July 1997*

The colour is starting to show some shift from purple to red; there are quite complex black cherry fruit aromas, tinged with earthy notes that also appear on the palate. Here some earthy/forest floor bottle-developed characters are starting to come through, held together by a reasonably firm tannin grip on the finish.

1988 ★★★★★ *July 1997*

Medium red–purple; a mix of aromas ranging from black cherry to slightly gamey (but pleasantly so) and soft vanillin oak lead into a many-flavoured wine with abundant sweet, ripe fruit. The winner of 15 silver medals, but never a gold, it is Pat Carmody's favourite vintage.

1987 ★★★★ *July 1997*

Medium red–purple; there is a full array of aromas running through game, liquorice and boot polish, all slightly feral. There are similar flavours on the palate, which has a slightly tart finish. A challenging wine, but not without appeal.

1986 ★★★★★ *July 1997*

Medium red–purple; the bouquet is firm, with a mix of game and liquorice; the palate is seriously complex, with a marvellous array of game, spice and liquorice flavours which have grip and length, yet are without aggression.

1985 ★★★★ *July 1997*

Medium to full red; the bouquet is rich, ripe and full of character, with a mix of black cherry and plum fruit. The palate is fine, with soft sweet tannins, and a European feel to it. The product of a very ripe year, and a trophy winner at the National Wine Show in Canberra.

1984 ★★★★ *July 1997*

Medium red; a clean, fresh and still relatively firm bouquet, which seems to hide the spice and black cherry fruit flavours that emerge immediately the wine enters the mouth. Delicate, but holding well, with fine tannins. A year in which, according to Pat Carmody, the vines started to come into balance, but a wine that was expected to last only two or three years when made.

1983 ★★☆ *July 1997*

Medium red; a rather off-putting nose with residue of the aspergillus rot which affected the vineyard that year. The palate is somewhat better, with hints of spice, and not overwhelmed by the mushroomy mould of the bouquet.

1982 ★★☆ *July 1997*

Very light rosé colour; an extremely attenuated bouquet leads on to an earthy palate with relatively little flavour. Carmody was using heading down boards to reduce extraction, as recommended by his teachers at (what is now) Charles Sturt University.

➡ Not Ready   ❯ Still evolving   🍾 Prime of its life   ⌀ Drink soon   🍶 Missed the boat

1981 ★★★ *July 1997*

Light to medium red; the bouquet is quite aged, but light and clean; there is distinctly more fruit and grip than the 1980 wine with some distinctly ripe cherry flavours, but no spice.

1980 ★★★ *July 1997*

Medium red, with a hint of tawny on the rim; the bouquet is of light to medium intensity, faintly earthy, and leads on to a light palate, almost a cross between Pinot Noir and Shiraz, with the tannins largely gone. Only 200 cases made.

1979 ★★ *July 1997*

Gas in the glass is evidence of a continuing malolactic fermentation in bottle; there are light touches of strawberry on the bouquet with some sweet, slightly caramelised flavours. Only 15 cases made, and most of the bottles exploded due to the malolactic fermentation.

★★★★★ Perfect   ★★★★☆ Close to perfect   ★★★★ Very good   ★★★☆ Expected

★★★ Short of standard   ★★☆ Undeserving   ★★ Decayed relic   NR No rating

cullen cabernet sauvignon
merlot 1977-1999

the anchors for this wine have been the 15 hectares of cabernet sauvignon, merlot and cabernet franc (which account for half the total Cullen estate plantings) and the continuous involvement of the Cullen family as winemakers: the late Dr Kevin Cullen, wife Diana, son-in-law Michael Peterkin (peripherally) and now daughter Vanya.

But there have also been changes. Some have been simple responses to vineyard conditions: while the blend is Cabernet Sauvignon-dominant, with Merlot and a little Cabernet Franc, it has varied in some years. More importantly, perhaps, was the introduction of the Scott-Henry trellis system at the end of the 1980s, resulting in grapes with better (i.e. lower) pH, colour and flavour. The impact on the wines from 1990 and onwards has been very obvious.

There has also been the expected ongoing challenge to make a better wine year by year. Between 1988 and 1994 inclusive a Reserve wine made its appearance, but has now been discontinued — a simple statement that all of the wine bottled under the Cullen Cabernet Merlot label is a good as it comes. So it is that the style has remained commendably stable: notwithstanding two years barrel ageing in French oak, these wines have tremendous structure and (at times) formidable tannins, resulting in a long-lived style.

It is the tannin structure of the wines of the 1990s which is so impressive relative to the earlier wines: the tannins are still present, but are softer and rounder, and will not threaten the balance of the wines as they do in some of the older vintages. Just as Leeuwin Estate makes the best Australian Chardonnay, so does Cullen make the best Cabernet Merlot.

First tasted in October 1994, updated, and later vintages added.

◀ *1999* ★★★★★   *April 2001*

Dense, deep, almost impenetrable red–purple; powerful, deep, dark blackberry and cassis fruit lead to the bouquet, the oak submerged in that fruit. The palate has tremendous depth and concentration, with a mix of blackberry, spice and cassis; the Cullen tannins are there aplenty, but in balance. An outstanding wine from an outstanding vintage, which really needs a sixth star to do it full justice.

◀ Not Ready   \ Still evolving   ▮ Prime of its life   ✓ Drink soon   ▯ Missed the boat

1998 ★★★★★ *March 2000*

Dense red–purple; the spotlessly clean, smooth bouquet is flooded with wonderfully rich cassis fruit; an imperious wine on the palate, with layer upon layer of fruit woven through with ripe tannins and oak.

1997 ★★★★★ *March 1999*

Medium to full red–purple; powerful, but perfectly balanced, dark berry fruit and oak on the bouquet is logically followed by a palate with great depth to the dark berry fruit, lingering but balanced tannins, and exemplary oak.

1996 ★★★★★ *October 1998*

Excellent, strong purple–red colour; the bouquet shows perfectly ripened fruit woven through with sweet, cedary oak; a beautifully balanced and structured palate with classic cassis fruit and fine, lingering tannins.

1995 ★★★★★ *January 1997*

Full red–purple; proclaims its class from the first second, with dark berry, dark chocolate and cedar oak skilfully interwoven; the palate is as concentrated as the bouquet promises with ripe, luscious fruit in a dark berry spectrum, perfectly balanced and integrated oak, and equally perfectly judged and controlled tannins.

1994 ★★★★☆ *October 1996*

Dense red–purple; in typical Cullen style, concentrated full and ripe with masses of blackcurrant fruit leading the bouquet; a massively concentrated and fairly tannic wine on the palate, although the oak has been held nicely in restraint. Simply needs a decade to open up.

1993 ★★★★☆ *October 1995*

Medium red–purple; a powerful and fragrant bouquet of medium to full intensity with cigar box oak and dark berry fruit. An intense yet finely structured wine, showing more of those cigar box flavours on the palate (together with fruit), finishing with persistent tannins.

1992 ★★★★★ *October 1994*

Dense impenetrable purple; a fine and clean, yet concentrated bouquet with perfectly ripened fruit and subtle oak. The palate is similarly concentrated yet fine, with supple tannins running through dark red berry fruit (and echoes of dark chocolate and mint), giving the wine great structure and length.

1991 ★★★★☆ *October 1994*

Medium to full red–purple; a ripe bouquet, almost luscious, with hints of dark chocolate and prune. Similar ripe flavours are evident on the palate with concentrated dark berry, plum and prune flavours, with sweet vanillin oak, rounded off by well-balanced, soft tannins on a long finish.

1990 ★★★★★ *October 1994*

Medium to full red–purple; the bouquet is solid, ripe and dense, with cassis, redcurrant and earth aromas. The wine is starting to open out on the palate, with softly luscious cassis/red berry fruit finishing with perfectly balanced tannins. The oak influence is evident but restrained.

classic wines

★★★★★ Perfect   ★★★★☆ Close to perfect   ★★★★ Very good   ★★★☆ Expected
★★★ Short of standard   ★★☆ Undeserving   ★★ Decayed relic   NR No rating

1989 ★★☆   *October 1994*

Medium red–purple; a rather astringent bouquet with soapy/gravelly aromas which follow through on to a tough, and again slightly soapy palate, reflecting a difficult growing season and seemingly high pH.

1988 ★★★☆   *October 1994*

Medium to full red–purple; slightly unusual aromas with overtones of coffee and caramel, as well as more typical earthy notes, and a touch of volatile lift. The palate likewise shows some of the caramel/toffee characters (possibly from oak) with some more conventional dark chocolate flavours, a tweak of volatility, followed by hallmark tannins on the finish.

1986 ★★★★★   *October 1994*

Medium to full red–purple; a clean, fresh bouquet with lots of red berry/cassis fruit and dusty oak. A wine in the mainstream of the style, almost a fulcrum between the old and the new, with nicely balanced fruit and tannins, promising to develop like the '77 and become more Bordeaux-like.

1985 ★★★★   *October 1994*

Medium to full red–purple; a quite fragrant bouquet with cassis fruit aromas along with some regional earth characters and faintly dusty oak. The palate is firm, with pronounced tannins; the wine has lots of character, but one wonders whether the tannins will outlive the fruit.

1984 ★★★★☆   *October 1994*

Medium to full red; the bouquet is much smoother and riper than the older vintages, showing some new oak influence. The palate is powerful and concentrated, with good dark berry fruit and abundant but well-balanced tannins.

1983 ★★★☆   *October 1994*

Medium red; a lifted fragrant bouquet of light to medium intensity with earth and berry aromas. The palate is relatively sweet and ripe, with some dark chocolate flavours, reminiscent of the '81 in style; thins out on the back palate, finishing with firm acid.

1982 ★★★★   *October 1994*

Medium to full red; somewhat earthy astringent aromas, with chocolate running through on the first impression, though opened up into more soft, fragrant characters with breathing. The palate shows strong cedary/cigar box/briary/earthy flavours which are attractive, but there is a question mark over the tannins, which are on the firm side.

1981 ★★★☆   *October 1994*

Medium to full red; a firm bouquet with some minty characters of medium intensity. The palate is distinctly firm, lacking fruit flesh, and finishing with pronounced acidity and tannins.

1977 ★★★★★   *October 1994*

Medium red; a fragrant, lifted bouquet with sweet earth, leaf and berry aromas, all strongly reminiscent of an aged Bordeaux. A lovely, mature wine on the palate, still holding lots of sweet berry and chocolate fruit on the mid-palate, finishing with soft tannins. Has never undergone malolactic fermentation.

━ Not Ready   ＼ Still evolving   ▮ Prime of its life   ⌀ Drink soon   ⎕ Missed the boat

Wheels have a habit of turning full circle; certainly the d'Arenberg wheel has done so. For the first 60 years, the Osborn family was content to grow grapes and then (from 1928) sell all the wine in bulk. It was not until the early 1960s that the first wine was sold in bottles bearing the distinctive diagonal red stripe and the d'Arenberg name.

This was a '61 vintage wine; two years later d'Arry Osborn made the 1967 d'Arenberg Burgundy which was to win seven trophies and 25 gold medals in a show record which, at the time, was unsurpassed. For good measure the following year he made a '68 Cabernet Sauvignon which won the 1969 Jimmy Watson Trophy.

D'Arenberg had arrived, and arrived in a big way. Yet within 16 years (in 1984) I wrote in my Australian Wine Compendium of the decline in the fortunes of the brand, suggesting that 'the styles are unashamedly traditional', and foolishly went on to say, 'I suspect it [the style] is a dying race'. How wrong can one be.

The rich, lush, opulently soft red wine style has come back with a vengeance; grenache has returned from the dead and, with the once-slighted shiraz, is making some of Australia's most eagerly sought wines — particularly in export markets. And indeed, these wines are a wonderful expression of terroir and variety, which age magnificently.

The 1961 to 1992 vintages were tasted in December 1992; subsequent vintages on release.

1999 ★★★★☆   February 2001
Medium purple–red; a very fresh and youthful bouquet with bright cherry jam varietal character is followed by a palate with excellent mouthfeel and balance; still a baby, but will make it.

1998 ★★★★☆   October 1999
Bright, spicy/peppery notes to clean red berry fruit aromas; lovely, juicy red berry fruit with spice and mint runs along the palate, finishing with soft, fine tannins.

1997 ★★★★★   November 1998
Excellent medium to full red–purple; the aromas are sweet, with blueberry and cherry, together with a hint of mint. The palate is very supple and elegant, with a silky, seamless mix of cherry, berry, mint and plum. Fine tannins on the finish. Top gold 1998 National Wine Show.

classic wines

★★★★★ Perfect   ★★★★☆ Close to perfect   ★★★★ Very good   ★★★☆ Expected
★★★ Short of standard   ★★☆ Undeserving   ★★ Decayed relic   NR No rating

33

1995 ★★★★★   *October 1997*
Strong purple–red; a rich and complex array of aromas ranging through liquorice, chocolate, game and mint lead into a wonderfully accessible and textured palate with sweet berryish fruit, hints of liquorice and game, finishing with soft tannins. The initial confection trap characters have disappeared.

1994 ★★★★☆   *December 1996*
Medium red–purple; a fragrant bouquet with a mix of spice, berry, game and faintly earthy notes, but no hint of the cowshed. The palate has excellent structure and mouthfeel, with those silky, sweet tannins adding to the flavour as well as the structure; softly lush and ripe, and a sheer delight.

1993 ★★★   *November 1995*
Medium red–purple; the bouquet is of medium intensity with sweet berry fruit and some slightly atypical minty aspects; the palate, too, shows some leafy/minty flavours out of the mainstream of the style.

1992 ★★★   *December 1992*
Medium to full red; a complex, ripe bouquet with some regional cowshed aromas. The palate has abundant ripe, sweet berry fruit, with just a hint of spice in the background.

1991 ★★★★☆   *December 1992*
Medium to full red; the bouquet is clean and smooth with gently sweet fruit, the palate showing an attractive blend of spicy shiraz and sweeter grenache flavours, finishing with those typical fine, soft tannins.

1990 ★★★★   *December 1992*
Full red; a very complex bouquet with abundant, ripe red berry fruit flavours which carry through to the palate, where spicy characters are also evident, finishing with well-balanced tannins.

1989 ★★★☆   *December 1992*
Good red colour, with full, sweet ripe berry fruit and just the faintest touch of spice on the bouquet. 60 per cent Shiraz, 40 per cent Grenache.

1988 ★★★★★   *December 1992*
A stylish and vibrantly peppery varietal bouquet, strongly reminiscent of the Rhône. The palate is similar to the '87, though slightly bigger; a complex, rich wine with lots of fruit flavour. 60 per cent Shiraz, 40 per cent Grenache.

1987 ★★★★★   *December 1992*
The colour is slightly more evolved, but the wine again shows lovely pepper spice aromas and flavours. The palate is still strong and lively, with excellent weight and structure. 50 per cent Shiraz, 50 per cent Grenache.

1986 ★★★★☆   *December 1992*
Relatively little colour change, but a quite different aroma and feel. The bouquet is sweeter and mintier than the older wines; the palate is concentrated with fresh fruit, a touch of mint and a faint hint of spice. Concentrated and stylish in a modern style. 100 per cent Shiraz, much of it pressings.

     ◄■ Not Ready   ➘ Still evolving   🍷 Prime of its life   ✓ Drink soon   🍾 Missed the boat

1982 ★★★★   *December 1992*

The bouquet is full, rich and ripe, altogether in a bigger spectrum. The palate is both strong and long, with tannins which are obvious but not abrasive. Primarily Shiraz.

1979 ★★   *December 1992*

A radical shift in style, with a rather ripe but dusty bouquet, and some gamey/farmyard flavours not helped by the very high alcohol of 14.5 per cent. 100 per cent Shiraz.

1976 ★★★★★   *December 1992*

Still retaining great colour, with a clean, very rich and ripe bouquet harking back to the best wines of the early '60s. Rich, full, ripe and chewy; an Australian classic. 100 per cent Shiraz; outstanding vintage year.

1975 ★★   *December 1992*

Good colour, but a rather earthy bouquet with diminished fruit; musty/earthy flavours dominate the palate. 100 per cent Shiraz.

1973 ★★☆   *December 1992*

Medium red, with clean, quite sweet fruit of medium weight, and promising rather more than the palate delivers, which is fractionally rough and hard, with distinct farmyard overtones. Blend of Shiraz and Grenache.

1972 ★★★   *December 1992*

Of light to medium weight, with some dusty/musty aromas, but the palate still has attractively sweet and soft fruit, and finishes well. Predominantly Shiraz, from a poor, wet vintage, and showing surprising quality.

1971 ★★★★   *December 1992*

Retaining good colour, with some of those dusty characters on the bouquet which ran through many of the older wines in the line-up. The palate is alive and well, with chunky, dusty/chocolatey fruit and quite high tannins providing a lingering finish. 100 per cent Shiraz.

1970 ★★★★☆   *December 1992*

While light in colour, a real surprise packet, with rich, chocolatey fruit aromas which are still fresh. The palate is at once fully aged yet balanced, with the fruit holding well and soft lingering tannins. Predominantly Shiraz; cool, wet summer.

1969 ★★☆   *December 1992*

Developed, light red in colour with light, faintly vegetal/bacterial aromas, leading on to a light palate with herbal/minty fruit characters. Shiraz and Grenache; nine weeks of rain during vintage.

1968 ★★   *December 1992*

Almost certainly a slightly corked bottle; has herb and mint characters, but a touch of astringency running throughout. Shiraz and Grenache.

1967 ★★★   *December 1992*

Notwithstanding the great reputation of this vintage, did not show particularly well, with distinct farmyard characters on both bouquet and palate. Certainly the wine is complex, but even more certainly it has seen better days. 75 per cent Grenache, 25 per cent Shiraz pressings.

classic wines

★★★★★ Perfect   ★★★★☆ Close to perfect   ★★★★ Very good   ★★★☆ Expected

★★★ Short of standard   ★★☆ Undeserving   ★★ Decayed relic   NR No rating

35

1966 ★★★   *December 1992*

Light red in colour, with a clean bouquet, but lacking richness. The wine is just holding on on the palate, but lacks the interest of the other old wines which preceded it. Blend of Shiraz and Grenache.

1965 ★★★☆   *December 1992*

A clean bouquet of medium intensity leads on to a wine with very pleasant dusty/cedary/cigar box characters, but without the fruit sweetness and richness of the oldest wines. Blend of Grenache and Shiraz.

1964 ★★★★☆   *December 1992*

A striking wine with soft, ripe almost voluptuous fruit aromas; in the mouth the wine is soft but very complex, in genuine Australian Burgundy style, a cross between French Burgundy and Rhône. Holding fruit and tannins well, with good balance. 100 per cent Shiraz.

1963 ★★★★★   *December 1992*

A quite remarkable old wine, holding its colour, with a full, smoothly fruity bouquet, very clean and showing a hint of mint. The palate is firm, complex and rich, with mouthfilling dark fruits, finishing with soft tannins. 50 per cent Shiraz, 50 per cent Grenache.

1961 ★★★★   *December 1992*

The colour is good, as is the bouquet, full rich and chocolatey, still in great condition. The palate shows very ripe fruit, verging on porty, but a great example of old Australian red style in a sweet mould. 100 per cent Shiraz.

de bortoli noble one botrytis semillon 1982-1999

I may be wrong, but I do not know of any other Australian table wine with a ten-year show record to equal that of the De Bortoli Noble One (as it has been called since 1990). Between 1982 and 1992 the various vintages had won 45 trophies and over 100 gold medals, and the wine has continued on its merry way since that time — and doubtless will continue to do so.

It is made from heavily botrytised semillon grown in the Murrumbidgee Irrigation Area. Successful attempts have been made with pedro ximinez (notably 1985) and, in a less luscious mould, gewurztraminer. Sauvignon blanc has not worked, so in the foreseeable future the wine will remain — as it always has been — 100 per cent Semillon.

Deen De Bortoli knew that McWilliam's had made a botrytised Pedro Ximinez way back in 1946, and as early as 1972 attempted his own version. That wine has developed considerable complexity, but lacks botrytis character. Son Darren tried with semillon in 1981 in his final year at Roseworthy, but once again botrytis failed to develop on the grapes due to the hot season.

In 1982 Darren succeeded beyond his (and his father's) wildest dreams: the wine won 10 trophies and 45 gold medals in a show career extending from 1982 to 1988. It set a pattern: barrel fermented in new French oak, and with exceptional richness and complexity. It was not made in 1989, but every other vintage has been of outstanding quality and remarkably consistent style.

First tasted in May 1993, updated, and later vintages added.

1999 ★★★★★   March 2001
Glowing green–yellow; the complex, intense and layered bouquet ranges through lime, marmalade and cumquat, the palate very intense and very well balanced, the lingering acidity stretching the finish on and on.

1998 ★★★★★   March 2000
Brilliant, glowing yellow–green; a rich, complex and luscious bouquet with butterscotch, citrus and subliminal oak is followed by a lively, fresh, peach, honey and lemon-flavoured palate; perfect acidity on the finish.

1997 ★★★★☆   March 1999
Bright, light yellow–gold; the bouquet has slightly unusual honey and candle wax aromas over citrus fruit. The palate is very long, with excellent acidity, and still evolving and developing; tasted very early in its life, and the rating may prove to be too low.

classic wines

★★★★★ Perfect   ★★★★☆ Close to perfect   ★★★★ Very good   ★★★☆ Expected
★★★ Short of standard   ★★☆ Undeserving   ★★ Decayed relic   NR No rating

1996 ★★★★★ *October 1998*

Glowing, deep golden yellow; as ever, almost impossibly rich with apricot, cumquat and lime aromas with well-balanced and integrated oak giving a hint of grated coconut. The palate provides more of the same, with fresh cumquat, coconut and vanilla flavours, long carry and finish.

1995 ★★★★☆ *February 1997*

Medium to full yellow–green; tasted soon after bottling, has all the potential to become a classic, with incredibly rich and sweet fruit on both bouquet and palate, and plenty of new oak still knitting together with the wine.

1994 ★★★★★ October 1996

Glowing yellow–green; the invariably complex array of aromas with tangy fruit, spicy lemony oak and some slightly unexpected florals. In the mouth, the ultimate in richness and complexity, with layer upon layer of flavour built in the style of the best French Sauternes, finished with excellent balancing acidity.

1993 ★★★★★ *November 1995*

Full gold; as always, a very complex bouquet with rich cumquat and mandarin fruit aromas together with pronounced oak. A complex wine on the palate with excellent structure; a spicy cut from the oak helps prevent the wine from cloying, as does the acid.

1992 ★★★★★ *May 1993*

Deep, glowing yellow–gold; complex apricot and cumquat fruit lifted by an appropriate degree of volatility, and noticeable oak. A very complex wine in the mouth, with the fruit and oak still coming together.

1991 ★★★★★ *May 1993*

Full yellow; typically complex, peach, cumquat and apricot aromas with well-balanced and integrated oak. The palate is similarly complex and luscious, with peach, mandarin and apricot fruit flavours interwoven with soft, spicy oak, and nicely balanced acidity.

1990 ★★★★★ *May 1993*

Full, glowing yellow; intense peach, apricot and marmalade aromas with hints of honey and butter, balanced by well–integrated oak. The palate precisely repeats the bouquet, with lusciously intense apricot and marmalade flavours, finishing with well-balanced acidity and appropriate oak. A prolific gold medal and trophy winner.

1988 ★★★★★ *May 1993*

Glowing yellow–orange; a very complex, rich and soft bouquet in the style of the '86, '85 and '83 wines. The palate is similarly soft and luscious, particularly on the entry to the mouth, then braced by good acidity on the finish.

1987 ★★★★★ *May 1993*

Medium to full yellow, with just a hint of orange, but bright; a very strongly botrytis-influenced wine with a distinct citrussy edge giving lift and intensity, here more in the style of the '82 and '84 wines. The palate is marvellous, still with fresh but intense fruit in a citrus/honey/cumquat spectrum; well-balanced oak, good acidity on the finish.

◄━ Not Ready   ❨ Still evolving   ❩ Prime of its life   ✐ Drink soon   ❨ Missed the boat

1986 ★★★★☆ *May 1993*

Medium to full yellow–orange; the bouquet shows pronounced tropical apricot aromas, with the oak a little more assertive relative to the fruit. There are similar sweet apricot-tinged flavours to the luscious palate, with the oak just a whisker assertive.

1985 ★★★★☆ *May 1993*

Medium to full yellow–orange; a complex aroma with pronounced botrytis lift and volatility, the aromas running in the dried apricot/mandarin peel/honeysuckle spectrum. Still has life in the mouth, partly from the volatility, and partly from natural acidity.

1984 ★★★★★ *May 1993*

Medium to full yellow–orange; fully bottle-developed, but marvellously complex and stylish Sauternes-like characters on the bouquet, with verve and bite. On the palate, powerful and structured citrus and apricot fruit; does start to dry out ever so slightly on the finish, but this is no bad thing.

1983 ★★★★ *May 1993*

Medium to full yellow–orange; some strange characters on the nose, with apricot and vanilla bean. The palate is full, rich and ripe, but again some of the strange characters of the bouquet. Almost certainly a slightly corked bottle.

1982 ★★★★★ *May 1993*

Medium to full yellow–orange; now fully aged, but retaining amazing complexity and richness with apricot, peach and marmalade aromas. The palate is rich and full, still filling the mouth with tropical/apricot flavours, soft and fleshy. The oak and acid are both well balanced and integrated.

classic wines

★★★★★ Perfect ★★★★☆ Close to perfect ★★★★ Very good ★★★☆ Expected
★★★ Short of standard ★★☆ Undeserving ★★ Decayed relic NR No rating

39

freycinet pinot noir 1988-2000

Situated on the east coast of Tasmania near Bicheno, Freycinet is vivid proof the existence of terroir (in the fullest sense of that term) in Australia. The vineyard is in an inverted U shape, opening out at the lower end and rising to close at the opposite end, with a mini-valley between the sides of the U.

It provides a unique site-climate. On the 42° South latitude line, the heat degree summation is a low 1250 heat degree days, but the sunshine hours are very high, and the pinot noir is typically picked a month prior to the end of the effective growing season. The rain falls mainly in the winter, the site is frost-free, largely wind-protected and a sun trap during summer.

Half a hectare of pinot noir was planted in 1980 on the north-facing side of the valley. That's even smaller than Romanee-Conti, and like Romanee-Conti, Freycinet has a worldwide audience, selling out immediately on release each year. The grapes are handpicked and fermented in a rotofermenter with the inclusion of 5 per cent to 10 per cent whole bunches, and pressed after five to six days fermentation. It is allowed to settle for a day or two, and is then taken to Troncais and Bourgogne barriques where it undergoes malolactic fermentation.

After ten months it will be given a coarse ('sticks and stones') filtration and bottled. Winemaker Claudio Radenti is adamant that he is not interested in feral or quasi-Burgundian characters. He wants the fruit to express itself, and that it does magnificently. The vintage notes (in brackets), incidentally, are supplied by Freycinet.

All except the 2000 were tasted in November 2000.

2000 ★★★★★   *June 2001*
Light to medium red–purple; initially fairly closed, progressively opening up to reveal spice and herb aromas; the tangy, vibrant palate has a spicy/sappy/plummy mid-palate, followed by a long, lingering finish. Carries its 1.45 degrees alcohol with aplomb.

1999 ★★★★   *November 2000*
Medium purple–red with the faintest touch of haze. Very powerful, strong, plum mint and spice fruit on the bouquet is followed by a ripe and powerful palate packed with dense fleshy, plummy fruit; hints of forest/stem/game peep through, and will develop with time. (There was slightly less sunshine than 1998; intermittent rainfall meant there was no need for irrigation at any time, but did lead to a touch of disease. Harvested 31 March at 25.5° brix; 3.5 tonnes picked.)

Not Ready   Still evolving   Prime of its life   Drink soon   Missed the boat

1998 ★★★★★ *November 2000*

Light to medium purple–red. An intense and complex bouquet with plummy, pure, ripe fruit intermingling with more savoury/foresty nuances, is still in the process of knitting together. The palate, likewise, has a complex mix of sweet plum and more savoury/foresty/tangy characters; fantastic length and finish. Four trophies Hobart Wine Show, including Best Tasmanian Wine and Best Wine of Show. (A textbook vintage with winter/spring rainfall then warm and dry throughout summer and autumn. Harvested 19 March at 24.5° brix; 4.5 tonnes picked.)

1997 ★★★★★ *November 2000*

A distinct colour shift to red–purple, though not particularly deep. The bouquet is full and intense, with sweet plum, mint and spice aromas supported by delicate oak. Rich plum and chocolate fruit flavours, supported by gentle spice and tannins, flood the mouth, yet the wine is quite elegant and lighter bodied than others, notwithstanding the low yield. (A good, sunny vintage with a hot summer and a cool autumn; small berries and bunches. Harvested 14 April at 25° brix; 2.5 tonnes picked.)

1996 ★★★★☆ *November 2000*

Light to medium red, slightly hazy. A complex and potent bouquet with a mix of plum, mint, earth and game leads into a palate which opens with plum and mint, but progressively lengthens with more savoury characters running through to the long finish. Starting to fully evolve. (One of the coolest years on record, a one in 20 event. Poor fruit set reduced yield, luckily given the cool and wet growing season. Harvested 15 April at 24° brix; 3 tonnes picked.)

1995 ★★★★☆ *November 2000*

Light to medium red, with just a hint of purple remaining. An aromatic bouquet with oriental spices on top of a powerful strawberry and plum underlay; the sweet mix of plum, strawberry, chocolate, mocha and forest harks back to the oldest wines, but still has plenty of power and intensity. Qantas Trophy Hobart Wine Show. (A dry November/December was followed by January rain and a humid summer with more rainfall at the end; less sunshine than 1994. Harvested 31 March at 24.7° brix; 6.5 tonnes picked.)

1994 ★★★★★ *November 2000*

Light to medium red, with no tawny hues. A vibrant and fragrant bouquet, with fresh plum, cherry and spice aromas is followed by a palate which is not overly rich or dense, but is long and intense with pure, gently sappy, pinot fruit. A lovely wine which has more than fulfilled its early promise. Qantas Trophy Hobart Wine Show. (A dry winter and a warm, dry early spring was followed by useful rain in October and 300 mm in December ending a drought. The rest of the summer was dry and hot; a very good vintage. Harvested 31 March at 24° brix; 6.5 tonnes picked.)

1993 ★★★☆ *November 2000*

Light to medium tawny–red, nearly identical to the 1992. Moderately sweet savoury/spicy/foresty aromas are followed by a palate with woodsy flavours and texture in fully mature mode, but with sparks of sweet plummy fruit coming off from time to time. (A difficult vintage, with a good start but a cool and wet summer (January/February) before fining up with an Indian Summer-type autumn. Some botrytis. Harvested 13 April at 25° brix; 4 tonnes picked.)

classic wines

★★★★★ Perfect ★★★★☆ Close to perfect ★★★★ Very good ★★★☆ Expected
★★★ Short of standard ★★☆ Undeserving ★★ Decayed relic NR No rating

1992 ★★★☆   *November 2000*

Light to medium tawny–red. The fragrant bouquet has some distinctly Burgundian secondary characters in a vegetal/earthy/stemmy mode. The flavours track the bouquet, predominantly foresty/earthy, finishing with pronounced acidity. Has lost the sweet plummy fruit it showed in 1995, but for some this will be a plus. (The season opened with a warm, dry start, but January was cool and wet; warmed up thereafter, and there was no more significant rain. Harvested 9 April at 25.6° brix; 6 tonnes picked.)

1991 ★★★★★   *November 2000*

Very strong colour, still with a predominantly red–purple hue. The bouquet is powerful and dense, packed with dark plum fruit; gamey Burgundian characters lurk underneath, adding complexity. A rich, concentrated and textured wine, with the tannins still holding. Amazing, given the relatively high yield. (A warm, dry spring was followed by a dry summer; an outstanding vintage. Harvested 3 April at 25° brix; 6 tonnes picked.)

1990 ★★★★   *November 2000*

Medium red tending to tawny. The aromas have some of the sweet caramel/mocha/spice of the '88, but not the same richness and intensity. The palate offers a mix of sweet plum, prune, spice and mocha; good length and holding well. (A cold winter was followed by a wet spring then a warm, dry summer and autumn. Harvested 11 April at 23.4° brix; 7.5 tonnes picked.)

1988 ★★★★★   *November 2000*

The colour is still quite strong; the wine needs careful decanting to eliminate fine sediment. A rich and complex bouquet even runs to touches of chocolate and liquorice; the palate is rich, ripe, sweet and luscious, still in outstanding condition. Touches of foresty/sou bois flavours add interest; still has a future. (An excellent growing season, hot (by Tasmanian standards) and dry, verging on drought. Harvested 17 March at 25° brix; 1.7 tonnes picked.)

◀ Not Ready   ↘ Still evolving   ▮ Prime of its life   ↗ Drink soon   ▯ Missed the boat

giaconda chardonnay 1986-1999

rick Kinzbrunner comes from the same school as Phillip Jones (of Bass Phillip) except that he (Kinzbrunner) is simply a mouse-quiet non-conformist rather than anarchist. The two share the same drive for cameo perfection, seemingly unconcerned about the harsh economic realities of such tiny scales of production. Their wines should cost hundreds of dollars a bottle, and would if they were made to similar standards of perfection in France or Italy.

The Giaconda wine comes from 1.5 hectares of chardonnay planted since 1982, field grafted with a mix of clones. No more than 700 cases are produced each year, and the wine sells out long before the subsequent vintage becomes available.

The wines made since 1986 are consistent in style, yet have evolved, and will continue to evolve, as Rick Kinzbrunner continuously refines his approach.

The use of 40 per cent new Allier and Vosges oak has not changed, nor the practice of roughly settling the wine overnight (after pressing) and transferring direct to barrel for inoculation (in new barrels) and wild yeast fermentation (in used barrels). The percentage of malolactic fermentation has changed from year to year, and Kinzbrunner is lengthening the period in barrel. Up to 1992 the wines spent a year; in 1993 he extended it to 18 months.

For all that, the wines are not flashy; they creep up on you, just like Rick Kinzbrunner does.

First tasted in November 1994, updated, and later vintages added.

1999 ★★★★ *April 2001*
Medium to full straw–yellow; typically complex nutty/toasty/cashew-accented bouquet leads into a full-bodied palate, with more of those ripe, complex nutty/spicy notes. The wine seems to thicken up somewhat on the finish, although not due to any excess alcohol.

1998 ★★★★★ *January 2000*
Medium yellow–green; the bouquet is very complex and high toned, with strong charry barrel-ferment oak; there is a great volume of flavour on the palate carrying through to an excellently balanced, long finish. Despite all that flavour, does not cloy.

1997 ★★★★★ *March 1999*
Glowing yellow–green; a typically complex bouquet, very Burgundian, with an array of secondary fruit aromas supported by subtle oak. The palate is no less interesting than the bouquet, with characters ranging all the way from creamy to minerally, and a touch of spicy oak emerging on the finish. Juicy fruity it isn't.

classic wines

★★★★★ Perfect   ★★★★☆ Close to perfect   ★★★★ Very good   ★★★☆ Expected
★★★ Short of standard   ★★☆ Undeserving   ★★ Decayed relic   NR No rating

43

1996 ★★★★★   *January 1998*

Medium to full yellow–green; a very complex bouquet with an array of toasty nutty bacony aromas to accompany the melon fruit is followed by a no less powerful and complex palate. Very Burgundian in feel and texture, it is already weighty by the normally reserved standards of Giaconda.

1995 ★★★★★   *November 1996*

Glowing yellow–green; a charry/high toast oak component comes through on the bouquet in slightly more assertive fashion than some of the Giaconda wines early in their life. On the palate there is that typically complex range of secondary flavours running through nutty to minerally, and the hallmark length on the finish.

1994 ★★★★★   *February 1996*

Light to medium yellow–green; as always, restrained, yet complex, with smooth but not heavy nutty/buttery/minerally aromas, showing the effects of barrel fermentation, malolactic fermentation and extended lees ageing. The palate is fine, elegant and reserved; a classic example of the Giaconda style with those flavours which creep up on you; finishes with well-balanced acid.

1993 ★★★★☆   *November 1994*

Light to medium yellow–green; the aromas are stony/minerally rather than overtly fruity, yet fresh as always; the oak is well balanced and integrated with vanillin hints. The palate is youthful and fresh, still settling down when tasted in November 1994, and absolutely in the Giaconda mainstream, and will build texture and richness as it ages.

1992 ★★★★★   *November 1994*

Light to medium yellow–green; complex apple, mineral and pear aromas intermingling with toasty oak. The palate is smooth, mouthfilling and round, with subtle toasty oak, the flavours so complex it is impossible to give a single fruit or other descriptor.

1991 ★★★★☆   *November 1994*

Light to medium yellow–green; there is some lift to the bouquet with fig and melon aromas; subtle oak as always. The palate is powerful, nutty and textured, seemingly showing more malolactic influence than normal, although this is not the case; lots of alcohol and very much the product of a ripe, warm vintage.

1990 ★★★★★   *November 1994*

Light green–yellow; a clean, crisp, firm bouquet with mineral and stone fruit aromas; subtle oak. The palate is elegant, fresh and lively with hints of melon and cashew; great balance and mouthfeel.

1989 ★★★★☆   *November 1994*

Medium to full yellow–green, by far the deepest of the range. The bouquet shows restrained malolactic influences, and is strongly reminiscent of many Napa Valley Chardonnays. The palate has a fraction more flesh than most with soft, mouthfilling dry fig fruit flavours.

1988 ★★★★☆   *November 1994*

Slightly brassy colour; yet another wine in the mid-stream of the Giaconda style on the bouquet, with attractive fruit showing some citrus and fig characters, and rather softer (and perhaps a little coarser) than the best wines, but delicious nonetheless.

1987 ★★★★   *November 1994*

Medium yellow–green; a restrained bouquet with nutty/minerally aspects showing the obvious malolactic influence. The palate is mouthfilling, quite French in character, and showing what appear to be some warmer fermentation characters, with a nutty finish.

1986 ★★★★★   *November 1994*

Light to medium yellow–green, bright and youthful. The bouquet is fine and elegant, still very young, with subtle oak. The palate is powerful and textured with the stone and stone fruit Giaconda characters to the fore. One would not guess it has not been through malolactic fermentation.

classic wines

★★★★★ Perfect   ★★★★☆ Close to perfect   ★★★★ Very good   ★★★☆ Expected
★★★ Short of standard   ★★☆ Undeserving   ★★ Decayed relic   NR No rating

45

grosset riesling 1981-2000

Where are few more fastidious winemakers than Jeffrey Grosset, who (many years ago) moved from Australia's largest winery, Lindemans Karadoc, to one of its smallest — his own. Even today, the quantities of each of the wines made are very small, reflecting his uncompromising attitude to fruit selection.

He makes two Rieslings, one labelled Watervale and the other Polish Hill. The original tasting featured alternating vintages between the two vineyards, in part because Grosset has not a single bottle left of some of the early vintages.

Although vintage variation played its usual role, and the luck of the draw decreed that the Polish Hill wines should have the majority of the best vintages (the even years) and the Watervale a number of off vintages which tell on the odd years, a clear distinction between the styles of the two wines emerged.

The Polish Hill wines are finer, drier and crisper, with delicate lime and citrus fruit; the Watervale wines are richer and fuller, with greater flavour and extract. Jeffrey Grosset always felt that the Polish Hill wines would be longer-lived, and so it has more or less been — although the higher residual sugar levels of the first t wo vintages slightly obscure the pattern (a bit of sweetness can be a great help to older wines).

Overall, yet another convincing demonstration of the Clare Valley's capacity to produce superb, age-worthy Riesling. Since 1998 tasting notes for both wines appear. Postscript: since 2000 the wines are bottled with Stelvin screw caps, underwriting their longevity.

First tasted in October 1994, updated, and later vintages added.

◄ *2000 Watervale* ★★★★★   *October 2000*
Light to medium yellow–green; the bouquet is quite rich, with more overt fruit than the wine often displays when young; the palate, likewise, is powerful, with considerable depth and length, the aftertaste full of authority, yet not aggressive.

◄ *2000 Polish Hill* ★★★★★   *October 2000*
Light to medium yellow–green; full, lime, mineral and a spicy grip to the powerful bouquet is followed by a generous, relatively open palate, again with a characteristic spicy edge.

1999 Watervale ★★★★★ — October 1999

There is a quiet precision in Jeffrey Grosset's demeanour wholly apposite to his mantle as heir-apparent to John Vickery as Australia's greatest Riesling maker. This wine is a classic, with far more lime and passionfruit than usual apparent at this early stage, providing a deliciously lingering finish.

1999 Polish Hill ★★★★★ — October 1999

Light to medium green–yellow; a crisp, clean bouquet which is utterly classic Clare Valley, minerally and less exuberant than the Polish Hill of the same year. The palate is lively and lingering, with more citrus fruit showing than in the bouquet; very good balance and length.

1998 Watervale ★★★★★ — October 1998

Light green–yellow; intense mineral, lime, spice and powdery aromas are followed by a similarly intensely-flavoured palate veering more towards lime and spice. A classically austere wine with a bone-dry finish. As good as ever.

1998 Polish Hill ★★★★★ — October 1998

Glowing yellow–green; as ever, a pure and intense celebration of Clare Riesling with lime, citrus and a hint of mineral on the bouquet. The palate is perfectly balanced, again showing pure varietal fruit character, with fine lime, citrus and herb flavours; perfectly balanced, with a lingering finish.

1997 Polish Hill ★★★★★ — November 1997

Light to medium yellow–green; a very fragrant bouquet with a distinct minerally edge to the herb and spice fruit. The palate is intense but fine, with tremendous grip and length to the finish; tighter and less evolved than the Watervale, but will literally flower with time in bottle.

1996 Polish Hill ★★★★★ — October 1996

Light to medium green–yellow; fragrant, flowery lime blossom aromas with some background hints of toast and spice. A wonderfully elegant and fine yet intensely flavoured wine on the palate, balanced and sculptured as only Grosset knows how.

1995 Watervale ★★★★★ — October 1995

Light to medium yellow–green; a supremely elegant bouquet, tight and discrete in classic Clare fashion, tinged with lime. A totally delicious wine to taste, with a long yet ultra-refined palate, gentle lime juice flavours, and a lingering yet clean finish.

1994 Polish Hill ★★★★★ — October 1994

Classic, youthful Riesling, light green in colour, with tangy lime aromas tinged with herbaceousness. A very intense, lingering palate with toast and lime flavours and a minimum of five years in front of it.

1993 Watervale ★★★★★ — October 1994

Bright, light green–yellow, with a highly floral, aromatic honeysuckle tinge to the bouquet. Delicious flavours and feel, with passionfruit aspects, long and lively in the finish.

classic wines

★★★★★ Perfect   ★★★★☆ Close to perfect   ★★★★ Very good   ★★★☆ Expected
★★★ Short of standard   ★★☆ Undeserving   ★★ Decayed relic   NR No rating

47

1992 Polish Hill ★★★★☆   *October 1994*

Bright and light in colour, with a very elegant bouquet in the lime/toasty spectrum, but with just a hint of the kerosene characters which have developed in the '84 and '86. In the mouth, fine, intense and lingering.

1991 Watervale ★★★★   *October 1994*

Medium yellow–green, with tangy lime and citrus aromas, and a well-balanced palate. The bottle in the line-up was slightly corked; could in fact be even better than this rating.

1990 Polish Hill ★★★★☆   *October 1994*

The colour is starting to show development but the bouquet is still intense and aromatic, with pronounced lime juice aromas. The palate is still extremely fine and tight; an elegant wine that is still evolving.

1989 Watervale HHI   *October 1994*

A fast developing wine which shows the influence of botrytis, medium to full yellow, with a lifted apricot-accented bouquet, and a rather soft, slightly blowsy palate.

1988 Polish Hill ★★★★☆   *October 1994*

The bouquet is clean, firm and relatively closed, with some toasty characters, signifying a transition phase in its development, but in the mouth comes alive, very much in the Polish Hill-style, with a long and intense flavour with touches of lime, and a tingling dry finish.

1987 Watervale ★★★☆   *October 1994*

Light to medium yellow–green in colour, with aromas tending to herbaceous. The palate is complex, not especially fruity, and rather firm on the finish.

1986 Polish Hill ★★★★   *October 1994*

Medium to full yellow, with a firm, lime and herb bouquet. Initially dry, toasty and very reserved, appealing more to the intellect than the tongue, but opened up in the glass to show some very attractive citrus and honey flavours.

1985 Watervale ★★★★   *October 1994*

Medium to full yellow, with a smooth honey-tinged bouquet, still surprisingly tight. The palate is attractive, with lively, tangy honey and lemon fruit, with good length and balance, finishing dry.

1984 Polish Hill ★★★☆   *October 1994*

Strong colour, still with some green hints; the bouquet is firm with a hint of classic developed kerosene Riesling character. The palate follows the bouquet, firm and tangy, with a touch of that kerosene cut; one wonders whether the wine might not have been better with a touch of residual sugar.

1983 Watervale ★★☆   *October 1994*

The product of a hot vintage, full yellow, almost into bronze in colour, the bouquet full and (atypically for Grosset) a little coarse. The palate, too, is big and a little coarse, though is certainly not broken up.

━ Not Ready   ❯ Still evolving   ▮ Prime of its life   ⌀ Drink soon   ⎕ Missed the boat

1982 Polish Hill ★★★★★ October 1994

Medium to full yellow, with just a touch of green remaining. The bouquet is quite Germanic in style with wonderful toasty lime aromas. An extremely elegant wine in the mouth, intense yet not heavy, with those Germanic lime notes and a long finish with a touch of sweetness from residual sugar.

1981 Watervale ★★★★ October 1994

Medium to full yellow, with a sweet, rich honey and toast bouquet in which the volatility becomes progressively more apparent as the wine sits in the glass. The palate shows lots of rich, honeyed fruit which fills the mouth, and finishes with appreciable but not excessive sweetness.

★★★★★ Perfect ★★★★☆ Close to perfect ★★★★ Very good ★★★☆ Expected
★★★ Short of standard ★★☆ Undeserving ★★ Decayed relic NR No rating

classic wines

49

hardys eileen hardy shiraz
1970-1998

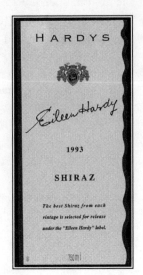

herein lies a cautionary tale. In 1970, Thomas Hardy decided it would honour the matriarch of the Hardy clan by naming the best red wine of the vintage in her honour. It was a 1970 McLaren Vale Shiraz, a wine which remains superb to this very day. But then the allure of other districts and other varieties, notably cabernet sauvignon, took hold and the wine wandered off on tangents.

In 1987 the fashion had waned; Shiraz was making its comeback, and the winemakers rather than the wine marketers had the final call in deciding what was the best red wine of the vintage. So, after a 17-year break, Eileen Hardy was once again a Shiraz.

The rebirth was based on a blend of Padthaway and McLaren Vale grapes; in the following year Clare Valley was added, and until 1991 the blend was Padthaway, McLaren Vale and Clare. In 1991 McLaren Vale became the dominant part, and by 1992 Padthaway was contributing only 20 per cent (although there is no predetermined or fixed formula).

The winds of change continued to blow in the 1990s. While the Shiraz continues to come from the best, and usually oldest, vineyards — thus giving the wine its power and concentration — American oak gradually gave way to French. Since 1996, indeed, only French oak has been used.

First tasted in November 1994, updated, and later vintages added.

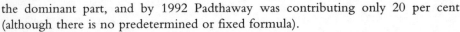

◄ *1998* ★★★★★   *March 2001*

Dense red–purple; there is the predictably dense and brooding dark cherry/dark plum fruit on the bouquet, the oak positive but not excessive. The palate is rich, full and savoury, with berry fruit still fleshing out on the back palate; continues the trend of recent years to refine the role of oak in the wine.

◄ *1997* ★★★★☆   *June 2000*

Full purple–red; the bouquet abounds with rich, red berry fruit allied with smoky, spicy oak. The palate is dense, packed with the flavour of black cherry, blackberry and mulberry and oak which will ultimately give cedary characters to the wine. All in all, a brooding giant which absolutely demands prolonged cellaring.

1996 ★★★★★   *May 1999*

Dense purple, very good for age; there is a distinct change in the character of the bouquet, with more savoury notes, and it is difficult to feel where the fruit stops and the oak starts. The answer comes on the palate; in relative terms, this is a fruit-driven — well, more fruit-driven — wine than all the others, with scented raspberry, chocolate, liquorice and black cherry fruit. The first of the Eileens to be matured in 100 per cent French oak, which certainly makes a contribution.

1995 ★★★★☆   *October 1997*

Medium to full purple–red; a rich and full bouquet with masses of ripe black fruits, dark chocolate and some liquorice; the oak is potent, but is justified. A wine which takes no prisoners, but which has fantastic palate flavour, bursting with liquorice, black cherry/berry and spice flavours surrounded by ultra-sophisticated vanilla oak.

1994 ★★★★☆   *July 1996*

Strong purple–red; an almost riotous array of intensely fragrant black cherry, liquorice, plum and spice fruit aromas lead on to a palate which is absolutely crammed with more of the same liquorice/black cherry/boot polish fruit flavours, the very essence of Shiraz.

1993 ★★★★★   *November 1994*

Medium to full red–purple; a ripe and concentrated bouquet with rich essencey/rose petal berry aromas with a background of high-toned oak. The palate is bursting with black cherry and blackcurrant fruit with great vinosity, matched by high-toned French oak; better balanced than the '92.

1992 ★★★★   *November 1994*

Medium to full red–purple; earthy, lifted fruit with pronounced toasty/charry oak, with a strong American influence. The palate shows the high-toned fruit character of many of the '92 reds from South Australia, but oak is very strong in the wine. Made in a particular style; it will be interesting to see whether the fruit or the oak triumphs with age.

1991 ★★★★★   *November 1994*

Full red–purple; a full and sweet bouquet with lots of chocolate and vanilla. The palate is quite luscious, with dark chocolate, liquorice and black cherry fruit, surrounded by heaps of charry oak which the fruit can (just) carry. An arresting show style with six gold medals to its credit.

1990 ★★★☆   *November 1994*

Medium to full purple–red; potent, high-toned, intense essencey fruit and oak. The palate shows lots of chocolate and briary fruit, with as much oak as the bouquet promises. The problem lies with the quantity of fruit and oak tannins, which take over on the finish and unbalance the wine. Atypical for 1990.

1989 ★★★   *November 1994*

Medium to full red, with a touch of purple. The bouquet is complex with hints of hay, straw, mint and earth. There is a similar array of mint, chocolate and earth flavours on the palate which, however, lacks vinosity on the mid-palate, before finishing with reasonably firm tannins. Very doubtful whether prolonged cellaring will pull the wine back into balance.

★★★★★ Perfect   ★★★★☆ Close to perfect   ★★★★ Very good   ★★★☆ Expected
★★★ Short of standard   ★★☆ Undeserving   ★★ Decayed relic   NR No rating

classic wines

1988 ★★★★☆   *November 1994*

Medium to full red–purple; that typically pungent, almost essencey combination of minty/berry fruit and oak which is the hallmark of the style. As one would expect, a powerful wine on the palate with lots of extract, tannin and chocolate/mint/berry fruit. Well-balanced, despite its power, and should age wonderfully well.

1987 ★★★☆   *November 1994*

Medium to full red–purple; a complex, fruit-driven bouquet with briar, liquorice and hints of the greener characters of the vintage, with a faintly gamey overtone. The palate is of medium intensity, with liquorice and leafy characters predominating; not intense, and is now at its best.

1970 ★★★★★   *November 1994*

Medium to full red; an absolutely classic bouquet with fragrant earth and chocolate varietal aromas, still holding its fruit. A nigh on perfect old, fruit-driven wine with classic McLaren Vale chocolate flavours, finishing with fine tannins. Delicious in every respect; if well corked and well cellared, will certainly live another ten years, probably 20.

◄ Not Ready   ＼ Still evolving   ▮ Prime of its life   ↙ Drink soon   ◻ Missed the boat

henschke cyril henschke cabernet
1978-1997

the first vintage of this wine (1978) was released in 1980 in memory of Cyril Henschke (1924–1979), Stephen Henschke's father, whose life had come to an abrupt and tragic end. While many, myself included, believe that the overall quality of the Henschke wines has improved since Stephen took over the reins, there can be no doubt that Cyril Henschke's vision (and skill) was responsible for Henschke being where it is today.

This wine is Stephen Henschke's recognition of that fact, and symbolic of his determination to respect and protect his legacy. In this his attitude closely parallels that of Alister Purbrick of Chateau Tahbilk.

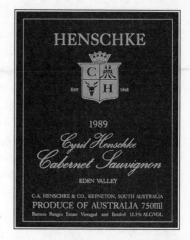

Right from the outset, the wine has won critical acclaim and consistent success in the show circuit. Up to 1986 it was made entirely from Eden Valley cabernet sauvignon (part estate-grown and part-purchased); in 1987, the first Merlot was introduced, and it now is a full-blown Bordeaux-style blend, typically 60 per cent Cabernet Sauvignon with roughly equal portions of Merlot and Cabernet Franc.

The wine is fermented in the same traditional fashion as the other Henschke red wines (open, wax-lined concrete fermenters with heading-down boards) and is matured for 21 months in new French oak. It is, as one would expect, a long-lived style, reaching the start of its plateau at around ten years of age, and promising to hold that plateau for another decade in the better vintages.

First tasted in November 1994, updated, and later vintages added.

1997 ★★★★
October 2000

Medium red–purple; the bouquet has a mix of very ripe, opulent cassis and blackberry fruit together with more fragrant cedary/foresty notes, promising much for the palate. Here, however, cedary, dusty tannins, part oak-derived, part from the fruit, disrupt the flow.

1996 ★★★★★
October 1999

Medium purple–red; a marvellously fine, elegant and fragrant bouquet featuring perfectly ripened cassis redcurrant fruit. The palate does not disappoint, being equally elegant and fine, particularly the absolutely beautiful tannins and gentle oak. It is fascinating to see how the fruit in the wine has soaked up the new oak.

classic wines

★★★★★ Perfect ★★★★☆ Close to perfect ★★★★ Very good ★★★☆ Expected
★★★ Short of standard ★★☆ Undeserving ★★ Decayed relic NR No rating

53

1995 ★★★★ *February 1998*

Medium to full red–purple; the charry oak which is evident in the other Henschke '95 wines, but which seems better-suited there, seems to bite somewhat on both the bouquet and palate of this wine. The palate flavours are of mint, red berry and leaf; again, a wine which seems distinctly off the pace of the best vintages.

1994 ★★★★★ *May 1997*

Medium to full red–purple; fabulous cabernet varietal aromas, with pristine cassis fruit tinged with a touch of green olive and supported by subtle oak leads on to a wine which floods the mouth with cassis/berry fruit; superb texture, supple and round, yet with the authority of Cabernet Sauvignon.

1993 ★★★★★ *October 1996*

Medium to full purple–red; a potent and intense bouquet with cassis tinged with olive in classic cabernet fashion; well-balanced and integrated oak. A glorious wine on the palate with wonderful fruit ranging through cassis to raspberry; impeccable oak handling and a very long, perfectly balanced finish. Deserves all its innumerable trophies.

1992 ★★★★☆ *October 1995*

Medium to full red–purple; a fragrant and complex bouquet with interwoven spicy oak and briary/berry fruit. A stylish wine on the palate with opulent use of high-toned spicy/charry oak; the oak level will come back with further time in bottle.

1991 ★★★★★ *November 1994*

Medium to full red–purple; a complex bouquet with ripe cassis/berry fruit married with charry/lemony oak, and overtones of Bordeaux from a ripe year. A marvellous wine on the palate, elegant, yet concentrated with dark briary/berry/cassis fruit of perfect ripeness, very good tannin balance.

1990 ★★★★★ *November 1994*

Medium to full red–purple; a concentrated, powerful and complex bouquet with many characters ranging from slightly gamey to cassis. The palate is powerful, concentrated and tannic, with dark berry/briary fruits; destined to be very long-lived.

1989 ★★★☆ *November 1994*

Medium to full red; out of the mainstream, with some leafy/minty characters. The palate, too, shows more mint and leaf than red berry fruits; the wine is, however, well balanced in terms of extract and oak.

1988 ★★★★★ *November 1994*

Medium to full red. A marvellously elegant, restrained and classic bouquet with pure cabernet varietal fruit aromas beautifully balanced by oak. The palate has red berry fruit flavours with an intriguing edge of coffee and chocolate, markedly different from the other wines, but totally appealing. The overall balance and structure of the wine is outstanding, finishing with fine-grained tannins.

1987 ★★★☆ *November 1994*

Medium red–purple; the vintage character which runs across so many of the 1987 Henschke wines comes again here, with rather leafy/gamey characters on both the bouquet and palate. There are some minty flavours, but the finish has a distinct green olive tang.

◄━ Not Ready   ❭ Still evolving   ❙ Prime of its life   ⌀ Drink soon   ⛝ Missed the boat

1986 ★★★★☆   *November 1994*

Youthful purple–red; the bouquet is very ripe with full cassis/berry fruit. The palate, too, shows incredibly ripe fruit, bordering on the extractive; there is lots of vanillin oak, too.

1985 ★★★★☆   *November 1994*

Medium red–purple; the bouquet is elegant, restrained, showing classic cool cabernet fruit. The palate feel is fine and elegant, with good acidity; the fruit and oak are perfectly balanced and integrated.

1978 ★★★★   *November 1994*

Medium red; very pronounced herbaceous varietal fruit drives the bouquet. The palate is very stylish and very varietal, with good structure, and finishing with firm acidity. (Rated great by Stephen Henschke.)

★★★★★ Perfect   ★★★★☆ Close to perfect   ★★★★ Very good   ★★★☆ Expected
★★★ Short of standard   ★★☆ Undeserving   ★★ Decayed relic   NR No rating

classic wines

55

perhaps the most extraordinary feature of Henschke's Hill of Grace Shiraz is that the vineyard was almost 100 years old before the wine made from it was separately bottled and given the Hill of Grace label. It is even more extraordinary when compared with Mount Edelstone, which became the first Henschke vineyard bottling in 1952. On the other hand, it is true that Penfolds Grange did not become a full commercial reality until 1955, following the first tiny experimental vintage in 1951. But the fact remains that the Hill of Grace vineyard, planted by Nicolaus Stanitzki in the 1860s, was purchased by Paul Gotthard Henschke on 17 December 1891, and had been in the family's hands for 67 years before the first vintage of 1958.

What is more, complete collections of Hill of Grace are even rarer than those of Grange, so the tasting I attended at Henschke in October 1998 was a chance of a lifetime. Andrew Caillard MW, the Sydney-based head of Langton's Wine Auctions and who knows more than anyone else about rare wine collections observed: 'I reckon there are about 30 to 40 complete collections of Grange in existence, but this is the only complete set of Hill of Grace.' Stephen Henschke underlined the point when he said: 'This is the first time I have ever tasted the complete range of Hill of Grace.'

The occasion was a celebration both of the 130th anniversary of Henschke (there is a touch of poetic licence in this calculation) and of 40 years of Hill of Grace 1958 to 1998 (no poetic licence there). Unlike some others, Henschke has never sought to compare Hill of Grace with Grange, and it is sheer coincidence that the last great Grange tasting (in August 1993) also covered 40 years (1951 to 1990).

The tasting, at the historic stone winery of Henschke, was divided into decades: '58 to '68; '69 to '78; '79 to '88; and '89 to '98. With almost alarming candor Stephen Henschke categorised each decade in turn. The first was 'The decade of ignorance', with minimalist or non-interventionist winemaking necessitated by a limited understanding of the chemical and biochemical processes involved, and by lack of sophisticated equipment.

The next decade, through to 1978, was that of 'The abuse of knowledge', which may seem a harsh assessment, but which is no more or less than the recognition that the bright, clean school of winemaking then prevalent resulted in the excessive use of sulphur dioxide, of fining and filtration, of obsessive attention to pH levels, and the exclusion of the pressings wine which had so sustained the wine in previous times.

The next period was 'That of the Young Turks', foremost of whom was Stephen Henschke, of course, for he had taken over winemaking responsibilities in 1979 after the premature death of father Cyril Henschke. He reversed the practice of selling off the pressings wine, which was kept separate but partially (often substantially) used in the final blend; he introduced new oak, but unhappy with the quality, began importing and seasoning his own oak which was then coopered by master barrel-maker A P John; he cooled and lengthened the

◄ Not Ready   ＼ Still evolving   ▮ Prime of its life   ⌇ Drink soon   ▯ Missed the boat fermentations; and finally moved to finishing the fermentation in the new oak barrels. The final decade has been 'That of Prue and the vineyard'. Prue Henschke, who like her husband studied both at Geisenheim and Charles Sturt University, is widely regarded as one of the foremost viticulturists in Australia, and manages the four separate vineyards including, of course, the jewel in the crown, the ever-so-gentle slope of the Hill of Grace.

Here the primary problem has been the mortality of the 'grandfather' vines planted in the 1860s. Gnarled and tortured (by age) into fantastic shapes, they superficially look strong, but often the massive, foreshortened trunk has largely rotted away, even attacked by white ants and other borers or pathogens, with just a small vein or two of living tissue carrying the nutrients (mainly water) from their large and deep root systems; 'tractor disease', even a very strong wind, or just sheer exhaustion, all take their toll.

A painstakingly process of field selection by Prue, her Geisenheim-trained assistant Uschi, and Prue's Uncle Louis, resulted in the propagation of examples of the best vines (via cuttings) in a nursery vineyard, and now the gaps where the old vines were have been filled with young vines protected by cones shaped identical to those you see on roads undergoing roadwork, albeit of different material; a compelling combination of new and old.

(The vintage condition notes come from a booklet published by Henschke to celebrate the 40th anniversary of Hill of Grace.)

First tasted in October 1998, updated, and later vintages added.

1998 ★★★★★ May 2001
Medium to full red–purple; powerful, luscious dark berry (blackberry/blackcurrant) aromas are supported by perfectly integrated oak. The palate has lots of depth, with layers of flavour offering a mix of plum and blackberry; excellent, ripe tannins run through to a long finish. (A classic year, with near-perfect growing conditions, and, in particular, during the harvest.)

1997 ★★★★ May 2001
The colour shows early signs of development, veering off total brightness. Cedar and spice are the dominant players on both bouquet and palate; the extract and tannins are at the lighter end of the spectrum, and I would expect the wine to develop quite quickly. (Certainly shows the cool growing season, with less than perfect ripeness.)

1996 ★★★★★ October 1998
Dense purple–red; exceptionally rich, ripe and lusciously sweet blackberry, blackcurrant and mint fruit aromas herald a great wine from a great vintage. There is a spectacular range of flavours on the palate, akin to an exotic version of the '86. (Average winter rainfall after drought years was followed by a mild spring and a mild, cool but windy summer. A cool, dry autumn provided an exceptionally long, slow ripening period and very good flavour development. A high-yield, high-quality year similar to 1990.)

classic wines

★★★★★ Perfect ★★★★☆ Close to perfect ★★★★ Very good ★★★☆ Expected
★★★ Short of standard ★★☆ Undeserving ★★ Decayed relic NR No rating

1995 ★★★★☆   *October 1998*

Medium purple–red; the bouquet is clean, moderately intense, with faint touches of green behind the sweet berry fruit, arguably adding complexity. The palate has unexpected richness and structure, with powerful yet ripe tannins; still very closed, and may develop exceptionally well with time. (The culmination of two drought winters, record spring frosts, poor fruit set and a hot, dry summer, then the coldest March on record seemed a recipe for disaster. Once again a warm April came to the rescue with very ripe grapes being harvested. Yields down by 30 per cent to 40 per cent; peppercorn-sized grapes on the bunches.)

1994 ★★★★☆   *October 1998*

Medium purple–red; vanillin oak is immediately evident on the bouquet, but without subduing the smooth supple fruit, showing none of the 'sauvage' characters of the '93. A lovely wine on the palate, although the oak is very evident, perhaps supporting, perhaps distracting from, the fruit. (A mild, dry summer with a slow start to vintage was followed by two weeks of hot weather which ripened everything at once. Stephen Henschke described it as the year of the 'black ferments', and regards it as having the potential of being one of the best ever vintages.)

1993 ★★★★★   *October 1998*

The colour is almost impenetrable, so dark and deep is it. The bouquet offers exotic, ripe, plum, prune, liquorice, berry and spice aromas, followed by a massively ripe and rich palate with the same array of flavours. A throw-back to the '61, and in many ways an atypical wine. (Was an extraordinary year, the wettest since 1851, much of the rain falling between September and December. Downy mildew threatened to run amok, but a severe hailstorm in December reduced the yields to below one-quarter of the average. The coolest February since 1950 followed, but the year was saved by an Indian summer in April. Good sugar and acid balance produced excellent concentration and flavour for the red wines.)

1992 ★★★★☆   *October 1998*

Medium purple–red; the clean and elegant bouquet has sweet, ripe but not dense fruit; a totally delicious palate with fruit in the blackberry to redcurrant range, a hint of spice and pepper, and almost milky tannins. The oak background is evident in the context of a slightly lighter wine. (A later, wet winter was followed by a dry, cool and long summer with the coldest January on record delaying harvest. Yields were high, only 10 per cent less than the record 1990 vintage.)

1991 ★★★★★   *October 1998*

Full red–purple; the bouquet is powerful, ultra-concentrated with dark briar, plum and anise aromas; the palate delivers all of the power, concentration and structure that the bouquet promises. A great wine, which will live and open up for years, but which is the polar opposite of the '90. (A short winter with below-average rainfall, a mild spring with early budburst and flowering and warm to hot summer resulted in the earliest vintage on record, with high sugar levels and below-average yields.)

1990 ★★★★★ October 1998

Full purple–red; a seamlessly smooth bouquet with perfectly ripened and balanced fruit woven through with subtle oak introduces a marvellously elegant wine, long and finely structured with gentle cassis and cedar. (An exceptional, picture book vintage in which every part of the season was exactly as it should be. Genuinely one of the great vintages of the twentieth century.)

1989 ★★★☆ October 1998

Light to medium red–purple; the bouquet is lighter, with slightly squashy berry fruit aromas, though clean and far from unpleasant. The palate is similarly pleasant, but going nowhere fast; simply doesn't have the concentration or style of the vintages preceding or following it. (A mild and wet winter was followed by a hot, windy start to spring, then a mild, dry summer, spoiled only by two weeks of excessive heat at the end of February. Picked mid-March at 22.5° brix.)

1988 ★★★★☆ October 1998

Medium to full red–purple; the bouquet shows classically balanced plum/berry fruit ripeness; the oak is sweet though quite strong. A very well-balanced and elegant wine on the palate, which, while smooth, does not have quite the weight and extract of the very best years. (An eventful year; excellent winter rains, hail damage in spring, rains during flowering and a very hot summer with ten days of century-degree heat in January followed by a cool misty February and another heatwave at the end of March. Picked 16–18 March at 23.9° brix.)

1987 ★★★★ October 1998

Medium to full red–purple; another register of fruit aromas, at least in the wines of the '80s, with a mix of quite pruney and very ripe aromas and then green mint/green pea characters. The complex palate likewise offers a mix of sweet and sour, liquorice and spice with a twist of green. Enjoyable now but drink quickly. (The third cool summer in a row, the coolest recorded since 1980; summer rains. Picked 2–3 April at 23° brix.)

1986 ★★★★★ October 1998

Superb, deep red–purple; smooth, concentrated and ripe blackberry and plum fruit is supported by subtle oak on the bouquet. A magnificent wine on the palate, with a cascade of dark berry fruits, wonderful rippling tannins, and great structure. Has another 30 years if properly cellared. (A dry winter with late rains, mild spring and a very cool summer (coolest since 1972) interrupted by two days of extreme heat on 5 and 6 March. Dry autumn with no rain after December. Picked 2–7 April at 22.3° brix.)

1985 ★★★★ October 1998

Strong purple–red; the bouquet is complex, with strong fruit and oak, but slight gamey canopy characters are evident. The slightly green streak shows through on the palate and, while not astringent, detracts somewhat from the wine. (The first of three cool summers, but with no rain for four months; the vines suffered water stress, had a large crop and ripened the fruit slowly. Picked 10–12 April at 22° brix.)

★★★★★ Perfect ★★★★☆ Close to perfect ★★★★ Very good ★★★☆ Expected
★★★ Short of standard ★★☆ Undeserving ★★ Decayed relic NR No rating

classic wines

59

1984 ★★★★★ *October 1998*

Medium purple–red; oak immediately evident for the first time on the bouquet, but complex, ripe fruit underneath came up progressively. A harmonious palate with dark plum, blackberry and just a hint of mint is followed by beautifully supple tannins on a lovely finish. (Good winter rains, warm, wet spring, mild summer and dry vintage conditions. Excellent vintage, picked 25 March–3 April at 23.4° brix.)

1983 ★★★★ *October 1998*

Excellent red–purple colour; the bouquet exudes lusciously sweet minty fruit and oak. The palate is very minty indeed with some of the ripe glossy cherry flavours of Barossa reds. (This was the vintage from hell, with frost, a severe hot, dry summer, floods, hail and bushfires. Very low yields; picked 9–18 March at 20.8° brix.)

1982 ★★★☆ *October 1998*

Medium red with hints of purple. The bouquet has faintly leafy/gamey overtones, strongly reminiscent of the Penfolds red wines of the same vintage. The flavours of the palate tend to track the bouquet, and despite a quite long finish, offers flavours I have never been able to come to terms with. Others will be more forgiving. (Very wet winter, mild spring and generally mild summer except for a heatwave just prior to vintage. Picked 17–26 March at 22.5° brix.)

1981 ★★★★★ *October 1998*

Medium to full red, still with some purple hues. The bouquet is powerful, with ripe plum and prune fruit; subtle oak. The palate is flooded with gorgeously ripe, textured, sweet plum, prune and chocolate fruit. (Average winter rains, mild spring and the hottest, driest summer since 1939, with cool dry conditions during harvest. Picked 27 March–3 April at 23.4° brix.)

1980 ★★★★★ *October 1998*

Bright red; the bouquet is clean, meltingly smooth, with sweet berry fruit and minimal oak influence. The palate has much more structure and extract than any of the wines of the '60s or '70s, with a range of ripe chocolate, sweet leather and more earthy flavours. (Good winter rains, mild spring, a relatively cool summer and dry conditions at harvest resulted in a great vintage producing superb quality. Picked 27–31 March at 22.3° brix.)

1979 ★★★★ *October 1998*

Medium brick–red; the bouquet is showing maturity, but is clean and with a mix of berry, leaf and earth. The palate has much sweeter fruit than the bouquet suggests, with hints of caramel and chocolate, and an appealing fresh finish. (A warm to hot summer and vintage, high yields and ripe fruit. Picked 20 March–3 April at 23.2° brix.)

1978 ★★★ *October 1998*

Light to medium red; the bouquet is light with leafy/tobacco aromas and fading fruit. On the palate faintly charry characters overlie light, sweet fruit. A batch of green American oak seems to have been the problem. (The season itself was low-yielding and of high quality, and an excellent vintage for reds. Picked 10–21 March.)

◄ Not Ready   ➘ Still evolving   ▲ Prime of its life   ✔ Drink soon   ▯ Missed the boat

1977 ★★★★ *October 1998*

Medium to full red; the bouquet is quite complex, with faintly dusty liquorice, bramble and earth aromas. The fully ripe, slightly brawny palate has the flavours promised by the bouquet; plenty of substance and extract. (Poor winter rains; a dry season, late vintage and below-average yields; picked 6–18 April.)

1976 ★★★★ *October 1998*

Clear, bright red; a fresh and clean bouquet with herb, anise and mint aromas of light to moderate intensity is followed by a fresh, relatively light-bodied but very attractive wine with sweet cherry fruit and soft tannins. (Good winter rains and high sunshine hours during a long summer produced high yields and lighter-style reds; perversely, all the pressings were sold off rather than incorporated.)

1975 ★★★★ *October 1998*

Medium red, with just some hints of brick starting to appear. The bouquet is clean, moderately intense with a gently sweet mix of berry and earth aromas. Elegance is the hallmark of the smooth, gentle medium-weight palate. Not complex, but eminently enjoyable. (Good winter rains; dry spring and summer with a hot February. Some rainfall in March reduced vine stress.)

1973 ★★★★ *October 1998*

Dark brooding red, with a touch of brown; ripe prune, plum and earth aromas are followed by a palate with rich, ripe prune and plum fruit flavours tracking the bouquet, interestingly without any of the chocolatey characters encountered elsewhere in the tasting. Very smooth texture and structure. (A cool start to summer followed by a hot January and a hot, wet February, before cooling off again. Above-average yields, but very ripe grapes.)

1972 ★★★★ *October 1998*

Exceptionally good bright red colour; the bouquet is clean and quite fresh but with the fruit showing an underlying leafy character. A powerful wine on the palate, long and persistent, but with a slightly green streak running through it. (Reasonable winter rains, moderate summer temperatures and rainfall all reducing water stress. Dry autumn with no rain until June. A classic year with near-perfect weather conditions producing excellent reds.) Perhaps my tongue got out of gear.

1971 ★★★☆ *October 1998*

Quite bright brick–red colour; the initially smooth bouquet shows moderate ripeness with a nice touch of chocolate, but then a hint of charry, almost petrolly, characters merge. The palate follows the bouquet with a mix of chocolate and more petrolly/earthy flavours; somewhat disappointing for what should have been a good vintage. (Hot and dry until April, when rain fell, but temperatures remained high.)

1970 ★★★ *October 1998*

Medium tawny, with just a touch of red; a relatively light, earthy, charry bouquet, showing little fruit initially, although a few sweet notes did appear after some time in the glass. The wine is pleasant on entry, but then dries up and weakens markedly on the finish. (Poor ripening conditions with 30 mm rain during the April harvest, poor colours and high acids.)

classic wines

★★★★★ Perfect ★★★★☆ Close to perfect ★★★★ Very good ★★★☆ Expected
★★★ Short of standard ★★☆ Undeserving ★★ Decayed relic NR No rating

61

1969 ★★☆   *October 1998*

Distinctly brown colour; strange woody/vegetal characters, sweet and sour suggesting imperfectly-ripened fruit. The palate is no better, the result of a poor vintage with unripe grapes and probably should not have been bottled or released. (A cool year; significant problems with mildew.)

1968 ★★★★☆   *October 1998*

Medium red–tawny. A clean, soft and smooth bouquet with gently sweet chocolate aromas heralds an interesting palate, with many flavours coming through and lingering in the mouth, ranging from slightly green leaf through to chocolate. Relatively low tannins; a wine to be drunk immediately for best enjoyment. (Poor winter rains; a very hot year with the drought period starting in September, partially broken by 70 mm rain in January and February. Continued hot to the very end of vintage.)

1967 ★★★★☆   *October 1998*

Medium to full red, with some tawny tints. Ripe chocolate and prune aromas not dissimilar to the '66. There was considerable bottle variation in the tasting; the best showing extremely ripe, luscious, almost Amarone-like flavours, though not the same weight. (Mediocre winter rains; a hot year, particularly in January, but with a drop in temperature thereafter.)

1966 ★★★★   *October 1998*

Medium red; a wine with more aggressive characters than most in the line-up, the bouquet ranging through spicy/earthy/charry and slightly riper fruit notes. The palate is relatively reserved, with echoes of those earthy/charry characters, and despite hints of the very ripe fruit, lacking the smooth vinosity of the best wines. (Hot, dry year with low yields and some shrivelled fruit at harvest.)

1965 ★★★   *October 1998*

Light to medium red; the bouquet is light, with slightly gamey/leafy characters; the palate is likewise light, lacking the sweetness and richness of the better wines, although it is reasonably well balanced. (Adequate winter rains; very dry and hot ripening period without rain; clearly, the vines struggled.)

1964 ★★★★☆   *October 1998*

Light to medium red; the bouquet abounds with extraordinarily sweet chocolatey aromas of medium intensity. The palate, likewise is medium bodied, but again precisely replicates that remarkable chocolate sweetness of the bouquet. Soft tannins; here other tasters liked the wine less than I did. (Good winter rains, a dry summer except for 30 mm of rain in February, followed by a dry autumn.)

1963 ★★☆   *October 1998*

Light to medium red; the aromas are very gamey with distinct dimethyl sulphide/unripe characters. The palate, likewise, is very green and leafy, with more of those dimethyl sulphide-derived characters. (A very dry January and February were followed by rains in late March through April.)

◄— Not Ready   ＼ Still evolving   ▌ Prime of its life   Drink soon   ▯ Missed the boat

1962 ★★★★
October 1998

Medium red which is still bright, and with virtually no tawny hues. The bouquet is of medium intensity, with a range of faintly minty/foresty/mossy/earthy notes. Similar characters appeared to me to run through the palate, which did not have over-much structure or tannins to support it. Other tasters liked the wine much more, and the cellar records of a warm year, excellent vintage at high baumé grapes (up to 13.5) suggest my impressions and tasting notes did not do the wine justice.

1961 ★★★★★
October 1998

Medium tawny red. The bouquet is complex, quite rich and sweet, with chocolate and more savoury aromas. The palate takes you through a roller-coaster ride, with rich, ripe fruit on the verge of portiness, sustained and balanced though by ripe tannins which run right through the mid to back palate, providing plenty of structure and life. The high point of the wine is its quite gorgeous finish. (No cellar records available of vintage conditions.)

1959 ★★★★
October 1998

Light to medium tawny red. The clean bouquet is much lighter than the '58, offering a mixture of earth, chocolate and leaf aromas. The palate is light, but smooth and well balanced; while not decaying, there is not much substance here for a prolonged life. (A late vintage, with a smaller crop than 1958. The wines were racked earlier than 1958, and the pressings were kept separate.)

1958 ★★★★★
October 1998

Medium red, with some tawny tints on the rim. The bouquet is amazingly rich and ripe with sweet chocolatey aromas, and no hint of drying out. The palate is no less rich and ripe, still quite dense, with chocolate and plum fruit, finishing with soft, lingering tannins. Well corked will hold for another 20–30 years. (Spring frosts caused minor damage; an early vintage with cold weather once the grapes were harvested.)

classic wines

★★★★★ Perfect ★★★★☆ Close to perfect ★★★★ Very good ★★★☆ Expected
★★★ Short of standard ★★☆ Undeserving ★★ Decayed relic NR No rating

63

henschke mount edelstone
1952-1998

the Mount Edelstone Vineyard was planted in the 1920s by Ronald Angas, the grandson of George Fife Angas, one of the founders of the Barossa Valley and who gave his name to one of its most important towns, Angaston. The Henschke family purchased the grapes for many years before acquiring ownership of the Vineyard from the Angases in 1974.

The first wine to bear the Mount Edelstone label was made in 1952. It had immediate success when first entered in the wine shows in 1956, but it was the wine of that vintage (1956) which really made the reputation of Mount Edelstone (and for that matter, Henschke). Over 40 years later, the wine is still superb; indeed, the remarkable feature of the Mount Edelstone tastings is the consistency of style and quality. There was a minor change of style in the 1970s when the pressings were excluded, but it was a short-lived change: they are once again incorporated.

One cannot deny the majesty and power of the Hill of Grace, but Mount Edelstone — planted on nearly identical soils only two kilometres away — has its own character, more spicy and lifted than Hill of Grace. As is appropriate and inevitable with a single-vineyard wine, vintage variation plays an important part in shaping the particular character of the wine of each year, but overall, I have the sneaking feeling that Mount Edelstone copes even better with the whims of nature than does Hill of Grace.

First tasted in November 1994, updated, and later vintages added.

1998 ★★★★★   *October 2000*
Medium red–purple; a fragrant and aromatic bouquet with spicy overtones to the berry and leaf fruit leads into a palate where spice, berry, cherry, leaf and mint are all present in abundance. The oak has been perfectly controlled throughout, and the wine finishes with excellent, fine tannins.

1997 ★★★★   *October 1999*
Medium red–purple; the bouquet is clean, but rather light and slightly leafy, tending simple. The palate is rather better, light but quite well balanced, with red fruits and some touches of sweet vanilla oak. Uncharacteristic tasting notes, perhaps for a wine going through a particularly difficult phase of its development.

◀ Not Ready   ❭ Still evolving   ❘ Prime of its life   ⟋ Drink soon   ☐ Missed the boat

1996 ★★★★★ *November 1998*

Medium to full red–purple; complex aromas run through the bouquet with nuances of pepper, liquorice and mint to the core of red cherry fruit. The palate is smooth, with cherry, mint and a touch of pepper all showing; the oak is sweet but not forceful, the tannins soft and supple. Top gold 1998 National Wine Show.

1995 ★★★★★ *February 1998*

Medium to full red–purple; a complex bouquet, with fragrant, spice, liquorice, earth and charry oak aromas all intermingling. The palate, too, is multiflavoured, with black cherry, liquorice and charry oak flavours. Fine tannins.

1994 ★★★★ *October 1996*

Medium to full red–purple; an unusually complex array of aromas with some floral/scented overtones and then more traditional and firmer earthy/ blackberry/bitter chocolate characters. The palate is firm, almost austere in the context of the Henschke style, with fine tannins and underplayed oak.

1993 ★★★★★ *October 1995*

Medium to full red–purple; a complex bouquet with abundant, soft cherry/berry fruit and perfectly balanced and integrated oak. There is mouthfilling dark chocolate and berry fruit on the palate, sophisticated use of French and American oak, and well-integrated and balanced tannins.

1992 ★★★★★ *November 1994*

Youthful purple–red; fresh, scented cherry/berry/spice aromas, reflecting a relatively cool vintage but showing lovely varietal character. There is delicious spicy/cherry/berry fruit on the palate with sweet vanillin oak. A luscious wine with everything going for it.

1991 ★★★★☆ *November 1994*

Deep, dark purple–red; the bouquet is rich, full and ripe with voluminous dark berry fruit. The palate is concentrated, powerful and aggressive, with slightly phenolic charry oak. Needs much time; could end up great.

1990 ★★★★★ *November 1994*

Medium to full red–purple; a complex spicy/earthy aroma with lots of red berry fruits. The palate is similarly complex with dark cherry, berry, chocolate and faintly gamey characters all evident. A many splendoured thing.

1989 ★★★★ *November 1994*

Medium to full red–purple; very ripe, almost jammy, with berry and mint aromas. The palate is likewise ripe, though not quite so extravagantly so as the bouquet, with attractive liquorice chocolate and cherry flavours. A pleasant, early-maturing wine in an off-beat fashion.

1988 ★★★★★ *November 1994*

Medium red–purple; some cedary/earthy aromas starting to develop on a fragrant bouquet, tinged with chocolate. In the mouth, an outstanding wine with sweet mid-palate red berry fruit and fine tannins woven throughout. Will be very long lived.

classic wines

★★★★★ Perfect ★★★★☆ Close to perfect ★★★★ Very good ★★★☆ Expected
★★★ Short of standard ★★☆ Undeserving ★★ Decayed relic NR No rating

65

1987 ★★★☆   *November 1994*

Light to medium red; most pronounced earthy/leafy herbal aromas, reminiscent of the '83. The palate shows extreme herbaceous/medicinal flavours, strongly suggesting the presence of some dimethyl sulphide. Has not developed gracefully, notwithstanding a show record which included six gold medals at national shows.

1986 ★★★★☆   *November 1994*

Medium to full red–purple; a concentrated bouquet with red berry fruits and a hint of charry/matchstick oak. A powerful wine on the palate with earth, spice and mineral flavours; the structure is good, the oak subtle.

1985 ★★★   *November 1994*

Medium red–purple; distinctly gamey/sweaty aromas, deriving either from canopy problems or possibly a slight bacterial infection. The palate shows more of the same sweaty/gamey characters, strongly pointing the finger at insufficient ripening; finishes hard in the mouth.

1984 ★★★☆   *November 1994*

Medium red–purple; another wine to lack the generosity one expects, with some leaf and game characters. There are spicy flavours on the palate, along with leafy notes; very much the product of a cool growing season, and slightly hard on the finish. May conceivably soften and improve with further bottle age.

1983 ★★★★   *November 1994*

Medium red; there are aromas of mint and earth on the bouquet, though not as ripe or lush as one might expect given the year. The palate is now nicely developed with traditional earthy, spicy Shiraz flavours, finishing with well-balanced tannins.

1982 ★★★★☆   *November 1994*

Strong red–purple colour, with a full, complex and rich bouquet, solid with sweet fruit and plenty of oak. In the mouth a big, rich, ripe fruity/minty wine with lots of tannin and extract. Perhaps it does lack the final finesse of the '78, but will be very long lived.

1978 ★★★★★   *November 1994*

Medium red–purple colour; a quite gorgeous bouquet, fragrant with wonderful liquorice and spice varietal character. The palate has abundant, gently sweet fruit, liquorice-accented, with fine-grained tannins; great length and style.

1972 ★★★   *November 1994*

Medium red colour; a lighter style with an interesting herbal/spice edge to the bouquet. In the mouth there are slightly green/herbal/malic characters reminiscent of the '65.

1967 ★★★★★   *November 1994*

As with many of the wines in the tasting, medium to full red with very little distinction or gradation between vintages. The bouquet is very rich and ripe with liquorice and dark chocolate. The palate, too, is wonderfully generous, rounded and soft, with chewy, ripe flavours and nice tannins. The longer it sat in the glass, the better it looked. Probably has another ten years in front of it.

◄ Not Ready   \ Still evolving   ▮ Prime of its life   ⬍ Drink soon   ▯ Missed the boat

1966 ★★★★★ *November 1994*

Medium to full red, with a youthful, clean bouquet full and liquorice-accented. The palate is mouthfilling, rich and rounded with lashings of dark chocolate and those typically fine, soft tannins. Beautifully balanced and structured.

1965 ★★★☆ *November 1994*

Medium red; a complex bouquet with sweet notes set against a faintly herbal edge. A cooler, more elegant style overall, with some slightly herbal/green edges to the fruit, though showing no signs of decay.

1962 ★★★★☆ *November 1994*

Medium brick–red; spotlessly clean, sweet chocolate and coffee-accented aromas, replicated in a gorgeously sweet, chocolate/toffee-flavoured palate which is delicate rather than cloying. The finish is starting to diminish, and the wine faded in the glass. Drink soon, and serve immediately after opening and decanting.

1961 ★★★★★ *November 1994*

Medium to full brick–red; powerful, concentrated bouquet, still in perfect condition. In the mouth a lovely wine with fully ripe dark chocolate, sweet rounded fruit and soft tannins.

1960 ★★★ *November 1994*

Light red; a clean, soft classic, gently earthy/ripe shiraz bouquet. The palate came as something of a disappointment, being rather lighter and thinner than the bouquet suggested. A product of a cooler vintage.

1958 ★★☆ *November 1994*

Medium to full red; ripe fruit, but volatility is evident in both the bouquet and palate; definitely on the down-hill run.

1956 ★★★★★ *November 1994*

The colour is still strong and red; the bouquet shows robust, complex sweet fruit with hints of earth. In the mouth the wine is remarkably powerful and still concentrated; there are plenty of tannins intermingling with pleasantly earthy/tarry notes. Remarkable old wine.

1952 ★★★★☆ *November 1994*

Brick–red, with a ripe caramel/truffle/mushroom bouquet. The palate is ripe, with lingering touches of dark chocolate and a sweet velvety texture and flavour. Holding on remarkably well, even though the bouquet shows telltale signs of age.

classic wines

★★★★★ Perfect   ★★★★☆ Close to perfect   ★★★★ Very good   ★★★☆ Expected
★★★ Short of standard   ★★☆ Undeserving   ★★ Decayed relic   NR No rating

houghton white burgundy

1982-2000

this is 'The Wine that Jack Built'—or so the saying might go. For it was the legendary Jack Mann who first made the wine in 1937; by the 1950s the blue stripe of Houghton White Burgundy was commonplace on the retail shelves of Eastern States retailers, the only wine from Western Australia to be able to claim that distinction. Moreover, Houghton was at the time owned by the UK-based Emu Wine Company, with all of the limitations of remote-control ownership and management.

Things turned for the better when Thomas Hardy acquired Emu Wines — better for both Hardy and Houghton, for the latter acquired the business for less than the true worth of its assets. Jack Mann retired, but the style of the Houghton White Burgundy was protected and indeed enhanced by far better white winemaking equipment and by a succession of gifted winemakers — Jon Reynolds, Peter Dawson, Paul Lapsley and now Larry Cherubino.

The wine itself has undergone some changes. In the early 1980s it was typically a blend of 65 per cent Chenin Blanc and 35 per cent Muscadelle, sometimes with a little Verdelho. Now Semillon and Chardonnay are included, although the Swan Valley and Gingin remain the geographic base.

It is bottled in batches throughout the year; 500 dozen of each bottling are retained, and at the end of the year the best batch is kept to one side as a Show Reserve, and released (after a typically very distinguished show record littered with trophies and gold medals) when six to eight years old.

First tasted in October 1994, updated, and later vintages added.

2000 ★★★★   *October 2000*

Arguably an article of faith, for it is more to do with five years time than today. Most will never know, happy to enjoy the gentle, passionfruit and tropical fruit aroma and flavour of today and eschew the rich, honeyed complexity of maturity.

1999 ★★★★   *October 1999*

If ever a wine suffers from schizophrenia, this one does. Designed (and doomed) to be consumed within hours of purchase, it will, however, turn from frog to prince around 2005, kissing not required. Fragrant yet delicate tropical passionfruit aroma and flavour, beguiling now, will be transformed into honeyed, luscious complexity with time.

◄■ Not Ready   ◣ Still evolving   🍷 Prime of its life   ⟋ Drink soon   🍶 Missed the boat

1998 ★★★★ *March 1999*

Light to medium yellow–green; a lively, attractive and aromatic bouquet with hints of passionfruit is replicated on the fresh, relatively light palate which will build weight and complexity over the next five years.

1996 ★★★★☆ *October 1996*

Light to medium yellow–green; a clean, fruit-driven bouquet with gentle tropical aromas of medium intensity, and a subliminal touch of oak. An elegant, fine and restrained palate; you really have to look at the history of the wine to understand its tremendous development potential.

1995 ★★★★★ *November 1995*

Light to medium yellow–green; the bouquet is spotlessly clean with attractive tangy fruit and a subtle touch of spicy oak. The palate is lively, fresh and crisp with fruit salad flavours, subtle spicy oak, and the faintest flick of residual sugar is balanced by good acid.

1994 ★★★★★ *October 1994*

Medium yellow–green; fruit-driven with abundant white peach and passionfruit aromas. The palate is clean and smooth, with gently peachy fruit, and a hint of melon; well weighted, well balanced, not too sweet and will develop well, if relatively quickly.

1993 ★★★★☆ *October 1994*

Medium yellow–green; rich, tropical peach and passionfruit aromas starting to subside as the wine commences to age. There are still strong passionfruit flavours on the palate, along with peach and melon; well structured and balanced, should develop nicely.

1992 ★★★★☆ *October 1994*

Medium yellow–green; starting to go into the transition stage, but is a tighter and more elegant wine than some in the line-up. The palate is fresh and clean, with some Semillon-like characters and some incipient toast starting to appear.

1989 ★★★★ *October 1994*

Medium to full yellow–green; has now developed rich, honeyed toasty/ buttery aromas, with obvious sweet fruit. The palate is big, rich and honeyed with abundant sweet fruit, so abundant that it in fact cloys fractionally on the finish.

1988 ★★★★★ *October 1994*

Medium to full yellow–green; a marvellously smooth bouquet, gently honeyed with lots of lightly browned toast, yet retaining freshness. The palate picks up on that freshness, with some herbaceous notes, good acidity and a particularly lively finish. Top gold medal at the Australian National Wine Show 1993.

1987 ★★★★★ *October 1994*

Medium to full yellow–green; a complex, rich and powerful bouquet with honeyed, nutty/buttery aromas. The palate is complex, rich and rounded, with the same honeyed fruit characters of the bouquet. Simply delicious.

classic wines

★★★★★ Perfect   ★★★★☆ Close to perfect   ★★★★ Very good   ★★★☆ Expected
★★★ Short of standard   ★★☆ Undeserving   ★★ Decayed relic   NR No rating

69

1986 ★★★★★   *October 1994*

Deep yellow; the bouquet is full and very toasty, with Semillon-like characters predominating. The palate is of light to medium weight, dry and toasty, and again far more like an aged Semillon than the complex fruit blend that it is. Well balanced; winner of three trophies and three gold medals.

1982 ★★★★★   *October 1994*

Bright, medium yellow–green; a tangy, lively bouquet, still remarkably fresh and herbaceous with hints of toast in the background. Still holding strong fruit on the palate, with firm acidity; has similarities to the '86 and '88.

howard park riesling 1986-2000

When John Wade left the security of the position of chief winemaker at Wynns Coonawarra Estate in 1985 to travel to a then little-known region in the far southwest corner of Australia he turned his back on many things, and effectively risked all. Ten years later he had achieved everything he could have hoped for, indeed more.

The first achievement was the Howard Park Riesling, making its debut in early 1987 with the 1986 vintage. If I had to nominate a single wine to demonstrate that the Mount Barker/Frankland region (or Great Southern, call it what you will) deserves to be rated alongside the Clare and Eden Valleys for the quality of its Riesling, it would be Howard Park.

Although made in tiny quantities, it has earned a thoroughly deserved reputation for exceptional quality, consistency and longevity. As the tasting notes indicate, none of the wines have started to fade; many have improvement in front of them; and only a few have yet plateaued. While the Leo Buring, Petaluma and Jeffrey Grosset Riesling tastings go back further, all are of equal importance in demonstrating just how superbly high-quality Australian Riesling ages in bottle.

John Wade has since moved on; Michael Kerrigan is the winemaker, the Birch family the owners. It is clear they jointly intend to jealously guard their inheritance.

First tasted in October 1994, updated, and later vintages added.

■ *2000* ★★★★☆   *October 2000*

Light to medium yellow–green; the bouquet is typically clean, crisp and fresh, with a range of mineral, herb, citrus and apple aromas. The palate is very tight and crisp, with powerful, minerally acid; an austere wine which really needs to be left alone until (say) 2004.

■ *1999* ★★★★★   *November 1999*

There have been changes aplenty at Howard Park, but not at the expense of this classic wine. Bright, light green–yellow, the delicately understated bouquet doesn't prepare you for the spotlessly clean, vibrantly lively palate with passionfruit, apple and lime flavours. A wine with an impeccable history, bred to stay.

★★★★★ Perfect   ★★★★☆ Close to perfect   ★★★★ Very good   ★★★☆ Expected
★★★ Short of standard   ★★☆ Undeserving   ★★ Decayed relic   NR No rating

classic wines

71

1998 ★★★★★   *October 1998*

Light to medium green–yellow; a beautifully intense wine with lime/citrus/tropical aromas, and a delicate, crisp palate in which passionfruit, lime and mineral flavours intermingle. Quite flawless.

1997 ★★★★★   *October 1997*

Light to medium yellow–green; pristine, lime-accented varietal riesling fruit aromas announce a wine which is on a plane all of its own, immaculately elegant and pure, yet intense. The flavours are predominantly lime, with a hint of pear, the finish crisp but lingering.

1996 ★★★★★   *October 1996*

Light to medium yellow–green; moves to the pace of its own drum, with an extra dimension of intensity and richness, yet not the least bit heavy on either bouquet or palate. There are voluminous Germanic lime flavours tinged with passionfruit, and a finish as long and as fresh as one could ever imagine.

1995 ★★★★★   *October 1995*

Light green–yellow; ultra-classic Riesling, elegant yet concentrated, with a mix of lime and toast to the bouquet. There is marvellous structure and grip to the palate; superb now, but with a decade in front of it. One of the great Howard Park Rieslings.

1994 ★★★★★   *October 1994*

Light green–yellow; intense, powerful and fragrant with toasty and lime fruit; no apparent yeast influence. A very powerful, intense and long flavour with those tightly structured lime flavours, and grip on the finish.

1993 ★★★★★   *October 1994*

Light green–yellow; classic, youthful fragrant and flowery aromas of toast and lime flood the bouquet. A beautifully bred wine on the palate, with classic structure and flavours; long and intense, yet fine.

1992 ★★★★   *October 1994*

Medium yellow–green; a complex bouquet with lime and many other fruit aromas showing a hint of botrytis. The palate is firm, with more obvious fruit flavours than many in the line-up; the acid is good, and the wine may come out of its transition phase with more time.

1991 ★★★★★   *October 1994*

Medium yellow–green; classic, tight, restrained bouquet with fine, tangy lime and lime rind aromas. The palate is as the bouquet promises, very tight, long and intense, with a lingering finish. There was a touch of botrytis, but it does not mark the wine.

1990 ★★★★☆   *October 1994*

A slightly corked bottle was tasted, which made the wine seem faintly blurred and broader. The structure was there, and the balance. The rating is something of a compromise between the wine as it was in the glass, and as it should be.

1989 ★★★★ October 1994

Medium to full yellow–green; a very complex bouquet, rich with some minerally aspects, and also obvious botrytis influence. The palate is luscious and rich in a Germanic, dry Auslese style; powerful and striking, and will appeal to many. 13.2 per cent alcohol thanks to the botrytis.

1988 ★★★★★ October 1994

Bright medium yellow–green. A perfectly smooth, rounded and fresh bouquet with lime/citrus aromas showing wonderful mature riesling character. The palate is perfectly balanced and tight, less sweet than the '86, and with a hint of classic kerosene character.

1987 ★★★★★ October 1994

Slightly more yellow hints showing in the colour, but still bright; full, rich and toasty, with luscious fruit aromas. The palate is soft and rich, with round, mouthfilling, almost honeyed flavours, but no sign of drying out.

1986 ★★★★★ October 1994

Glowing green–yellow; potent, intense lime aromas which magically combine power and elegance. The palate has near-perfect weight, balance and composition, showing no signs of fading; fine yet flavourful, with an attractive touch of sweetness.

★★★★★ Perfect ★★★★☆ Close to perfect ★★★★ Very good ★★★☆ Expected
★★★ Short of standard ★★☆ Undeserving ★★ Decayed relic NR No rating

howard park cabernet sauvignon
merlot 1986-1998

What do Opus One and Howard Park Cabernet Merlot have in common? Much more than one might imagine. Each wine was created, marketed and established its reputation without having either a vineyard or a winery of its own. Both are Bordeaux-type blends, with the precise composition varying from one year to the next, and each now has a winery it can call its own. It is the scale which is different: Opus One is a $20 million, 20 000 cases joint venture between Mouton Rothschild and the Mondavi family.

The Howard Park winery may be state-of-the-art, but it is strictly functional and the volume of Howard Park will not rise above 2000 cases a year for the foreseeable future.

Prior to 1990, the wine was predominantly or (in 1988) wholly Cabernet Sauvignon, and labelled as such. The '90 was 70 per cent Cabernet Sauvignon, 20 per cent Merlot and 5 per cent each of Malbec and Shiraz; the '91 was 70 per cent Great Southern Cabernet Sauvignon and 30 per cent Margaret River Merlot; the '98 was 75 per cent Cabernet Sauvignon, 13 per cent Cabernet Franc, and 12 per cent Merlot sourced from the Great Southern and Margaret River regions. What is consistent is the extraordinary refinement, balance and polish of each successive vintage.

First tasted in October 1994, updated, and later vintages added.

1998 ★★★★★ *October 2000*

Medium to full red–purple; sweet berry fruit and sweet, spicy French oak support a bouquet showing good ripeness and no volatile acidity problems whatsoever. The palate confirms the convincing return to form, notwithstanding the challenges of the growing season. The wine has a seductive structure, and soft, persistent tannins.

1997 ★★★★ *October 1999*

Medium red–purple; the bouquet is clean, without any untoward lift, but the fruit is quite light. An elegant style on the palate, with delicate fruit sustained by spicy Troncais oak; well-balanced, fine tannins.

◄ Not Ready   ➘ Still evolving   ▮ Prime of its life   ◢ Drink soon   ⎕ Missed the boat

1996 ★★★★☆   *October 1998*

Medium red, with some softening in the purple hue. The bouquet is fragrant and complex, with that typical spicy/cedary oak of Howard Park; the palate has admirable structure with cedary, foresty flavours, soft, fine tannins, and sweetness deriving partly from the fruit and partly from the Troncais oak. A welcome return to form.

1995 ★★★☆   *October 1997*

Medium to full red–purple; from this point on I have real problems with the wine. Like the curate's egg, it is great in parts, but not others. The 'others' derive from the degree of what is euphemistically called lift and technically called volatile acidity. There are wonderful dark berry and dark chocolate flavours together with that sweet, cedary oak, but I cannot help but notice the volatility. Others may be less pedantic.

1994 ★★★★★   *October 1996*

Full red–purple; a superb mix of blackcurrant, cassis and briar fruit with gently spicy French oak on the bouquet leads on to an unusually concentrated yet not heavy wine on the palate with layer upon layer of flavour, cassis/blackcurrant/blackberry fruit and fine, lingering tannins. Bordeaux seldom does better than this.

1993 ★★★★★   *October 1995*

Medium to full red–purple; quite marvellous dark berry/blackcurrant fruit interwoven with fine, spicy French oak; spotlessly clean and of the highest imaginable quality. The palate is perfectly structured and balanced with supple blackcurrant fruit, subtle spicy oak, and fine-grained tannins; as good as they come.

1992 ★★★★★   *October 1994*

Medium to full purple–red; a powerful, classic wine in the mainstream of the Howard Park style, spotlessly clean and with less opulent fruit than the '91. On the palate, immaculately balanced and structured, with near-perfect berry fruit ripeness in a highly disciplined style, finishing with lingering tannins.

1991 ★★★★☆   *October 1994*

Medium to full purple–red; the bouquet has luscious, sweet berry and cherry fruit, and that seamless integration of high-quality French oak that is there, but you don't really notice it. The palate is seemingly the ripest and sweetest of all of the wines in the line-up, and also one of the most powerful; the tannins are still showing, but will soften well before the fruit starts to go.

1990 ★★★★★   *October 1994*

Bright purple–red. By far the most powerful wine on the bouquet with dark berry fruit and cedary, sweet oak. The palate is concentrated, powerful and intense, with dark briary/berry fruits and subliminal oak. Will go down the track of the '86, but conceivably end up as the greatest of the wines made up to '92.

classic wines

★★★★★ Perfect   ★★★★☆ Close to perfect   ★★★★ Very good   ★★★☆ Expected
★★★ Short of standard   ★★☆ Undeserving   ★★ Decayed relic   NR No rating

1989 ★★★★★ *October 1994*

Medium to full red–purple; a relatively soft and spicy bouquet with harmonious sweet plum, berry and cassis aromas, touched by charry oak. The palate is lusciously complex and rich, with perfectly ripened fruit flavours and equally perfectly balanced oak. The year had none of the problems encountered in the Eastern States. 13 per cent alcohol.

1988 ★★★★★ *October 1994*

Medium to full red–purple; an elegant and stylish bouquet exhibits the hallmark balance and integration of fruit and oak. The palate is glorious, with wonderful sweet berry fruit on the mid-palate, then a very long, relatively dry finish, reflecting 28 days maceration on skins. Will live for a decade, probably two.

1986 ★★★★★ *October 1994*

Bright red–purple of medium intensity. The aromas are strongly reminiscent of Bordeaux, with fine, cedary aspects and the seemingly inevitable balance and ripeness of fruit. In the mouth, the wine is eerily like a moderately mature, high-quality Bordeaux. There are fine-grained tannins, cedar and cigar box nuances, and no particular fruit flavours dominate, yet all the cabernet fruit is there. Ten years minimum before it tires.

Not Ready ⟍ Still evolving ▮ Prime of its life ⌟ Drink soon ⛾ Missed the boat

huntington estate cabernet
sauvignon 1973-1998

bob and Wendy Roberts have created a remarkable family-owned estate, with daughter Susan (married to Richard Tognetti, director of the Australian Chamber Orchestra) now in charge of winemaking. It is a family with a breathtaking range of skills and interests, most centred on wine and music, with the annual Huntington Festival a major event on the Australian musical calendar.

Yet this Mudgee-based winery has never received the recognition it deserves for its red wines. Space constraints meant that only one Cabernet release from each vintage has been included: Huntington Estate uses a complicated series of bin numbers prefixed with the letters FB (full-bodied) or MB (medium-bodied), and often several releases will be made each year.

What is more, all things are relative. While the division between FB and MB is a valid one for most wineries, Huntington medium-bodied wines would appear full bodied, the Huntington full-bodied wines undoubtedly so. But there is a wonderful continuity of style: these are wines of exceptional generosity of fruit and fullness of structure. One might expect the young wines to be harsh and tannic, but they are not. Certainly, they benefit enormously from cellaring for at least five and frequently ten years, but it is easy to see where they are headed (and not so difficult to drink a bottle or two while they are young).

The 1973 to 1991 vintages were tasted in May 1995; other vintages on release.

1998 Bin FB16 ★★★   *February 2001*
Medium red–purple; cedary/dusty/earthy cabernet varietal aromas are followed by a palate with sweet berry at the core, finishing with quite pronounced tannins. A vintage slashed by hail just before veraison. Only 300 cases made.

1997 Bin FB35 ★★★★   *March 2000*
Medium red–purple; the bouquet has a range of cedar, earth and berry aromas; cassis and chocolate flavours are the staple of a rich, round palate finishing with ripe tannins.

classic wines

1995 Bin FB30 ★★★★☆   *January 1998*

Medium purple–red; as one would expect, there is pronounced varietal character in an earthy blackberry spectrum; overall of light to medium intensity. The palate, too, shows firm varietal cabernet fruit, with sweet flavours coming through on the mid to back palate before firm tannins stiffen up the finish. Subtle oak.

1994 Special Reserve ★★★★   *January 1998*

Medium to full red–purple; the bouquet is rich and full with a mix of cassis, blackberry and mint fruit aromas. The same mix of cassis and mint runs through a smooth palate, finishing with soft, fine tannins.

1993 Bin FB27 ★★★★   *May 1997*

Medium to full purple–red; a solid, briary/earthy bouquet with dark fruits and subtle oak. The wine is as substantial on the palate as the bouquet suggests, with chewy/briary/earthy cabernet flavours, lingering tannins and subtle oak throughout.

1991 Bin FB ★★★★☆   *May 1995*

Deep purple–red in colour, with a very ripe and potent earth/mint and cassis berry bouquet. A massively potent wine, tight and tannic. (No bin number allocated at time of tasting.)

1990 Bin FB23 ★★★★★   *May 1995*

Similarly dense purple–red colour with a clean, smooth and stylish bouquet redolent of chocolate and mint. The powerful palate has the balance for long cellaring and needs much time, with lots of fruit and persistent tannins.

1989 Bin FB32 ★★★★★   *May 1995*

Once again, dense purple–red with virtually no colour change evident. The bouquet is concentrated, inky and youthful, with dark berry fruits to the fore. In the mouth, it is rich, voluptuous, concentrated and ripe, a radical departure from the preceding vintages and seemingly a throwback to the style of the very early wines. The tannins are particularly well balanced.

1988 Bin MB20 ★★★☆   *May 1995*

A radical colour shift, with all of the youthful purple tones disappeared. The bouquet is tightly composed and structured, with clean, smooth berry fruit. A much lighter-bodied style which is smooth, clean and well balanced with nice mouthfeel.

1987 Bin FB14 ★★☆   *May 1995*

Bright purple–red, but the wine lacks the richness and sweetness of the majority, with slightly stalky/herbal aromas and quite herbaceous varietal fruit on the palate, which lacks the vinosity one expects of this line.

1986 Bin FB8 ★★★☆   *May 1995*

The fresh purple–red colour introduces a complex bouquet with overtones of Coonawarra: stalky, earthy and sweet berry/cassis notes are all present. The palate is more towards medium bodied than full bodied, and is remarkably fresh and indeed slightly unformed. Time may fill out the slightly thin entry to the mouth.

1985 Bin FB25 ★★☆   *May 1995*

Despite its youthful purple–red colour, and its potent, striking, essence-fruit bouquet, I would prefer to drink this wine sooner rather than later, because volatility is evident in both the bouquet and palate, and is likely to intensify with age.

1984 Bin FB16 ★★★★★   *May 1995*

Strongly coloured, with classically varietal Cabernet aromas, herbaceous without being green or lean. The same extraordinarily precise cabernet varietal character is evident on the palate, suggesting a cool growing season. While muscular and lean, it is not the least bitter, having wonderful length and balance.

1983 Bin FB9 ★★★   *May 1995*

The colour is lighter and more developed and the aromas more earthy than fruity. The structure is quite strong, and although not aggressively tannic, simply needs more flesh and fruit.

1982 Bin FB18 ★★   *May 1995*

A faintly smelly/eggy/dusty bouquet is echoed in a slightly bitter, earthy and stalky palate.

1981 Bin FB13 ★★★★☆   *May 1995*

A strongly-coloured, very ripe wine with an earthy/briary/chocolate bouquet leading on to a concentrated palate with lots of fruit extract and tannins. Very big but marvellously balanced.

1980 Bin MB9 ★★☆   *May 1995*

Medium red colour, with a clean, faintly leafy and relatively light bouquet. The palate is, as the bouquet promises, on the lean side, with a faintly lactic character.

1979 Bin FB29 ★★★★★   *May 1995*

A glorious wine, still full red, with even a hint of purple. The bouquet is complex and stylish with masses of dark berry fruits, a touch of pleasant earthiness and minimal oak. In the mouth it is no less impressive, marvellously elegant, with fresh red berry fruits, perfect tannins and just a touch of oak.

1978 Bin FB16 ★★★   *May 1995*

Medium to full red, with lifted, fragrant and ripe earth and chocolate aromas. In the mouth the wine is very potent with some mint flavours before the tannins take over, tannins which will outlive the fruit.

1977 Bin MB17 ★★   *May 1995*

An altogether lighter style, both in colour, aroma and body. There are slightly petrolly overtones to the bouquet, and lighter, leafier flavours throughout.

1976 Bin MB18 ★★★☆   *May 1995*

Another lighter wine, initially leafy but the aroma of which came up in the glass. The palate, too, has much more substance than the bouquet suggests, with some dark chocolate flavours and good tannins. Just needs that little bit more flesh.

classic wines

1975 Bin FB9 ★★★★   *May 1995*

Medium to full red in colour, with quite fresh, sweet cherry-accented fruit with hints of spice and cedar. While much lighter than the '74, on the palate, more lifted, with the spicy cherry notes of the bouquet reappearing.

1974 Bin FB2 ★★★★★   *May 1995*

Incredibly, still retaining just a hint of purple in the colour with firm, youthful and strong dark chocolate fruit and echoes of new oak on the bouquet. The flavours are of dark chocolate, dark berry with a hint of mint; a great mature wine which is wonderfully harmonious, and has the substance to live.

1973 ★★★☆   *May 1995*

Some tawny hues are appearing in the colour, while the sweet, dusty aged bouquet is not unlike an old Bordeaux, with mint, chocolate and cedar all there. In the mouth, clearly an old wine, but certainly hanging in and is still well balanced, even if its fruit is now fading.

jamiesons run 1985-1998

Jamiesons Run may seem an odd inclusion, and in a sense it is. If it qualifies, it certainly does so under the heading 'new classic', for its first vintage was 1985, and the 1997 tasting was held by Mildara Blass to celebrate its tenth birthday.

But when you stop to consider its show record, the entitlement to inclusion becomes less argumentative. Every vintage between 1986 and 1994 (other than the '92) won at least one gold medal at national wine shows. Cumulatively, the nine vintages won 26 gold medals and six trophies — including the much coveted Jimmy Watson Trophy in 1989 (for the 1988 vintage).

Nor does classic have to mean rare and expensive — Houghton White Burgundy is the white wine correlative to Jamiesons Run. Both show the commercial face of Australian winemaking at its best, although I would be less than honest if I suggested that either should be expected to repay very extended cellaring.

Indeed, changing fermentation techniques — notably the arrival of 22 rotary fermenters or vinomatics at Mildara's Coonawarra winery — are likely to produce even softer (and faster maturing) wines in the future. Given that most Jamiesons Run will be consumed within days or weeks of purchase, this is as it should be. But nature has a way of coming up with vintages such as '90, '91, '96 and '98, and Coonawarra is in any event a special place in which to grow grapes and make wine.

First tasted in August 1997, updated, and later vintages added.

1998 Reserve ★★★★★
February 2001

Medium to full red–purple; the bouquet has more charry/toasty oak than the standard wine, and deeper, more powerful fruit. A complex, rich and powerful palate ranges through blackberry and blackcurrant fruit plus sustained tannins. The best Reserve so far.

1998 ★★★★☆
February 2001

Medium red–purple; the moderately intense bouquet is quite fragrant, with sweet blackberry and mulberry fruit. Most attractive sweet berry, cassis, plum and blackberry fruit flavours are supported by a nice touch of oak and fine tannins. Has evolved very well since being bottled.

classic wines

1996 Reserve ★★★★☆ *October 1998*

Medium red–purple; the moderately intense bouquet is clean, with attractive earthy/berry fruit and subtle oak. The palate is firm but not harsh or aggressive, with a similar mix of earth, mint and red berry flavours; subtle oak, soft tannins.

1996 ★★★★☆ *January 1998*

Strong red–purple; a fragrant, potent mix of berry, leaf, spice and earth aromas lead into a wine of excellent weight and structure, right back to the best. Sweet red cherry, mint and blackberry flavours run through the palate; subtle oak.

1995 ★★★★ *August 1997*

Youthful purple–red, as one would expect. The bouquet is similarly youthful, with red berry, mint, leaf and earth aromas. Light cherry fruit and soft tannins on a pleasant palate mark a wine that is still improving but that will mature fairly quickly. It would seem to show the influence of increased vinomatic fermentation. 77 per cent Cabernet Sauvignon, 11 per cent Shiraz, 6 per cent Cabernet Franc, 3 per cent Malbec, 3 per cent Merlot.

1994 ★★★☆ *August 1997*

Medium to full purple–red; the bouquet is clean, with red berry fruits particularly noticeable in the line-up when compared to the older wines, although there is that vineyard touch of leaf and mint. Much lighter in body than the '93 on the palate, and has developed quickly since first released. Would not appear to be particularly long lived, and seems a little acidic. 59 per cent Cabernet Sauvignon, 23 per cent Shiraz, 10 per cent Cabernet Franc, 5 per cent Merlot, 3 per cent Malbec.

1993 ★★★★☆ *August 1997*

Dark, almost opaque colour; ripe, concentrated dark berry fruits with hints of dark chocolate fill the bouquet, and are matched by opulently ripe red berry and dark chocolate flavours on a quite luscious, but not over the top, palate. Well-balanced tannins; an impressive wine teetering on the very brink of top rating. 55 per cent Cabernet Sauvignon, 30 per cent Shiraz, 12 per cent Merlot, 3 per cent Malbec.

1992 ★★★★★ *August 1997*

Medium purple–red; a quite distinctive bouquet, fragrant and stylish, with a mix of cedar, leaf, earth and game, and true Bordeaux overtones. The palate lives up to the bouquet, with silky feel and texture, and good length. 45 per cent Cabernet Sauvignon, 40 per cent Shiraz, 10 per cent Merlot, 5 per cent Cabernet Franc.

1991 ★★★☆ *August 1997*

Still retaining distinct purple tinges, and a distinct break in the colour spectrum from the older wines. The bouquet is potent, with a hint of volatile lift, and ripe dark berry/gamey fruit. A powerful palate, quite rustic, with some angular edges and even a touch of roughness. Abundant character; for a dark night and a thick steak. 55 per cent Cabernet Sauvignon, 36 per cent Shiraz, 4 per cent Merlot, 3 per cent Cabernet Franc, 2 per cent Malbec.

Not Ready   Still evolving   Prime of its life   Drink soon   Missed the boat

1990 ★★★★★ *August 1997*

Medium red–purple; the bouquet shows quite powerful fruit with some minty/leafy notes, and an attractive touch of cedar/cigar box followed by a truly excellent palate that has an extra degree of fruit sweetness and an extra dimension of flesh. Fully justifies the reputation of the vintage; at its peak but will live. 47 per cent Cabernet Sauvignon, 39 per cent Shiraz, 6 per cent Merlot, 5 per cent Cabernet Franc, 3 per cent Malbec.

1989 ★★★ *August 1997*

Medium red–purple; the bouquet has predominantly earthy notes, with some cedar and leaf; a pleasant palate, with a mix of leaf, mint, earth and cedar, holding some tannins. All in all, a good outcome for the vintage. 80 per cent Shiraz, 12 per cent Cabernet Sauvignon, 5 per cent Merlot, 3 per cent Cabernet Franc.

1988 ★★★☆ *August 1997*

Medium purple–red; the bouquet is attractive; elegant and well balanced with gently sweet fruit and some spice. The palate opens up with elegance, but then rapidly starts to show that it is on the decline from what was quite obviously a richer and stronger wine earlier in its life — and in particular when it won the Jimmy Watson Trophy in 1989. 80 per cent Shiraz, 10 per cent Cabernet Sauvignon, 5 per cent Merlot, 3 per cent Cabernet Franc, 2 per cent Malbec.

1987 ★★☆ *August 1997*

Medium red, with just a hint of purple; a distinctly gamey/leafy bouquet shows a fundamental lack of fruit ripeness. The palate is quite astringent overall, with green, gamey canopy characters; a captive of the vintage. 67 per cent Cabernet Sauvignon, 24 per cent Shiraz, 5 per cent Merlot, 4 per cent Cabernet Franc.

1986 ★★★★★ *August 1997*

Medium red–purple; there is a hint of volatile lift on the bouquet, but it is not excessive; the aromas are in the cedar/earth/leaf secondary, bottle-developed phase. The palate is most appealing, with considerable richness and ripeness, and dark chocolate overtones to the fruit; finishes with soft but persistent tannins. 58 per cent Shiraz, 33 per cent Cabernet Sauvignon, 9 per cent Cabernet Franc.

1985 ★★★★ *August 1997*

Medium red–purple; the bouquet is clean, with pleasantly ripened fruit of medium intensity; showing a range of fragrant cedary/earthy characters, reminiscent in some ways of mature Bordeaux. Vanillin/coconut oak is more obvious on the palate than it is on the bouquet; a soft, fully mature wine just holding on at the end of its plateau. 70 per cent Cabernet Sauvignon, 20 per cent Shiraz, 5 per cent Malbec, 3 per cent Merlot, 2 per cent Cabernet Franc.

classic wines

| ★★★★★ Perfect | ★★★★☆ Close to perfect | ★★★★ Very good | ★★★☆ Expected |
| ★★★ Short of standard | ★★☆ Undeserving | ★★ Decayed relic | NR No rating |

jasper hill emily's paddock

emily's Paddock is much smaller than Georgia's Paddock, with only 3.2 hectares of shiraz and a little cabernet franc (typically resulting in a blend of 95 per cent Shiraz and 5 per cent Cabernet Franc). It catches the morning sun earlier with its northeasterly aspect (Georgia's has a northwesterly aspect) and is a little steeper and drier. All of this adds up to yields averaging 2.5 tonnes to the hectare, half that of Georgia's at a still-extremely low 5 tonnes to the hectare.

The vineyards are one kilometre apart, but share the same Cambrian soil (derived from rock older than 500 million years) which is over 3 metres deep; friable, red-brown gravelly loam with high levels of iron.

The policy of minimal intervention in the vineyard is carried through in the winery for both Georgia's and Emily's Paddock. Ron Laughton does not acidify the wines, and fines them only when necessary.

As with Georgia's Paddock, the high alcohol levels of more recent vintages (15.5 degrees seems standard) causes much discussion and no little controversy. That it contributes to the character of the wine is beyond doubt; whether it is a necessary part of the makeup is less clear, although Ron Laughton (who should know) has answered in the affirmative.

First tasted in November 1998, updated, and later vintages added.

◄ 1999 ★★★★★   *April 2001*

Dense purple–red; the immensely complex and rich bouquet has a range of spice/heather/herb/plum aromas, with a slightly savoury substrate. The palate has an arpeggio of flavours centred on notes of dark chocolate and prune, but absolutely not limited to those characters. Oak and tannins well managed and well balanced.

◄ 1998 ★★★★★   *April 2001*

Dark, deep red–purple; the bouquet has everything: plum, prune, spice, blackberry, liquorice and lots of shoe-leather aromas (sweet, not sour). The massively flavoured palate has all the flavours imaginable, but with high-toned spiced/brandied prune and plum flavours, mixed with dark chocolate, predominant.

◄ Not Ready   ＼ Still evolving   ▸ Prime of its life   ∕ Drink soon   ⛾ Missed the boat

1997 ★★★★★ *November 1998*

Dense, youthful purple–red. The extremely rich, ripe and concentrated bouquet offers liquorice, cardamom and mint; the palate, likewise, has an amazing concentration of exotic spices (cardamom, etc) and sweet liquorice fruit, fruit which has gobbled up the oak.

1996 ★★★★★ *November 1998*

Strong, deep red–purple; the heady bouquet is crammed with pure, dark cherry/cherry pip fruit, followed by cascades of flavour on the palate, running through dark cherry, coconut and mint plus appropriate tannins.

1995 ★★★☆ *November 1998*

Medium purple–red; a quite striking bouquet with cherry jam and that ubiquitous touch of mint. The palate shows similar, ultra-ripe jammy fruit flavours. A tiny vintage which was only packaged in magnums, of which there were 400.

1994 ★★★★☆ *November 1998*

There is an atypical slightly dull edge to the colour, but the bouquet poses no problems, with an aromatic spicy lift to the mint and red berry fruit supported by coconut oak. A big wine on the palate with a fair swag of oak contributing to the overall sweetness; finishes with soft tannins.

1993 ★★★★ *November 1998*

Medium purple–red; sweet caramel and mint aromas are immediately obvious when the wine is swirled; the palate, likewise, offers a mixture of caramel and mint, followed by slightly green notes on the finish.

1992 ★★★★★ *November 1998*

Medium to full red–purple; the rich and full bouquet has gloriously smooth red berry/black cherry/redcurrant fruit with a substrate of mint. The palate is equally entrancing, with lots of substance in both the fruit and oak components which are perfectly balanced. The long carry and finish is supported by lingering tannins.

1991 ★★★☆ *November 1998*

Medium to full red–purple; the potent, indeed aggressive bouquet is utterly different from that of Georgia's from the same vintage. The palate carries the same story, with powerful, grippy pyrazine characters. A wine which tastes as if it had gone feral in the vineyard.

1990 ★★★★★ *November 1998*

Medium to full red–purple; while the fruit on the bouquet is not especially ripe or powerful it is very complex, with a core of sweet berry fruit, a slice of mint and a touch of sweet liquorice. The palate is a revelation; beautifully smooth and balanced despite all the power which reveals itself, the opulently ripe fruit balanced by lingering tannins. Drink now or in another ten years.

1989 ★★★★ *November 1998*

Medium red, with some of the purples dissipating. The moderately intense bouquet has red berry and quite sweet briary aromas; the palate is fresh and clean, with quite crisp acidity; it may well be the pH is quite low, and if so, might be deceptively long-lived.

classic wines

★★★★★ Perfect ★★★★☆ Close to perfect ★★★★ Very good ★★★☆ Expected
★★★ Short of standard ★★☆ Undeserving ★★ Decayed relic NR No rating

85

1988 ★★★★☆   *November 1998*

Medium purple–red; another wine with great fragrance on the bouquet: cherry pip fruit supported by subtle oak. The substantial palate has ripe cherry and cherry pip flavours woven through with persistent but not harsh tannins. Subtle oak.

1987 ★★★★   *November 1998*

Medium purple–red; the bouquet has an earthy fragrance with touches of mint and liquorice. Some of those earthy notes appear on the palate, but it does have a core of sweet fruit. An elegant wine and an undoubted success for a cool vintage.

1986 ★★★☆   *November 1998*

Medium purple–red; fragrant red cherry and mint aromas are accompanied by an unusual touch of oriental spice. The relatively light palate has the same red cherry and mint fruit of the bouquet, with soft, supple tannins. Some would rate the wine higher, and it did tremble on the brink of four stars.

1985 ★★★   *November 1998*

Medium to full red–purple; the ripe fruit on the bouquet offers a mix of prune, plum, earth and a touch of mint, suggesting slightly uneven ripening. The palate echoes the bouquet, with ripe pruney characters offset by slightly grippy, green tannins on the finish.

1984 ★★★☆   *November 1998*

Medium purple–red; earthy/charry/stemmy aromas are followed by a palate which still retains a fair degree of flavour and flesh, but which has echoes of the charry/burnt match notes of the bouquet. Very good by any standards other than those of Jasper Hill.

1983 ★★★★★   *November 1998*

Striking, full red–purple colour, a total contrast to the '82. The bouquet is exceptionally rich and ripe, yet not the least jammy, simply very complex. A wine of great structure and richness, with soft chocolatey fruit and tannins which run through the entire length of the palate, yet never threaten it. Super stuff.

1982 ★★☆   *November 1998*

Light to medium red–purple; quite fragrant, clean albeit sappy aromas precede a wine which is still drinkable but is fading fast, and was once much better. Just for the record, there was no Cabernet Franc included.

jasper hill georgia's paddock
1982-1999

georgia's Paddock Shiraz comes from a 12-hectare planting completed between 1975 and 1976, with small plantings after the bushfires of 1987. As with Emily's Paddock, the wine is named after owners Ron and Elva Laughton's daughter. The vines were not irrigated when young, and did not produce their first crop until 1982. It hardly needs be said they remain dry-grown.

No artificial chemicals have ever been applied to the soil or the vines. No herbicides, no insecticides and no fungicides other than elemental sulphur and Bordeaux spray (copper sulphate) have been used, entitling the vineyards to organic status, although they are not formally registered as such.

The annual rainfall of 575 mm falls in winter and spring, but the deep soils retain moisture well, and carry the vines through to between 13.5 to 14 degrees baumé by the commencement of vintage during the first half of April. The net result is wines with exceptional colour, flavour and longevity, and which mount a powerful argument in support of the view that Heathcote is the best region in Australia for the production of rich, long-lived Shiraz.

I discuss the alcohol issue — identical for each of the two wines — in the introduction to Emily's Paddock, and it does not need repeating here. Suffice to say I am not here to second-guess the style, but simply to rate the wines within its context.

First tasted in November 1998, updated, and later vintages added.

1999 ★★★★★   *April 2001*

Dense purple–red; an almost impenetrable array of black fruits dominate the bouquet, with some savoury aspects, and well-balanced and integrated oak. The strong, dense and potent palate has lots of bitter chocolate flavours along with the riper black fruit spectrum of the bouquet; a long, lingering finish has powerful but balanced tannins, and likewise oak. I have beaten the alcohol horse enough to say no more.

1998 ★★★★★   *April 2001*

Dense purple–red; a rich, ripe bouquet has a cascade of aromas running through leather, liquorice, prune and plum, slightly more savoury, perhaps, than Emily's of the same vintage. The palate is loaded with intensely rich and sweet blackberry, plum, prune and spice flavours; the tannins are balanced, as is the oak, but it is undeniable you feel the alcohol.

classic wines

★★★★★ Perfect   ★★★★☆ Close to perfect   ★★★★ Very good   ★★★☆ Expected
★★★ Short of standard   ★★☆ Undeserving   ★★ Decayed relic   NR No rating

1997 ★★★★★   *November 1998*

Full, deep purple–red; the bouquet is quite overwhelming, with scented, spicy, exotic aromas tumbling out of the glass. The palate is no less rich and ripe with plum and cherry fruit still locked in arm-to-arm combat with the tannins. The rating is, to a degree, an article of faith.

1996 ★★★★☆   *November 1998*

Dense red–purple; the bouquet is almost overpowering in its luscious sweetness, augmented by some coconut oak. A massively powerful and structured wine on the palate with layered fruit flavours and sweet oak.

1995 ★★★★★   *November 1998*

Medium to full purple–red; the bouquet has abundant cherry pip and black cherry fruit supported by subtle oak; the wine shows very deft handling of oak and tannins, allied with beautifully ripened fruit. Lots of substance and structure.

1994 ★★★★   *November 1998*

Medium to full purple–red; the aromas are quite different from the vintages immediately preceding it, offering cherry, mint and a hint of coconut. The palate is quite firm, with berry and mint flavours; well structured, but not in the same luscious idiom.

1993 ★★★★★   *November 1998*

Medium to full red–purple; the bouquet is very complex, rich and concentrated with abundant plummy/briary fruit and subtle oak. The palate is quite outstanding in its richness, complexity and depth, arguably the best of all of the Georgia's, and certainly with decades in front of it.

1992 ★★★★★   *November 1998*

Medium to full red–purple; the bouquet is quite lovely, with masses of red cherry fruit; the palate is utterly seductive, beautifully balanced, long, sweet and succulent, with tannins barely noticeable but definitely present. Can be drunk now or in 20 years with more or less equal enjoyment.

1991 ★★★★★   *November 1998*

Very strong, dense colour; the bouquet oozes opulently ripe and rich plummy/ liquorice fruit. The palate offers a full panoply of rich, ripe Shiraz flavours, finished off with tannins which are still softening, but which are ripe. Has a great future.

1990 ★★★★   *November 1998*

Medium to full red, with some purple hues. The bouquet is quite challenging, with new oak/candle wax aromas and powerful fruit underneath that somewhat strange overlay. The wine comes into its own on the palate, with smooth, powerful red and black cherry fruit; there is, however, a hint of green tannin in the finish.

1989 ★★★☆   *November 1998*

Light to medium red, with just a touch of purple; the bouquet is clean, but not particularly intense, and with slightly earthy overtones. The palate has similarities to the '84, showing the dilution of a wet vintage but helped by some degree of fruit sweetness.

1988 Georgia's and Friends ★★★   November 1998

Medium to full red, tinged with purple and still quite deep; the bouquet is firm with some leafy astringency coming from the fruit. The palate has more power than the '87, but those green fruit characters do persist. Made partly from Georgia's grapes and partly from friends'.

1987 Friends ★★★   November 1998

Medium red, with just a touch of purple; the bouquet is firm, with some vegetal herbaceous aromas (DMS) and also a touch of mint. The palate exhibits herb, mint and spice flavours, well made but very different because of the circumstances of the year, when the crop was destroyed by fire and the grapes were provided by the Laughtons' numerous friends.

1986 ★★★★☆   November 1998

Medium to full red; the bouquet is positively luscious, with meltingly sweet fruit and a dusting of mint. Earthy characters latent in the bouquet come up on the palate, which is less luscious than the bouquet suggests, but on the other side, has plenty of structure.

1985 ★★★★★   November 1998

The brilliant but deep red–purple colour does not deceive; intense, dark berry and liquorice aromas run through a ripe, rich but clean bouquet, flowing into a rich, dark berry-flavoured palate with hints of briar and appropriately firm tannins. Another wine without a foreseeable end point.

1984 ★★★   November 1998

Medium red; the bouquet is relatively light, with some red berry fruit and touches of mint. The palate is quite firm, with slightly green fruit characters and a relatively high acid profile. A product of what must have been a very cool vintage.

1983 ★★★★★   November 1998

The dense, deep colour is extraordinary, but no more so than the potent, powerful dark berry aromas, incredibly youthful and intense. The palate offers layer upon layer of flavour, sweet, ripe and dense, replete with soft tannins. A quite superb wine which will live for decades.

1982 ★★★★   November 1998

Medium red, still with a touch of purple, impressive at this age. The bouquet has considerable fragrance and youth, with spotlessly clean, sweet earthy/berry fruit. The palate shows more signs of age, but is still smooth and silky, with very soft, fine tannins, good length and acidity.

classic wines

★★★★★ Perfect   ★★★★☆ Close to perfect   ★★★★ Very good   ★★★☆ Expected
★★★ Short of standard   ★★☆ Undeserving   ★★ Decayed relic   NR No rating

knappstein riesling 1977-2000

born into one of the great wine families of the Clare Valley, it was logical that Tim Knappstein should elect to study oenology at Roseworthy Agricultural College (now part of Adelaide University). However, his graduation as dux of the course, and his immediate success with the Leasingham Rieslings Bin 5 and Bin 7, could not have been foreseen. Together with his uncle, Mick Knappstein, he helped make Stanley Leasingham a household name — and ironically created the situation which led to a takeover offer from H J Heinz which was too good to refuse, but which also led in due course to Tim Knappstein's Enterprise Wines.

Times have changed since. First came the acquisition of the business by Petaluma, and then the decision by Tim and Annie Knappstein to move to their Lenswood Vineyard in the Adelaide Hills. Andrew Hardy has been the winemaker for a number of years now, and the winery name has been shortened to Knappstein Wines. The quality of the Riesling, however, has not changed.

First tasted in October 1994, updated, and later vintages added.

◄ 2000 ★★★★☆   *October 2000*

Light green–yellow; there are distinct herb and spice overtones to the lime fruit of the bouquet; a young, intense, powerful spicy/chalky palate begs for time.

◄ 1999 ★★★★   *October 1999*

Light yellow–green; a fragrant and spicy bouquet, with some mineral and subliminal lime aromas. A wine which begs for time in the bottle, with a very tight mineral and spice flavoured palate, and a dry finish.

\ 1997 ★★★★☆   *October 1997*

Light to medium yellow–green; an attractively rich bouquet with sweet citrus aromas; a marvellously balanced and modulated wine in the mouth, with abundant mid-palate lemony fruit followed by a fine, dry, lingering but not phenolic finish.

▮ 1996 ★★★★☆   *October 1996*

Light green–yellow; clean, fresh and bracing, with lime, a touch of mint and of toast on the bouquet, classy Clare; the palate is spotlessly clean, fresh and elegant with mineral, lime and toast flavours and, as one would expect, without any phenolic heaviness whatsoever. Guaranteed to age with grace.

▮ 1995 ★★★★   *March 1996*

Light green–yellow; there are clean and smooth lime and toast aromas. The quality of the grapes was very poor, but the wine has turned out extraordinarily well given its start in life, with gentle lime and tropical fruit flavours. Has fair length; perhaps needed a touch more acid.

◄ Not Ready   \ Still evolving   ▮ Prime of its life   ✒ Drink soon   ⎁ Missed the boat

1994 ★★★★☆   *October 1994*

The product of an excellent vintage; the bouquet is fine, floral and toasty, with some citrus/herbal notes. The palate has many flavours, predominantly spicy/toasty, but early in its life was not particularly fruity.

1993 ★★★★   *October 1994*

Bright, light green–yellow, with some spicy aspects and the fruit aroma and fragrance slightly subdued, although lime characters did come up in the glass. An elegant wine, with a well-balanced, long palate; once again the fruit slightly diminished, perhaps due to the typical evolution of Riesling in the bottle.

1992 ★★★☆   *October 1994*

Bright, light green–yellow; a crisp, fresh and tangy bouquet, with some toasty notes. The entry to the mouth shows lively citrus and lime flavours, but the finish is slightly furry, perhaps due to some botrytis influence.

1991 ★★★   *October 1994*

The start of many vintages with remarkably consistent and attractive glowing yellow–green colour. The bouquet shows some spicy edges to slightly broad fruit, with those same spicy aspects carrying through to a faintly flat finish. Marginally disappointing in the line-up.

1990 ★★★★★   *October 1994*

Brilliant colour; a lovely wine with very pure, concentrated lime juice aromas and an elegant, yet long and intense palate. A classic now, but with a tremendous future; balanced and harmonious.

1989 ★★★☆   *October 1994*

The colour is good, but not quite as brilliant as most. A complex, fuller style, with a toasty lime bouquet. Holding remarkably well on the palate with quite intense fruit flavours, and little obvious signs of the botrytis of the year.

1988 ★★★☆   *October 1994*

Bright green–yellow of medium depth; the bouquet is quite fresh, with lime, lemon and toast aromas, the palate full bodied, but lacking the intensity and tight acidity of the best wines.

1987 ★★★   *October 1994*

Slightly disappointing colour, with brown tinges. The bouquet is flat, suggesting some oxidation, but the palate is rather better, with quite good lime and toast on the mid-palate, finishing slightly dry. A bottling plagued by cork problems.

1986 ★★★★★   *October 1994*

Remarkable glowing yellow–green, with a wonderful, intense lime and toast bouquet. A classically concentrated palate, with powerful lime and toast flavours, and a long finish.

1985 ★★★★   *October 1994*

Glowing yellow–green, with aromas of honey, lime and toast. The wine is round, full and smooth in the mouth, with good balance; not particularly concentrated, but attractive nonetheless.

★★★★★ Perfect   ★★★★☆ Close to perfect   ★★★★ Very good   ★★★☆ Expected
★★★ Short of standard   ★★☆ Undeserving   ★★ Decayed relic   NR No rating

classic wines

91

1984 ★★★★   *October 1994*

Bright, full yellow–green; fairly firm and reserved bouquet with more lime juice than toast. A firm, crisp wine, quite restrained and perhaps a fraction hollow on the finish — but scores for its freshness.

1983 ★★★★☆   *October 1994*

A fantastic result for the year, glowing yellow–green in colour, with a very rich, almost Germanic, honeyed lime and toast bouquet. The palate is full-blown, totally seductive, full and rich with those Germanic lime flavours from the bouquet. Infinitely better than the year would suggest.

1982 ★★☆   *October 1994*

The colour is still good, but the bouquet shows slightly dry/leafy aspects, significantly less fruity than the other wines in the line-up. The palate, too, shows somewhat leafy, dried-out characters as the fruit is starting to fade.

1981 ★★★★   *October 1994*

Brilliant green–yellow, with a firm bouquet, predominantly lime and toast, but a faint touch of riesling kerosene character. The palate is firmly constructed, with tight citrus and lime flavours, and a firm finish.

1980 ★★★★★   *October 1994*

One of the great Rieslings, unfortunately not present in the tasting, but rated on its known track record. If you have the wine in the cellar, you are lucky.

1979 ★★★★☆   *October 1994*

Glowing green–yellow. The bouquet is slightly firmer than the older wines in the line-up, still with very good lime and toast fruit. The palate shows some slightly tough edges, but still has masses of lime fruit, with hints of other flavours, even into white peach.

1978 ★★★★★   *October 1994*

With the '77, the deepest-coloured wine in the tasting, but still bright. The bouquet is full and rich, with toast and lime bottle-developed aromas similar to the '77. In the mouth, full, rich and soft, with an amalgam of lime, toast and honey flavours. Holding perfectly on the finish.

1977 ★★★★☆   *October 1994*

Glowing green–yellow; a classically rich lime and toast bouquet, generous, with little sign of age. The palate is rich and mouthfilling with lime, camphor and toast flavours. It does show very slight signs of drying out on the finish, although what appears to be a touch of residual sugar does help.

lake's folly cabernets 1966-1999

dr Max Lake's place in history is secure: it was he who led the way for hundreds of weekend winemakers who sought to briefly escape from the pressure of their busy professional lives to indulge in their passion — wine. When he started taking soil samples from the lee of the Brokenback Range, the locals were mildly curious. When they learned he intended to plant a vineyard and make wine, they thought he was mad. When told he intended to plant cabernet sauvignon, they knew he was mad.

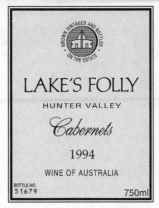

It was 1963, the red wine boom was but a twinkle in the eye of the still nascent consumer; the business lunch marked by beer or spirits, but seldom wine; and the Hunter Valley was a sleepy, shrunken hollow with only 460 hectares of grapes, compared to 1800 hectares in 1876.

Max Lake not only proved that a dedicated wine lover with no formal training could make good wine, but could make what would quickly achieve international recognition as a wine of great character, finesse and style.

In due course, son Stephen Lake quietly assumed the mantle, and no less quietly set about making even better wines. In May 2000 the estate was sold, but Stephen continued as a consultant, and little should change.

The numbers in brackets are the Folly's own rating, out of ten, which I give in each case for the purpose of comparison.

First tasted in November 1994, updated, and later vintages added.

1999 ★★★★☆   *January 2001*
Medium red–purple; the bouquet is sweet and ripe, with a distinctive mix of small, dark berry fruit and earth. The palate opens with ripe, soft, fleshy fruit before distinctly regional savoury/earthy characters take over towards the finish; the parts need time to come together.

1998 ★★★★★   *March 2000*
Healthy, full red–purple; a distinctly regional, gently earthy/savoury cast to the fruit will doubtless raise a question in the minds of some, but for me the wine is spotlessly clean. A perfectly made wine on the palate, with cassis fruit the anchor for both the texture and structure; exemplary tannin and oak handling completes the picture.

1997 ★★★★★   *April 1999*
Medium to full red–purple; the bouquet is chock-full of cassis/berry fruit supported by perfectly handled oak. The palate is as beautifully constructed as any young wine can be; cassis berry fruit, fine-grained tannins, great length, and again that impeccably-handled oak. The best Folly for years, perhaps ever.

★★★★★ Perfect   ★★★★☆ Close to perfect   ★★★★ Very good   ★★★☆ Expected
★★★ Short of standard   ★★☆ Undeserving   ★★ Decayed relic   NR No rating

classic wines

93

1996 ★★★★ *January 1998*

Medium red–purple; a quite austere bouquet with earthy/leathery aromas bordering on the astringent. Loosens up slightly on the palate, which is predominantly driven by austere earthy cabernet, speaking of the terroir, but with definite hints of violets and mint to provide softer notes.

1995 ★★★☆ *January 1997*

Medium red; a strongly regional, earthy/leathery bouquet, neither luscious nor generous. There is somewhat more to be found on the palate, but, overall, has to be taken as an article of faith.

1994 ★★★★☆ *January 1996*

Light to medium red; the bouquet is clean, but, as seems so often to be the case, surprisingly light in terms of fruit concentration. The palate is delicately structured; very fine tannins running through the wine are a feature, giving an even flavour and texture profile from the moment of entry to the finish. The harmony and balance make the wine easy to overlook.

1993 ★★★★★ *November 1994*

Medium red–purple; clean and smooth, with a characteristic vineyard dark plum fruit character; elegant and of light to medium intensity. The palate is spotlessly clean, with plummy fruit, subtle oak and soft tannins. (10)

1992 ★★★★ *November 1994*

Medium red–purple; of typical light to medium intensity, with hints of spice and briar, but overall clean, smooth and elegant. The palate is well balanced and composed with a touch of plum and rather more spice and briary characters. Soft tannins as ever. (8)

1991 ★★★★ *November 1994*

Medium red–purple; the bouquet is of medium to full intensity, clean and ripe, with plum and briar fruit and subtle oak. The palate is generous, with the trademark berry and plum fruit, although one might have expected a little more weight richness on the mid to back palate given the reputation of the year. (9.5)

1989 ★★★★☆ *November 1994*

Medium red–purple; the aromas are clean with spicy, plummy fruit of medium intensity, and subtle vanillin oak. A delicious wine on the palate which has the fruit richness and sweetness absent from many of the wines in the line-up of intermediate age, finishing with soft, sweet tannins. (9)

1988 ★★★ *November 1994*

Medium red; somewhat leafy, earthy, bitter and astringent aromas. The palate is better than the bouquet promises, with some leafy/gamey characters, but is still relatively astringent, and it is unlikely age will do much for it. (7)

1987 ★★★★ *November 1994*

Light to medium red, with a touch of purple; the bouquet is smooth, with faintly minty overtones. An attractive, albeit relatively light-bodied palate with mint, spice and briar all there. (7.5)

Not Ready ⟍ Still evolving ▮ Prime of its life ⟋ Drink soon ⨅ Missed the boat

1985 ★★★☆ *November 1994*

Medium to full red, with just a hint of tawny; the bouquet is of medium intensity, with earthy/briary/berry fruit and nicely integrated oak. The palate is relatively powerful with tarry/earthy fruit characters, marred fractionally by a slightly soapy finish. (8)

1983 ★★☆ *November 1994*

Medium red; distinct sweaty/gamey/leafy/earthy aromas to the bouquet, followed by very pronounced gamey/sweaty/leafy characters on the palate, sour and sulphidic. A major disappointment for the year. Was the bottle typical? (7.5)

1981 ★★★★ *November 1994*

The colour is retaining more red hues than brown; the bouquet clean with supple fruit of light to medium intensity. The palate is attractive, with sweet, supple berry fruit of medium intensity. As ever, the oak impact is minimal, the tannins soft, and the wine has pleasant mouthfeel and balance. (9)

1978 ★★★ *November 1994*

Light to medium red, with just a hint of purple; the bouquet is rather light with some vegetative/tobacco aromas which are varietal but not rich. The palate seems to be starting to tire and thin out somewhat with some rather green, stemmy tannins. A drought year with considerable stress. (9)

1977 ★★★ *November 1994*

Medium red; the bouquet is of light to medium intensity with sappy/gamey/leafy aromas, the palate showing a similar spectrum of flavours, with the fruit starting to drop and dry out. (7)

1976 ★★★☆ *November 1994*

Medium to full red–tawny; a cedary/leafy bouquet which, like the palate, is showing distinct cabernet varietal character. A little tough on the palate, and reminiscent of Bordeaux in a difficult year. (6)

1975 ★★★★ *November 1994*

Light red–tawny; a faintly earthy/spicy bouquet with fruit still holding. There are some very interesting flavours on the palate with a touch of sappiness, but smooth, finishing with fine tannins. (7)

1973 ★★★☆ *November 1994*

Light red–brown; the bouquet initially a fraction soft and dilute but came up, with echoes of sweet fruit starting to appear. An attractive aged, gentle wine on the palate with soft tannins, and flavours of earth and bark. (7)

1970 ★★★★ *November 1994*

Quite brown in colour, but an attractive bouquet with complex regional/secondary earth and berry aromas. A most pleasant wine on the palate with secondary cigar box flavours, a hint of mint, and vestigial tannins holding the structure together.

classic wines

1969 ★★★★★   *November 1994*

Deceptively brown in colour, but a rich bouquet with gentle sweet earthy aromas, and neither tar nor sulphide. The palate is rich with flavours of forest floor leaf and spice, together with some sweet earth and leather notes. Aged but elegant, and holding. (10)

1968 NR
Not tasted. Wet vintage. (6)

1967 NR
Not tasted. Good vintage. (6)

1966 NR
Not tasted. Dry, hot. (7)

⬤ Not Ready   ◥ Still evolving   ▮ Prime of its life   ✎ Drink soon   ⬯ Missed the boat

lake's folly chardonnay 1974-1999

max Lake has recounted the establishment of the Folly's Chardonnay thus: 'Our Chardonnay is another bit of serendipity. With the idea of making some champagne [sic], in 1969 we obtained some CSIRO nursery imports, but these turned out to be pinot blanc. Next year we obtained a different variety from the NSW Department of Agriculture. Our first manager refused to look after it, with the result that we did not bottle a wine from those vines until 1974. The favourable attention it generated was the dawn of a new realisation. People seemed happy enough to fund my taste for French champagne, so we never did go on to make any fizz.' (*Memoirs of a Folly*, Max Lake, 1994.)

Restricted though the production of the Cabernet is, that of the Chardonnay is tiny, and my tastings of it over the early years were sporadic. I have to admit to having been most impressed with the 1994 tasting, and not a little surprised. It is one of the relatively few Chardonnays in Australia which is actually likely to improve with four or five years bottle age, and hold for a decade.

The style is Chablis-like, the use of oak restrained, employment of forcing techniques such as skin contact eschewed. When winery propaganda describes a wine as being a 'food style' it is usually to distract attention from the fact that it either tastes of nothing at all or nothing pleasant. The Lake's Folly Chardonnay is a genuine food style.

The numbers in brackets (up to 1993) are the Folly's own rating, out of ten, which I give in each case for the purpose of comparison.

First tasted in November 1994, updated, and later vintages added.

1999 ★★★★★ January 2001
Brilliant yellow–green; the bouquet offers a complex yet subtle interplay between fruit, oak and malolactic fermentation, with no one character dominant. The palate is intense and much tighter than most, if not all, Hunter Valley Chardonnays, with the same seamless integration of all of its components.

1998 ★★★★☆ March 2000
Medium yellow–green; tangy melon/stone fruit aromas are woven through subtle oak, complex but smooth. The palate lacks the final intensity promised by the bouquet; very neat handling, but does not quite follow through on the finish. Time may change my perspective.

1997 ★★★★★ February 1999
Medium yellow–green; the bouquet is very smooth, with seamless integration of fruit and oak and gentle peach/melon aromas. The wine has an unexpected delicacy and elegance on entering the mouth, and gently builds on this to provide a really attractive mouthfeel. Bang on the quality of the '96.

classic wines

★★★★★ Perfect ★★★★☆ Close to perfect ★★★★ Very good ★★★☆ Expected
★★★ Short of standard ★★☆ Undeserving ★★ Decayed relic NR No rating

1996 ★★★★★   *January 1998*

Glowing yellow–green; a complex yet elegant bouquet with multi-layered mineral/ stone fruit characters, giving a Burgundian tang and grip. A stylish wine in which the winemaker's thumbprints are very evident, yet still retains a core of tight fruit in a highly structured wine with secondary characters giving complexity. Outstanding.

1995 ★★★★☆   *January 1997*

Bright yellow–green; a typically elegant and subtle bouquet with understated fruit and tightly controlled oak. There is more of the same on the carefully crafted palate, which has style, class and a long finish, but which creeps up on you stealthily.

1994 ★★★★☆   *January 1996*

Medium to full yellow–green; a concentrated and quite complex bouquet, tangy with those slightly burnt edges so commonly found in Hunter Valley white wines, and subtle but evident oak. The palate is an exercise in restraint, neither extroverted nor floral, with tightly knit and perfectly balanced fruit and oak. Long carry and finish.

1993 ★★★★☆   *November 1994*

Medium yellow–green; a quite tight and powerful bouquet with toasty/smoky fermentation aromas reminiscent of the Tyrrell's '93 Vat 47. The palate is generous with similar peachy fruit, a hint of toast and vanillin oak. (9)

1992 ★★★★☆   *November 1994*

Medium yellow–green; complex fruit and oak aromas which are tightly knit and in the Folly mainstream. The palate is lively, tangy and more citrussy, and still slightly lean. Should build marvellously with time. (9.5)

1991 ★★★★   *November 1994*

Medium to full yellow–green; soft, full ripe peach aromas which are just a fraction coarse. The palate is big, soft, generous honeyed/peach fruit showing the hot year; slightly hard alcohol on the finish. (8)

1990 NR   *November 1994*

Two bottles tasted, both corked, one badly so, the other faintly. There seems to be elegant fruit there. Cork taint was a real problem in Lake's Folly up to 1990. (6.5)

1989 ★★★★★   *November 1994*

Brilliant green–yellow; elegant, lively, tangy, melon and citrus fruit to the bouquet. The palate is definitely on the lighter side, but is very elegant and crisp. One wonders precisely in which direction it will head. (8)

1988 ★★★   *November 1994*

Medium to full yellow; a firm, rather herbaceous style which lacks generosity and vinosity on both bouquet and palate, all suggesting insufficiently-ripened fruit. (6.5)

1986 ★★★★   *November 1994*

Medium to full yellow; a big, full, buttery bouquet with a whisper of volatility. A full-blown wine which seems to me to be in compartments which have never really come together. Other tasters liked it much more. (8.5)

1985 ★★★ *November 1994*

Quite deep colour; the bouquet is broad, slightly flat and smelly. The palate, too, is tending to dry out a little, showing some coarseness and hints of oxidation. (7)

1984 ★★★★★ *November 1994*

Brilliant light green–yellow; the bouquet is very much alive with lovely melon/citrus fruit and charry/toasty oak. The palate is elegant, smooth and tightly structured with melon and citrus fruit, finishing with clean acidity. A rating entirely at odds with that of Lake's Folly. (5)

1983 ★★★★☆ *November 1994*

Medium yellow–green; a big, slightly honeyed bouquet with relatively subdued fruit aromas. A similarly big wine on the palate with generous malty/honey/peachy fruit. (9)

1982 ★★★★☆ *November 1994*

Glowing yellow–green; a complex, rich and stylish bouquet, with some tang to the fruit, and oak in balance. There is a distinctly French feel to the structure and flavour, with touches of vegetal and mineral tastes. Many things happening here; finishing with good acidity. (8)

1981 ★★★★☆ *November 1994*

Medium to full yellow; clean, honey/mead/peach aromas which are in good condition. The wine is nicely balanced and composed, neither fat nor blowsy. Exceptional for such a hot year and still holding remarkably well. (9)

1980 NR

Not tasted. Like all the wines from this point backwards, considered past it's best by Lake's Folly. (7)

1980 NR

Not tasted. Like all the wines from this point backwards, considered past its best by Lake's Folly. (7)

1979 NR
Not tasted. (5)

1978 NR
Not tasted. (6)

1977 NR
Not tasted. (6)

1976 NR
Not tasted. (9)

1975 NR
Not tasted. (6.5)

1974 NR
Not tasted. (10)

classic wines

leeuwin estate art series cabernet sauvignon 1979-1994

Producing Australia's greatest Chardonnay would not have any downside if it were the only wine made by Leeuwin Estate. But of course it is not, and it tends to overshadow the other wines of the Estate. Yet from the very first day, Leeuwin has strived to produce the finest possible wines from a winery which is equipped as well as any in the world, and using the strictest selection criteria in determining which wines will be released under its top labels (the Art Series) and which under its lesser labels (now known as Prelude).

Thus the oldest wine in this tasting (the '79) was not in fact released under the Art Series label, and was held for even longer than the usual four years for Cabernet Sauvignon. As a young wine it was not considered worthy of release under any Leeuwin label, but — as the note indicates — it matured magnificently, and was a bargain when finally released in the second half of the 1980s.

Overall, the Leeuwin Estate Cabernets are wines with great intellectual appeal and unusual refinement. They are at the opposite end of the spectrum from the easy-come, easy-go style of standard Australian commercial red wines; even in the context of the Margaret River, they are in the leaner, more elegant mould, but yet unmistakably of the region. Needless to say, they age superbly.

First tasted in October 1994, updated, and later vintages added.

◄■ 1994 ★★★★   *February 1998*

Medium red–purple; the bouquet is of medium intensity, with a mix of cedary, earthy and more briary aromas. The palate has attractive texture and flavour, with chocolate, briar and cedar overtones to the red fruits. Almost milky soft tannins run through the length of the palate.

◄■ 1993 ★★★★☆   *April 1997*

Medium to full red–purple; concentrated, classic cabernet fruit aromas, primarily of cassis but with hints of sweet earth and subtle oak. The palate is powerful, again showing classic, dusty blackberry/cassis fruit with balanced but lingering tannins on the finish.

◄■ 1992 ★★★★★   *October 1996*

Strong red–purple; full, ripe cassis fruit on the bouquet is surrounded by attractive cigar box oak, more evident than in previous vintages. A powerful wine on the palate with masses of blackcurrant and dark chocolate fruit with balanced but persistent tannins. I much prefer this wine to the '91.

◄■ Not Ready   ＼ Still evolving   ▮ Prime of its life   ⟋ Drink soon   ▯ Missed the boat

1991 ★★★
October 1995

Medium to full red–purple; tasted on four separate occasions, twice in show or blind tastings, twice in open tastings, and on every occasion I detected characters in the wine which I find off-putting, yet it has received high praise in many quarters. To me there is a hint of gaminess and astringency which may be derived from the canopy, may be from sulphide or may be from bacterial action — or perhaps none of the above. Whatever, I cannot come to terms with the wine.

1990 ★★★★★
October 1994

Full red–purple; the bouquet is of medium ripeness with blackcurrant and cherry fruit aromas. The palate has lots of sweet blackcurrant/cassis and plum fruit balanced by fine, cedary tannins. Gives the impression that it will mature slightly quicker than its predecessors, but be none the worse for that, and is the product of an unusually good vintage.

1989 ★★★★★
October 1994

Full red–purple colour, with the typical gravelly, potent edges to the blackcurrant fruit and some cedary notes in the bouquet. In the mouth, textured and rich, with layer upon layer of flavour including a touch of chocolate; lots of tannins and needing lots of time.

1988 ★★★☆
October 1994

Full red–purple; a gravelly, complex and concentrated bouquet which is still obviously immature. The palate shows some slightly softer mulberry notes, and slightly riper fruit, lacking the austere intensity of some of the other wines. There is a suspicion this might have been a slightly corked bottle.

1987 ★★★★☆
October 1994

Medium to full red–purple; a stylish, potent, concentrated bouquet with herbaceous overtones leads on to an extremely powerful and intense wine which cries out for time. It may or may not scale the final heights of greatness.

1986 ★★★★☆
October 1994

Medium to full red–purple; the bouquet is much riper than the '85 with briary, bramble, blackcurrant, mint and pepper aromas all intermingling. In the mouth an attractive melange of flavours, with a touch of sweetness balanced by lots of tannin; a serious wine.

1985 ★★★☆
October 1994

Medium to full red–purple. The bouquet is potent with herbaceous/ capsicum aromas, like a Bordeaux from a less than fully ripe year. The palate is leafy, briary and cedary, in fairly extreme style and lacking fruit generosity, yet will still clearly improve.

1979 ★★★★☆
October 1994

Medium to full red; there are abundant, complex secondary aromas of briar, cedar and leaf on the bouquet, leading on to a palate with touches of dark chocolate tinged with cedary/earthy notes. The structure of the wine is Bordeaux-like, with fine-grained tannins.

classic wines

★★★★★ Perfect	★★★★☆ Close to perfect	★★★★ Very good	★★★☆ Expected
★★★ Short of standard	★★☆ Undeserving	★★ Decayed relic	NR No rating

leeuwin estate art series
chardonnay 1980-1998

LEEUWIN ESTATE

1990
Margaret River
Chardonnay

PRODUCE OF WESTERN AUSTRALIA

the relationship between yield and quality is obvious to all makers and most consumers of red wine. High-yielding vines produce red wines which are dilute in flavour, low in extract and tannin, and — most obviously of all — light in colour. The implications for white wine quality are much less widely understood, partly because there is little discernible difference in the colour of a young white wine made from low-yielding, as opposed to high-yielding vines.

But one of the reasons Le Montrachet produces the greatest white wine in the world is the incredible concentration in the flavour of the grapes from the very low-yielding vines — which produce less than two tonnes per acre.

So it is at Leeuwin Estate, where Block 20 (one of five blocks of chardonnay on the estate) always produces the core of the Art Series Chardonnay. Yields never exceed 2.5 tonnes to the acre, and are frequently less than 2 tonnes per acre. Most producers would regard 4 to 5 tonnes as acceptable for top quality wine, with yields rising to 10 tonnes per acre in the riverlands.

But it is also true that the low yields have to come from healthy, balanced vines, and preferably be achieved naturally — that is, without bunch thinning. The ancient, deep, laterite/granite soils and the strongly maritime-influenced climate combine to give Leeuwin Estate just this result. Shortly put, this is Australia's greatest Chardonnay, and one of the great wines of the world.

Please note that Murphy's Law has resulted in a range of tasting dates; most of the wines from 1982 onwards were tasted in February 2001.

◄ 1998 ★★★★★   *February 2001*

Light to medium green–yellow; toasty barrel-ferment oak mingles with nectarine and grapefruit in a manner very reminiscent of the '97 when it was first released; the palate has tight grapefruit and melon together with a touch of cashew, with excellent length and acid balance. Yet another great wine from Leeuwin.

1997 ★★★★★   *February 2001*

The bottle in the tasting in February 2001 showed a very advanced golden–yellow colour, utterly at odds with a bottle tasted only five months previously; once again, random oxidation at work. I am therefore substituting the tasting note of 5 October 2000.

Back to its best, reminiscent of the great 1987, and produced from microscopic yields. Vibrant yellow–green, it has a complex array of melon, cashew, cream and fig aromas followed by a multi-layered and textured palate with seamless integration of fruit and oak. Developing slowly.

1996 ★★★★★   *February 2001*

The colour is deeper than it should be at this relatively early phase of its life, but my recollection is that it started with an extra bit to the hue. The hallmark complex nutty/toasty barrel-ferment character is offset against that other hallmark, piercing melon, nectarine and fig fruit. The wine flows across the tongue, very even and very long, again with that persistence of flavour, and precise acidity on the finish.

1995 ★★★★★   *February 2001*

Excellent, glowing yellow–green; a strongly Burgundian and very complex bouquet with nutty/toasty barrel-ferment characters is followed by a commensurately long, intense and concentrated palate ranging through cashew, chestnut, citrus and spicy oak, finishing with grainy, lemony acidity.

1994 ★★★★★   *February 2001*

Brilliant medium green–yellow; fresh, vibrant and elegant citrussy/nectarine/melon aromas are supported by perfectly judged oak on the bouquet. A lovely, vibrant and fresh palate with a scintillating array of citrus and melon fruit; the oak is no more than there in the background, the length of the palate sustained by perfect acidity.

1993 ★★★★★   *February 2001*

Medium to full yellow–green; toasty hazelnut/cashew malolactic input gives extra complexity to the underlying tangy fruit; a rich, layered and complex palate with cashew/hazelnut/honey/citrus flavours providing lots of mouthfeel and length. An excellent year for white wines in the region, and the wine has matured superbly, throwing off its uncertain start.

1992 ★★★★★   *February 2001*

This bottle, without question, was the subject of random oxidation, with an unnaturally deep, yellow–gold colour. I therefore provide the note and the ranking from tasting the wine in October 1995.

Light to medium yellow–green; the bouquet is as stylish as ever, with tangy melon and white peach fruit married with high-quality French oak and all the signs of sophisticated winemaking, together with an element of bottle maturation. The palate is marvellously balanced and constructed, with fine, long citrus and melon fruit, the oak evident but in no way assertive. A quite lovely wine right up with the best of the Leeuwin Estate Chardonnays.

★★★★★ Perfect   ★★★★☆ Close to perfect   ★★★★ Very good   ★★★☆ Expected
★★★ Short of standard   ★★☆ Undeserving   ★★ Decayed relic   NR No rating

classic wines

103

1991 NR   *February 2001*

One of the bottles in the March 2001 tasting which went on an unscheduled trip around Australia in blazing heat before arriving at the tasting. The colour was very deep, and the wine showed some slight astringency which may or may not have been due to cork and/or the rough treatment it had received. On the other hand, the notes from the 1994 tasting also make reference to some 'slightly rough characters' on both bouquet and palate. All in all, sufficient uncertainty to not rate the wine.

1990 ★★★★★   *February 2001*

Good medium yellow–green; the bouquet is slightly subdued, with melon and fig set against more buttery/toasty/oaky characters. The powerful palate is effectively a replay of the bouquet, toasty, figgy and round on the mid-palate, then good acidity and length. I am not entirely convinced this bottle was fully representative.

1989 ★★★★★   *February 2001*

Bright, deep gold; a toasty, brandysnap, honey, caramelised bouquet still shows new oak influence. The palate is quite different, with surprising bite, life and freshness; very long, with lingering citrus and grapefruit; fine acidity to close.

1988 ★★★★   *February 2001*

Full yellow–gold; a toasty/nutty/honeyed bouquet shows distinct hints of maderisation, the palate rich and full, with elevated alcohol giving a slightly hot finish. From a hot, low-yielding and early vintage, and absolutely showing those influences.

1987 ★★★★★   *February 2001*

Full golden–yellow; an exceedingly complex bouquet, with terrific intensity, and overt characters of Burgundy, is a forefather of the 1995 vintage. The powerful, complex and long palate, with layers of fruit flavour building towards the finish provides the wine with quite fantastic length. Always was a classic, and still is. Really deserves a sixth star.

1986 ★★★★☆   *February 2001*

Full yellow–gold; the fruit aromas of the bouquet range through nectarine, fig, apricot and mandarin, suggesting a touch of botrytis from a rain-affected vintage. The palate, however, largely shrugs off those characters, with smooth, gently sweet fruit, tailing-off ever so slightly on the finish. Here, too, the wine tasted in 1994 was off-song, but no problems this time.

1985 ★★★★★   *February 2001*

Again, marvellous colour; a tangy, smoky, gunflint bouquet with the mix of faintly vegetal and grapefruit character of Burgundy is accompanied by complex cashew notes. The palate is still fresh and lively, with great grip and focus, and a long, lingering finish. Yet another of the wines to have as much affinity with Burgundy as Australia. Shows a cool and late vintage.

1984 ★★★★☆ *February 2001*

Deep yellow–gold; a potent and complex bouquet still with youthful smoky/charry edges of the kind found in the 1987 and 1995 vintages. The palate is long and complex, but not as rich as some on the mid-palate; the length is good. The bottle tasted in October 1994 was undoubtedly the subject of random oxidation; this was a much better bottle.

1983 ★★★★★ *February 2001*

Brilliant, medium green–yellow; the bouquet falls in two parts, on the one hand fresh, fine nectarine, fig and hazelnut, and on the other toasty barrel- ferment characters with an echo of Burgundy. The palate is exceptionally tight, fresh and youthful, a veritable Peter Pan. Took a long time to come around in bottle following a hot vintage and rapid fermentation.

1982 ★★★★★ *February 2001*

Has a bright gold colour, flecked with green, leading into a rich and clean bouquet with lots of peach and nectarine. The voluptuously sweet fruit of the palate gives the wine a richness and mouthfilling flesh beyond most white wines. Less Burgundian than others in the line-up, but there is no sin in that.

1981 ★★★★★ *October 1994*

Another tiny crop affected by problems during flowering which gave rise to an extraordinarily complex and concentrated bouquet, with a Burgundian vegetal bite. The palate shows the same characters, with an amazingly sweet mid-palate fruit reminiscent not just of Burgundy, but also Le Montrachet.

1980 ★★★★★ *October 1994*

Yet another very low-yielding year thanks to problems in spring. Like the '81, a magnificent surprise, with the colour still strong, the bouquet rich and potent with melon, grapefruit and honeysuckle aromas. In the mouth the wine has tremendous depth and complexity, round luscious and mouthfilling, but balanced by perfect acidity. Be aware, however, that this note and the previous were made in 1994.

★★★★★ Perfect   ★★★★☆ Close to perfect   ★★★★ Very good   ★★★☆ Expected
★★★ Short of standard   ★★☆ Undeserving   ★★ Decayed relic   NR No rating

leo buring riesling 1963-1997

arguably, this tasting — held in the Barossa on 23 April 1997 — ranks second only to the Penfolds Grange tastings in significance. Just as Grange is the quintessentially Australian red wine, so is Leo Buring Riesling the quintessential white wine.

Until 1992 more riesling was crushed each year in Australia than chardonnay, and for much of the time span covered by this tasting, Riesling and Semillon together accounted for 90 per cent of all premium bottled white wine sales.

But the importance of Riesling could not — and cannot — be measured simply by statistics. It has an extraordinary capacity to age (and improve) in bottle, a capacity proven in the nineteenth century when 50-year-old German Riesling was (relatively) common and brought higher prices than first-growth Clarets. And the second-oldest bottle of wine I have tasted was a 1727 Rudesheimer Apostlewein from Germany.

What also made this tasting so remarkable was that it was presided over by John Vickery, who made all the wines and who in fact provided the oldest vintages from the last few bottles in his private cellar. He is to Riesling what Max Schubert was to Shiraz: unchallenged as the greatest Riesling practitioner, able to take the variety onto another plane.

As John Vickery himself pointed out, the wines in the tasting had done it the hard way, cellared in less than ideal conditions, moved on a number of occasions, and given ordinary corks in the first instance. If you have these wines in a good cellar, and the corks have held, you are indeed lucky. (The 1997 tasting played a pivotal role in the Stelvin screw-cap renaissance.)

Additional notes come from an earlier vertical tasting and from subsequent tastings of new releases.

◀ 1997 Eden Valley ★★★★☆   *March 2000*
Light green–yellow; the aromatic bouquet offers a mix of lime, lemon and mineral; the palate is still delicate and youthful, with herb, lemon and lime flavours and nice length to the finish.

▮ 1995 Eden Valley ★★★★☆   *October 1999*
Medium yellow–green; a highly aromatic bouquet with strong, toasty fruit is followed by a powerful petrol and toast-flavoured palate. Unusual in two respects: first, the degree of development, and second, the essentially old-fashioned style. Big appeal to traditionalists.

◀ Not Ready   ◣ Still evolving   ▮ Prime of its life   ✎ Drink soon   ▯ Missed the boat

1994 Eden Valley ★★★★★   *December 1998*

Medium yellow–green; the bouquet is starting to unfold with sweet lime fruit at the core of still-building complexity. The palate is amazingly fresh, lively and youthful with lingering delicate lime flavours on the finish. Will go on for years; it is not surprising this is only a partial release, with a portion held back for further release in the future.

1992 Leonay Watervale ★★★★☆   *April 1997*

Glowing yellow–green; a rich, soft and toasty bouquet with some citrus in the background and the first signs of varietal kerosene aromas developing. Now full, rich and flavoursome, with smooth lime and toast, seemingly reaching its peak, and will hold it for years to come.

1991 Leonay Bin DWV17 ★★★☆   *November 1994*

Light to medium yellow–green; very toasty nettle, herbs and apple aromas with some slightly burnt fermentation aromas. The palate has soft, citrus flavours, even with a touch of white peach and a fair finish.

1991 Leonay Eden Valley ★★★★☆   *October 1996*

Glowing yellow–green; a soft, clean, quite full bouquet with gentle lime and toast aromas leads on to a rich, highly flavoured palate, showing bottle-developed Riesling character at its best.

1991 Leonay Watervale ★★★★★   *November 1998*

Strong yellow–green; there are classic toast, honey and lime aromas in abundance on the bouquet, the palate showing lots of bottle development but still with years and years in front of it. It is well balanced, with lovely toast and lime flavours running through to the finish. Gold medal 1998 National Wine Show.

1990 Leonay Bin DWT17 ★★★★   *November 1994*

Light to medium yellow–green; a firm, tight, fresh and crisp bouquet in classic style. The palate is bright and fresh, with quite intense lime flavours, a hint of passionfruit; good balance and length.

1990 Leonay Eden Valley Bin DWT17 ★★★★☆   *September 1994*

Light to medium yellow–green; a firm, tight, fresh and crisp bouquet in classic style. The palate is bright and fresh, with quite intense lime flavours, a hint of passionfruit; good balance and length.

1989 Barossa Valley Bin DWS26★★★★☆   *April 1997*

Medium yellow–green; a rich, ripe and toasty bouquet with gently tropical fruit leads into a wine with distinctly tropical/pineapple fruit flavours on the palate, tinged with lime. The wine has good feel, weight, balance and length.

1988 Leonay Watervale Bin DWR13★★★★   *April 1997*

Medium yellow–green; strong, pronounced toasty aromas and flavours — almost into vanilla — drive the wine throughout. Slightly heavy towards the finish.

1985 Green Label Eden Valley ★★★★★   *April 1997*

Amazingly pale and bright green–yellow; the bouquet is powerful and intense with lime/citrus fruit, the palate no less powerful and long. Tangy lemony flavours finish with crisp acidity, and the wine will surely live forever.

★★★★★ Perfect	★★★★☆ Close to perfect	★★★★ Very good	★★★☆ Expected
★★★ Short of standard	★★☆ Undeserving	★★ Decayed relic	NR No rating

classic wines

1985 Green Label Barossa ★★★☆ *April 1997*

Medium yellow–green; the bouquet is quite rich, with hints of honey, toast and more tropical notes. A full-bodied wine on the early and mid-palate, but hollows out towards the finish, and is slightly short.

1984 Eden Valley Bin DNB29 ★★★★☆ *April 1997*

Medium yellow–green; a mix of toasty, tangy citrus and honey aromas are followed by a palate that initially showed camphor/lime characters, suggesting it is starting to age, but which got better and better the longer the wine sat in the glass and was retasted. A remarkably long palate; perilously close to top rating.

1981 Watervale Bin DWK7 ★★★ *April 1997*

Medium to full yellow–straw; hints of camphor and lime on a slightly coarse and somewhat volatile bouquet; the wine is rather heavy on the palate, with toasty/charry notes. Apparently, never a good wine, with lots of stress from a very hot vintage.

1980 Bin DWJ25 ★★★☆ *November 1994*

Light to medium yellow–green; the bouquet is youthful with slightly green aspects to the herbal/lime/toast aromas. The palate is relatively light and soft, with lime/camphor flavours, fractionally stripped.

1980 Bin DWJ18 ★★★ *November 1994*

Medium yellow–green; soft, lime and toast aromas lacking intensity. The palate is pleasant, without fault, showing some lime and toast flavours, but generally lacking intensity.

1979 Eden Valley Bin DWI16 ★★★★★ *April 1997*

Wonderful bright yellow–green colour; complex lime, toast and honey aromas of medium to full intensity lead into a classically constructed and flavoured wine with identical flavours to those of the bouquet, and a touch of fruit sweetness on the back palate before moving into a long, dry finish.

1978 Watervale Bin DWH21 ★★★★☆ *April 1997*

Even better colour than the '79, glowing and brilliant yellow–green. The bouquet is firm, tangy and fresh with aromas of herb and lime. The palate, too, has tangy grassy/herbal/lime flavours, with good balance and acidity.

1978 Bin DWH23 ★★★★☆ *November 1994*

Medium yellow–green; the bouquet is firm with some kerosene and mineral notes, and a hint of toast. A lighter style on the palate with fresh lime and toast flavours; not intense but holding well.

1977 Barossa Eden Bin DW246 ★★★★ *April 1997*

Full yellow–green; aromas of lime, with touches of nettle and mint lead into a wine of fair length and balance, showing more of those camphor and lime flavours of the bouquet.

1977 Watervale Bin DWG37 ★★★★ *April 1997*

Medium to full yellow–green; an intense bouquet with an amalgam of lime, honey and toast leads on to a full, rich palate, that is perhaps a fraction heavy and slightly phenolic, particularly on the finish, but that has lots of flavour.

◀━ Not Ready ＼ Still evolving ▮ Prime of its life ⌁ Drink soon ⎁ Missed the boat

1976 Bin DWF25 ★★★☆ *April 1997*

Medium yellow–green; a slightly blowsy bouquet with potent, tropical/pineapple honey and camphor aromas. The palate is soft and a fraction blowsy, relatively developed and lacking intensity.

1975 Watervale Bin DWE13 ★★★☆ *April 1997*

A slightly dull, out-of-condition colour, tinged with brown and protein haze. The bouquet is toasty, with slightly earthy/minerally notes, the palate solid but difficult to assess given the colour.

1975 Eden Valley Bin DWE17 ★★★★★ *April 1997*

Brilliant green–yellow; a magnificent bouquet with lime, citrus and toast, and as fresh as a daisy. In the mouth, a great wine at the absolute peak of its power, with perfect harmony, length and balance, and an exquisite blend of lime juice and honey flavours, finishing with good acidity. Really needs an extra star to do it justice.

1975 Watervale Bin DWE18 Spatlese ★★★★★ *November 1994*

Glowing yellow–green; rich, toasty honeyed aromas lead on to a rich, very full-bodied and harmonious palate with luscious lime and honey flavours. The wine does not cloy on the finish, and should be exceedingly long lived. A winner of 21 gold and 22 silver medals.

1973 Barossa/Watervale Eden Bin DW33 ★★★★ *April 1997*

Medium to full yellow–green; abundant ripe, honeyed, gently toasty fruit on the bouquet is repeated on a round, rich and full-flavoured palate.

1973 Watervale Spatlese Bin DWC14 ★★★★☆ *April 1997*

Yellow–orange; the bouquet is soft and rich with some mandarin/dried fruit aromas. The wine floods the mouth with its richness and fruit (rather than residual sugar) sweetness. A wine which either needs to be served fully chilled or with food.

1973 Barossa Bin DWC11 ★★★★★ *April 1997*

Medium to full yellow; an unusual but most attractive bouquet with overtones of crème caramel to the more conventional honey and toast aromas. A delicious palate, rich, full and rounded, with lime and honey flavours running through a long finish.

1973 Eden Valley Bin DWC17 ★★★★★ *April 1997*

Medium to full yellow; a wonderful essence of regional and varietal character on the spotlessly clean and youthful bouquet with intense but soft lime juice aromas; the palate is very powerful, intense and long. A wine of the highest quality that, if well corked and cellared, will live for another decade at least.

1973 Watervale Bin DWC15 ★★★★★ *April 1997*

Bright, glowing medium to full yellow–green; the bouquet is still fragrant, with herb, lime and toast aromas mixed with a touch of honey. A lovely wine, initially gently toasty but which builds and unfolds on the mid- to back-palate, finishing with soft acidity.

classic wines

★★★★★ Perfect   ★★★★☆ Close to perfect   ★★★★ Very good   ★★★☆ Expected
★★★ Short of standard   ★★☆ Undeserving   ★★ Decayed relic   NR No rating

109

1972 Eden Valley Bin DWB15 ★★★★★   *April 1997*

Absolutely brilliant colour, light to medium yellow–green. An extraordinarily youthful and intense bouquet with a mix of herb, mineral and lime aromas introduces a wine that is the epitome of Riesling — long and fine — and in perfect condition. Both this and the Watervale of the same year take Riesling into another dimension of quality.

1972 Watervale Bin DWB13 ★★★★★   *April 1997*

Medium yellow–green; a wonderfully fresh and intense bouquet with lime and herb aromas is followed by a wine that floods the mouth, richer and rounder than the Eden Valley of the same year, and sheer perfection.

1972 Barossa/Watervale/Eden DW33 ★★★★☆   *April 1997*

Medium yellow–green; an impressively tight, quite racy bouquet with herb and mineral notes is followed by a fresh, tight and youthful palate, with excellent structure. Absolutely outstanding for a large-volume, cheap commercial wine at the time of its release.

1971 Eden Valley Bin DWA15 ★★★★☆   *April 1997*

Glowing yellow–green; the bouquet almost certainly showed slight cork taint, imparting a slightly charry note, but could not obscure the tremendous length to the fruit on the palate, nor the soft, lingering acid finish. The rating is something of a compromise; it is almost certain a sound bottle would receive top points.

1970 Watervale Bin DWZ13 ★★★★   *April 1997*

The colour shows distinct signs of browning, yet is still bright. The bouquet is highly unusual, with penetrating lime, cinnamon spice, mandarin and cumquat aromas. The palate follows down the same unusual track, with voluminous camphor/cumquat lime and spice flavours.

1970 Eden Valley Bin DW110 ★★★★★   *November 1994*

Bright medium yellow–green, despite a relatively low-filled bottle. A wonderfully youthful bouquet with fresh lime, honey and toast aromas. The palate is still vibrantly fresh with rounded lime/citrus flavours, a long finish with perfect acid.

1968 Bin DW95 ★★★☆   *November 1994*

Medium to full yellow with just a hint of green. The bouquet has aromas of toast and honey, and just a hint of lime, but is starting to tire. There are lime and camphor flavours on the mid-palate, but as it is starting to dry out on the finish, harder phenolics are starting to appear.

1968 Bin DWX14 ★★★   *November 1994*

Deep gold; very advanced honey/apricot/lime/camphor aromas with a faintly musty overtone. The wine has plenty of flavour still, but is drying out and becoming tough as it maderizes.

1967 Eden Valley Bin DWW22 ★★★★★   *April 1997*

Bright medium to full yellow–green; an incredibly fresh bouquet showing perfect lime and honey varietal character is followed by a graceful, elegant and long palate. A wine that was initially austere, but that has matured magnificently with age.

1966 Eden Valley Bin DWV12 ★★★★★   *April 1997*

The glowing yellow–green colour is absolutely remarkable, the bouquet exceptionally fresh, with lime and honey, and just a hint of charry/toasty character in the background. The palate displays a wine that is beautifully balanced, still holding its varietal integrity, and with a very long finish. Still a great classic.

1965 Barossa Bin DW58 ★★★   *April 1997*

Full yellow; the bouquet shows some maderisation, with hints of cumquat, but is far from decayed, and the palate likewise still has some soft cumquat and lime fruit, tinged with camphor.

1963 Chateau Leonay Bin DW55 ★★★   *April 1997*

The colour shows its age, with straw–brown tinges, and the bouquet is maderised, although not unpleasant. The palate is holding far better than the bouquet suggests, though it is slightly phenolic. These were the last two bottles from John Vickery's personal cellar.

★★★★★ Perfect   ★★★★☆ Close to perfect   ★★★★ Very good   ★★★☆ Expected
★★★ Short of standard   ★★☆ Undeserving   ★★ Decayed relic   NR No rating

lindemans hunter river shiraz
(burgundy) 1959-1995

lindemans 1959 Bin 1590 Burgundy is one of the greatest Hunter Valley wines, on a par with the best of Maurice O'Shea's light-bodied dry reds — for Bin 1590 is not a leviathan like the 1965 Bin 3110, nor some of the bigger O'Shea wines. Over the years I have drunk many bottles of this wine: it is now exceedingly rare, and it may be I will not taste it again. In a sense, I do not wish to — I would prefer to remember the sheer perfection of the bottle tasted for this work in November 1994.

The quality since 1959 has been more consistent than with the Semillons; high-quality grapes have been available in most years — essential, given that these wines were made with little or no oak influence until the mid-1980s and were typically bottled at the end of the year in which they were made, a little known fact.

The older labels are a challenge: usually Burgundy, sometimes Claret, with a part-changing, part-repetitive four-figure Bin Number system. The first two numbers ascended with the years, though without any particular rhythm, while the last two represented the quality: 00 the show bin, 03 the commercial (early) release, the 10 a special wine not seen every year.

As the notes show, the best wines will live for 40 years or more, and only the weakest will not happily see out ten years. They have their own inimitable style, and are a vital part of Australia's wine heritage.

First tasted in November 1994, updated, and later vintages added.

◀ **1995 Bin 9003** ★★★☆   *December 1999*

Medium red; the bouquet is of medium intensity, with earthy, distinct varietal character surrounded by soft vanilla oak. The palate is likewise of medium weight, with earthy/chocolatey flavours and soft tannins running through to the finish. Pleasant but not great.

1994 Bin 8803 ★★★☆   *March 1998*

Dark red; the aromas are typically complex, with a mix of plum, sweet leather and earth fruit aromas. The palate is well balanced, with a mix of plummy and more earthy flavours, with those unmistakable tannins of the region, which become positively silky with age.

◀ Not Ready   ＼ Still evolving   ▌ Prime of its life   ⌁ Drink soon   ⌷ Missed the boat

1991 Reserve Bin 9200 ★★★★

August 1996

Medium red–purple; soft, rich and ripe fruit in an earthy/minty/berry spectrum is supported by quite pronounced but not excessive oak. A powerful and rich wine on the palate, with a mix of mint, berry and earth in typical regional style. Finishes with soft tannins. Likely to improve further with age.

1990 Bin 8003 Burgundy ★★★★★

November 1994

Medium red–purple. A complex bouquet with some spice and medicinal aromas over bright berry fruit underneath. The palate has abundant, vibrant varietal spice which is fruit, not oak, derived. The finish is perfectly balanced, the structure likewise; a lovely wine.

1989 Bin 7803 Burgundy ★★★☆

November 1994

Medium red; a scented bouquet with some lift, together with mint, leaf and herbal characters. The palate is distinctly minty, leafy and earthy, and not generous. It may be in an ugly transition phase, but one wouldn't be sure.

1988 Bin 7600 Burgundy ★★★★★

November 1994

Medium to full red; a quite rich bouquet with traditional earth and chocolate aromas. On the palate, an interesting throwback to some of the older wines in the tasting, with attractive chocolate and earth edges to red berry fruits, finishing with well-balanced tannins. Outstanding for a relatively unfashionable Hunter vintage.

1987 Bin 7403 Burgundy ★★★★★

November 1994

Medium to full red; some new oak apparent on the bouquet which is not entirely integrated, and seems fractionally green. The palate is very much better than the bouquet suggests with sweet fruit, and well-balanced tannins providing excellent structure and complexity.

1986 Bin 7203 Burgundy ★★★★☆

November 1994

Medium red; a clean, varietally-driven bouquet of spice and berry. The palate is lively, fresh and clean; of medium weight overall with nicely balanced red berry and spice flavours.

1982 Bin 6400 ★★★☆

November 1994

Medium red; a faintly baggy/earthy bouquet, the fruit lacking richness. The palate is curiously unformed, with clean red berry fruit, finishing with soft tannins. Really shows early bottling characters.

1980 Bin 5900 ★★★

November 1994

Medium red, with a touch of tawny; the bouquet is clean with some red berry/cherry fruit. The palate is remarkably fresh but not especially ripe, and again simple and unformed, finishing short. Could develop, but it is inherently unlikely.

1975 Bin 5103 ★★☆

November 1994

Medium red–tawny; a rather baggy vegetal aroma, lacking sweet fruit. The palate is likewise light and lacking fruit richness; a saving grace is that the tannins are soft and balanced.

★★★★★ Perfect   ★★★★☆ Close to perfect   ★★★★ Very good   ★★★☆ Expected
★★★ Short of standard   ★★☆ Undeserving   ★★ Decayed relic   NR No rating

1973 Bin 4800 ★★★★★   *November 1994*

Medium red; a clean and smooth bouquet with gently earthy regional overtones to ripe, sweet berry fruit. In the mouth absolutely in the mainstream of Hunter Shiraz, soft and round fruit with gently earthy overtones, and soft tannins.

1972 Bin 4700 ★★★☆   *November 1994*

Medium tawny–red; fragrant, but with some medicinal/herbaceous aromas. The palate is quite similar, with herbaceous/minerally notes; lighter bodied, with soft tannins.

1970 Bin 4000 ★★★★☆   *November 1994*

Medium to full red, with a hint of tawny. A concentrated and complex bouquet of earth, leather and mineral notes. The palate, too, is concentrated, with excellent earth and chocolate regional fruit, finishing with firm tannins.

1969 Bin 3910 ★★★☆   *November 1994*

Medium tawny–red; the bouquet is clean, with a complex array of fruit aromas running from sweet berry through to chocolate and earth. The palate is likewise complex with earth and chocolate flavours, less ripe than the bouquet, and finishing with persistent tannins.

1968 Bin 3700 ★★★☆   *November 1994*

Medium red–tawny; a faintly funky bouquet with fractionally gamey/sweaty/medicinal notes. The palate is complex, but starting to dry out on the mid-palate, and finishing with slightly hard tannins.

1967 Bin 3603 ★★★★   *November 1994*

Medium red–tawny; a smooth, sweet bouquet of medium weight with some chocolate fruit. The palate is nicely balanced and smooth, with no off-characters, finishing with appropriately balanced tannins and acidity.

1966 Bin 3300 ★★★☆   *November 1994*

Medium red–tawny; a radical change from the older vintages, with earthy/mineral/herbal/medicinal aromas. The palate is an inevitable letdown after the '65 with herbal/liquorice and medicinal flavours again apparent. Very different from Bin 3303 of the same year.

1965 Bin 3100 Burgundy ★★★★☆   *November 1994*

Note that this was not a good example, proving the old adage of no great old wines, only great old wine bottles. Incredibly deep red; the bouquet explosively potent and concentrated with dark briar, chocolate and liquorice fruit. The palate shows signs of oxidation; massively concentrated but not particularly expressive or fruity. Is normally every bit as great as the Bin 3110.

1965 Bin 3110 ★★★★★   *November 1994*

Dark, deep red with some faint tawny characters on the rim. The palate is fragrant, powerful and extremely complex, like a bigger version of the Bin 1590, featuring an array of aromas through earth to berry, but all sweet. The palate is incredibly complex and multifaceted, with tannins running throughout hugely concentrated and powerful briary chocolate fruit. Properly corked, it will live for another 30 or 40 years. 14.5 per cent alcohol.

◄━ Not Ready   ◥ Still evolving   ▮ Prime of its life   ◢ Drink soon   ⨅ Missed the boat

1964 Bin 2950 ★★★★ *November 1994*

Full tawny–red; a solid, rich, dark chocolate and liquorice bouquet leads on to a big, rich full-bodied and powerful palate which is briary rather than fruity; it is almost certain that the tannins will outlive the fruit.

1963 Bin 2585 ★★★★☆ *November 1994*

Medium to full tawny–red; a complex bouquet with earth, mint and mineral characters all present, and some volatility evident. A punchy wine, driven by that touch of volatility, but with very traditional flavours and good length. Holding well other than the volatility.

1963 Bin 6600 ★★★★☆ *November 1994*

Youthful red; attractive red berry, chocolate and earth fruit, a return to top form after some disappointing vintages preceding it. The palate is very ripe, almost but not quite jammy, with sweet cherry fruit, finishing with soft tannins.

1961 Bin 1970 ★★★★ *November 1994*

Medium to full tawny; exceptionally rich bouquet with loads of dark chocolate and sweeter berry fruit, then some more gamey/earthy notes. Complex, ripe, earthy/gamey/chocolate flavours, then with a hint of regional hay/straw, finishing with pronounced tannins. Starting to lose its fruit.

1959 Bin 1590 ★★★★★ *November 1994*

Medium to full tawny–red; a gloriously fragrant and complex bouquet with a magnificent array of aromas from sweet berry through liquorice to sweet leather. On the palate a superb example of Hunter Valley Hermitage; they simply do not come any better than this. Sweet fruit comes on the mid to back palate, finishing with soft tannins on a dry, yet not drying, farewell.

lindemans limestone ridge shiraz
cabernet 1959-1998

there are those who believe that St George Cabernet Sauvignon is Lindemans' best Coonawarra red wine, but I would be most surprised if Limestone Ridge did not have the largest band of loyal followers who buy the wine year in, year out. It comes from the first vineyard planted by Lindemans after it acquired Rouge Homme from the Redman family in 1965, and takes its name from the fact that it sits astride the main north/south ridge in Coonawarra. Here the terra rossa soil is thinner than usual, the underlying limestone closer to the surface and harder to break. Thus planting the 20 hectares of shiraz and 4 hectares of cabernet sauvignon between 1967 and 1968 caused unusual problems for the planting crew.

The first 'true' vintage of Limestone Ridge was 1973, but way back in the late 1960s Lindemans released a one-off 1959 Limestone Ridge wine (under an entirely different parchment label) made from 100 per cent shiraz and which it had inherited with the purchase of Rouge Homme. The other significant 'one-off' was the release of a 100 per cent Cabernet Sauvignon from the 1976 vintage (principally in magnum).

The wine is a variable blend of Shiraz (55 per cent to 80 per cent) and Cabernet Sauvignon, and is matured in a mix of new American and French oak hogsheads for 20 months — with the American oak inevitably dominating.

The 1959 to 1992 vintages were tasted in November 1994; subsequent vintages on release.

1998 ★★★★★　　　　　　　　　　　　　　　　　　*February 2001*
Medium to full red–purple; clean, ripe black cherry and berry fruit with spicy overtones and well-managed oak on the bouquet foreshadow a quite delicious palate, with a core of sweet, black cherry fruit surrounded by fine tannins and positive oak.

1997 ★★★★☆　　　　　　　　　　　　　　　　　　*February 1999*
Medium to full red–purple; lusciously ripe plummy/cherry fruit is swathed in high-quality oak on the bouquet. The same ripe cherry and plum fruit runs through a seductive palate with a long, soft finish. Oak certainly makes its contribution, but does so in balance and harmony with the fruit.

◄■ Not Ready　　　＼ Still evolving　　　▮ Prime of its life　　　◢ Drink soon　　　▯ Missed the boat

1996 ★★★★★   *September 1999*

Medium to full red–purple; the wine has quite lovely richness and concentration, with perfectly ripe berry fruit and well-balanced and integrated oak. The palate is no less seductive, with streams of sweet plum, raspberry and cherry fruit supported by gently sweet oak. Outstanding; the best Limestone Ridge for many years, possibly ever.

1994 ★★★★★   *January 1998*

Medium to full red–purple; a powerful, concentrated bouquet with excellent fruit and oak balance and integration; the palate is well balanced and composed, with briar, chocolate and red berry fruit together with generous vanilla oak, finishing with moderate tannins. A typical '94 vintage, not fleshy, but powerful. A prolific gold medal winner in shows.

1993 ★★★★★   *January 1997*

Medium to full red–purple; a generous, softly sweet and fragrant bouquet with mulberry/plum fruit and soft vanilla oak leads on to a rich, rounded and mouthfilling palate. There is a seamless integration of ripe mulberry-accented fruit and creamy vanillin American oak. The best of the Lindemans trio from this vintage.

1992 ★★★   *November 1994*

Medium to full red–purple; attractive, clean, juicy berry fruit, quite ripe, with prominent oak. A well made wine with spicy/cherry/berry fruit and masses of oak; not as concentrated as the '91 and will develop quickly.

1991 ★★★★★   *November 1994*

Medium to full red–purple; clean, concentrated plum, cherry and spice fruit aromas with perfectly balanced and integrated oak. On the palate, exceptionally concentrated in comparison to all others in the line-up, with lots of round, mouthfilling plum cherry and raspberry fruit, finishing with good tannins.

1990 ★★★★☆   *November 1994*

Medium to full red–purple; solid, smooth cherry/berry fruit with hints of mint on the bouquet and nicely handled oak. Fresh, flavoursome and smooth on the palate with red berry fruits and nice dusty vanillin oak, finishing with soft tannins.

1989 ★★★☆   *November 1994*

Medium to full red–purple; clean red berry and mint fruit aromas, once again showing well-handled oak. The palate is light and fresh, starting to show obvious development, but with no errant fruit, and the tannins are supple. A success for a difficult year.

1988 ★★★★   *November 1994*

Medium red–purple; the bouquet is of light to medium intensity with clean, pleasantly ripe shiraz with well-balanced nutty oak. The palate has a range of flavours from red berry, plum through to more vegetal mint, finishing with soft vanillin oak.

1987 ★★★   *November 1994*

Medium red, starting to brown; an amalgam of leafy/gamey/earthy/minty aromas which are not terribly attractive; the palate, too, has an array of herbal, medicinal and green leaf flavours, finishing with soft tannins.

★★★★★ Perfect   ★★★★☆ Close to perfect   ★★★★ Very good   ★★★☆ Expected
★★★ Short of standard   ★★☆ Undeserving   ★★ Decayed relic   NR No rating

1986 ★★★★★ *November 1994*

Strong red–purple; fresh, sweet fruit with a hint of mint, and coffee-tinged oak. The palate shows positive, sweet red berry fruit of good intensity, with a nice touch of new oak, finishing with soft tannins.

1984 ★★★☆ *November 1994*

Medium to full red; distinctly sweeter than the older wines, riper, almost jammy, with a hint of volatility on the bouquet. The palate has plenty of ripe, sweet red berry fruit flavours, with a soft finish. There is an element of sweet and sour to the wine.

1982 ★★★★ *November 1994*

Medium to full red–purple; there is ample berry and plum fruit in the wine, which is still quite fresh. The problem lies with the oak, which, even at this stage does not seem to be integrated or balanced, and the question is whether it will ever become so. A formidable show record including a trophy, nine gold, five silver and seven bronze medals.

1981 ★★★☆ *November 1994*

Medium red showing obvious development; a complex bouquet with a mix of vegetal, mint and riper tobacco aromas. The palate is solid, with flavours of earth, chocolate, mint and spice, finishing with firm tannins.

1980 ★★★★ *November 1994*

Medium red, again with a hint of brown starting to appear. A potent, striking bouquet with fruit aromas running the full spectrum from medicinal/leafy/gamey through to riper berry. The palate, too, is potent and powerful, with obvious dimethyl sulphide giving a tangy medicinal edge; in fairly extreme style. Love it or hate it.

1979 ★★★ *November 1994*

Light to medium red; a fairly plain, thin and inexpressive bouquet with some medicinal/dimethyl sulphide characters. The palate is ripe with simple, squashy berry characters and slight coffee/chocolate overtones, finishing with soft tannins.

1978 ★★★ *November 1994*

Medium red; a powerfully medicinal bouquet showing dimethyl sulphide. The palate is striking, with pronounced Coonawarra pie and peas characters, again indicating dimethyl sulphide; simply not my style.

1977 ★★☆ *November 1994*

Medium tawny–red; the bouquet is sweet and sour, with chocolate to green mint. The palate is astringent and stemmy, with green herbal fruit. Possibly a slightly corked bottle.

1976 ★★★☆ *November 1994*

Medium to full red; a complex and potent bouquet showing the range of medicinal and herbal aromas which so mark this period, together with some characters vaguely reminiscent of the Hunter. The palate, too, is idiosyncratic in its high-toned, high alcohol profile, with those strange medicinal characters.

◀ Not Ready 🮰 Still evolving 🮲 Prime of its life 🮱 Drink soon ⎕ Missed the boat

1976 Cabernet Sauvignon ★★★★★   *November 1994*

Medium to full red. A ripe, clean bouquet with abundant sweet fruit almost into chocolate, but with a varietal herbal edge. The palate, too, shows an intriguing flavour mix of dark chocolate and more herbaceous notes; good structure, and well-balanced tannins.

1973 ★★   *November 1994*

Aged, high pH colour. The bouquet is tired with earthy/mushroom characters coming on top of leaf and mint. The palate shows similar flavours to the '72, but is tougher and more tannic. Not an attractive wine.

1972 ★★☆   *November 1994*

Medium tawny; aged camphor, green mint and earth aromas leading on to a palate with distinctly vegetal, minty, gamey characters.

1971 ★★★   *November 1994*

Medium red–tawny; clean but aged aromas of toffee, chocolate, leaf and mint. A pleasant old wine, still retaining some vestigial fruit sweetness on the palate with touches of toffee and coffee, finishing with soft tannins.

1959 ★★★★☆   *November 1994*

Medium red; a clean and fragrant bouquet with herbs, spice and toffee aromas. Perhaps a faded old lady, but still holding its fruit and structure, finishing with fine tannins and showing aged varietal earth characteristics throughout.

★★★★★ Perfect   ★★★★☆ Close to perfect   ★★★★ Very good   ★★★☆ Expected
★★★ Short of standard   ★★☆ Undeserving   ★★ Decayed relic   NR No rating

lindemans st george cabernet sauvignon 1973-1998

I f one wished to present a work-case study of the development of Cabernet Sauvignon in Australia over the past 25 years, one could hardly do better than use St George — particularly if the object were to show the failures as well as the successes.

It has to be remembered that when Lindemans planted this choice block of land with 12 hectares of cabernet sauvignon in 1969, the total Australian production of cabernet in that year was 1250 tonnes. Ten years later it had risen to 20 000 tonnes, and by 2000 it had soared to 159 000 tonnes with further growth in sight.

So Australian viticulturists and winemakers have been on a sharp learning curve, a curve made even more challenging by innovations in viticulture, many of them pioneered in Coonawarra — first mechanical harvesting and pruning, and then minimal (read no) pruning. In the midst of this came the appearance of DMS, or dimethyl sulphide, a substance originating in grapes which have ripened in a shaded canopy but which can increase alarmingly after the wine has been bottled. Like substances such as trichloranisole (cork taint) or methoxypyrazine (the base flavour compound of cabernet sauvignon) it can be tasted in sub-microscopic quantities.

All of these factors are reflected in St George, from its Jimmy Watson Trophy in 1981 to its less glorious moments. As with Limestone Ridge, since 1986 things have improved out of sight, but again as with Limestone, prolonged cellaring may prove unrewarding.

First tasted in November 1994, updated, and later vintages added.

◄ 1998 ★★★★★   *February 2001*
Medium to full red–purple; while the varietal character is clearly defined in a strong, blackcurrant/cassis mode, the bouquet is distinctively elegant, a character which enhances the tightly knit palate. There are no surprises with the flavours of blackberry and blackcurrant, nor the lingering tannins on the finish.

◄ 1997 ★★★★★   *October 2000*
Medium red–purple; the bouquet is already showing some attractive bottle-developed savoury/cedary overtones to the fruit; the palate, on the other hand, is rich and surprisingly dense, with abundant blackberry/blackcurrant fruit, lingering, ripe tannins and well-integrated and balanced French oak. A great success for the year.

   ◄ Not Ready   ◣ Still evolving   ◢ Prime of its life   ◢ Drink soon   ⬮ Missed the boat

1996 ★★★★☆ *September 1999*

Medium to full red–purple; the bouquet is quite earthy and relatively austere, raising a question mark about the particular bottle, although the palate came through strongly with ripe, rich chunky cassis-flavoured fruit backed up by plenty of tannin providing a sturdy structure.

1995 ★★★★☆ *October 1998*

Medium to full red–purple; the bouquet is sweet and smooth, with well-balanced fruit and oak; the palate is even more attractive, with sweet chocolate and mint-flavoured fruit, well-above-average tannin structure, and nicely judged oak. The best of the trio from 1995.

1994 ★★★☆ *January 1998*

Medium to full red–purple; the bouquet is quite oaky, with charry/earthy varietal fruit, and the palate has lots of earthy astringency, very much a child of '94, and looking particularly ungainly in early 1998.

1993 ★★★☆ *January 1997*

Medium red–purple; a soft, faintly cedary/earthy bouquet which is not especially rich leads on to a pleasant wine on the palate with red berry, leaf and earth flavours, finishing with soft tannins. The main problem seems to be a lack of concentration.

1992 ★★★★☆ *November 1994*

Medium red–purple; ripe, sweet berry and mint fruit with pronounced charry French oak. The palate is high-toned, with fresh red berry fruit and spicy, charry oak still to integrate.

1991 ★★★★★ *November 1994*

Medium to full red–purple; a smooth, clean, fine and elegant bouquet with well-balanced and integrated oak. The palate is full bodied with ripe plum and berry fruit, showing above-average concentration, and the same very well-integrated and balanced oak evident on the palate. The tannin structure, too, is good; four gold medals.

1990 ★★★★★ *November 1994*

Medium to full red–purple; a complex bouquet which has another dimension in fruit weight and intensity compared to the wines of the ensuing (older) vintages, with abundant dark berry, plum and cassis fruit and nicely balanced and integrated oak. The palate is full, rich and round, with abundant plum and cassis fruit, and lingering tannins.

1989 ★★★☆ *November 1994*

Medium to full red, still with a touch of purple; pleasantly complex berry fruit with a hint of charry oak on the bouquet leads on to a light, pleasant early-maturing wine on the palate, again showing some charry oak.

1988 ★★★★☆ *November 1994*

Medium to full red–purple; clean, smooth cherry and berry fruit with attractive cedary oak. A quite fresh wine on the palate which has a real touch of class and elegance, finishing with soft tannins.

classic wines

★★★★★ Perfect ★★★★☆ Close to perfect ★★★★ Very good ★★★☆ Expected
★★★ Short of standard ★★☆ Undeserving ★★ Decayed relic NR No rating

1987 ★★★ *November 1994*

Medium red, starting to brown off; the bouquet is rather leafy and minty with hints of caramel and toffee from the oak. The palate is lean, leafy and minty, ageing fast.

1986 ★★★★★ *November 1994*

Medium to full red–purple; the bouquet is firm with red berry, earth and green leaf aromas of cool-ripened cabernet, with a hint of charry oak. The palate is holding well, with complex red berry fruits, rounded tannins and supple oak.

1985 ★★★★ *November 1994*

Medium to full red; a relatively complex bouquet with briar, cedar, tobacco and earth aromas intermingling. The palate is rather more concentrated and fruity than the bouquet suggests, with attractive cherry and plum fruit balanced by cedary/briary oak.

1984 ★★★☆ *November 1994*

Dark red; surprisingly ripe, plummy fruit aromas on the bouquet with briary, maceration undertones. The palate too, has ripe plum and berry fruit flavours which are not intense but which are still holding. There are some more leafy, lifted characters which may soon take control of the wine.

1982 ★★★☆ *November 1994*

Medium red; the aromas are quite fragrant and clean with pleasant leafy/minty aspects. The palate, too, shows quite fresh stemmy/minty/leafy flavours, vaguely reminiscent of Bordeaux. Fractionally hard in the mouth.

1981 ★★★ *November 1994*

Very developed and tired-looking colour; the bouquet, too is tired with plain, earthy/chocolatey aromas, leading on to a minty/earthy/leafy palate lacking sweetness, although finishing with soft tannins. Hanging in there — just.

1980 ★★★★ *November 1994*

Two bottles tasted; the best features of each chosen. Medium red; fragrant, leafy/herbal aromas showing moderate dimethyl sulphide, and subtle oak. The palate is markedly herbaceous and tangy, and still lively, albeit in an extreme style.

1979 ★★ *November 1994*

A very tired, thin, baggy and oxidised wine which, while not obviously corked, was very likely a poor bottle.

1978 ★★★ *November 1994*

Medium red; a potent, leafy/tobacco-accented bouquet showing more of the dimethyl sulphide characters, which come through on the intense, biting flavour of the palate, finishing with a trace of bitterness.

1977 ★★★ *November 1994*

Medium red; the bouquet is ageing, with distinct leaf and mint aromas, and a hint of earth. The palate is a little fresher and brighter, though far from rich, with leaf and mint flavours once again predominant.

← Not Ready　　↘ Still evolving　　❚ Prime of its life　　🍷 Drink soon　　▯ Missed the boat

1976 ★★★☆   *November 1994*

Medium red–tawny; a soft, gently earthy bouquet with the fruit fading. The palate is pleasant in a fully mature style, with faded sweet fruit and some earthy/leafy notes starting to take over.

1973 ★★☆   *November 1994*

Medium red; the bouquet has lost all of its primary fruit, with aged herb and earth notes predominate. The palate, too, is well past its best, with some faint sweet tobacco characters lingering.

★★★★★ Perfect   ★★★★☆ Close to perfect   ★★★★ Very good   ★★★☆ Expected
★★★ Short of standard   ★★☆ Undeserving   ★★ Decayed relic   NR No rating

classic wines

123

mcwilliam's mount pleasant elizabeth 1975-1997

times have changed for the face of one of the enduring white wine classics of Australia, but inside the bottle the wine remains the same. It has moved from the slender Riesling bottle, once the standard package for Hunter Semillon, to the squat Burgundy shape along with a change in glass colour from dark green to lighter, dead-leaf green. There has been a major label redesign, with the focus on the word Elizabeth, and 'Hunter Valley Semillon' has been added in reasonably prominent type on the front label. Ever-fewer restaurants now include the wine in their list of Rieslings where it once occupied a prime spot. (Semillon was once called Hunter River Riesling.)

The wine is made without any artifice, although given the vast volume in which it is made, there are some surprising facts. Roughly half is estate-grown, half purchased from contract growers, most hand-picked. Winemaker Phil Ryan believes the Glen McWilliam-designed drainers into which the crushed grapes are put before pressing also play an important role in rapidly separating the free-run juice.

The making is simplicity itself: cold fermented, no hint of oak, and bottled by mid-year before being given two years corkage. The show judges have acknowledged its quality: every release between 1981 and 1997 had received at least one gold medal, and up to 2001 had accumulated 26 trophies and 161 gold medals.

Note: I have included the intermittent release of top-of-the-range Lovedale (prior to 1980 called Anne) in the notes.

The majority tasted in April 2001; the remainder in November 1994.

1997 ★★★★☆   *April 2001*
Glowing yellow–green; a powerful bouquet, with a mix of toast and honey on the one hand, and lime and herb on the other. Yet again, the wine has flavour, length and grip, with good acidity; still remarkably fresh.

1996 ★★★★   *April 2001*
Bright, light yellow–green; a rich and smooth bouquet with a mix of lemon, citrus and honey aromas, the palate is particularly fresh, with a touch of carbon dioxide still evident, and less developed.

◀ Not Ready   ❩ Still evolving   ▮ Prime of its life   ⬗ Drink soon   ⬭ Missed the boat

1996 Lovedale ★★★★★　　　　　　　　　　　　　　　　April 2001
Bright, light green–yellow, with some carbon dioxide apparent in the glass. The bouquet is at once complex and intense, with a faint hint of some of the vaguely French characters which appear from time to time in these wines. The palate is brilliantly fresh, lively and intense, with sweet lemon juice flavours and a pure finish.

1995 ★★★★　　　　　　　　　　　　　　　　　　　　　April 2001
Light to medium yellow–green; clean, fresh and lively, with lemony/citrussy fruit still dominant on the bouquet. The palate is lively, fresh and crisp, with delicate herbaceous fruit; doesn't appear to have the fruit intensity of the best years, and the finish is slightly grippy at this juncture. May be simply going through one of those development phases.

1995 Lovedale ★★★★　　　　　　　　　　　　　　　　　April 2001
Light to medium yellow–green, showing a fair amount of carbon dioxide when first poured. The bouquet is clean, fresh and elegant, but not particularly expressive; the palate, likewise, is lively and fresh, with a touch of spritz from the carbon dioxide; definitely needs more time to resolve itself when it will almost certainly receive a significantly higher rating.

1994 ★★★★☆　　　　　　　　　　　　　　　　　　　　April 2001
A developed yellow–gold colour, not dissimilar to the 1987 (for example); the bouquet is right in the Elizabeth slot, rich, and with honeyed/toasty aromas already in full flight. There is a good entry to the mouth and mid-palate fruit, with a touch of lemon peel, closing with fresh acidity. Does seem to lighten off ever so slightly on the finish.

1993 ★★★★★　　　　　　　　　　　　　　　　　　　　April 2001
Golden yellow; sweetly complex aromas run from honey and toast to citrus/mandarin to more herbaceous notes. The palate has a complex array of flavours, opening with honey and mandarin, then more herbal characters to the fresh, crisp, bone-dry finish.

1992 ★★★★☆　　　　　　　　　　　　　　　　　　　January 1997
Full yellow–gold; surprisingly, as developed, if not more developed, than the '91 at the same stage, with rich toasty/buttery aromas and an equivalently rich, toasty/buttery/vanilla-flavoured palate.

1991 ★★★★★　　　　　　　　　　　　　　　　　　　　April 2001
Deep, glowing gold; a rich and ripe bouquet with honeyed buttery/toasty/ nutty aromas is followed by a mouthfilling, full-bodied, old-style white burgundy palate. The complex array of flavours runs from some sweet, ripe fruit characters on the one side, and mineral at the other extreme. Drink sooner rather than later, but may surprise with its tenacity.

1990 ★★★★★　　　　　　　　　　　　　　　　　　　　April 2001
Glowing yellow–green; the bouquet is complex, with some of the tangy cross-cut of the 1996 Lovedale and the 1989 Elizabeth. The palate is intense, long and lingering, leading from buttered toast on the mid-palate to lemony acidity on the finish.

classic wines

★★★★★ Perfect　　★★★★☆ Close to perfect　　★★★★ Very good　　★★★☆ Expected
★★★ Short of standard　　★★☆ Undeserving　　★★ Decayed relic　　NR No rating

125

1989 ★★★★☆ *November 1994*

Medium yellow; a very complex bouquet with some of the slightly vegetal/French characters of the Tyrrell's Vat 1 of the same year. The most complex, multiflavoured wine in the entire range, with unusual herbaceous characters, which are deceiving because they must be derived from the grapes, but give all the appearance of having come from changed fermentation techniques (they did not).

1988 ★★★☆ *April 2001*

Deep colour; a very developed bouquet and palate; has always been one of the fastest-maturing Elizabeths, but random oxidation/bottle variation seems to be an additional concern.

1987 ★★★★☆ *April 2001*

Glowing golden–yellow; a rich bouquet with layers of aroma, initially honey and toast, then citrus, and finally mineral, is followed by a complex mid-palate reflecting the many flavours of the bouquet, but then thinning out fractionally on the finish.

1986 Lovedale ★★★★★ *November 1994*

Medium to full yellow; a complex bouquet with quite potent hay and straw aromas, and a hint of honey. On the palate, softer, riper and more rounded than the '84 Lovedale, more in the mould of the '79. Pleasant honeyed fruit, finishing with nice acidity. A wine which does show considerable bottle variation.

1986 ★★★★★ *April 2001*

Full golden colour; the intense bouquet shows some lifted characters attributable to a likely touch of volatile acidity. The lively and intense palate has lemon rind flavours, again with a touch of lift. The rating is perhaps a little generous, and given on a non-technical assessment.

1984 Lovedale ★★★★★ *April 2001*

Bright green–gold; intense, complex and fine varietal fruit character comes through with crystal clarity in the multifaceted herb, lemon and grass aromas. The palate is similarly intense and long, with a mix of citrus, lemon and mineral flavours, the finish — if it were possible — adding even more to the breed and finesse of a truly great wine.

1984 ★★★★☆ *November 1994*

Medium to full yellow; a firmer style with some herbaceous notes and other characters not dissimilar to the '89. The palate is much the firmest and most grippy of the older wines, showing pronounced herbaceous varietal flavour and texture.

1983 ★★★★★ *November 1994*

Medium to full yellow; smooth, honeyed and rich with lots of buttery toast aromas and hints of stone fruits. The palate is round, full and soft, with honey and butter flavours and textures, with a faint echo of the stone fruits of the bouquet.

1982 ★★★★★ *April 2001*

Glowing golden–yellow; a rich, honeyed/toasty/lemony bouquet is followed by a lively, intense palate with lemon and citrus overtones to the more honeyed characters of the mid-palate. A terrific wine, with a long, lingering finish.

◀ Not Ready ＼ Still evolving ▮ Prime of its life ✎ Drink soon ⏀ Missed the boat

1981 ★★★★☆   *April 2001*

Golden–yellow; a rich, ripe honeyed/buttery bouquet has a most attractive mineral substrate which still provides some freshness. The flavoursome palate has a range of sweet nutty/honeyed/buttery flavours, round and mouthfilling.

1979 Anne ★★★★★   *November 1994*

Medium to full yellow–straw; soft, gently toasty aromas with some leatherwood honey. The palate is rich and concentrated, almost plush; much riper and softer than the older Elizabeths; utterly seductive mouthfeel.

1975 ★★★★★   *November 1994*

Medium to full yellow–green; strong, fragrant champagne toast and nut aroma; the palate is full of sweet honeyed/nutty/buttery fruit, showing no signs of fading, and finishing with good acidity.

1975 Anne ★★★★★   *November 1994*

Medium to full yellow; a rich, exceptionally powerful and stylish bouquet with strong herbaceous varietal fruit in the family of the '84 and '89 wines. The palate is still at the peak of its condition, again with those strong varietal fruit flavours, and a lingering bite to the finish.

★★★★★ Perfect   ★★★★☆ Close to perfect   ★★★★ Very good   ★★★☆ Expected
★★★ Short of standard   ★★☆ Undeserving   ★★ Decayed relic   NR No rating

classic wines

127

mcwilliam's mount pleasant
maurice o'shea 1937-1954

the memory of Maurice O'Shea is perpetuated with an annual trophy given by McWilliam's for outstanding contribution to the wine industry. The presentation dinner is an important event in the wine calendar, attended by most of the leading figures in the industry.

But his memory also lives on in the wines he made between 1925 and 1956, during which time McWilliam's had progressively acquired ownership of the winery. He made wines with an almost haunting elegance and finesse, wines which are palpably the work of an artist. He could also produce the occasional blockbuster, such as the 1947 wine acquired by Hardys, awesome in its power.

O'Shea bestowed these wines with enigmatic names; Mountain C, Mountain A, Mountain D, Henry I, II and III, KY, BL, KS, HT, Richard, Charles, Florence, Elizabeth, normally tacking on the variety and quite often adding 'Light Dry Red' or 'Full Bodied Red'. Most of the Christian names and initials were those of O'Shea's friends, but also indicated the source of the wine. Thus TY and Richard were Tyrrell's wines, Charles was from Elliot, and HT from Tulloch.

One of O'Shea's greatest talents lay in his ability to recognise the quality of a just-fermented wine; another lay in his skills as a blender. Those who have tasted 1937 Mountain A (as I did in 1983) will need no persuasion that O'Shea was capable of making the perfect wine. As with the Seppelt Preece wines, these notes come from a range of tastings.

1954 Bin 54/30 Claret ★★★   *April 1996*
Medium red; a fragrant, somewhat lifted charry/earthy/tarry bouquet in which the Hunter component dominates. Some volatility intrudes to sharpen and harden the palate, although this wine, too, settled down with food. Almost certainly a blend of Hunter and McLaren Vale material.

1954 Robert Hermitage ★★★★★   *April 1996*
Still retaining marvellous colour in terms of both depth and hue; very rich and ripe fruit aromas in a liquorice, prune and sweet earth spectrum lead on to a palate which is every bit as powerfully rich and ripe as the bouquet suggests. There are more of those liquorice and prune flavours, a hint of boot polish (which does not detract) and quite powerful tannins on the finish. A wine which responded marvellously well to food. From the fourth vintage of the Rosehill Vineyard.

1954 OP Hermitage ★★★★   *June 1991*
Light tawny–red in colour; two bottles tasted, the lesser bottle still showing good fruit under slight break-up characters, with the better wine showing classic, gentle tarry/earthy Hunter aromas and flavours, and good tannins on the finish.

➤ Not Ready   ❭ Still evolving   ❙ Prime of its life   ⌁ Drink soon   ⬮ Missed the boat

1954 Richard Hermitage ★★★★★ *November 1994*

Medium red, with a touch of tawny; in wonderful condition, gloriously fragrant and spotlessly clean with classic gentle earth Hunter Shiraz aromas. While the tannins have entirely softened on the palate, there is still amazingly sweet fruit, with a range of secondary flavours almost impossible to describe. Tasted 1994; in the dark green bottle (the pale bottles are usually lesser wines). As with all these old wines, considerable bottle variation.

1953 Philip Hermitage ★★★★☆ *April 1996*

Medium red, but still quite bright; a lifted and fragrant bouquet with those ever so typical earthy/charry/tarry overtones, yet with no astringency or bitterness. A glorious wine on the palate which caresses the mouth, a pinot component giving it the texture of an old Burgundy, and even some of the flavours. '53 was a great vintage; and the first to use the name 'Philip', although under the old picture label.

1952 Pinot Hermitage NR *April 1996*

Although 1952 was a wet vintage, Maurice O'Shea recorded that it produced 'two magnificent wines' (and he was not given to hyperbole), 1952 Stephen and 1952 Pinot Hermitage. The Pinot Hermitage won 47 show awards in an era when only first, second and third prizes were awarded; unhappily, the bottle was severely corked.

1952 Stephen Hermitage ★★★ *April 1996*

Strongly coloured; a wine which on both bouquet and palate was agreed by all 12 tasters present to have an intense coriander character. Eucalypt mint and sweet fruit flavours and aromas gradually unfolded, but the coriander won the day. A strange and atypical bottle; made from the Old Paddock and Old Hill mountain vineyard blocks, and won 15 show awards.

1949 HT Hermitage ★★ *July 1987*

A wine which had thrown a huge crust, with the wine in solution degenerated to a pale orange colour. The colour was an accurate omen of what was to come: overwhelming volatility. Bottled in a spirits or methylated spirits bottle, and the cork had failed.

1947 Hermitage (ex-Thomas Hardy) ★★★☆ *March 1994*

A wine of incredible colour, still impenetrable, with no brown hues evident. The bouquet is equivalently massive, with an almost unbelievable concentration of hay, straw and liquorice aromas. The palate is similarly, almost excessively, concentrated, with extreme regional hay/straw characters, and some atypical Hunter characters, including fearsome tannins. Will live forever.

1946 KS Hermitage ★★★★★ *July 1987*

Medium red, with almost no signs of tawny; the bouquet has flawless, sweet fruit with hints of red cherries and is spotlessly clean. In the mouth, absolute perfection, smooth, sweet, velvety fruit on the mid-palate, and a long, lingering finish. Elegance personified.

★★★★★ Perfect   ★★★★☆ Close to perfect   ★★★★ Very good   ★★★☆ Expected
★★★ Short of standard   ★★☆ Undeserving   ★★ Decayed relic   NR No rating

129

classic wines

1945 Hermitage (ex–Thomas Hardy) ★★★★★   *March 1993*
(No other label details.) One of the most perfect Australian wines I have ever drunk. The colour is still strong red, with few, if any, brown tinges. The bouquet is perfection, wonderfully regional, perfectly smooth, with no particular fruit or mineral component dominant. The wine is satin and silk in texture, with touches of liquorice in the sweet, dark fruits; an infinitely complex wine with wonderful balance, showing no hint of decay.

1945 Bin H4 ★★★★★   *April 1996*
Deep red, quite remarkable; a massively concentrated, powerful and initially closed bouquet, astonishing for a wine of this age; opened up gradually to show some aromas of earth and mint. By far the fullest bodied of all of the wines tasted in the evening, sweetly rich and velvety, with the tannins evident but balanced. If O'Shea used some wine from Baileys in northeast Victoria in certain of his wines, he may well have used a touch in this. (Another bottle opened in February 2000 as equally magnificent and youthful.)

1945 Henry II ★★★★★   *April 1996*
Another wine with excellent bright red colour; opened up quite gloriously with sweet, scented fruit on the bouquet, although it did tend to collapse a little over time. No less totally delicious in the mouth, lingering and silky, with dark cherry and briar flavours, and perfect acid and tannin balance. A blend of Pinot Noir and Hermitage, although not labelled as such.

1944 Mount Henry ★★★★★   *April 1996*
Full brick–red; an amazingly fragrant bouquet, with layer upon layer of aromas which unfolded, to reveal cedar, cigar box, dark cherry and a trace of regional earth and tar. Literally flooded the mouth with its voluptuous sweetness, silky, long and lingering, with that sweetness carrying right through the mid to back palate. The quintessence of all that is great in the Hunter Valley. Once again, there has to have been some Pinot in this wine.

1944 Pinot Hermitage Light Dry Red ★★★★★   *October 1994*
Medium to full red; an extraordinarily complex, rich and intense bouquet with those very typical hay/straw characters and a touch of Waterbury's Compound. The palate is of medium to full weight, with liquorice, hay and sweet chocolate all showing, and substantial tannins still present. Looks 10–15 years old; archetypal Hunter of a ripe year.

1944 BL Hermitage Light Dry Red ★★★★★   *June 1991*
Medium red, with just a touch of tawny; a wine in superb condition with a great bouquet showing a touch of that ripe, regional hay character leading on to a palate with richly deep and sweet fruit, finishing with very fine, soft tannins.

1943 Mountain D ★★★★★   *April 1996*
Like all of the wines from '43 to '45 in this tasting, possessed extraordinary colour; the bouquet has that haunting combination of earth, liquorice and dried prune, together with notes of coffee bean and vanilla. A magnificently sweet and rich palate, yet not a scintilla of portiness or heaviness. A triumphant conclusion to a great tasting.

1942 Ty Hermitage ★★★★☆ *July 1987*

Light red, with a very heavy crust thrown in the bottle. The bouquet opened up, initially showing wet dog and straw aromas but then breathing off into a classic, soft, gently earthy Hunter. A lovely old velvety wine in the mouth, with a little volatility, totally within expected or tolerable limits, and the wine in fact improved over an hour or so in the glass.

1937 Mountain A Dry Red ★★★★★ *June 1984*

A wine which will live with me for the rest of my days. The colour was faded almost to the point of orange, but that was the only hint of senility. The aromas fragrant, distinctively and definitively regional, yet neither tarry nor sour. The palate ethereal in its delicacy, light and smooth, but with a soft, intense lingering finish.

★★★★★ Perfect   ★★★★☆ Close to perfect   ★★★★ Very good   ★★★☆ Expected
★★★ Short of standard   ★★☆ Undeserving   ★★ Decayed relic   NR No rating

mcwilliam's mount pleasant OP & OH shiraz (hermitage) 1967-1998

OP & OH stands for Old Paddock and Old Hill, planted respectively in 1880 and 1920. The vines are dry-grown (there is no possibility of irrigation) and average around 1 tonne to the acre over the years, with a maximum of 2 tonnes, and in years such as 1991 and 1965, yielding next to nothing.

OP & OH made its appearance as a blend in 1967, and over the intervening decades has produced some of McWilliam's finest red wine. The tiny production from the OP & OH vineyards may be supplemented by grapes from the Eight Acre Vineyard (planted in the 30s and 40s) and from some of the best shiraz around the winery. However, total production is very small, often less than 1000 cases a year.

It is not made every year: vintages produced so far are 1968, '70, '76, '82–'85, '87–'90 and '94–'99. The '99 will be released late in 2002.

Fermentation methods have become more sophisticated over the years to the point where since 1998 pre-fermentation cold maceration is employed for two days, and after a six-day ferment, the wine is pressed and allowed to complete the last stages of its primary and malolactic fermentation in American oak barrels (80 per cent new, 20 per cent one year old) before being racked and then returned to the same barrels for 18 months maturation.

Older vintages tasted in November 1994, younger vintages mainly in June 2001.

1998 ★★★★   *June 2001*
Full red–purple; a concentrated bouquet with a mix of dark berry, blackberry, plum, spice and earth leads into a wine with masses of flavour reflecting the bouquet; a great example of style and terroir coming from old vines; excellent balance to the finish.

1997 ★★★☆   *March 2000*
Medium to full red–purple; the bouquet is clean and quite concentrated with plummy fruit and a touch of mint. The palate offers more of the same in a more savoury/earthy caste, but lacks depth, and in particular, the brilliant fruit of the '96. •B•

1996 ★★★★   *June 2001*
Medium to full red–purple; a powerful, complex bouquet with an array of licorice, blackberry and leather aromas, together with a hint of game is followed by an extremely powerful palate, with excellent typicity in a slightly austere/savoury mode which only adds to the quality of the wine.

Not Ready   Still evolving   Prime of its life   Drink soon   Missed the boat

1995 ★★★★ *June 2001*

Very good red–purple; the fragrance which often marks the O'Sheas is evident on the bouquet with its complex array of spice and berries; the smooth yet complex medium-bodied palate has a mix of berry, chocolate, earth, spice and cedar, finishing with finely balanced tannins. More developed than some, but by no means distressingly so.

1994 ★★★★ *June 2001*

Medium to full red; a spicy, savoury, earthy bouquet with some berry notes is followed by a tense, taught palate with a certain degree of earthy astringency; long and slightly severe, but still opening up.

1990 ★★★★ *November 1994*

Light to medium red–purple; clean, fresh, gentle red berry fruit aromas with a hint of vanilla and mint. The palate is nicely structured, with a perfect balance between fruit tannins and oak, and plenty of length to the finish.

1989 ★★★☆ *November 1994*

Medium to full red, with a hint of tawny; a briary/earthy/woodsy bouquet with some sweeter fruit notes hiding underneath. A powerful wine on the palate, driven more by tannins than by fruit, and tougher than all of the others.

1985 ★★★★ *November 1994*

Good red colour; a complex bouquet with earth, liquorice, red fruits, and a touch with Hunter tar. The palate has some of the gently plummy fruit of the '91 alongside more stemmy characters, finishing with soft tannins.

1984 ★★★☆ *November 1994*

Medium red–tawny; the bouquet is of light to medium intensity, tending sappy and leafy with hints of earth. The palate is smoother and fractionally riper than the bouquet suggests, finishing with soft tannins. Drink soon.

1967 ★★★★★ *November 1994*

Medium to full red; a classic aged Hunter with all of the traditional aromas ranging from soft earth to leather through savoury mushrooms. The palate is classically balanced and structured, briary/woodsy/earthy/leathery flavours all intermingling, finishing with quite persistent tannins. Six trophies and 19 gold medals.

★★★★★ Perfect   ★★★★☆ Close to perfect   ★★★★ Very good   ★★★☆ Expected
★★★ Short of standard   ★★☆ Undeserving   ★★ Decayed relic   NR No rating

mcwilliam's mount pleasant maurice o'sh

shiraz 1987-1998

first made in 1987 in honour of the master winemaker Maurice O'Shea, who presided over Mount Pleasant from 1921 until his death in 1956. Like its half-sister, OP & OH, it is not made every year. Vintages so far produced are 1987, '88, '91 and '93 to 2000. The 1999 will be released late in 2002, the 2000 a year later.

Like the OP & OH, the Maurice O'Shea Shiraz is not vintaged every year. In the years in which it is made, it is sourced entirely from the Old Hill Vineyard planted in the 1880s by the King family, and purchased by Maurice O'Shea in 1921.

The wine is cold-macerated for 48 hours before the initiation of fermentation via specially selected yeasts, and after seven days is pressed and taken direct to new American oak hogsheads to complete primary and malolactic fermentation on lees. Thereafter the wine is racked and returned to the same barrels, where it spends the remaining 18 months at a constant 15°C.

Some older vintages tasted in November 1994, most younger vintages in June 2001.

1998 ★★★★   *June 2001*
Deep red–purple; the bouquet is slightly more lifted than the OP & OH of the same year, with spicy/savoury/berry aromatics. Flavours of chocolate, licorice and leather are supported by a complex texture in the mouth, with tannins running through from the start to the finish.

1997 ★★★★   *October 2000*
Medium red–purple; a restrained, earthy, regional bouquet is followed by a palate with rather more sweet berry fruit, classy, fine-grained tannins, and subtle oak. A wine at the very start of its life, and may blossom with further bottle age.

1996 ★★★★   *June 2001*
Medium red–purple; the bouquet is quite fragrant, with regional spice, cedar, earth and leather aromas to the fore, fruit to the back. The palate turns 180°, with excellent fruit on entry, then a savoury austerity to the finish, the tannins needing to soften a little more. Gold medal 1998 National Wine Show.

1995 ★★★★   *October 1997*
Medium to full red–purple; a wonderfully complex bouquet with hints of licorice, leather and sweet bramble is followed by a classic Hunter palate in a true O'Shea mould, with savoury flavours and a silky texture and structure.

   ▬ Not Ready   ❱ Still evolving   ❰ Prime of its life   ⌀ Drink soon   ⎁ Missed the boat

1994 ★★★★   *November 1997*

Very strong red–purple; a rich, full and sweet bouquet with dark plum and dark cherry fruit introduces a classic Hunter red, with concentrated plummy/earthy fruit; not heavy, but long. A great result for the vintage.

1993 ★★★★   *June 2001*

Medium to full red, quite developed, with the first hints of brick emerging; strong terroir is immediately evident on the bouquet, with an attractive mix of sweet earth, licorice, leather and spice, characters which are reflected on the palate, which has good tannins, and is still on the way up.

1991 ★★★★   *November 1994*

Strong red–purple; rich and concentrated, with lots of smooth plum/cherry fruit and minimal oak input. Deep, plummy/briary fruit on the palate, not the least extractive or rough; will live forever; finely balanced tannins.

1988 ★★★★   *June 2001*

Medium tawny-red; the bouquet has the fragrance which has marked so many of these O'Shea wines, with an array of spicy/cedary and earthy aromas. The palate has considerable weight and concentration, with licorice and cedar flavours augmented by well-balanced tannins. Has a long way to go before it starts breaking up.

1987 ★★★★   *November 1994*

Medium to full red, relatively deep in the line-up; a clean bouquet with a complex array of aromas from chocolate to dried prunes, with faintly earthy/dusty notes. Much the ripest and richest palate of the older wines, round, full and fleshy, with hints of chocolate, getting close to its peak but will hold.

★★★★★ Perfect   ★★★★☆ Close to perfect   ★★★★ Very good   ★★★☆ Expected
★★★ Short of standard   ★★☆ Undeserving   ★★ Decayed relic   NR No rating

classic wines

135

moss wood cabernet sauvignon

1973-1998

If ever an argument needed to be mounted for the importance of terroir — or the very special character of the Moss Wood Vineyard — this wine provides it. For it is different from all of the other Margaret River Cabernet Sauvignons, yet exceptionally consistent in style over the years it has been produced. This consistency prevails notwithstanding the progressive ageing of the vines; the change of winemakers (from founder Bill Pannell to current owner/winemaker Keith Mugford); the changes in the use of oak and oak type; the absence of malolactic fermentation prior to 1981; the introduction of a small percentage of cabernet franc and merlot since 1989; and significant improvements to the vineyard trellis and canopy management.

There is a suppleness, a softness which the other Margaret River Cabernets do not have. Yet the wines age as well as any, sustained by their soft tannins and the length of flavour which is there right from the outset.

These are truly wines made in the vineyard; they are fruit-driven rather than oak-driven. Notwithstanding this, since 1995 Keith Mugford has extended the barrel ageing from 18 months to two years, and in consequence abandoned the idea of the Special Release wines made intermittently between 1980 and 1991.

First tasted in October 1994, updated, and later vintages added.

1998 ★★★★★   *March 2001*
Full, deep red–purple; a dense, ripe bouquet offers blackberry, chocolate, gentle spice and nice oak; the palate has equally attractive texture and depth, the tannins and oak woven through a range of savoury/blackberry/ blackcurrant flavours.

1997 ★★★★   *August 2000*
Medium red, with some purple hues, showing development. The bouquet is complex, with savoury/earthy aromas definitely in the secondary phase. The palate is complex and rich, with a mix of savoury/briary/foresty characters running through blackberries, chocolate and vanilla.

1996 ★★★★☆   *March 1999*
Medium to full red–purple; a concentrated bouquet with soft, berry and earth flavours supported by subtle oak is, like the palate, in typical Moss Wood style. The palate has complex yet fine secondary flavours, with earth, berry and chocolate merged with oak and finishing with lingering tannins.

◄ Not Ready   ➘ Still evolving   ♟ Prime of its life   ✄ Drink soon   ▯ Missed the boat

1995 ★★★★★   *October 1997*

Medium to full purple–red; a smooth gently sweet textured bouquet with that very special character of Moss Wood, a particular softness which is quite unique. The palate is in precisely the same mould, with soft, luscious mouthfilling blackcurrant and dark chocolate fruit flavours with perfectly integrated and balanced sweet oak. The tannins, likewise, are extraordinarily supple and fine.

1994 ★★★★★   *October 1996*

Strong red–purple; much more concentration and depth than the '93, with dark fruits and gently earthy overtones. The palate confirms the impression of the bouquet, with plenty of weight and power to the blackcurrant fruit and tannins. Subtle oak as always; '94 was a great success for Moss Wood cabernet.

1993 ★★★★☆   *October 1995*

Medium red–purple; in typical Moss Wood style, a clean, elegant bouquet with harmonious fruit and oak balance and integration, but not particularly fruity or rich; the understated palate has cedar/cigar box flavours with fine tannins and understated fruit. A pleasure to drink.

1992 ★★★★   *October 1994*

Medium to full purple–red; the bouquet is clean, of medium intensity with sweet blackcurrant and redcurrant fruits, and even a touch of violet; gentle oak. Tasted early in its life, and may rate even higher with bottle maturation; medium to full fruit style with good tannins and overall elegance.

1991 Special Reserve ★★★★★   *October 1994*

Dense red–purple in colour, with a powerful, concentrated bouquet showing briary/dark fruits. In the mouth there is abundant rich, blackcurrant/raspberry fruit backed by gently spicy oak. An excellent ripening season with no stress.

1991 ★★★★   *October 1994*

Medium to full red–purple. The bouquet is somewhat closed in, but is clean and with hints of spice to the fruit. In the mouth the wine is still fractionally hard, with firm dark cherry and berry fruits, and subtle oak.

1990 Special Reserve ★★★★★   *October 1994*

Medium to full red–purple; distinctly more textured than the standard wine of the same vintage; the fruit is wonderfully balanced in ripeness, neither overripe nor green, neither over-extracted nor under-extracted. In the mouth, beautifully balanced and sculptured, with black cherry fruit and perfectly integrated oak. Another ten years will not tire the wine. Made in what Keith Mugford regards as possibly the best season ever.

1990 ★★★★☆   *October 1994*

Medium red–purple; some gamey notes lurk in the bouquet, with hints of cedar and tobacco; the primary fruit seems subdued, with the secondary characters yet to develop. The palate is much more attractive, with perfectly ripened dark berry/cherry fruit and fine tannins.

★★★★★ Perfect   ★★★★☆ Close to perfect   ★★★★ Very good   ★★★☆ Expected
★★★ Short of standard   ★★☆ Undeserving   ★★ Decayed relic   NR No rating

137

1989 ★★★   *October 1994*

Slightly dull colour, suggesting a higher pH level. The bouquet is starting to build some fragrance, very good given the vintage; the palate has some gamey notes typical of the year, but has reasonable extract and tannins; altogether a creditable result given the appalling vintage — the worst ever, says Mugford.

1988 ★★★   *October 1994*

Medium red–purple; the bouquet has a degree of fragrance with sappy/leafy overtones, and just a hint of soapiness. The palate lacks the generosity of the better wines, being a fraction mean, with leafy, green characters. A low-cropping year with a very hot finish to the season which stressed the vines.

1987 Special Reserve ★★★★☆   *October 1994*

Medium to full red, with less purple than the standard wine. The bouquet is complex, rich, concentrated and lush, although the palate is more elegant with good tannin structure and great length. Will live for 15 years at least.

1987 ★★★★☆   *October 1994*

Medium to full red–purple; the bouquet is complex, pleasantly herbaceous varietal character with a touch of lift and attractive cedary oak. A well-balanced and structured palate with dark fruits offset by a touch of herbaceousness, and a long finish. A dry, mild vintage producing wines of very good balance.

1986 ★★★★☆   *October 1994*

Medium to full red; a complex, concentrated bouquet with herbaceous notes yet generosity; there is an element of lift which adds to the attraction. The palate is concentrated and well balanced, with dark berry fruits and a firm tannin structure. The product of a good growing season with small yields.

1985 ★★★   *October 1994*

Medium to full red. Youthful red berry fruits are evident, but the overall impression is closed and slightly hard, suggesting a whisper of sulphide. The palate is a similar mixture of good and less attractive characters; there are the same red fruits, but once again hard edges intrude.

1984 ★★☆   *October 1994*

The colour shows distinct development, with brown tinges starting to develop; a thinner, leafier style with reasonably good varietal character, but won't improve. A dry vintage, but the grapes did not ripen enough, and it shows in the wine.

1983 Special Reserve ★★★☆   *October 1994*

Strong brick–red; the bouquet is complex, with leafy, cedary and caramel/vanillin notes all intermingling, and a touch of volatility. The palate is well balanced, with complex flavours and fair tannins, but I preferred the standard wine of the same year, which seemed fresher.

1983 ★★★★   *October 1994*

Dense red, with some brick-tinged hues. The bouquet is quite concentrated; cedary/briary, but with a solid underlay of dark fruits. In the mouth the same attractive dark fruit flavours are present; it is well structured with plenty of tannins. An early vintage which produced wines considered round, ripe and tannic.

1982 ★★☆

Medium to full brick–red. A distinctly herbaceous bouquet, clean with some lift; the palate shows some sharpish, slightly volatile characters, possibly deriving from bird damage to the fruit. A vintage marked by some rain.

1981 ★★★

Identical colour to the '82; the bouquet has a hint of camphor, but seems to herald the hardness of the bouquet; while there is plenty of concentration, the tannins really are tough and hard. A low-yielding vintage, indeed noted for its hard tannins.

1980 Special Reserve ★★★★☆

Strong brick–red colour; the bouquet is solid, smooth and with sweet fruit backed by some cedary notes; total contrast to the standard wine. The palate is elegant, well balanced and finishing with soft, fine tannins. Made in an excellent year, second only to the '90. Retasted March 2001; still superb, and in great condition.

1980 ★★☆

Medium brick–red; this may well have been a poor bottle, as it showed hay/straw oxidation characters on both the bouquet and palate, and the judgment may be harsh.

1979 ★★★

Medium to full brick–red. The bouquet shows some slightly dank, dried leaf characters, suggesting the fruit was slightly underripe. On the palate the wine is herbaceous and again fractionally hard; there are similarities to the '77, but without the same fruit concentration. In fact made in what was regarded as a good season.

1978 Dry Red ★★☆

Brick–red, with pleasant, soft caramel/leafy characters. The flavours are in the leafy/cedary range, and although lacking richness, far from a bad wine given its downgrading to Dry Red.

1977 ★★★★☆

While the colour is now brick–red, the bouquet is very youthful, with striking, potent herbaceous varietal fruit and some cedary notes. The palate is no less potent and powerful, indeed outstanding if you accept the herbaceous elements; lots of concentration, and impeccable balance. A good growing season, with a dry vintage.

1976 ★★★★

Brick–red; a fine, aged bouquet with complex and fragrant cedar and cigar box aromas. In the mouth, an extremely attractive cedary/briary wine with very good balance, in no way indicative of its very high alcohol (14.5 per cent). A heatwave vintage with very ripe fruit.

1975 ★★★

Definitely starting to show its age with the colour and the bouquet, although retaining elegance and finesse. There are fractionally herbaceous flavours, much less ripe than the '76, but the tannins are nicely balanced. From a very good, cool growing season with fruit picked in perfect condition.

classic wines

★★★★★ Perfect   ★★★★☆ Close to perfect   ★★★★ Very good   ★★★☆ Expected
★★★ Short of standard   ★★☆ Undeserving   ★★ Decayed relic   NR No rating

139

1974 ★★★   *October 1994*

Medium to full brick–red; attractive old wine with dark chocolate aromas; the palate is fairly tannic and the fruit is starting to fade, but still drinking well. Tastes far riper than the cool year and relatively low alcohol would suggest.

1973 ★★   *October 1994*

While the colour is still quite good, the bouquet is leafy and soapy, with a lantana edge, which follows through on to the palate. Now simply an old wine.

▬ Not Ready   ➘ Still evolving   ▮ Prime of its life   ⬧ Drink soon   ▯ Missed the boat

moss wood semillon 1977-2000

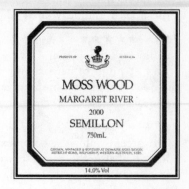

MOSS WOOD
MARGARET RIVER
2000
SEMILLON
750mL

14.0% Vol

the Moss Wood Semillons were produced in a wood-matured and unoaked version each year, and both versions were in fact tasted — the unoaked from its first vintage in 1977, the wood-matured from its inception in 1983. I have elected to give the tasting note for the best wine from each vintage, although I should hasten to add that the wood-matured wines from both 1986 and 1983 were outstanding, even though I have described the unoaked versions. However, since 1994 only an unoaked version has been produced.

As in so many things, Moss Wood marches to the tune of a different drum with its Semillon. The usual Margaret River Semillon is crisp and very herbaceous, frequently blended with the Sauvignon Blanc which it so closely resembles. The Moss Wood Semillons, by contrast, are richer and smoother, with wonderful mouthfeel, perhaps due to the higher-than-average alcohol (for Semillon).

This generosity of flavour and texture manifests itself from an early age, yet in no way imperils the ageing capacity of the wines from the better vintages. It also means that the use of oak is not simply for the purpose of propping up otherwise deficient fruit — although it was interesting to see how (in 1994) the wood-matured wines dominated the younger group, the unoaked versions the older wines.

First tasted in October 1994, updated, and later vintages added.

2000 ★★★★   *December 2000*
Light green–yellow; the bouquet is clean, but despite the power from 14 degrees alcohol, is not particularly aromatic; the power really comes through on the rich, mouth-coating mid-palate, and the dry but long finish.

1999 ★★★★   *October 1999*
Light to medium yellow–green; the bouquet is clean, light and crisp, tending more to mineral than herbal citrus. The palate is well balanced and smooth, yet to open up its underlying fruit character.

1998 ★★★★☆   *October 1998*
Light to medium yellow–green; the bouquet is powerful, with interesting, European overtones, perhaps suggesting the deliberate use of some solids in the juice. In the mouth, the wine has that extra dimension of weight (without sweetness) of Margaret River, easily carrying the massive 14.5 degrees alcohol.

classic wines

1997 ★★★★☆   *October 1997*

Medium to full yellow–green; voluminous aromas, rich, full and complex introduce a full-bodied, multiflavoured wine with tropical fruit flavours.

1995 ★★★★★   *December 1996*

Medium yellow–green; a marvellously powerful, rich and concentrated bouquet with just a hint of herbaceousness lurking in the background. The palate follows the bouquet, albeit more trenchantly, with the herbal notes more obvious, but by no means excessive. Tremendous impact and length.

1994 ★★★★★   *November 1994*

Light green–yellow; a complex, concentrated and intense bouquet with some faintly herbal notes, more to white Bordeaux in style. The palate is as powerful and concentrated as the bouquet promises, again with those overtones of white Bordeaux, and the richness so particular to Moss Wood.

1993 ★★★★   *October 1994*

Light to medium yellow–green, with a tangy/tropical bouquet still showing some yeast influence when tasted three months after vintage. The palate was clean, with good intensity and balance, abundant mouthfeel and not overly herbaceous. Spring hail reduced the crop in a mild growing season.

1992 Wood Matured ★★★★☆   *October 1994*

Light to medium yellow–green. The bouquet is well integrated and subtle, gently smoky spicy oak with tangy fruit. The same sophisticated spicy oak handling is evident on the palate; the fruit is not especially powerful, but the wine is well balanced. Similar vintage to '93 except for slightly higher yields.

1991 Wood Matured ★★★★   *October 1994*

Light to medium yellow–green. Stylish, smoky Vosges-like oak which is well balanced and integrated on the bouquet. On the palate, the spicy clove oak is a little dominant at this point but should evolve and come together with time. A difficult year for semillon with excessive yields.

1990 Wood Matured ★★★   *October 1994*

Frankly, disappointing given the outstanding growing season. The colour is bright and vivid, and the oak is far from overdone, but the wine shows volatility on both bouquet and palate which for me, at least, intruded. Redeemed in part by the length of the finish; others may be more tolerant of the volatility.

1989 Wood Matured ★★★☆   *October 1994*

Medium to full yellow–green; a developed bouquet with moderately sweet fruit and faint hints of oxidation. The palate is soft, with sweet fruit and gently vanillin oak now at its peak. Relatively speaking, very successful for a terrible vintage which started hot and finished cold.

1988 ★★★☆   *October 1994*

Medium to full yellow colour; clean, strongly herbaceous aroma in pungent Margaret River style. The palate is similarly strongly herbaceous; well made, with good length. A low-yielding year which was good until the February heat.

◀━ Not Ready   ↘ Still evolving   ▮ Prime of its life   ⚗ Drink soon   ⬓ Missed the boat

1987 ★★★★★　　October 1994

Bright green–yellow, with a very fresh, citrus-tinged bouquet, smooth, harmonious and youthful. In the mouth, a lovely wine with the same freshness, harmony and balance of the bouquet, with the flavours more towards citrus than herbaceous. A copybook, dry vintage.

1986 ★★★★★　　October 1994

Glowing green–yellow; the bouquet has wonderful varietal character with a hint of herbaceousness and toasty characters building in the background; still youthful. The palate shows powerful, intense classic semillon, superbly structured with hints of White Bordeaux; a low-cropping year.

1985 ★★★★　　October 1994

Bright deep yellow–green; some volatility, which slightly masks the fruit, but is acceptable. A relatively powerful wine with a touch of volatility which does not unduly hurt the palate; honey and butter characters starting to evolve. A cool start to vintage was followed by a very hot end of February.

1984 Wood Matured ★★★★★　　October 1994

Medium to full yellow; the bouquet is smooth and rich, with plenty of depth and style, and still fresh. The palate is altogether stylish, gently herbaceous, still showing a hint of spicy oak, and holding very well. Note that some bottles of this vintage were corked. A cool, dry copybook vintage.

1983 ★★★★★　　October 1994

Bright yellow–green; a glorious honey, toast and butter bouquet, fresh and showing no signs of fading. The palate is beautifully balanced, dry, toasty with crisp acidity. A wonderfully elegant wine which is not a powerhouse but has everything there. A very good growing season after a wet winter.

1982 ★★★★★　　October 1994

Bright, medium to full yellow–green. The bouquet is exceptionally smooth and youthful, with good varietal tang and cut. A very powerful, stylish wine in the mould of the '86; a long, intense palate with an amalgam of honeyed and more tangy/cabbagey characters. A marvellous outcome for a wet vintage.

1981 ★★★★★　　October 1994

Bright green–yellow; the bouquet is relatively herbaceous, still fresh and young, and just a hint of volatility. The palate is rich and multifaceted, with layers of honeyed/buttery fruit interwoven with more tangy flavours. A powerful and impressive wine from a mild growing season similar to 1992.

1980 ★★★★☆　　October 1994

Glorious, glowing yellow–green hues introduce a stylish wine with that intriguing combination of smoothness interwoven with a varietal tangy bite. The palate is still powerful and strong, with honeyed/buttery fruit which is not the least bit flabby, although the wine is at its peak. From a very good vintage.

classic wines

★★★★★ Perfect　　★★★★☆ Close to perfect　　★★★★ Very good　　★★★☆ Expected
★★★ Short of standard　　★★☆ Undeserving　　★★ Decayed relic　　NR No rating

143

1979 ★★   *October 1994*

Full yellow in colour, the first wine in the line-up to show any signs of excess development. There are hints of oxidation (hay/straw) on the bouquet, and the palate is quite sweet, suggesting either botrytis or residual sugar.

1978 ★★★   *October 1994*

Full yellow, similar to the '79; a rich, very honeyed/buttery bouquet, just starting to lose its freshness. The palate is again fully aged, slightly past its peak but still drinking well in a soft, slightly maderised style. From a near-perfect year with a fine, dry summer after good spring rains.

1977 ★★   *October 1994*

Medium to full yellow; the bouquet is fractionally dilute, possibly the result of young vines, and on the palate the wine is clearly tiring and past its best. A year marked by some late season vintage rain.

— Not Ready   Still evolving   Prime of its life   Drink soon   Missed the boat

mount langi ghiran langi shiraz
1981-1999

the entitlement of Langi Shiraz to classic status should not be in doubt. Way back in 1984, long before terroir became a cliché, I wrote about the terroir of Mount Langi Ghiran in my *Australian Wine Compendium*; even by then, it was evident that this is a special place.

Since then, there have been many changes, all adding to Langi's importance. Trevor Mast, merely a consultant winemaker in 1984, became the co-owner in 1987, and in 1996 Riquet Hess (former CEO of H. Sichel of Blue Nun fame) became Mast's new partner in the venture.

The vineyards have steadily grown, one 9-hectare block now permanently enclosed in a highly sophisticated high-clearance net (like a giant aviary), and a new winery built.

Fermentation still takes place in open, oblong, lined concrete vats, the only concession to ever-increasing production being a pneumatic punch-down system. Once fermentation is completed, the must is fed by gravity into the Bucher press waiting underneath the vats.

The wine is matured in a mix of American (two-thirds) and French (one-third) barrels, one-third new, one-third second use, and one-third used for the third time.

The result is a wine which is fruit-driven; speaking strongly of its place and of the climate of each particular vintage. In some years (typically the cooler vintages) the wine is strongly spicy, in other years less so. The laid-back Trevor Mast is quite happy to accept the cards which nature deals him, but will, of course, try to maximise the outcome. The brief vintage comment (in brackets) at the end of the majority of the tasting notes is that of Trevor Mast.

Tasted in April 2001.

◀ *1999* ★★★★☆   *April 2001*
Deep colour; a powerful bouquet with layer upon layer of dark fruit and spice is followed by a rich palate with a mix of spice, pepper and red and black fruits, together with a hint of fennel. (Contrary to much of Victoria, an excellent vintage. Harvested 5 May.)

1998 ★★★★★   *April 2001*
Medium to full red–purple; lots of sweet plum and berry fruit together with a touch of new oak on the bouquet is followed by a full, rich and sweet palate. There is ripe fruit throughout which has little or no spice, but rounded tannins provide a sure structure for a long life. (An excellent growing season and harvest conditions. Harvested 20 April.)

★★★★★ Perfect   ★★★★☆ Close to perfect   ★★★★ Very good   ★★★☆ Expected
★★★ Short of standard   ★★☆ Undeserving   ★★ Decayed relic   NR No rating

classic wines

1997 ★★★★   *April 2001*

Medium to full red–purple; a very complex array of dark berry, plum, spice and liquorice fruit aromas with smoky oak adding to the mix on the bouquet. A smooth, rounded palate with lush fruit and noticeably soft tannins which suggest the wine will develop reasonably quickly. There is also a fleeting touch of green to the flavour. (A difficult year (for unspecified reasons); harvested 5 May.)

1996 ★★★★★   *April 2001*

Medium red–purple; an immensely appealing, fragrant bouquet has spicy black cherry, plum and liquorice aromas. The palate continues in much the same vein, with lovely, sweetly savoury/spicy fruit and fine tannins to support a lingering finish. (Trevor Mast's favourite vintage for drinking at the moment. Harvested 10 May.)

1995 ★★★★☆   *April 2001*

Medium to full red–purple; the clean bouquet has abundant sweet cherry and plum fruit with a nice touch of oak. Sweet plummy fruit on the palate takes the wine out of the spicy spectrum; the tannins are balanced, but the wine is just a fraction short. (Medium crop; harvested 18 April in ideal conditions.)

1994 ★★★★   *April 2001*

Medium red–purple; the savoury, spicy bouquet is quite elegant, showing a touch of oak not evident in the older wines. The palate is pleasant, with spice and vanilla in a light to medium-bodied and not particularly concentrated frame. (A lighter crop; the wine was quite tight in structure for its first two years. Harvested 13 May.)

1993 ★★★★★   *April 2001*

Medium to full red–purple, very impressive. A powerful, rich and complex bouquet is filled with spice, black fruits and liquorice. The palate has great depth and richness, layered and textured, with perfect tannin balance. Great now, but will hold for many years. (Reduced crop, wet spring and perfect autumn. Harvested 6 May.)

1992 ★★★★☆   *April 2001*

Excellent red–purple, still bright and clear. The bouquet confirms the promise of the colour, with primary fruit aromas of small berry and cherry, fresh and lively. The palate is similarly lively and youthful, and still developing, although there is just a question mark about the depth to sustain it over a long term. May be a Peter Pan, eternally youthful. (Great acid-fruit balance, very vibrant spice and tannins. Harvested 24 April.)

1991 ★★★★☆   *April 2001*

Medium red–purple; ripe fruit shines through the mix of sweet spice and plum aromatics on the bouquet. The palate is quite weighty, with black fruit flavours and a moderately tannic finish. (A racy wine when young, with great balance of tannin and acid; very fruit-driven. Harvested 24 April.)

1990 ★★★★★ *April 2001*

Light to medium red, with just some hints of purple remaining. Has the typical Langi fragrance, with a mix of spice, berry and earth. The wine really fills the mouth with almost melting sweetness mixed with liquorice; fine, supple, long tannins sustain a truly delicious, elegant wine. (A warmer growing season with medium crop and soft tannins. Harvested 18 April.)

1989 ★★★★ *April 2001*

Medium red; still with fragrant spice, leather and earth aromatics. Precisely the same flavours come through on the fresh palate, which does, however, seem to lack a little sweetness and vinosity on the mid to back palate. (Trevor Mast indicated the wine had been poorly stored and was not indicative of a vintage which, while wet, produced wines of great colour and intense spice at Langi Ghiran. Harvested 28 April.)

1988 NR

Not available for tasting. An abnormally warm season produced a very spicy wine which, according to Mast, is still drinking superbly; elegant and great depth. (Harvested 28 March.)

1987 ★★ *April 2001*

Medium red, with that dull edge indicating a high pH. Green leaf/spice aromas lead into a distinctly tart and sharp palate with high acidity and all the hallmarks of unripe grapes. (A poor, wet vintage produced green fruit. The wine was in fact recalled shortly after it was released. Harvested 16 May.)

1986 ★★★★★ *April 2001*

Medium red–purple, excellent for age; dense, ripe blackberry, liquorice and spice aromas lead into a similarly powerful palate with dark, bitter chocolate and liquorice accents to the fruit; lingering tannins provide good structure and balance. (A great vintage with a big crop which nonetheless produced a very intense wine. Harvested 1 June.)

1985 NR

Not tasted. Trevor Mast's notes indicate a very cool year, producing an overtly spicy, medium-bodied palate which is a touch green. (Harvested 21 May.)

1984 ★★★★ *April 2001*

The depth of the colour is not great, but the red hue is good. A sweet, smooth, gently ripe bouquet has an attractive mix of leather and spice aromas. The elegant palate is supple and smooth, far more conventional in its taste than the preceding wines, and still a fine wine. (A cool year with a relatively big crop, always in a spicy mode. Harvested 13 June.)

1983 ★★★☆ *April 2001*

Surprisingly strong and deep red; the bouquet is still quite dense, with complex earth, spice and chocolate aromas. A very powerful palate, with the tannins very much in evidence and adding to the impact of the fruit. Those tannins are starting to dry out the palate and grip on the finish, and will undoubtedly outlive the fruit. (A drought year from start to finish. Harvested 24 April.)

classic wines

★★★★★ Perfect	★★★★☆ Close to perfect	★★★★ Very good	★★★☆ Expected
★★★ Short of standard	★★☆ Undeserving	★★ Decayed relic	NR No rating

1982 NR
Not available at the Langi Ghiran tasting; a brief note made by me in 1984 was 'a little clumsy, with big, sweet fruit flavours and some varietal spice'. Has almost certainly started to fade now.

1981 ★★★ April 2001
Slightly dull red, suggestive of fairly high pH. Fragrant spice and leather mark a distinctly aromatic bouquet; liquorice, leaf and spice flavours are strikingly similar to an aged southern Rhône style. Fermented and matured in concrete tanks situated in the Fratin brothers' cowshed, and given no time in oak. A remarkable old relic.

Not Ready Still evolving Prime of its life Drink soon Missed the boat

mount mary pinot noir 1979-1999

Dr John Middleton is Victoria's — and the Yarra Valley's — answer to the Hunter Valley's Dr Max Lake. Indeed, he started home winemaking and grape growing around the same time as Dr Lake, but it was not until 1977 that Mount Mary produced its first wine (a Cabernet) and 1979 that its first Pinot Noir was made.

But together with Seville Estate — owned by John Middleton's partner in the local medical practice, Dr Peter McMahon — Mount Mary announced to the world that the Yarra Valley was one of those rare spots in which the capricious pinot noir grape can readily produce great red table wine which, with a few years bottle age, can taste uncannily like a fine French Burgundy.

The core of the Mount Mary Pinot Noirs lies in the site selection (it is 100 per cent estate-grown, single-vineyard wine) on a gentle north-facing slope enjoying the grey soils so favoured by the founding father of the nineteenth-century Yarra Valley, Hubert de Castella. The conservative viticultural practices — no irrigation and limited bud numbers — are also important in producing low yields of high-quality fruit.

The making techniques used are likewise conservative: as little interference as possible with the natural flavour of the grapes, and only minimal use of new oak. The wines often take two or three years to start showing their latent complexity, and — by the standards of many Pinot Noirs — are relatively long lived. At their best they are a magical rendition of the variety.

Three tastings: April 2001, January 2001, and May 1994.

1999 ★★★★★   *April 2001*

Excellent hue, bright, light to medium red–purple. Pure varietal character is evident on the bouquet with fragrant plum and cherry fruit. Stylish palate has the hallmark silky mouthfeel in a light- to medium-bodied frame. Very interesting to taste the wine so young (April 2001), as you can see the breed of the wine, and the pure fruit with which it starts. Shows absolutely no sign of any vintage problems

1997 ★★★★★   *January 2001*

Strong, deep colour, particularly for Mount Mary. A potent, powerful and still surprisingly youthful bouquet has a complex array of dark, plummy fruits and spices, together with a hint of forest. The palate is potent and with ripe, dark plum and spice fruit and a near-hidden touch of sous bois.

classic wines

★★★★★ Perfect   ★★★★☆ Close to perfect   ★★★★ Very good   ★★★☆ Expected
★★★ Short of standard   ★★☆ Undeserving   ★★ Decayed relic   NR No rating

149

1996 ★★★★★   *April 2001*

Light to medium red–purple; a super-fragrant bouquet has a range of aromas ranging through lively cherry and strawberry to more savoury. The palate is delicate, almost caressing with its silky textures, once again offering a combination of sweet and more savoury fruit.

1995 ★★★★☆   *April 2001*

Light to medium red–purple; similar to the 1996, but with slightly more brick appearing. A fragrant, high-toned bouquet with some savoury/foresty characters starting to emerge flows through into the palate. This opens with the same sappy/foresty characters, but also has some quasi-citrus notes together with an appealing spicy finish.

1994 ★★★★☆   *January 2001*

Medium to full red; the bouquet is very complex, with a mix of sappy/spicy/forest floor aromas which are lifted (but not volatile) allied with a hint of game. The palate is long and sappy, with quite high acidity, reflecting a cool vintage. A wine which polarises opinions.

1993 ★★★★☆   *April 2001*

Light red, with just a touch of brick on the rim; a light but strongly varietal array of earthy/savoury/spicy secondary aromas lead into an unexpectedly long and intense palate. Here the impact is at once striking and persistent, not unlike some 1972 Burgundies, and begging for the right food. Extremely interesting.

1992 ★★★★★   *January 2001*

Light but clear red; a fine, elegant and fragrant bouquet, almost ethereal, leads into a long, super-fine palate, with a lovely hint of sweetness at its core, and a lingering, silky finish.

1991 ★★★★   *January 2001*

Light red; a lively and fragrant bouquet with sappy/earthy aromatics is followed by a refined and long palate, far from the fruit-driven style of some of the other Yarra Valley Pinots of this vintage.

1990 ★★★★   *May 1994*

Light red–purple. The bouquet is light, fresh and clean with red cherry and strawberry fruit. The palate is in marked contrast to the '89, still youthful and tending simple at this juncture, but the flavours are correct in the red cherry/strawberry spectrum. While it needs time, does not appear likely to be especially long lived.

1989 ★★★★★   *May 1994*

Light to medium red–purple; the bouquet is appealing, with complex, fragrant spicy, plum and cherry aromas. The palate is totally delicious with a range of complex but bright flavours ranging from sappy to sweetly ripe; good mouthfeel.

1988 ★★★☆   *May 1994*

Light to medium red–purple; the bouquet is youthful, with multifaceted aromas from primary pinot through to distinct farmyard, with an almost bonox/meaty edge. A powerful wine on the palate with lots of character, although a slightly distracting edge of roughness runs through it.

◄── Not Ready   ╲ Still evolving   ♠ Prime of its life   ⌒ Drink soon   ☐ Missed the boat

1987 ★★★☆ *May 1994*

The colour is developed, with some distinct browning. The bouquet is quite Burgundian, although the fruit is subdued. Throughout the wine, and continuing on the palate, there is a suggestion of higher than desirable pH; a wine on the sappy side, lacking the sweet fruit of the '86.

1986 ★★★★★ *May 1994*

Light to medium red–purple; the bouquet is redolent of fresh, varietal fruit in the black cherry spectrum, and virtually no oak evident. The palate shows wonderfully clean, firm pinot which is developing very well. A wine which offers the best of both worlds, the complexity of age but still with good fruit, perfect balance and a long finish.

1985 ★★★★☆ *May 1994*

Light to medium red, with just a hint of purple remaining. The bouquet is complex and full of character with plum, cherry and earthy notes. The palate is no less complex, with quite ripe, dark plum and cherry fruit, and again an echo of those earthy characters of the bouquet.

1984 ★★★★ *May 1994*

Light to medium red–purple; primary varietal pinot fruit characters are still lingering in a slippery/sappy mould, complexed by a touch of plum. There are many flavours on the palate ranging from minty to plum to sappy; a racy style with good acidity.

1983 ★★★★ *May 1994*

Still holding some red–purple hues, and of light to medium depth. The bouquet is ripe, with distinct farmyard overtones, and a whisper of toffee-like character. A luxuriantly ripe and rich wine on the palate with plum, tobacco and prune flavours which come together well.

1982 ★★★☆ *May 1994*

Medium tawny–red, deeper than the older wines, and with more red than brick hues. The bouquet is quite fragrant with attractively sappy notes, and a hint of mint. The palate has retained good character and length, even if the fruit is starting to dry out a little, and the tannins intrude somewhat on the finish.

1981 ★★★ *May 1994*

Onion-skin colour and distinct caramel overtones to the bouquet. The palate shows more of the same, with slightly singed/caramel flavours and finishes rather short.

1980 ★★★☆ *May 1994*

The colour is slightly deeper than either the '79 or the '81. There are some meaty/earthy farmyard characters on the bouquet which are not unpleasant, but which come again on the palate, together with a touch of prune. There are some tannins left, but the wine is now at the very end of its plateau.

1979 ★★★★ *May 1994*

Light reddish–brown in colour, verging on onion skin; the bouquet is light but fragrant, still undeniably pinot in aroma, with background earth and tobacco characters. An old but graceful wine in the mouth, fully aged, with secondary flavours now dominant, but the balance still good. Finishes slightly short.

classic wines

| ★★★★★ Perfect | ★★★★☆ Close to perfect | ★★★★ Very good | ★★★☆ Expected |
| ★★★ Short of standard | ★★☆ Undeserving | ★★ Decayed relic | NR No rating |

mount mary quintet cabernets

So far as I know, John Middleton was the first to use the economical name Cabernets to encompass the complex blend of Cabernet Sauvignon, Merlot, Cabernet Franc, Malbec and Petit Verdot — all of the varieties of Bordeaux — which go to make up this classic wine. Others have followed suit, so the wine is now called Quintet.

The Mount Mary Vineyard, on its own discrete, gentle north-facing slope, is one of the best in the Yarra Valley. The soils are the sandy grey loam so favoured by Hubert de Castella, and great care has always been taken with the viticulture, and the trellis system much improved in recent years. The vineyard is not irrigated, and yields are low, but the vines seldom show any signs of stress.

Dr Middleton has always believed that the primary role of the winemaker should be to protect and reflect the quality of the fruit from the vineyard. Thus the fermentation régime and the use of oak is not intended to change the character of the grapes. The corollary is that the wines do mirror the conditions of each vintage, and that there is rather more variation between vintages than is generally supposed.

Since the Yarra Valley has a climate which is cooler than Bordeaux, and cabernet sauvignon does not normally ripen until late April, it is not so surprising that vintage variation should occur. It is an accepted part of the makeup of great French wines: why not here?

Principally tasted in April 2000.

1999 ★★★★☆   *April 2001*

Bright but full purple–red; clean and rich blackberry and cassis fruit aromas are married as impeccably as always with the oak. The smooth, medium-bodied wine flows evenly across the palate, with soft, fine tannins and no hint of green. A great result for a wetter-than-usual vintage.

1998 ★★★★★   *October 2000*

Medium purple–red; the bouquet offers a mix of ripe cassis, blackberry and raspberry aromas with subtle but evident oak. The long, even palate has near-identical cassis and blackberry flavours, supported by fine, lingering tannins and subtle oak. Reflects the '98 vintage; by the standards of Mount Mary, quite full.

1997 ★★★★★   *April 2000*

Medium red–purple; red berry, mint and leaf, and just a hint of oak, run through the fragrant bouquet. The palate is fine, supple and elegant, with redcurrant and cassis supported by the barest hint of oak. As with all these wines, fruit-driven and not a hair out of place.

1996 ★★★★★　　　　　　　　　　　　　　　　　　　*April 2000*

Medium red–purple; the bouquet is very similar to that of the '97, with that Mount Mary fragrance and echoes of gum leaf and mint accompanying the redcurrant fruit. The palate has touches of softer, slightly plummier fruit, and is long and silky, supported by very fine tannins.

1995 ★★★★★　　　　　　　　　　　　　　　　　　　*April 2000*

Medium red–purple, identical to the '96 and '97; delicate spicy notes are the first impression on the bouquet, followed by a fragrant mix of earth, berry and mint. The immaculately balanced and proportioned palate has a slightly softer profile than the youngest wines, but utterly captivates with its red berry and subliminal flavours.

1994 ★★★★☆　　　　　　　　　　　　　　　　　　　*April 2000*

The colour is a pigeon pair with the '93, bright, and just showing the first hints of change; the typically elegant bouquet runs through cassis, mint, earth and savoury spice lurking in the background. The powerful palate faithfully reproduces the flavours promised by the bouquet, welded together to give that silky mouthfeel and balance.

1993 ★★★★★　　　　　　　　　　　　　　　　　　　*April 2000*

Similar colour to the '94, showing just a touch of development; the aromas open up with herb, earth and berry, then unfold to display rich cassis. The palate is softening just a touch, exactly as you would want it, but still flooded with cassis, blackberry and black cherry flavour.

1992 ★★★★★　　　　　　　　　　　　　　　　　　　*April 2000*

Medium red–purple; introduces a run of eerily similar wines running through to the 1997, with the lush cassis berry starting to soften a little, and a hint of the spicy savoury characters which will develop with further age. An elegant palate has hints of cedar together with the red berry fruit, finishing with soft, fine-grained tannins.

1991 ★★★★☆　　　　　　　　　　　　　　　　　　　*April 2000*

Medium red–purple; the bouquet is distinctly spicy, with splashes of mint and cassis, but has an overall softness; the palate is very accessible, with softer, riper fruit than the other wines of the '90s, tinged with spice, the oak, as ever, imperceptible.

1990 ★★★★★　　　　　　　　　　　　　　　　　　　*April 2000*

Strong, bright red–purple; the bouquet has intense, sweet berry fruit leading into a palate with great texture and mouthfeel, the dark berry flavours joined by a touch of bitter chocolate.

1989 ★★☆　　　　　　　　　　　　　　　　　　　　　*May 1994*

Distinctly light in colour, with a sappy/leafy/gamey bouquet and identical characters on the palate. Disappointing wine from a poor vintage.

1988 ★★★★★　　　　　　　　　　　　　　　　　　　*April 2000*

Excellent purple–red; the intense and powerful bouquet runs through cassis and blackcurrant to more cedary, spicy, savoury aromas. The palate has an absolutely marvellous extra depth of texture, voluptuous and velvety, yet retaining the finesse and purity which runs through all these wines.

classic wines

★★★★★ Perfect　　★★★★☆ Close to perfect　　★★★★ Very good　　★★★☆ Expected
★★★ Short of standard　　★★☆ Undeserving　　★★ Decayed relic　　NR No rating

1987 ★★★☆ — *May 1994*

Medium to full red–purple; the aromas are of dark berry, plum and touches of earth. An attractive, well-balanced wine which has matured relatively quickly, with slightly leafy aspects, and soft tannins.

1986 ★★★★★ — *April 2000*

Excellent colour for its age; the bouquet is classic, with fragrant cedar, cassis, blackberry and spice coming through with clarion clarity. The palate is a distillation of pure Cabernet Sauvignon, slightly earthy but pristine. Like many of its compatriots, has got younger, not older, over the last six years.

1985 ★★★★★ — *April 2000*

Medium red–purple; once again that family fragrance of spice and cedar surrounds the fresh fruit of the bouquet, which seems to have gained a second life. The palate, likewise, is beautifully balanced with perfectly married flavours and textures.

1984 ★★★★★ — *April 2000*

Strong red–purple; the bouquet has great fragrance, classic Cabernet, with concentrated cassis/blackberry fruit which leads into a superlative palate, balanced, and rich without being overripe. Silky Rolls Royce power.

1983 ★★★ — *May 1994*

The colour is on the light side with slightly dull aspects. Light fruit with distinct farmyard characters; the palate is quite tannic, and again those farmyard characters come through; the wine is rather hollow overall.

1982 ★★★★☆ — *April 2000*

Similar colour to the 1981; the bouquet is complex, with a mix of sweet berry set against more savoury/spicy characters. The palate is very elegant and tight, but the barest touch of green does manifest itself throughout.

1981 ★★★★★ — *April 2000*

Greater depth of colour and at the point of change, with some purple along with the red hues. The bouquet is ripe, rich, sweet and plushy, with dark berry, plum and spice. A very rich wine and concentrated by the standards of the day, with tannins still poking through on the finish, though without threatening the wine. A wine which has evolved marvellously well, the ripeness which once seemed to unbalance it and make it atypical of the Yarra Valley now standing it in good stead. Ditto the tannins.

1980 ★★★★☆ — *April 2000*

Medium red; the aromas are arresting, with wild herb, spice, echoes of lavender and even a touch of liquorice, all cocooned in cedary oak. The palate has lingering, intense mint, herb and red berry emerging on the finish. A much better bottle (or better wine) than that tasted six years ago.

1979 ★★★★★ — *April 2000*

Medium red, still with a hint of purple; much younger and more vibrant fruit ranging through sweet cassis, almost into sandalwood is evident, but with a faintly foresty background. The complex palate has many flavours, with lovely sweet, ripe cassis/plum fruit and fine, ripe tannins on the finish.

1978 ★★★★☆   *April 2000*

The colour is bright and strong, but has lost all of its purple hues, moving towards brick–red; the bouquet has a range of fragrant savoury, spicy, cedar, cigar box aromas; the sweeter fruit is starting to dissipate on the palate with more savoury/slippery/green characters emerging, but the texture and the structure of the wine is holding.

1977 ★★★★☆   *May 1994*

Medium to full red, with just a hint of tawny starting to show through; very attractive aromas which are sweet with cedar, camphor and briary characters. The palate is similar, now fully mature but yet well balanced and has plenty of substance to hold it.

★★★★★ Perfect   ★★★★☆ Close to perfect   ★★★★ Very good   ★★★☆ Expected
★★★ Short of standard   ★★☆ Undeserving   ★★ Decayed relic   NR No rating

orlando lawson's padthaway shiraz

In July 1999 the first ever vertical tasting of Lawson's Shiraz presented to the media and/or trade was held in Melbourne. Given that, together with Jacaranda Ridge, it is Orlando's super-premium standard-bearer, this may seem a belated presentation, but its style took time to evolve.

The one constant in Lawson's since its first vintage in 1985 has been the vineyard block, planted in 1968 by the grazier who then owned the surrounding 160-hectare property. It is only 2.8 hectares, and (apparently) was established for decorative purposes in front of his house on a sandy ridge.

Orlando purchased the grapes, and their quality led to the acquisition of the whole property in 1988 and to the planting of an additional 100 hectares of vineyard. While Orlando has no regrets about the acquisition and planting, the 'new' vineyard does not produce Shiraz with the same flavour and quality of that of the founding block. That block is especially magical, for it routinely yields 12 to 15 tonnes per hectare without in any way diminishing its quality; production thus averages 2000 cases a year.

It is released when it is four to five years old, having spent 18 months in new American oak and another two and a half years in bottle. Between 1985 and 1990 various winemakers used various oak and fermentation combinations, and while every vintage won at least two gold medals, the style varied considerably, but has since slipped into a smooth groove.

The outstanding features of the 15-vintage line-up were the consistently excellent colour, the soft yet mouthfilling fruit, and the touches of mint and eucalypt, particularly in the younger vintages, together with a stylish dressing of American oak.

(Vintage notes in brackets from Philip Laffer, Orlando, and emphasises the best, rather than the worst, features of each vintage.)

Tasted in July 1999.

◀ *1998* ★★★★★   *July 2000*

Dense, youthful purple–red; there is lots of oak present, but also lots of concentrated dark berry fruit with just a faint hint of mint. The palate is powerful, concentrated and with excellent tannin structure. Has everything it takes, and should be an outstanding wine. 100 per cent American oak. (The 1998 vintage was perhaps the best of the decade. Warm sunny conditions and little rainfall, both prior to and during vintage, concentrated flavours and resulted in deep colours.)

   ◀ Not Ready   ❭ Still evolving   ❘ Prime of its life   ◢ Drink soon   ☖ Missed the boat

1997 ★★★★ *July 1999*

Very good colour; the bouquet is still coming together, with minty fruit and slightly angular oak; inevitably, less concentrated than the '96. Minty eucalypt flavours on the palate are supported by quite persistent tannins. 100 per cent American oak. (Vintage was preceded by a sustained hot period in February, while March was the coolest it had been in many years. These conditions delayed flavour ripeness but, once achieved, resulted in rich strong colours, attractive aromas and impressive structure.)

1996 ★★★★★ *July 1999*

Strong red–purple; very concentrated and complex fruit running through plum and mint, with some charry oak notes which are wholly appropriate. A marvellous wine on the palate; much the most concentrated in the line-up, with liquorice, dark berry and spice flavours. The oak is well balanced, and the finish long. Relatively speaking, deserves a sixth star. 100 per cent American oak. (The 1996 vintage was preceded by mild summer temperatures with little rainfall. The vintage conditions throughout February to April were warm and dry resulting in concentrated varietal flavours and deep colours.)

1995 ★★★☆ *July 1999*

Medium red–purple; the bouquet is fragrant and strongly minty, with vanilla oak providing a pleasant counterbalance. An elegant wine on the palate with lively flavour, but does fade fractionally on the finish, thereby inviting the oak to fill the space. 100 per cent American oak. (Vintage was preceded by a long dry spell during budburst and flowering. The dry spring conditions served to reduce vine vigour and crop loads, however, timely rainfall in January and February ensured the vines produced fruit of full ripeness and flavour development.)

1994 ★★★★★ *July 1999*

Excellent bright red–purple hue. There are lovely sweet fruit aromas on the bouquet running through mint, red berry and plum woven through with vanillin oak. The palate is ripe, fine and smooth; the 100 per cent American oak contribution is substantial and on one of three occasions I have tasted the wine seemed intrusive (but not on the others). (An excellent vintage. A warm and mild growing season, and a long dry autumn ensured that the grapes were harvested at full ripeness with strong colour, intense varietal characters and balanced structure.)

1993 ★★★★☆ *July 1999*

Strong, youthful red–purple; the bouquet is quite powerful, with lots of dark berry, plum and mint fruit aromas. On both bouquet and palate the fruit carries the oak with relative ease. The abundant sweet berry and chocolate fruit have both texture and depth. A surprise packet. 100 per cent American oak. (Cool and wet conditions in spring and early summer preceded the 1993 vintage, delaying ripening and reduced the crop level to the lowest it had been for many years. Warmer temperatures towards harvest produced fruit of full ripeness with strong colour, balanced structure and generous varietal flavour.)

classic wines

★★★★★ Perfect   ★★★★☆ Close to perfect   ★★★★ Very good   ★★★☆ Expected
★★★ Short of standard   ★★☆ Undeserving   ★★ Decayed relic   NR No rating

1992 ★★★☆   *July 1999*

Youthful purple–red; the bouquet is quite fragrant and lively, with mint and dark berry fruit, but American oak does play a major role in shaping the aromas. The palate is seductive but, once again, is oak-dominated. To be fair, I am sure that others will be far more tolerant of the oak, and would give the wine a commensurately higher rating. 100 per cent American oak. (The 1992 vintage was favoured by a mild spring during flowering followed by a long cool ripening period throughout summer and autumn. The congenial vintage conditions gave rise to rich wines of deep colour, intense flavour and excellent structure.)

1991 ★★★★★   *July 1999*

Dense, deep red–purple; a powerful, concentrated bouquet with liquorice, black cherry and high-quality coffee/vanilla American oak. The palate is rich, complex and sweet with plummy dark fruit flavours running through to the mid-palate, and smoky vanilla oak kicking back in on a long, powerful finish. Predominantly American oak with a small percentage of French. (The 1991 vintage was preceded by a cool spring and a long, warm and dry summer. The vintage conditions gave rise to wines of full flavour, deep colour and strong varietal definition.)

1990 ★★★★☆   *July 1999*

Medium red–purple, slightly advanced for its age. The bouquet was relatively disappointing at the outset, even slightly stale, although it has undoubted concentration of dark fruit characters on the bouquet. There is great depth to the dark fruit flavours which easily carry the quite subtle oak. In very different style, no doubt due to the oak used, and some grip to the finish. Given the reputation of the 1990 vintage, fractionally disappointing. 100 per cent French oak. (The 1990 vintage is recognised as one of outstanding quality, particularly for red wines. The near perfect conditions during spring and the absence of temperature extremes in the summer ripening period resulted in excellent fruit at optimum maturity.)

1989 ★★★★   *July 1999*

Appealing bright red, with a touch of purple. There are fresh redcurrant and cherry fruit aromas with nicely balanced and integrated oak on the bouquet, and lively redcurrant, cherry and mint flavours on the palate. A fresh and lively wine, and a great outcome for what was regarded as a pretty difficult vintage, irrespective of the vintage notes provided by Orlando. 100 per cent American oak. (The 1989 growing season was relatively cool until March, when warmer temperatures prevailed. The result was intense varietal fruit characters and flavours.)

1988 ★★★★   *July 1999*

Medium red; the bouquet is moderately intense, with a mix of smoky/charry oak, gently sweet berry fruit and a hint of mint. The sweet vanillin oak tends to come up on the palate, and, together with quite firm tannins, poses a challenge to the fruit flavour. I strongly suspect others will have far less problem with the balance between oak and fruit. 100 per cent American oak. (Conditions throughout the 1988 growing season were warmer than preceding years which, coupled with reduced crop levels, produced bigger, richer wines than those of previous vintages.)

1987 ★★☆ *July 1999*

Medium to full red; there are slightly cabbagey/dusty overtones to the wine, with a strong streak of astringency running throughout. I personally thought this was a poor bottle, although Philip Laffer didn't see a major problem. Matured in a mix of French and American oak. (The 1987 vintage was characterised by excellent fruit quality due to the cool extended ripening period, which gave structure and length.)

1986 ★★★★☆ *July 1999*

Strong red, again with the barest hint of brick, and even retaining some purple hues. The bouquet is sweet and quite rich with good oak integration and balance. The ample fruit that runs through into the palate has dark berry and chocolate flavours, but neither spice nor mint. The oak is once again well-balanced, the structure helped by gentle but persistent tannins. Matured in predominantly American oak; the remainder French. (A cool spring and early summer, with a warmer final ripening period, led to the 1986 vintage being one of the best for the decade.)

1985 ★★★★ *July 1999*

Medium but bright red, with the barest hint of brick-red on the rim. The bouquet is smooth and clean, with soft vanilla overtones. A pleasant, soft and smooth palate, with vanilla, red berry and chocolate with some tannins on the finish. Will probably hold but won't gain much. Matured in predominantly French oak, the balance American. (The 1985 vintage was characterised by excellent fruit quality due to the cool extended ripening period prior to vintage.)

penfolds bin 128 coonawarra
shiraz 1980-1998

in 128 did not appear in either the first or second edition of *Classic Wines*, perhaps due to the fact that of all of the Penfolds Bin range red wines it has the lowest profile notwithstanding its impeccable breeding as a 100 per cent Coonawarra-based wine.

The explanation is due to the fact that until the late 1970s Bin 128 was relatively light bodied and matured in American oak. Since that time a number of positive changes have been made, first the introduction of French oak from the 1980 vintage, and since the mid-1980s an increasingly rigorous fruit selection.

The tasting notes come from the Rewards of Patience tasting held in September 1999, and which span the 1980 to 1997 vintages inclusive. One of the most noticeable features of the tasting was the importance of colour: it is tempting to say that the ranking could be done on colour alone; that would be a gross exaggeration, but the colour variation was significant and did closely correlate with the final ranking of the wine. For the record, the grapes all come from company vineyards in Coonawarra and the wine spends 18 months in French oak hogsheads, 20 per cent of which are new, 80 per cent being one and two years old.

All except the 1998 were tasted in September 1999 at the Penfolds Rewards of Patience tasting.

1998 ★★★★★ February 2001
Medium to full red–purple; the bouquet is clean, with abundant, ripe dark plum/dark cherry fruit which has soaked up the oak; the palate is powerful, with much more concentration than usual, and in particular, tannins; has a very long life in front of it.

1997 ★★★★ September 1999
Good medium to full red–purple colour; the bouquet is inevitably less concentrated than the '96, with cherry and hints of sweet shoe leather. A nice wine in the mouth, with attractive berry flavours together with hints of mint and leather; fine tannins; give the impression it will develop quite quickly over the next five years.

1996 ★★★★★ September 1999
Excellent full red–purple. Gorgeous black cherry fruit oozes from the glass, concentrated and stylish. There is perfect dark cherry/blackberry fruit in abundance on the seductive palate, the soft tannins beautifully balanced and integrated, as is the oak. A great classic.

◄ Not Ready   ◣ Still evolving   ◗ Prime of its life   ◢ Drink soon   ☐ Missed the boat

1995 ★★★☆   *September 1999*

The colour is somewhat lighter and weaker than the older wines from the 1990s. The bouquet, too, is similarly lighter and weaker than the wines of the 1990s which precede it, with berry, leaf and a hint of mint. A pleasant wine, quite well balanced but which shows the indifferent vintage conditions in Coonawarra.

1994 ★★★★   *September 1999*

Medium to full red–purple; the bouquet is quite concentrated with dark berry fruit and a hint of the earth which runs through so many of these wines. An attractive palate, but rather less rich and concentrated than the bouquet suggests, and while it should hold its form for another three to five years, will not benefit from further cellaring.

1993 ★★★★☆   *September 1999*

Medium to full red–purple; a solid mix of dark cherry, blackberry and chocolate on the bouquet is followed by a palate with considerable fruit substance and structure, quite concentrated, and with the dark berry fruit still evolving.

1992 ★★★★☆   *September 1999*

Medium to full red with just a touch of purple. The quite intense bouquet has attractive, fresh cherry and liquorice fruit. The perfectly balanced palate has dark cherry fruit and an echo of the liquorice of the bouquet. All in all a surprise packet, and very nearly rated five stars.

1991 ★★★★   *September 1999*

Strong colour, but more developed and without the brightness of the '90. The bouquet is clean, predominantly of blackberry and cherry but with some hints of chocolate and earth. The palate has plenty of power and life, with berry fruit but then an unexpected touch of astringency towards the finish. It is just possible this was not a good bottle.

1990 ★★★★★   *September 1999*

Distinctly deeper colour, medium to full red–purple; the bouquet is still evolving, with clean, smooth, red and black cherry fruit supported by subtle but evident oak. The wine has great structure, with soft tannins running through classic shiraz fruit. Utterly delicious.

1989 ★★★☆   *September 1999*

Medium to full red; the bouquet is quite aromatic with an attractive touch of spice and leads into a pleasing palate with berry, spice and earth flavours; a particularly good outcome for a more than ordinary vintage. Drink soon, though.

1988 ★★★★   *September 1999*

Medium to full red; the smooth bouquet has berry-accented, smooth, gently sweet fruit. The palate is likewise gentle, with a mix of berry, earth and chocolate supported by soft tannins. As good now as it will ever get.

1987 ★★★☆   *September 1999*

Medium to full red; the moderately intense bouquet is pleasant enough, but some tobacco/stemmy characters indicate the cooler vintage. The palate still offers some pleasing flavour, but doesn't have the rich fruit to justify cellaring.

1986 ★★★★★   *September 1999*

Medium to full red; a marked colour change from this vintage onwards, deeper and with far more red than brick. The bouquet is richer and more concentrated than the wines which precede it, with dark berry fruit prominent and just a few touches of chocolate and earth. The palate is in another dimension altogether, with lovely dark berry and dark chocolate fruit to the fore. A particularly well-balanced wine.

1985 ★★★☆   *September 1999*

Medium brick–red; the quite sweet and rich earth and chocolate aromas hark back to those of the '80. There is some berry and earth fruit on the palate, although not as appealing as the bouquet, and finishing with fractionally dry tannins.

1984 ★★★   *September 1999*

Medium brick–red; there is some astringency to the fruit aromas with green leaf characters. The palate is well enough balanced but, consistently with the bouquet, lacks sweet fruit in its heart.

1983 ★★★   *September 1999*

Medium brick–red; the light bouquet has some pleasantly sweet chocolate aromas, but the palate is definitely on the downwards slope, with light caramel chocolate flavour.

1982 ★★★☆   *September 1999*

Medium brick–red, quite fragrant and sweet but lighter even than the '81, notwithstanding a hint of spice and leaf still lingering. The palate is a logical continuation, with hints of that '82 vintage character of so many of the Penfolds reds coming from the flashes of green dimethyl sulphide.

1981 ★★★☆   *September 1999*

Medium brick–red; the bouquet is moderately intense, with slightly less fruit sweetness and slightly more leaf and earth aromas than the '80. The palate is fully mature, with some remnants of chocolate and berry fruit, but has seen far better days.

1980 ★★★★★   *September 1999*

Medium to full brick–red; a rich, sweet mature bouquet with a mix of earth and chocolate aromas; a quite lovely, mature red with soft berry, chocolate and earth flavours, still supported by lingering tannins. While rated at its peak, should nonetheless be drunk by (say) 2003 for maximum enjoyment.

penfolds bin 389 cabernet shiraz

first made in 1960, Bin 389 quickly became known as 'Poor Man's Grange', a dual reference to its far cheaper price and to the fact that the new barrels employed to make Grange were passed on after one use to mature Bin 389. In fact, new oak is also used in the making of Bin 389, though never extravagantly — around 20 per cent.

While the varietal blend has remained more or less 60 per cent Cabernet Sauvignon and 40 per cent Shiraz — varying slightly from one vintage to the next — the regional base has changed significantly over the years. The first wines were made from grapes produced on the defunct Auldana Vineyard (now suburban housing adjacent to Magill Estate), but the net gradually spread across the Barossa Valley and beyond.

For some years now the wine has been sourced from vineyards in the Barossa Valley, Coonawarra, Padthaway, McLaren Vale, Langhorne Creek and the Clare Valley. This spread has added to, rather than detracted from, the quality and complexity of the wine. It gives the winemakers greater scope to deal with seasonal variation, and to achieve balance by blending rather than chemical manipulation — a central tenet of Max Schubert's winemaking philosophy.

While Bin 389 does not have the exceptional longevity of Grange, the best vintages age superbly for 20 years or more. And if anyone should ponder on the question of the synergy from the blend of Cabernet and Shiraz, Bin 389 provides the answer.

All except the 1998 were tasted in September 1999 at the Penfolds Rewards of Patience tasting.

◄ *1998* ★★★★★   *February 2001*
Full red–purple; dense, dark berry, dark chocolate, and savoury/spicy aromas are a backdrop for a palate full of cassis, blackberry and chocolate supported by a great depth of ripe tannins. Needs a decade to really start strutting its stuff, but will undoubtedly do so.

◄ *1997* ★★★★   *September 1999*
Medium purple–red; surprisingly well-integrated and balanced fruit and oak, with lively cassis accents. The palate, too, offers attractive mint and berry flavours plus a slice of vanilla courtesy of the oak.

classic wines

★★★★★ Perfect   ★★★★☆ Close to perfect   ★★★★ Very good   ★★★☆ Expected
★★★ Short of standard   ★★☆ Undeserving   ★★ Decayed relic   NR No rating

163

1996 ★★★★★   *September 1999*

Medium purple–red; an ultra-fragrant bouquet with juicy, cassis cabernet fruit aromas, not powerful but infinitely seductive. Perfect grapes made into perfect wine provide a silky smooth yet powerful palate with plum and cassis fruit, finishing with quite marvellous tannins.

1995 ★★★☆   *September 1999*

Medium to full red–purple; the Achilles Heel of the vintage is there, although not blatantly; overall the aromas are rather lighter and more minty/earthy. The palate has a range of minty berry and leafy flavours; the oak seems a little pencilly. Perhaps a harsh judgment or possibly a less than perfect bottle.

1994 ★★★★★   *September 1999*

Full purple–red; yet another almost broodingly powerful wine, with masses of dark, layered cassis and chocolate fruit aromas. The same multiplicity of flavours run through the palate with prune, dark plum, liquorice and spice all present. Part of a range of 1994 wines from Penfolds which were a revelation.

1993 ★★★★   *September 1999*

Full red–purple; another powerful bouquet, with dark berry/dark chocolate fruit together with splashes of charry oak/savoury characters. The palate is opulent and mouthfilling, with ripe prune/mulberry fruit and fairly firm tannins.

1992 ★★★★☆   *September 1999*

Medium to full red–purple; the bouquet is quite fragrant, although for some reason the cedary/vanillin oak is a little more obvious than in most of the wines. From this point attractive plum, blackberry, chocolate and cedar flavours take over, followed by quite firm tannins.

1991 ★★★★☆   *September 1999*

Dark red–purple; profound, ripe blackberry/liquorice/spice aromas drive the bouquet. The palate offers ripe prune/blackberry/blackcurrant fruit, with the tannins now well balanced and integrated. Could quite conceivably become a five-star wine with time.

1990 ★★★★★   *September 1999*

Dark red–purple, so dark it briefly stains the glass when swirled. The powerful, concentrated yet supple bouquet is redolent of blackcurrant fruit, a hint of liquorice and much more; the round, rich and mouthfilling palate, oozing cassis and chocolate fruit, finishes with perfect tannins. A classic wine from a great vintage. It is difficult to see the end point for the development of this wine.

1989 ★★★☆   *September 1999*

The colour is holding surprisingly well, still red–purple. The bouquet is not particularly intense, but is fresh and lively; the palate is easy drinking, and has in fact held very well over the past five years, but still seems too big to be opened and enjoyed.

1988 ★★★★★   *September 1999*

Medium to full red–purple, still bright; really outstanding cabernet sauvignon drives this wine from start to finish, with fragrant, ripe cassis cabernet flavours complexed by more spicy/savoury notes on the bouquet lead into a quite delicious palate, with ripe cassis fruit balanced by firm but ripe tannins. Has developed far better than one could have ever imagined.

1987 ★★★☆   *September 1999*

Medium red; a fragrant bouquet with a mix of berry, mint and leaf. The palate is still fresh, with a mix of mint, leaf, berry and vanilla flavours finishing with soft tannins. Drink sooner rather than later.

1986 ★★★★★   *September 1999*

Medium to full red; a very clean and elegant bouquet which is now showing signs of development, with cedary/savoury overtones. The palate is similarly elegant and very well balanced and structured, but has developed a little more quickly than anticipated, and is now at its peak.

1985 ★★☆   *September 1999*

Medium red–brown; the leafy, soapy/stemmy aromas disappoint, as does the palate, which is no better than the bouquet. Near identical notes and rating to the prior occasion.

1984 ★★★   *September 1999*

Medium to full red, but slightly dull; the bouquet is leafy/earthy/hay/straw more than it is savoury; the palate showed some redeeming features with a touch of dark chocolate to balance the leafy characters, but lacks richness. In fact performed slightly better than it did five years ago, but this should not encourage anyone to cellar it.

1983 ★★★★   *September 1999*

Medium to full brick–red; a mix of liquorice, plum, spice, berry and mint fruit aromas are all in a ripe spectrum, complexed further by some charry/smoky notes. A big, powerful and ripe wine in a true reflection of the vintage, finishing with powerful tannins.

1982 ★★★   *September 1999*

Shows some of the characters common to all of the 1982 vintage wines from Penfolds, although less trenchantly so. Medium red–brick; some dimethyl sulphide/green canopy aromas are followed by soft, sappy green fruit on the palate; there are some cedary flavours, and at least the tannins are balanced. Nonetheless, not a wine to cellar.

1981 ★★★   *September 1999*

Like the 1980, was nearly identical with the wine tasted five years ago. Medium red–brick; the bouquet has a mix of potent savoury/leafy cabernet aromas with sweet chocolatey characters from the Shiraz. The palate is savoury, leafy but decidedly tannic.

classic wines

★★★★★ Perfect   ★★★★☆ Close to perfect   ★★★★ Very good   ★★★☆ Expected
★★★ Short of standard   ★★☆ Undeserving   ★★ Decayed relic   NR No rating

165

1980 ★★☆   *September 1999*
Medium red–brick; interesting sweet and sour aromas, scented and verging on the cosmetic. Strong herbal fruit flavours are over the top and at odds with the style.

1978 ★★★   *September 1999*
A wine which has significant cork taint problems. The bottles sampled in the last Rewards of Patience tasting were corked; so was the first at this tasting. The second did not appear to be tainted, but showed some green fruit aspects on the light to medium bouquet, and slightly green cabernet fruit flavours dominate the palate, taking it out of the mainstream style.

1977 ★★★★   *September 1999*
Medium brick–red; the moderately intense bouquet opens with sweet chocolate-accented aromas followed by more savoury secondary characters. The palate is elegant in a lighter-bodied and well-balanced way. Showed very much better than in 1994.

1976 ★★★★★   *September 1999*
A major surprise, showing very significantly better than it did on the last tasting five years ago. Medium to full brick–red; the bouquet has a mix of ripe dark berry and liquorice aromas with more savoury/tarry/briary notes. The fruit on the palate is far sweeter and more powerful than the bouquet suggests; the only question mark is whether the tannins will outlive the fruit.

1975 ★★★☆   *September 1999*
Medium brick–red, very similar to the older wines. The bouquet offers a range of soft earthy/savoury notes together with some chocolate. There are a range of earthy/savoury/leafy flavours interwoven with some riper characters on the palate; you can see the interplay of the varieties.

1971 ★★★★★   *September 1999*
This has always been a classic wine, and continues to be so, gaining a new lease of life over the past five years. Medium brick–red; the bouquet is marvellously complex with a mix of chocolate, liquorice and leaf/mint aromas. The palate is no less complex and powerful with a mix of chocolate, liquorice and coffee followed by persistent, ripe tannins on the finish. A great bottle of a great wine.

1970 ★★★★   *September 1999*
Medium brick–red; quite scented, with a mix of charry, earthy, cedary and chocolatey aromas. A nicely balanced palate with the juxtaposition of leathery and chocolatey/berry fruit flavours. The tannins are starting to dry off a little.

1966 ★★★★☆   *September 1999*
Medium to full brick–red; a sweet, fully aged bouquet with savoury complexity; you can sense the softness which will come in the mouth. The palate opens with soft chocolate and berry fruit before finishing with a tweak of Cabernet-type flavour on the finish. Has developed noticeably over the past five years.

◄■ Not Ready   ＼ Still evolving   ▌ Prime of its life   ◢ Drink soon   ▯ Missed the boat

penfolds bin 707 cabernet sauvignon 1964-1998

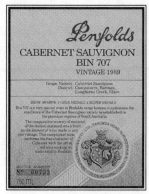

W hen Penfolds made the first of this famous line in 1964, there was only a minuscule amount of cabernet sauvignon grown in Australia; only 500 tonnes were crushed in that year, compared with 270 000 tonnes in 2001. The plantings were scattered and small, but one was in the Kalimna Vineyard, which Penfolds had acquired in 1945, and made a superb Cabernet in the same year. Subsequently Max Schubert made a tiny quantity of experimental Grange from cabernet sauvignon, drawing on the same source, but abandoned the idea of using cabernet simply because the grape was in such short supply.

Plantings increased steadily over the 1960s, but nowhere near rapidly enough to cope with the then-emerging red wine boom. So much so, that notwithstanding the extreme popularity of the wine among connoisseurs, Penfolds stopped making the wine after the 1969 vintage, electing to use its precious supplies in building Bin 389.

Production was recommenced in 1976, and the wine has established itself as Australia's premier commercial Cabernet Sauvignon. It is made from a blend of Coonawarra, Barossa and Eden Valley grapes, vinified in a fashion similar to Grange, with the fermentation finished in American oak barrels.

The style is opulent, rich and long lived, distinctively Penfolds yet no less distinctively Bin 707: there is no other Australian Cabernet Sauvignon quite like it. Its endless series of trophies, first places and gold medals in shows, exhibitions and tastings around the world bear eloquent testimony to its quality.

All except the 1998 were tasted in September 1999 at the Penfolds Rewards of Patience tasting.

◀ *1998* ★★★★★　　　　　　　　　　　　　　　　　　　　　　　　　*April 2001*
Dense, deep purple–red; intense, almost juicy, dark berry fruit is matched with excellent oak handling on the bouquet. The wine floods the mouth with ripe, cassis/blackberry fruit accompanied by fine tannins throughout, the oak perfectly balanced and integrated.

◀ *1997* ★★★★☆　　　　　　　　　　　　　　　　　　　　　　　*September 1999*
Dark purple–red; a wine which continues that high-toned, lusciously aromatic fruit of the '96, with some cedary oak. There is plenty of weight and stuffing to the palate, where cassis and vanilla intermingle, rounded off with lingering tannins.

classic wines

★★★★★ Perfect　　★★★★☆ Close to perfect　　★★★★ Very good　　★★★☆ Expected
★★★ Short of standard　　★★☆ Undeserving　　★★ Decayed relic　　NR No rating

167

◄■ *1996* ★★★★★   *September 1999*

The colour is slightly less dense than the '94, but nonetheless an excellent, full purple–red. The bouquet is complex, aromatic and scented, with charry oak still integrating with the plum/cassis fruit. A wine which looks positively elegant on the palate compared with the blockbuster '94; fragrant, high-toned flavours with fine, supple tannins.

1995

Not made.

◄■ *1994* ★★★★★   *September 1999*

Dense, deep red–purple. An immensely powerful and concentrated bouquet with blackberry and chocolate fruit, still folded in on itself but which promises to open up marvellously in due course. There is likewise masses of blackcurrant, blackberry and chocolate fruit running through the entire length of the palate.

◄■ *1993* ★★★★☆   *September 1999*

Dense red–purple; blackberry, blackcurrant and plum fruit is seamlessly woven through with oak on the bouquet. A very powerful wine stacked with very ripe fruit on the palate which is slightly gauche and doesn't quite fulfil the promise of the bouquet. Who knows what time will bring?

🍾 *1992* ★★★★★   *September 1999*

Dense red–purple; classic cabernet blackberry/blackcurrant fruit with a hint of pine forest on the bouquet leads into a wine with vibrant flavours and texture. Supple, slurpy fruit flavours run from cassis to plum, finishing with soft tannins. Yet another great '92 wine from Penfolds, yet another surprise.

🍾 *1991* ★★★★★   *September 1999*

Medium to full red–purple; fragrant plum, cedar and vanilla aromas attest to the superb oak handling evident in all of these wines. The palate has plenty of power, with dark plum and briar/savoury fruit with quite persistent tannins on the finish. Still evolving.

🍾 *1990* ★★★★★   *September 1999*

Full red, with touches of purple. It has an infinitely seductive mix of sweet cassis, plum and mulberry fruit aromas, yet not the slightest hint of overripeness. The supple, silky palate has great balance and length, with all the flavours promised by the bouquet, yet not at all over-done. A sheer privilege and pleasure to taste (and, better still, drink).

🍶 *1989* ★★★★   *September 1999*

Medium to full red; an exotic and aromatic mixture of mint, prune and plum on the bouquet lead into a wine which has developed exceptionally well, with lovely sweet plum flavours and soft tannins. I fancy its plateau period will not be terribly long, and that it should be drunk within the next three to five years.

🍶 *1988* ★★★★☆   *September 1999*

Medium to full red; a marvellously subtle, perfectly composed and balanced bouquet in typical Penfolds '88 vintage style which consistently shows that elegance. Ethereal hints of mint and smooth cassis join together on a long, velvety palate.

1987 ★★★★
September 1999

Medium to full red, an ultra-fragrant bouquet with aromas of berry, scented pine and sandalwood. The palate has most attractive sweet berry and plum fruit which dips very slightly before the tannins come again on the finish.

1986 ★★★★★
September 1999

Full, bright red; perfectly ripened sweet cassis berry fruit wafts from the glass, complex and multi-dimensional. A classic, mature cabernet palate, opening with cassis and berry, then with a touch of austerity on the finish courtesy of the perfect tannins.

1985 ★★★☆
September 1999

Medium red; some of the Coonawarra-type earthy/vegetal secondary cabernet characters are starting to appear on the bouquet; the palate has a range of leafy, berry and faintly minty flavours, the tannins being fractionally grippy. As previously, a total style contrast to the '84.

1984 ★★★★
September 1999

Medium to full red; complex and perfectly ripened varietal cabernet aromas run through well-handled oak on the bouquet. A lovely wine in the mouth, with gentle cassis running throughout, the tannins perfectly balanced, as is the oak. Has developed superbly over the past five years.

1983 ★★★★☆
September 1999

Medium red; predominantly sweet berry aromas dominate the bouquet, with some more minty/gamey notes in the background. Back to the mirror-smooth, gently sweet fruit palate-style of the best of the older wines; the previously strong tannins have softened right out.

1982 ★★☆
September 1999

Medium red; a wine which shrieks of dimethyl sulphide on both bouquet and palate. Others may be less harsh in their reaction, but I simply do not like this character in small doses, let alone large.

1980 ★★★☆
September 1999

Medium to full red; strong, leafy, herbaceous overtones to the sweet berry fruit of the bouquet announce a positively flavoured wine, but with an olive/herb streak running through, and firm tannins rip on the finish. For whatever reason, showed much better on the previous occasion.

1979 ★★★★
September 1999

Full red; there is a range of sweet chocolate, mint and leaf aromas on the bouquet which are showing remarkably well. The palate has soft, predominantly sweet, flavours which are much more appealing than on the previous tasting five years ago.

1978 ★★★★
September 1999

Full red, healthy and bright; the bouquet is clean and smooth, with elegant, gently sweet fruit and subtle oak. The palate picks up where the bouquet leaves off, in elegant style; cedar, earth and some berry fruit flavours are supported by soft tannins on the finish.

classic wines

★★★★★ Perfect ★★★★☆ Close to perfect ★★★★ Very good ★★★☆ Expected
★★★ Short of standard ★★☆ Undeserving ★★ Decayed relic NR No rating

1977 ★★★   *September 1999*

Medium to full red; cooler vintage aromas with slight vegetal/olive/game/earth aspects to the bouquet. The palate is complex and multiflavoured with some sweet caramel, berry and mint flavours before slightly green tannins on the finish.

1976 ★★★★★   *September 1999*

Full red; fragrant aromas showing a marked shift into cassis berry fruit. The palate is beautifully sweet, with flowing cassis and fine tannins there in the background; truly, a lovely wine.

1969 ★★★★☆   *September 1999*

Once again, glowing brick–red. A powerful, complex blackberry, briar and leather bouquet, then a palate full of chocolate and dark briary/berry fruit. A powerful wine, the tannins running throughout the palate but well balanced.

1968 ★★★☆   *September 1999*

Like all of the first six wines, glowing brick–red. The bouquet is quite fragrant with touches of anise and sweet leather, but nuances of caramel and berry on the mid-palate are losing the battle with the tannins which run throughout; a wine which is starting to dry out.

1967 ★★★★   *September 1999*

Glowing brick–red; the bouquet is clean, lacking a little of the resplendent generosity of the previous wines. There are very slight vegetal characters on the palate with a whisper of anise, but has that same mirror-smooth texture and fine tannins.

1966 ★★★★★   *September 1999*

Full, glowing brick–red; holding superbly, with ripe berry, echoes of cassis; great varietal character and showing no signs of tiredness. A gorgeous palate, with ripe berry fruit flavours, hints of chocolate and soft tannins running through a long finish. A mixture of velvet and silk; quite remarkable.

1965 ★★★★☆   *September 1999*

Glowing brick–red; a tangy bouquet showing obvious volatility yet not to the point of fault or distraction. There are hints of charry earthy characters on entry to the mouth, then smoothing out into a long, even palate; the tannins are largely gone and it is acidity which is holding the wine up.

1964 ★★★★★   *September 1999*

Glowing brick–red; sweet berry fruit is still evident on the bouquet surrounded by mocha, coffee and a touch of chocolate. A lovely old wine with no sign of structural breakup, almost mirror smooth, and a fresher bottle than that tasted five years ago. 100 per cent Kalimna cabernet from the 1880 plantings.

Not Ready   Still evolving   Prime of its life   Drink soon   Missed the boat

penfolds grange 1951-1996

It is impossible to overstate the importance of Penfolds Grange to the Australian wine industry. One could argue that had the late Max Schubert not commenced his pioneering work in 1951 someone else would have done so sooner or later. Disproving a negative is an impossible task, and the fact remains that it was Schubert — and that when he set about fashioning Grange, he did so with the creative brilliance of a Michelangelo or a Mozart.

That his vision was decades in front of its time, and was entirely misunderstood by many of those who might have been expected to understand it best, has been well documented. Suffice it to say that the establishment of Penfolds as one of the greatest red winemaking companies in the world can be directly attributed to Grange.

Curiously, Grange has never been an estate wine: right from the beginning, Schubert spread his net far and wide, hunting out parcels of old, dry-farmed, low-yielding shiraz from diverse mesoclimates to provide a natural chemical and flavour balance to the base wine.

Among a range of unusual making procedures (including the addition of powdered tannins and the deliberate encouragement of volatility) his masterstroke was to finish the primary fermentation in new, small American oak barrels. Taken together, the choice of fruit and winemaking techniques produced wines of quite extraordinary complexity and longevity: I really needed another scale (an extra star or two) to do justice to this breathtaking range of wines.

The notes come from two tastings: the Anders Josephson tasting in 1994 (an extraordinary tasting event which featured every Grange made between 1951, the experimental vintage, and 1990) and the Rewards of Patience tasting in September 1999. The 1996 was tasted in April 2001.

Finally, on re-reading the tasting notes one feature stands out: how infrequently the oak contribution is mentioned, particularly in the older wines.

◄ *1996* ★★★★★   *April 2001*

Medium to full red–purple, still bright after five years, vibrant cherry and plum fruit aromas more than handle the oak on the bouquet; the palate is sumptuous, but not heavy, the cherry and plum flavours tracking the bouquet. The wine has a very long finish, with fine, integrated tannins. Destined to become one of the great Granges.

◄ *1995* ★★★★☆   *September 1999*

Strong purple–red; rich, ripe red and black cherry fruit, sweet as it can be, matched with good oak on the bouquet. There is plenty of power and ripeness to the palate, with no sign of a lesser vintage; good tannins and length.

classic wines

★★★★★ Perfect   ★★★★☆ Close to perfect   ★★★★ Very good   ★★★☆ Expected
★★★ Short of standard   ★★☆ Undeserving   ★★ Decayed relic   NR No rating

171

1994 ★★★★★   *September 1999*

Medium to full purple–red; excellent concentration and balance of dark plum and cassis fruit interwoven with oak on the bouquet; the palate has powerful, dense dark berry plum and liquorice fruit, strong tannins and hallmark vanilla oak.

1993 ★★★★   *September 1999*

Medium to full red–purple; certainly has abundant character on the bouquet with rich, ripe, faintly jammy fruit. The palate, likewise, has big, ripe plum and prune fruit; overall looks a trifle gauche in this line-up.

1992 ★★★★☆   *September 1999*

Medium to full purple–red; the bouquet is redolent of liquorice, leather and minty berry fruit, and the palate has that bright, breezy raspberry and liquorice fruit of the vintage, finishing with soft, fine tannins.

1991 ★★★★★   *September 1999*

Medium to full red–purple; a voluptuous and potent bouquet with cherry and plum fruit which is ripe but not jammy, much in the mould of the '83. The palate is showing much more than the '90 vintage, ripe, and with bold cherry and plum fruit, touches of liquorice and soft but persistent tannins.

1990 ★★★★★   *September 1999*

Medium to full red–purple; there is not a hair out of place on the sweet, elegant and fragrant bouquet. The palate has an abundance of soft redcurrant, cherry and mocha chocolate fruit (and oak), finishing with very fine, persistent tannins.

1989 ★★★★   *September 1999*

Medium to full red–purple; those ripe, raisiny characters of the vintage come rocketing through the ultra-voluptuous bouquet. The palate offers plum and prune flavours, akin to overripe Grenache; a strange one, but far from unattractive.

1988 ★★★★★   *September 1999*

Medium to full red–purple; fragrant, scented and lifted raspberry, cherry and mint aromas; the lift is coming from the fruit, not volatile acidity. A totally delicious wine on the palate, very elegant, smooth and satiny; not showy.

1987 ★★★★☆   *September 1999*

Medium to full purple–red; the bouquet is powerful yet firm and still remarkably closed, releasing liquorice, earth and berry only after prolonged coaxing. The palate doesn't really show the cool vintage, with nice cherry/berry fruit and soft, slightly dusty tannins.

1986 ★★★★★   *September 1999*

Medium to full purple–red; the bouquet is absolute perfection, with smooth, sweet, plum/cherry fruit which has soaked up the new oak; you know the oak is there, but it is largely hidden. A perfectly constructed wine, seamless in every respect; all the flavour you could ever wish for. Really deserves a sixth star.

1985 ★★★★   *September 1999*

Medium to full red–purple; the bouquet is firm, and with some of the slightly green, minty aromas which run through many of the 1985 Penfolds reds. The palate is of medium weight, with a mix of thyme, mint, herb and berry, finishing with soft tannins.

◄━ Not Ready   ❧ Still evolving   ♠ Prime of its life   ⟋ Drink soon   ⏟ Missed the boat

1984 ★★★★★
September 1999

Medium to full red–purple; quite fragrant, with sweet cherry, plum and mint aromas. The palate has wonderful mouthfeel, soft and silky, with strong chocolate flavours making their appearance. An elegant, seductive wine which seems even younger than when previously tasted, but still has the 'drink me now' tag around its neck.

1983 ★★★★★
September 1999

Strong red–purple; lusciously ripe cherry plum fruit on the bouquet, rich and welcoming. Dense, ultra-ripe but not jammy mint and morello cherry flavours are surrounded and supported by smooth, rippling tannins. Decades to go.

1982 ★★★★
September 1999

Light to medium red, with just a hint of purple. The bouquet is lighter, with slightly hessiany/green canopy characters giving it some Bordeaux-like characters. The palate has soft, caramel, crème brûlée notes before finishing with soft tannins. An odd wine from an odd red wine vintage for Penfolds.

1981 ★★★★☆
September 1999

Medium to full red–purple; the aromas are complex, running through briar, earth, cedar and dark berry. The palate offers all of the same flavours in a complex matrix; the tannins, previously threatening, are now in balance.

1980 ★★★☆
September 1999

Medium to full red–purple; the bouquet is particularly attractive and welcoming, with a mix of chocolate, cherry, cassis and vanilla, all very sweet. A potent, long, lingering palate with glossy plum, cherry and chocolate flavours.

1979 ★★★★☆
September 1999

Medium red–purple; the bouquet opens attractively with soft fruit, but then volatile acidity manifests itself, a characteristic which follows through onto the palate. Chocolate and cherry flavours are matched by fairly aggressive tannins; seems to me in a rebellious mood, and probably best left alone for the time being. Was more attractive when younger, and will likely be more attractive in the years ahead.

1978 ★★★★
September 1999

Lighter colour but still bright and predominantly red. There are sweet, earthy Shiraz aromas, much lighter than most in the line-up. On the palate, smoky/earthy Shiraz flavours appear, quite reminiscent of an aged Hunter red. Overall, soft easy drinking; soft tannins.

1977 ★★★
September 1999

Excellent colour; a clean, quite intense berry/briar/earth bouquet with nicely balanced oak is followed by a palate on which some slightly assertive green tinges manifest themselves. Not a great Grange, but a far better bottle than that at the Josephson tasting.

1976 ★★★★★
September 1999

Strong red–purple, a wonderful array of liquorice, berry and chocolate aromas foreshadow a powerful and wonderfully complex wine on the palate, with rich, chocolate and berry flavours. Should be very long lived; lovely tannin balance.

★★★★★ Perfect ★★★★☆ Close to perfect ★★★★ Very good ★★★☆ Expected
★★★ Short of standard ★★☆ Undeserving ★★ Decayed relic NR No rating

1975 ★★★★ *September 1999*

A marked colour change to dark red; some slightly vegetal canopy characters are somewhat unexpected on the bouquet; the palate is powerful, with flavours of leaf, berry and mint, again in that quasi Cabernet spectrum. Definitely out of the mainstream.

1974 ★★★ *September 1999*

Brick–red; some sweet earth aromas, but almost inevitably lacks fruit intensity. The tannins take over fairly abruptly on the palate, but this apart, not bad for a perfectly dreadful vintage decimated by mildew.

1973 ★★★★ *September 1999*

Medium brick–red; continues the theme of some volatile acidity, lifting chocolate, berry and fruit aromas. The palate is markedly sweet with slightly jammy berry fruit; there are hints of fruit pickle contributed, doubtless, by the element of volatile acidity.

1972 ★★★★☆ *September 1999*

Medium brick–red; potent, powerful mint and dark berry fruit aromas are lifted to a degree by some volatile acidity. The palate is powerful, concentrated with briary/savoury fruit flavours; not quite up to the form which showed at the Josephson tasting, but not far short of it. A wine which has always suffered from some bottle variation; a bargain when you find a good one.

1971 ★★★★★ *September 1999*

Medium brick–red; an intensely complex bouquet with that controversial whisk of volatile acidity, sweet earth and truffle. The palate is equally complex, with flavours of plum, prune and truffle; the extremely long finish is due in part to that touch of volatile acidity.

1970 ★★★★ *September 1999*

Medium brick–red; sweet, soft berry, honey, raisin, spice and earth aromas are followed by more sweet, raisiny berry fruit on the palate. Out of the mainstream, but nice nonetheless, particularly if drunk soon.

1969 ★★★★ *November 1994*

Medium red; a touch more concentrated than the 1970, with a smooth bouquet showing mint, sweet earth and dark chocolate aromas. The palate is quite firm, with good structure; surprisingly alive and taut.

1968 ★★★★☆ *November 1994*

Medium red; similar to the '69 and '70 with its soft berry, earth and chocolate aromas, although complexed by some smoky characters. On the palate, smoky and chocolatey flavours, of lighter weight but beautifully balanced tannins. At its peak.

1967 ★★★★★ *November 1994*

Medium to full red; a wine which instantly proclaims its quality on its bouquet which is firmer, richer and more complex and concentrated than the three vintages which followed it. The palate, too, reveals a substantial wine, powerful, structured and concentrated with flavours of briar, forest, dark berry fruits and bitter chocolate all there. Well-balanced and integrated oak.

◄ Not Ready 	 ＼ Still evolving 	 ▮ Prime of its life 	 ↗ Drink soon 	 ◻ Missed the boat

1966 ★★★★★   *September 1999*

Medium to full brick–red; a very fresh and firm bouquet, almost with Cabernet notes, ranging through dark berry and mint; a touch of volatility does not detract from the wine. The palate precisely tracks the bouquet, sweetness building all the while, again somewhat reminiscent of Cabernet Sauvignon and, in this limited sense, not typical of previous tastings. Still, that hardly matters.

1965 ★★★★   *November 1994*

Medium to full red; a fragrant seductive bouquet but with some aged earth and chocolate characters starting to develop. The palate is powerful, with chocolate and prune flavours, followed by a slightly drying, grippy tannin finish. Doubtful whether the fruit will outlive the tannins.

1964 ★★★☆   *November 1994*

Medium to full red. A complex bouquet with hints of game, leaf, forest floor and earth which become even more obvious on the palate, almost degenerating to the barnyard level. Others were more forgiving of the wine.

1963 ★★★★★   *September 1999*

Medium to full brick–red; a rich and complex bouquet with gloriously sweet plum, cherry, spice and cedar aromas. An amazingly rich and voluptuous palate, crammed with glistening plum and chocolate fruit flavours, finishing with soft, supple tannins.

1962 ★★★★★   *November 1994*

Medium to full red. A complex yet supremely elegant bouquet with fragrant cedar, earth and tobacco aromas, strongly reminiscent of a great Bordeaux. The palate is supremely elegant, with wonderful harmony, balance and length, and an extraordinarily intense finish.

1961 ★★★☆   *November 1994*

Dark red; the bouquet appears to show elevated volatility, although the chemical analysis suggests otherwise. A big, brawny wine on the palate with angles all over the place; some chocolate fruit remaining, but starting to go over the edge.

1960 ★★★★☆   *November 1994*

Bright red of medium depth; there is a certain amount of volatile lift on the bouquet with cedar, garden mint, vanilla and chocolate all apparent. An interesting wine on the palate, with a sweet middle tinged with caramel and vanilla, finishing with firm tannins. The volatile acidity seemed to increase as the wine sat in the glass.

1959 ★★★☆   *November 1994*

Medium red; the bouquet is slightly astringent and tough, almost suggesting the presence of some sulphides. The palate, however, is firm, and not as astringent as the bouquet suggests it will be, though equally not particularly complex.

1958 ★★★☆   *November 1994*

Medium to full red; a firm, earthy bouquet in which the absence of any new oak is very noticeable. On the palate there is lots of ripe sweet fruit, with nicely balanced tannins; a wine crying out for oak. I liked it more than others did.

★★★★★ Perfect   ★★★★☆ Close to perfect   ★★★★ Very good   ★★★☆ Expected
★★★ Short of standard   ★★☆ Undeserving   ★★ Decayed relic   NR No rating

1957 ★★★★☆   *November 1994*

Medium to full red; a lovely wine with near-perfect aged shiraz on the bouquet, leading on to a sweetly fruited, chocolate-accented palate, finishing with lingering, soft tannins. A major surprise.

1956 ★★★★★   *November 1994*

The colour is amazing, still red–purple. The bouquet is very complex and rich with layered chocolate, berry and earth aromas. A superb old wine on the palate, still 100 per cent there, with intense berry, plum and chocolate fruit flavours. I liked it much more than the rest of the panel.

1955 ★★★★   *September 1999*

Bright brick–red; there are quite marked charry/earthy notes on the bouquet, with sweet fruit underneath. As always, a powerful wine in terms of its fruit; simply not a good bottle. Significant variation is emerging here; at its best, still a supremely great wine, but both the bottle tasted at the Josephson tasting in *November 1994* and this bottle disappointing.

1954 ★★★★★   *November 1994*

Extraordinary colour, still strong red. A powerful, almost cabernet-like aroma, clean, with no sign of decay. On the palate rich and powerful, with those hallmark mint, berry and chocolate flavours, finishing with soft tannins. In wonderful condition; has power and length still.

1953 ★★★★★   *September 1999*

Amazing colour, still with predominantly red hues; in perfect condition, with sweet berry and more spicy/savoury notes giving great complexity to the bouquet. The palate is crammed full of supple, sweet, lingering cherry, blackberry and chocolate fruit, with a fantastic finish and aftertaste. The tannins are gone, but it doesn't matter a scrap. Consistent tasting notes over 25 years; utterly unique.

1952 ★★★★★   *November 1994*

Extraordinary colour for its age, still vibrant; a very complex bouquet with powerful red berry and chocolate flavours, rich and vibrant. The palate has wonderful red berry fruit flavours, hints of chocolate and tannins holding in perfect balance. An extremely long finish. Very nearly as freakish as the '53.

1951 ★★★   *November 1994*

The colour faded, the bouquet tired and faintly smoky. The palate, too, is pale and tired, not representative of what the wine might or should be. Two bottles opened in similar or worse condition.

◄ Not Ready   ◣ Still evolving   ▮ Prime of its life   ◢ Drink soon   ▯ Missed the boat

penfolds kalimna bin 28
shiraz 1971-1998

bin 28 was one of the undervalued jewels in the Penfolds' crown, but as the reputation of Australian Shiraz spread around the world in the latter part of the 1980s, Bin 28 received the recognition it long deserved. Indeed, in the 1991 International Wine challenge (held in London and the largest and most prestigious show in the English-speaking world) Bin 28 was named Red Wine of the Year thanks to the 1987 and 1988 vintages. It is ironical that — relatively speaking

— these should be two of the less exciting releases of recent vintages, which have gone from strength to strength.

The wine takes its name from, and was originally largely sourced from, Penfolds' Kalimna Vineyard, which it acquired from D & J Fowler in 1945, and which is the single most important source of premium quality grapes for Penfolds. While the 145 hectares of vines continue to provide an important part of Bin 28, it is today a multi-region blend sourced from the Barossa Valley, Clare Valley, McLaren Vale and Langhorne Creek, the respective contributions varying according to vintage conditions.

It is matured in second and third use American oak barrels passed down through the Grange, Bin 389 and similar programmes. But as Penfolds' chief winemaker John Duval points out, the principal emphasis is on the lush varietal fruit, providing a wine which does not demand prolonged cellaring — but which rewards those with patience.

All except the 1998 were tasted in September 1999 at the Penfolds Rewards of Patience tasting.

1998 ★★★★★   *February 2001*

Full red–purple; the smooth, dark cherry and spice fruit together with a touch of vanilla oak on the bouquet leads into a strongly structured and concentrated palate. Here dark berry, plum and some more savoury characters are bound up with lingering tannins; patience will be richly rewarded.

1997 ★★★★   *September 1999*

Medium red–purple; youthful plummy fruit with some earthy/charry notes on the bouquet introduces a pleasant, indeed pretty, wine which lacks the intensity of the '96 and won't go on forever, but by any other comparison is a good wine.

classic wines

★★★★★ Perfect   ★★★★☆ Close to perfect   ★★★★ Very good   ★★★☆ Expected
★★★ Short of standard   ★★☆ Undeserving   ★★ Decayed relic   NR No rating

1996 ★★★★★ *September 1999*

Medium to full purple–red; marvellous blackberry, dark cherry and plum fruit bursts through the bouquet and fruit-driven palate. Soft tannins are woven throughout, guaranteeing a 20-year life for this classic.

1995 ★★★★ *September 1999*

Medium purple–red; the bouquet is clean and smooth, with attractively ripe sweet plum fruit; the highlight of the palate is excellent, soft tannin structure which runs throughout the plum, chocolate and berry flavours. This was not a bad vintage for Shiraz in the Barossa Valley.

1994 ★★★★☆ *September 1999*

Medium to full red–purple; smooth, opulent plum and berry fruit with hints of more savoury/chocolatey characters run through to a most attractive palate, with plum, berry, leather and liquorice flavours all present, sustained by balanced tannins.

1993 ★★★☆ *September 1999*

Medium to full red; the bouquet shows riper aromas with chocolate and berry counterpoised against briar and earth. The palate veers more towards the sweet berry and plum spectrum, but has lingering tannins and some of the earthy undertones of the bouquet. All in all, somewhat schizophrenic.

1992 ★★★★★ *September 1999*

Excellent, youthful dark red, tinged with purple; the bouquet exudes dark cherry and vanilla fruit promising and duly delivering a velvety smooth, voluptuous and totally seductive palate. One of a number of wines which have developed exceptionally well since the Rewards of Patience tasting in 1992.

1991 ★★★★☆ *September 1999*

Medium to full red; expressive cherry and berry fruit aromas, with a touch of earth, lead into a wine which is complete in every sense; powerful fruit in a dark berry spectrum with lots of tannins that mark the palate which, while exuberant, is not over the top. Destined for a long life, and the rating may be churlish.

1990 ★★★★★ *September 1999*

Deep red tinged with purple, great colour. Luscious dark plum, cherry and vanilla aromas showing perfect fruit ripeness; the great depth and power of the fruit is the key to an outstanding wine; the tannins simply hold the fruit in place. There is every reason to suppose this wine will develop as well as the '71.

1989 ★★★☆ *September 1999*

Medium red; the bouquet has slightly stewy yet fragrant berry and mint fruit, the palate ripe, jammy, spicy berry fruit. All in all, fruit characters which will crumble quickly.

1988 ★★★★ *September 1999*

Medium to full red; the bouquet is more intense and weighty than expected, with solid, dark briar and berry fruit. The palate tracks the bouquet with savoury fruit characters; neatly balanced tannins to close.

1987 ★★★★
September 1999

Medium red; the bouquet seems to have freshened up, offering a subtle marriage of berry, mint and earth; an elegant, harmonious and well-balanced wine which has developed unexpectedly well, surprising for a cool vintage.

1986 ★★★★★
September 1999

Dark red; the bouquet is powerful with a mix of dark berry/briary/chocolate fruit and a touch of oak. The palate is powerful and concentrated, with lots of grip running through the middle to the finish. Has years in front of it.

1985 ★★★☆
September 1999

Medium red-brick; the bouquet is of light to moderate intensity, with slightly charry overtones to sweet cherry and chocolate fruit. The palate is pleasantly soft, but seems to have lightened off and developed rather quickly.

1984 ★★★
September 1999

Medium brick–red; the bouquet is clean, but not especially complex, with some plum and prune fruit lurking in the background. The palate lacks concentration, and, relatively speaking, is quite plain and weak.

1983 ★★★★☆
September 1999

Medium to full red, with a hint of brick; lots of ripe fruit ranging through plum, prune, earth and chocolate on the bouquet is followed by a palate with the depth and power of a warm vintage. Here sweet plum, prune, berry and mint flavours flood the mouth, and the tannins are softening, which is all to the good.

1982 ★★☆
September 1999

Medium red, with just a touch of brick; the bouquet shows very strong DMS fruit character distinctive of the vintage. The palate is light, and in a style which has never appealed to me, nor ever will.

1981 ★★★★☆
September 1999

Medium to full red-brick; the bouquet is concentrated and complex, with ripe fruit in the plum/berry/prune spectrum. A real mouthful, with abundant berry, chocolate and plum fruit backed by strong tannins. Just entering the peak of its development potential.

1980 ★★★☆
September 1999

Medium brick–red; the wine is lighter than the '79, and seems to have evolved very quickly over recent years. The palate is pleasant and smooth with a mix of dark berry, chocolate and earth, but, like the bouquet, is ageing quickly. Conceivably an unrepresentative bottle.

1979 ★★★
September 1999

Medium to full brick–red; the bouquet is quite striking, with a mix of charry/earthy/gamey/meaty aromas. There is lots happening on the palate, with some of the characters of the '77 evident, but the gamey finish is off-putting.

classic wines

★★★★★ Perfect	★★★★☆ Close to perfect	★★★★ Very good	★★★☆ Expected
★★★ Short of standard	★★☆ Undeserving	★★ Decayed relic	NR No rating

179

1978 ★★★   *September 1999*

The colour is more youthful, with red hues more dominant. The bouquet has gently sweet plum/prune/berry fruit, the oak, as always, subtle. The palate has similar fruit to that of the bouquet, but an astringent, green grip to the tannins mars the finish. Those tannins will certainly outlive the fruit.

1977 ★★★★☆   *September 1999*

Dark brick–red; there is a powerful attack on the bouquet with a mix of earth, liquorice and cigar aromas. The palate is stacked with personality, with the flavours replicating all the characters of the bouquet, and running through to a long finish. A major surprise completely at odds with the last Rewards of Patience tasting.

1976 ★★★   *September 1999*

Slightly darker brick–red colour, without the olive hues; the aroma shows obvious aged, secondary characters, with savoury earth and chocolate. The palate has slightly fresher mid-palate fruit, but then tannins come on the finish.

1975 ★★★★   *September 1999*

Brick–red; almost olive/mahogany. The bouquet is surprisingly powerful, with leathery Shiraz varietal character followed by a powerful and striking palate with a mix of caramel, chocolate and earth flavours. Fully mature, and full of character.

1971 ★★★★★   *September 1999*

Brick–red; a very complex bouquet with strongly bottle-developed chocolate, earth and vanilla aromas. On the palate, sweet, soft flavours coalesce into each other; with its silky texture the wine is still superb to drink now but must surely start its decline within the next five years.

◄━ Not Ready   ➘ Still evolving   ▮ Prime of its life   ⌀ Drink soon   ⎕ Missed the boat

penfolds koonunga hill shiraz
cabernet 1976-1999

most Australians have a degree of difficulty in facing up to the achievement of excellence. Whether one calls it knockabout humour or cultural cringe does not matter: it is deeply embedded in our national psyche. Thus to proclaim this wine as the greatest example in the world of a large-volume commercial red wine costing less than $15 does not come easily. Yet I believe it to be so.

It was first made in 1976; while it drew its name from a vineyard established in 1973 which provided part of the grapes, it also included components of Bin 28 and Bin 389. The white wine boom had caught everyone by surprise, and red wines were in surplus.

The resulting wine was an instant success, and so it should have been, for it was essentially made in the same way as its more illustrious brothers, yet sold for a fraction of the price. Since that time, production has increased tenfold: each vintage now occupies more than 4000 barrels. Yet the quality has been maintained, indeed improved, while the price (in real terms) has decreased.

In every way, it is a freakish wine. Handmade from premium area grapes not including riverlands sources, matured in real oak, bulk-bottled and binned, it is a wine of real substance, character and style. Most vintages improve for a decade, the best for 15 years or more, yet most of the wine is consumed within days of purchase, providing endless satisfaction at an almost derisory price.

All except the 1999 and 1998 were tasted at the Penfolds Rewards of Patience tasting in September 1999.

1999 ★★★★   *December 2000*

Medium red, with just a touch of purple; the bouquet is solid, with dark berry fruit and touches of chocolate and earth; the medium-bodied palate is well balanced; a supremely honest wine with skilled oak and tannin management in an average year.

1998 ★★★★☆   *October 2000*

Penfolds has zealously protected the quality of Koonunga Hill since its birth, though production has increased tenfold. The bouquet is complex, with blackberry, chocolate and subtle vanilla oak from genuine barrel maturation; the palate has the texture and mouthfeel lacking in many wines at this price point, rich and flavoursome.

classic wines

★★★★★ Perfect   ★★★★☆ Close to perfect   ★★★★ Very good   ★★★☆ Expected
★★★ Short of standard   ★★☆ Undeserving   ★★ Decayed relic   NR No rating

1997 ★★★★   *February 1999*

Medium to full red–purple; quite rich and ripe blackberry and chocolate fruit aromas with a hint of vanilla on the bouquet leads into a palate as honest as the day is long, with solid ripe fruit, good tannins and the barest touch of American oak. This is not a wine about sophistication or elegance, simply straightforward flavour.

1996 ★★★★★   *September 1999*

Medium to full red–purple; a weighty but clean bouquet with dark berry, cassis and plum fruit is followed by a palate which is literally oozing with fruit and class; here dark berry, plum and chocolate fruit flavours are balanced by substantial tannins. Should develop along the lines of the '90 vintage.

1995 ★★☆   *September 1999*

Medium red, with just a touch of purple. The palate has distinct fruit sweetness, with dark berry, liquorice and chocolate, but the palate comes as a major disappointment, with disjointed stewy fruit and quite harsh tannins. It is inherently improbable that time will cure the problems.

1994 ★★★★☆   *September 1999*

Medium red–purple; the bouquet opens with some faintly gamey characters, but then touches of spice and red berry come through. An elegant, medium-bodied wine with sweet berry fruit, a hint of chocolate, and quite firm tannins.

1993 ★★★★★   *September 1999*

Medium to full red–purple; the bouquet has ripe, concentrated briary/berry fruit with a hint of the hallmark chocolate. The palate is powerful, ripe and rich, with dark berry and dark chocolate flavours supported by balanced but quite pronounced tannins. A major surprise.

1992 ★★★★   *September 1999*

Medium red–purple; smooth cassis and redcurrant fruit, with the barest hint of more savoury/earthy characters. There is fresh, powerful blackcurrant and red berry fruit on the palate, but the tannins are a tad aggressive, and the wine needs more time.

1991 ★★★★★   *September 1999*

Medium red–purple; complex berry, cedary and faintly minty fruit of the bouquet is followed by a palate with excellent structure, flavour and balance, adding a touch of spice to the mix. Tannins run right through the palate without aggression; a very different style from the '90, but nonetheless first class.

1990 ★★★★★   *September 1999*

Medium to full red–purple, bright and clear, and outstanding for a ten-year-old wine. There is a glorious mix of cassis, dark berry, liquorice and leather on the bouquet. The wine floods the mouth with cascades of fruit, ripe and generous. What a wine, which, at the time of its release, sold for less than $10 a bottle.

1989 ★★★☆   *September 1999*

Medium to full red; the bouquet is quite fragrant with an interesting mix of tea-leaf and more jammy flavours. The unusual palate has more of that slightly jammy, stewy fruit, but is far from unpleasant. Many of these fruit characters are repeated across the spectrum of Penfolds red wines from the difficult 1989 vintage.

   ◀ Not Ready   ◥ Still evolving   ⬤ Prime of its life   ⬌ Drink soon   ⬚ Missed the boat

1988 ★★★
September 1999

Two bottles opened, neither totally convincing. Medium red; the bouquet is quite earthy and charry, with not a lot of fruit remaining, and quite aggressive. There is a little more berry fruit on the palate than the bouquet suggests, but tending leafy/savoury/gamey.

1987 ★★★★
September 1999

Medium red–brick; the bouquet is distinctly savoury, almost minerally, quite firm and showing a touch of oak. The palate is powerful and long, with good structure and some grip. A truly excellent outcome for a cool vintage.

1986 ★★★★☆
August 1993

Medium brick–red; the moderately intense bouquet has echoes of slightly charry/petrolly oak, but elegant fruit is there too. On the palate, relatively sweet chocolate characters have come up; the wine is showing far better than it did in the previous Rewards of Patience tasting.

1985 ★★★★
September 1999

Medium brick–red; the bouquet is surprisingly fragrant with some spice running through the sweet berry, chocolate and mint fruit. The palate, too, is lighter but with attractive, sweet chocolate and spice flavours, finishing with appropriately soft tannins.

1984 ★★★★
September 1999

Medium brick–red; the bouquet has a pleasant mix of berry, chocolate, leaf and mint aromas. The elegant palate has a similar mix of flavours, finishing with near-perfect tannins.

1983 ★★★★
September 1999

Medium to full brick–red. An attractive wine with aromas of cedar, cigar box and the inevitable chocolate. The palate is a throwback to the '76, rich, ripe and sweet, with lingering but not aggressive tannins.

1982 ★★★☆
September 1999

Medium brick–red; again, some hints of green, perhaps reflecting a move to more Cabernet Sauvignon in the blend. The palate, by contrast, is elegant, harmonious, and well balanced, with more fruit sweetness than evident on the bouquet.

1981 ★★★
September 1999

Medium brick–red. There is an unexpected touch of fruit astringency, perhaps due to vine stress in the face of the drought conditions of the vintage. Similar characters show through the palate.

1980 ★★★☆
September 1999

Medium to full brick–red. A powerful bouquet showing some stemmy characters. Given the overall style, relatively austere yet texturally smooth and well-balanced. Simply lacks generosity.

1979 ★★★★
September 1999

Slightly lighter colour; the bouquet is sweet and smooth with some berry fruit but less concentrated. A truly pleasant wine on the palate with lighter-bodied tannins; however, soft and well balanced.

classic wines

★★★★★ Perfect ★★★★☆ Close to perfect ★★★★ Very good ★★★☆ Expected
★★★ Short of standard ★★☆ Undeserving ★★ Decayed relic NR No rating

1978 ★★★★☆   *September1999*

Medium to full brick–red. The bouquet is rich and complex with distinct berry notes plus savoury touches plus chocolate. The palate opens with quite lively savoury fruit, but that hallmark chocolate sweetens the wine up.

1977 ★★★★★   *September 1999*

Medium to full brick–red; the aromas of the bouquet run more in a savoury/earthy spectrum, but have considerable character. The palate tracks the bouquet, but with added touches of chocolate, liquorice and berry. The maturity rating is designed to encourage those lucky enough to have it in their cellar to drink it sooner rather than later, rather than a statement about the wine as it is today.

1976 ★★★★★   *September 1999*

The glorious mature fruit of the bouquet is rich, sweet and ripe; likewise the abundant, rich and ripe fruit on the palate, with its touch of chocolate, and nuances of cedar and cigar box, is little short of amazing.

Not Ready   Still evolving   Prime of its life   Drink soon   Missed the boat

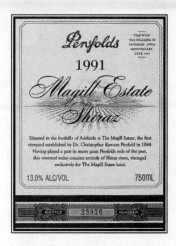

in some ways, this wine is the ultimate testimonial to the skills of the Penfolds winemaking team. Conceived in 1983, it deliberately runs counter to the mainstream of the company's red winemaking philosophy and techniques.

For a start, it is a single-vineyard wine, made from a single variety. True, that vineyard is one of the most historic in Australia. It marks the site of the birth of Penfolds in 1844 where Dr Christopher Rawson Penfold built his house (which survives marvellously intact) and planted his first vines. The 5.2-hectare vineyard which remains today is but a fragment of the 100 hectares which existed at the start of the 20th century, and the vines are not especially old, having been planted between 1951 and 1985. The hillside plantings are but a few minutes drive from the centre of Adelaide, the quality of the grapes beyond doubt, and the sense of history is palpable. So to devote the 50 tonnes of grapes to make around 3000 cases of Magill Estate makes eminent sense, even if outside the normal scope of Penfolds winemaking.

But it departs in another significant respect. It represents a conscious and wholly successful attempt to produce a far more elegant style; French, rather than American, oak, earlier picking, and cooler fermentation temperatures have been used to produce a wine which marches to the tune of a different drum, yet — tantalisingly — stays within the family. The corollary is Clos de Mesnil of Krug, at once different yet the same.

All except the 1998 were tasted in September 1999 at the Penfolds Rewards of Patience tasting.

1998 ★★★★★   *May 2001*

Strong purple–red; a warm, complex, highly scented bouquet of sweet berry/leather/liquorice/cedar and vanilla is a great opening stanza. The warmth of the bouquet flows through to the entry of the palate, layers of black fruits then unfolding, all supported by excellent use of oak and soft tannins. By far the best Magill Estate to date.

1997 ★★★★   *September 1999*

Medium to full red–purple; a highly scented bouquet with very ripe, juicy berry fruit characters. The palate has more of those juicy berry flavours together with a hint of mint. A good wine, but not great. 13.5 degrees alcohol.

classic wines

★★★★★ Perfect   ★★★★☆ Close to perfect   ★★★★ Very good   ★★★☆ Expected
★★★ Short of standard   ★★☆ Undeserving   ★★ Decayed relic   NR No rating

185

1996 ★★★★★   *September 1999*

Medium to full red–purple; stylish, perfectly ripened black cherry and plum fruit drives a sweetly harmonious bouquet. A wine with magnificent texture and structure on the palate with long, lingering satiny tannins on the finish. The oak is not the least bit assertive. 13.5 degrees alcohol.

1995 ★★★★☆   *September 1999*

Dense, dark red–purple, showing a massive colour shift. The bouquet is very rich, with plum, prune and chocolate aromas which are replicated on the palate. An amazing wine which once again emphasises that while 1995 may have been a poor vintage for the Limestone Coast Zone, and perhaps for Cabernet generally, it was a good year for Shiraz from Adelaide and north. 13.5 degrees alcohol.

1994 ★★★★★   *September 1999*

Medium to full red, with some purple tinges remaining. There are distinctly earthy/charry notes (predominantly ex-oak) over sweet, dark plum fruit. The wine really struts its stuff on the palate, with lovely, sweet, succulent plummy fruit; smooth and sensual. 13 degrees alcohol.

1993 ★★★★   *September 1999*

Medium to full red; ripe fruit with some pruney overtones running through subtly woven cedar and vanilla oak. The palate is ripe, full and fleshy with berry and vanilla flavours, followed by some tannin grip on the finish. 12 degrees alcohol.

1992 ★★★☆   *September 1999*

Medium to full red; the bouquet is quite savoury, with less obvious fruit (just a dash of plum) and lots of cedar/vanilla oak. The palate lacks the density of the better wines in the tasting, with light minty/leafy berry fruit and cedary oak. Drink soon; likely to continue its downward path at a fair clip. 13 degrees alcohol.

1991 ★★★★★   *September 1999*

Medium to full red; ripe, liquorice and plum-accented fruit with seamless oak on the bouquet. A rich, ripe mouthfilling wine with plum, sweet leather, spice and finishing with persistent, ripe tannins. 13 degrees alcohol.

1990 ★★★★★   *September 1999*

Medium to full red, quite developed. A complex bouquet interwoven with plum, cherry, liquorice, cedar and mint seamlessly married to the oak. Still very much on parade, with plum, black cherry and chocolate followed by soft, lingering tannins on the finish. Slightly disappointing given the vintage and the way the wine tasted five years ago. I have vacillated between 4.5 and five stars, finally opting for the latter, but without great conviction. 13.5 degrees alcohol.

1989 ★★★★   *September 1999*

Medium red with some brick hues on the rim. The bouquet has some of those slightly stewy, ripe fruit characters of the vintage but is undeniably generous. There is ripe prune and plum fruit on the forepalate, with a slight dip in the middle before tannins come on the finish. Has lost the Rhône Valley spice it had when younger. 12.5 degrees alcohol.

1988 ★★★★★   *September 1999*

Medium to full red; a clean, sweet plum, cherry and mint bouquet; as with all the wines, the oak is subtle. The palate has by far the sweetest fruit of the older brigade, with lovely soft, dark plum and touches of liquorice and chocolate. 12 degrees alcohol.

1987 ★★★★   *September 1999*

Medium to full red–brick; quite ripe and sweet with a mix of berry, chocolate and leather. The palate offers a quite attractive array of cedary/leathery/berry fruit with an overall impression of sweetness before moving into a tannic finish. Has some time on its side. 12 degrees alcohol.

1986 ★★★★   *September 1999*

Medium to full red; a quite elegant plum and cherry bouquet, complexed with some cedary notes. Undoubtedly the elegant style being looked for at the time, but it is noticeable how rapidly the luscious fruit of five years ago has faded. Still a good wine, but should be drunk by 2003. 11.5 degrees alcohol.

1985 ★★★★   *September 1999*

Much deeper colour, with red rather than brick hues. The bouquet has ripe, dark berry and chocolate fruit supported by smoky oak. The palate has soft plummy/chocolatey fruit starting to show signs of dipping; the tannins, too, are softening (which is a good thing). 11.7 degrees alcohol.

1984 ★★★   *September 1999*

Light to medium brick; some slightly soapy/gamey aromas on the leafy, cedary bouquet. On the palate there is leaf, mint and some caramel, the fruit of youth almost entirely dissipated. 12.5 degrees alcohol.

1983 ★★★   *September 1999*

Light to medium brick–red; the bouquet is light, with some cedary elegance, but also some very advanced earthy/woody aromas. The palate is likewise fully developed, having well and truly passed its best. Has shown disconcertingly rapid development over the last five years. 12.2 degrees alcohol.

penfolds special bin show reds
1956-1996

It is right and proper that Grange should be regarded around the world as Penfolds' — and Australia's — greatest red wine. But on and off since 1962 Penfolds has produced individual wines which the chosen few who drink them recognise as being significantly better than Grange.

The forerunners made in the 1950s were experimental wines which explored other varieties and areas — a 1960 blend of Cabernet and Mataro was one of the more arcane. When Penfolds re-entered the show ring in 1962, the focus shifted to wines of special quality, and in that year Max Schubert vintaged what many regard as Australia's

greatest red wine of the past 40 years or so: 1962 Bin 60A, a blend of two-thirds Coonawarra Cabernet Sauvignon and one-third Kalimna Shiraz.

In 1963, a string of Bins (Bin 61, 62, 63 and 64) were made, Bin 61 being quite magnificent. In 1966 Bin 620 — a Cabernet Shiraz entirely from Coonawarra — was made, but the following year Bin 7 reverted to the Coonawarra–Kalimna blend, and was followed by 1980 Bin 80A and 1990 Bin 90A, truly magnificent wines. More recently the Kalimna Block 42 Cabernet Sauvignon, made from 100-year-old vines, has joined this unique band.

All were tasted in September 1999 at the Penfolds Rewards of Patience tasting.

◀ **1996 Block 42 Kalimna Cabernet Sauvignon ★★★★★**
September 1999   Medium to full red–purple; a paradigm of everything Cabernet Sauvignon should be: the fragrant cassis/redcurrant fruit and perfect oak integration of the bouquet is followed by an intensely flavoured yet elegant wine on a very long palate flooded with cassis and redcurrant fruit, and crowned with fine tannins on the finish.

◀ **1993 Cellar Reserve Cabernet Shiraz ★★★★☆**   September 1999
Dense red–purple; very rich, ripe and concentrated cassis and prune fruit aromas are followed by a similarly dense and concentrated palate. Perhaps it lacks a little of the finesse of the other great wines, but still a monument and may well merit five stars as it begins to approach maturity around 2015.

◀ **1990 Bin 920 Coonawarra Cabernet Shiraz ★★★★★**
September 1999   Deep red–purple; there is fragrant, sweet fruit, an essence of cassis and plum on the bouquet, balanced with subtle oak. A massive wine with layer upon layer upon layer of flavour in the mouth. Nowhere near ready to drink; exceptional concentration. Leave until 2020.

◀ Not Ready   ＼ Still evolving   ▮ Prime of its life   ⟋ Drink soon   ▯ Missed the boat

1990 Bin 90A Coonawarra Cabernet/Barossa Valley Shiraz

★★★★★ *September 1999* Deep purple– red; glorious cassis raspberry fragrance to the bouquet; the palate has fantastic complexity with layers of fruit, tannin and oak welded together into a balanced and harmonious whole. A truly great classic, to be left until 2010.

1982 Bin 820 Coonawarra Cabernet Shiraz ★★★★

September 1999 Medium to full red; a faint touch of dimethyl sulphide which, however, actually adds to the complexity of the wine's bouquet. That character, however, is far more obvious on the palate, and is not to my personal taste. Others will be more forgiving.

1980 Bin 80A Coonawarra Cabernet/Kalimna Shiraz

★★★★★ *September 1999* Medium to full red–purple; a wonderfully elegant and fragrant bouquet with fine and pure cassis/berry aromas balanced by fine, cedary oak. The palate is perfection, with cascades of cassis fruit running through to a long, lingering, supple finish.

1973 Bin 170 Kalimna Shiraz ★★★★★   *September 1999*

Medium to full red–purple; an extraordinary wine with a marvellous array of liquorice, cherry and spice recalling high-quality northern Rhône wines; much better than the '73 Grange. The palate lives up to the bouquet with great texture, and all of the flavours of the bouquet, framed by lovely tannins.

1973 Bin 169 Coonawarra Claret– ★★★★   *September 1999*

Strong red–purple; for once the bouquet does not pierce the senses, with slightly baggy, green canopy characters. There is powerful cassis berry fruit on entry to the mouth followed by grippy tannins on the finish; confirms the suspicions about the bouquet, but in any other context the wine would no doubt shine.

1967 Bin 7 Coonawarra Cabernet/Kalimna Shiraz ★★★★★

September 1999 Medium red–purple; an ethereal, lifted fragrance wafts from the glass giving a sense of ripe plums, cassis and cedar. Again, that silken texture shot through with the rippling flavours promised by the bouquet and sustained through to a long finish.

1966 Bin 620 Coonawarra Cabernet Shiraz ★★★★☆

September 1999 Medium red–purple; a fine, elegant, restrained savoury berry/earthy bouquet very typical of mature Coonawarra Cabernet Sauvignon. A lighter style on the palate, elegant, even a touch of austerity; classic Claret style. It is a wine which does show considerable variation, with some bottles quite abrasive. This was a good one.

1963 Bin 64 Kalimna Cabernet ★★★★★   *September 1999*

Deep, vibrant red. The bouquet is flooded with voluptuously rich and ripe essence of cassis and a wholly acceptable twist of volatility. The palate has very ripe cassis moving into notes of plum and prune; a staggering mouthful which, consistently with its sister wines from 1963, does show some volatility on the finish. The first Jimmy Watson Trophy winner.

★★★★★ Perfect   ★★★★☆ Close to perfect   ★★★★ Very good   ★★★☆ Expected
★★★ Short of standard   ★★☆ Undeserving   ★★ Decayed relic   NR No rating

1962 Bin 60 Kalimna Shiraz/ Coonawarra Cabernet ★★★★★ *September 1999*

Medium to full red; there is great aromatic complexity to the bouquet, showing pristine Cabernet and a spicy twist from the Shiraz component. The palate has extraordinarily fresh, youthful fruit, yet paradoxically is marvellously elegant. A fruit-driven wine with a very long finish and soft tannins. A sister to the famous Bin 60A, simply with more Cabernet Sauvignon and less Shiraz, but otherwise identical.

1962 Bin 60A Coonawarra Cabernet Kalimna Shiraz ★★★★★ *September 1999*

Medium to full red; you can lose yourself in the depth of this wine which has that magical complexity of aromas which almost defy description. The palate has a glorious silken texture, with the flavours shining like a hologram. Arguably the greatest Australian red wine made in the twentieth century.

1961 Bin 58 Kalimna Cabernet ★★★★★ *September 1999*

Exceptionally good colour for a wine of its age, still full red. A fantastic bouquet, with rich cassis berry, full of life and, it must be admitted, a touch of volatility which in no way impairs enjoyment of the wine. The palate delivers all that the bouquet promises with perfectly ripened classic cabernet sauvignon. While obviously mature, has an indefinite future if the cork holds and the wine is well cellared.

1956 Bin 136 Magill Burgundy (Shiraz) ★★★★★ *September 1999*

Medium brick–red, tinged with mahogany; soft, sweet, earthy shiraz varietal fruit aromas with a whisper of chocolate fill the bouquet which is still holding well. Sweet cherry flavours mark the entry to the mouth, followed by a marvellous twist of spice and liquorice on the finish.

━ Not Ready   ❯ Still evolving   ♦ Prime of its life   ✎ Drink soon   ▯ Missed the boat

When the late John Davoren made the first vintage of St Henri in 1956 he took a path diametrically opposed to that chosen by Max Schubert for Grange. Instead of defying convention, Davoren followed it. To this day, indeed, St Henri remains a conventional proving the virtue of honesty. It is appropriate that the label should have been a copy of one which had been in use around the turn of the twentieth century.

Davoren's idea was to make a wine which would be of similar quality to Grange, but which employed conventional winemaking techniques, relying largely on the integrity of the shiraz which forms the core of the wine. It is matured for 18 months in old 2000-litre casks and used hogsheads, which play an important role in shaping the texture and structure of the wine but which impart only the slightest nuance of oak flavour.

The vineyard source has shifted from Auldana (which is no more) to the full spectrum of South Australia's best regions: shiraz from the Barossa Valley, McLaren Vale, Clare Valley, Langhorne Creek and Eden Valley; and a variable but small percentage of cabernet sauvignon from Coonawarra and the Barossa Valley.

Over the years, I have participated in four major vertical tastings of St Henri, all of which lead to the conclusion the majority of the wines made prior to 1986 have become austere and astringent. Since then, and particularly with the 1990 and subsequent vintages, there has been significant change for the better.

All were tasted in September 1999 at the Penfolds Rewards of Patience tasting.

1997 ★★★★   *September 1999*

Medium red–purple; youthful with that moderately intense, fragrant, juicy berry fruit of the vintage is followed by a palate also typical of the year, medium bodied, with chocolate/savoury/berry flavours and light tannins. Should develop reasonably quickly from this point on.

1996 ★★★★★   *September 1999*

Medium to full red–purple; a piquantly ripe and fragrant bouquet, crammed with prune, plum and berry fruit leads seamlessly into a juicy, fruit-driven palate loaded with blackcurrant, prune and plum fruit, finishing with plush, soft tannins on the lingering finish.

1995 ★★★☆   *September 1999*

Medium red–purple; the sweet bouquet has a mix of blackcurrant, plum and mint fruit which swells out on the sweet mid-palate, but then softens noticeably on a slightly short finish. Possibly an unrepresentative bottle.

classic wines

★★★★★ Perfect   ★★★★☆ Close to perfect   ★★★★ Very good   ★★★☆ Expected
★★★ Short of standard   ★★☆ Undeserving   ★★ Decayed relic   NR No rating

1994 ★★★★★   *September 1999*

Medium to full red–purple; the bouquet is rich and dense, with strong chocolate, liquorice, blackberry and mint aromas. Yet another power-packed, racy 1994 wine which has really come into its own over the past few years. Masses of blackberry, prune, chocolate and minty fruit run through to a long finish.

1993 ★★★★   *September 1999*

Medium red–purple; clean, quite sweet blackberry, plum and mint fruit on the bouquet lead into a relatively light yet quite fleshy palate, which is delicious now but does not appear to have the structure for prolonged cellaring, contrary to the impression the wine gave when first released.

1992 ★★★   *September 1999*

Light to medium red–purple; the earthy/savoury bouquet signals a momentary return to the style of the past, although there is more sweetness to the fruit on the mid-palate, before gritty tannins reimpose themselves on the finish.

1991 ★★★★☆   *September 1999*

Medium to full red–purple; the bouquet is powerful, but has less fruit expression than the 1990 with slightly charry overtones. The wine opens up on the palate, with rich, full chocolate/plum/blackberry/cherry flavours and well-balanced tannins.

1990 ★★★★★   *September 1999*

Medium to full red–purple; the bouquet is rich, with smooth, ripe plum and blackberry fruit underpinned by an attractive hint of spice. The palate manages to be at once intense yet elegant and understated, with the structure to guarantee a long life.

1989 ★★★☆   *September 1999*

Medium red, with some purple hues remaining; extremely ripe dried prune/plum/ liquorice aromas are repeated on the opulent prune, plum and spice-flavoured palate; the softness of the structure and acidity point to immediate drinking.

1988 ★★★★☆   *September 1999*

Medium red–purple; a clean, smooth and relatively sweet minty/blackberry bouquet is followed by what can only be called an elegant and civilised palate, now at its peak.

1987 ★★★★   *September 1999*

Medium to full red; the clean bouquet has evolved very well over the past six years, with pleasantly ripe, sweet plummy fruit, the palate, likewise, showing unexpected sweetness on the middle, before drying out fractionally on the finish. Will never be better than it is now.

1986 ★★★★☆   *September 1999*

Medium red; a powerful wine in all respects, with a mix of sweet, blackberry/liquorice and more earthy/savoury characters on the bouquet. The palate has more of the blackberry fruit of the bouquet with a touch of chocolate; the once-formidable tannins have softened and come into balance.

◄ Not Ready   ❧ Still evolving   ❦ Prime of its life   ✆ Drink soon   ⬓ Missed the boat

1985 ★★★☆   *September 1999*

Medium red; the bouquet is clean with some sweet plum, prune and mint fruit, the palate retaining some of the same sweet fruit but giving signs it won't hold out for much longer.

1984 ★★★   *September 1999*

Medium tawny-red; a light, leafy bouquet lacks sweetness, but is clean. The palate doesn't have a great deal of character, but the balance is pleasant, and the wine seems to have regained a second wind.

1983 ★★★☆   *September 1999*

Medium red; a complex bouquet with ripe fruit under a dash of lemon; the palate, likewise, has some of the same sweet and sour flavours, but has undeniable flavour and has supple, rather than astringent, tannins.

1982 ★★   *September 1999*

Medium red, with just a touch of tawny; the aromas are quite fresh, ranging through earth, leaf and mint; there is more of the same on the palate, which seems to have become more green and astringent with dimethyl sulphide more evident, over the past few years, and is fading quickly.

1981 ★★★★   *September 1999*

Medium red–tawny; like the 1971, a controversial wine with some dimethyl suphide characters. If you accept these, this is one of the best of the middle–aged St Henris. It is not a wine I would personally choose, but I recognise its strong points.

1980 ★★★   *September 1999*

Medium red–tawny; the bouquet is clean, quite fragrant, with hints of berry; while the flavours are in the herbaceous spectrum, the palate is reasonably well structured and balanced, and still holding on (just).

1979 ★★☆   *September 1999*

Medium tawny–red; fairly typical earth, cedar and tobacco aromas are followed by a rather earthy, astringent palate which is now well past its best.

1978 ★★★☆   *September 1999*

Light to medium red–tawny; the bouquet has some lift to the stemmy/leafy/earthy aromas, but the wine takes a distinct turn for the better on the palate, with pleasant earth, chocolate and mocha flavours, finishing with soft tannins.

1977 ★★★   *September 1999*

Dull, blackish red, with earthy/hessiany aromas, and a mix of earth, chocolate and hessian on the palate.

1976 ★★★★   *September 1999*

Dark red; intense, complex gamey/chocolatey/liquorice aromas are followed by an extremely concentrated and powerful palate, with the austere tannins providing a steel backbone. Like full-bodied Italian red wines, should be great with food, but is hard going on its own.

★★★★★ Perfect   ★★★★☆ Close to perfect   ★★★★ Very good   ★★★☆ Expected
★★★ Short of standard   ★★☆ Undeserving   ★★ Decayed relic   NR No rating

classic wines

193

1975 ★★☆   *September 1999*
Brick–red, with hints of brown; coffee, chocolate and earth aromas also provide the mid-palate flavours of chocolate and berry, but then tough, astringent tannins dry out the finish.

1974 ★★★   *September 1999*
Medium red–tawny; the bouquet has quite sweet chocolate aromas, amazing for the worst vintage in living memory in South Australia. There are ultra-ripe stewed/dried prune flavours on the palate which, once again, are an unexpected outcome for a vintage ruined by downy mildew.

1973 ★★☆   *September 1999*
Medium red–tawny; dried leaf/compost/hay aromas are followed by a very astringent palate. Either the wine has completely cracked up, or was a tainted bottle.

1972 ★★★   *September 1999*
Dark red; the bouquet seems to have some of the crushed green, grape-stem characters of the 1971, with sweet and sour fruit flavours on the mid-palate before dry tannins close up the finish.

1971 ★★★★   *September 1999*
Medium to full red, with a hint of brick; a pungent and assertive bouquet with some stemmy overtones to plum and liquorice fruit. An extremely controversial wine on the palate, powerful and complex, but with an underlying hint of green austerity. From a great vintage year for Penfolds, and most other tasters rate the wine more highly than I do.

1970 ★★☆   *September 1999*
Tawny–brick; a very earthy bouquet with notes of leather and tobacco is followed by a palate dominated by rather dry and bitter tannins, tannins which outgun the remnants of sweet fruit on the mid-palate.

1969 ★★   *September 1999*
Tawny–brick colour; most unusual crushed leaf/coriander aromas are followed by a palate which provides a truly wild ride, with high volatile acidity and acid.

1968 ★★★★   *September 1999*
Tawny–brick–red; while the aromatics of the bouquet are all in the secondary phase of their development, ranging through cedar, tobacco and coffee, both the bouquet and the palate have quite surprising sweetness in a chocolate/coffee spectrum.

1967 ★★★   *September 1999*
Brick–red; fragrant coffee and mocha aromas with touches of cedar and tobacco are a promising opening, but rather earthy/charry flavours on the palate take away from the attraction of the plum pudding flavours.

1966 ★★★★☆   *September 1999*
Medium to full tawny–red; a solid and rich bouquet offers a mix of dark, bitter chocolate and mint, with just a touch of volatile lift. The palate has good balance and structure, with abundant chocolate and berry fruit, and a pleasing sweetness on the finish and aftertaste augmented by gently chewy tannins.

◄— Not Ready   ＼ Still evolving   ▮ Prime of its life   ✒ Drink soon   ∪ Missed the boat

1965 ★★★
September 1999

Medium tawny–red; there is a distinct lift of volatility which doesn't, however, totally spoil the bouquet; that volatility lifts the chocolate, cedar and leather flavours of the palate, but is rather intrusive.

1964 ★★☆
September 1999

Medium tawny, almost no red; an earthy, leathery, somewhat astringent bouquet; the mid-palate has dried out, and the wine is way past its best.

1963 ★★★★
September 1999

Medium tawny–red; the bouquet is right in the mainstream of the style, with earthy/mushroomy austerity and a touch of cedar. The palate is altogether more appealing, with chocolate, cedar, earth and Marmite flavours.

1962 ★★★☆
September 1999

Medium tawny–red; the bouquet is substantial, but again showing that slight austerity to the fruit which is clearly part of the style, yet avoids being green or mean. The palate likewise shows a mix of chocolate and earthy austerity; a cerebral wine.

1961 ★★★★★
September 1999

Medium to full tawny–red; a firm and complex bouquet with a mix of austere fruit and sweeter, truffle aromas. A most attractive palate, with a core of chocolate wrapped within more savoury characters, and a long finish.

1960

Not tasted.

1959 ★★★
September 1999

Medium tawny–red; earthy astringency and some oxidation on the bouquet are followed by a palate with strong roast coffee and more earthy flavours, and a slightly sharp finish.

1958 ★★★★☆
September 1999

Medium tawny–red; a fragrant bouquet with sweet cedary/earthy aromas, and no hint of astringency. Remarkably together on the mid-palate, still quite smooth with sweet fruit with leathery overtones; fades slightly on the finish.

1957

Not tasted. The first commercial vintage following an experimental vintage in 1956.

classic wines

★★★★★ Perfect   ★★★★☆ Close to perfect   ★★★★ Very good   ★★★☆ Expected
★★★ Short of standard   ★★☆ Undeserving   ★★ Decayed relic   NR No rating

195

Unlike the other wines in the Petaluma portfolio, which have all had a regional, indeed specific vineyard, base since inception, the Chardonnay has reflected a vinous odyssey by Brian Croser around Australia. Specific details of the regional source of each wine are given with the tasting note of each vintage, but there has been a gradual progression from 100 per cent Cowra (New South Wales) to 100 per cent Piccadilly Valley (South Australia).

PETALUMA

1994 CHARDONNAY

750ml
PRODUCE OF AUSTRALIA BOTTLED AT PICCADILLY SA

Given these wanderings, the style of the wine has remained remarkably consistent over the years. It would be idle to suggest that Brian Croser was able to conjure up something entirely magical from the pre-Piccadilly Valley fruit sources, or that the wines have the secret of eternal youth. The lesson from all but one or two producers (Leeuwin Estate is the most obvious example) is that the older generation Chardonnays cannot compete with their younger siblings.

The obvious question is whether we will be saying the same thing in another ten years of the present-day wines. The answer is yes; for one thing, many of the Piccadilly Valley vineyards are still relatively young. For another, makers are still going through a sharp winemaking learning curve.

What is more, Brian Croser has kept a balance with this wine, resisting the temptation to puff it up yet not unduly retard its development. The main change has been the introduction of the ultra-premium Tiers Chardonnay, sourced from the best blocks in Petaluma's ownership.

(Petaluma's own assessment given in brackets at the end of each note up to 1992.)

First tasted in November 1994, updated, and later vintages added.

1998 ★★★★   *October 1999*
Light to medium green–yellow; a clean, finely balanced bouquet with nectarine, fig, a touch of cashew and a hint of mineral all present. A refined style, with gentle creamy/cashew flavours and subtle oak. Delicate and understated; will develop.

1997 ★★★★   *November 1998*
Very light green–yellow; an extremely delicate, unevolved and faintly minerally bouquet is followed by a delicate, crisp apple and melon-accent palate which needs some years to open and build. As it does, will doubtless rate higher points.

1996 ★★★★★   *November 1997*
Spotlessly clean, it ripples with a marvellous array of fruit aromas and flavours ranging from stony-minerally through citrus-grapefruit to tropical, yet retains exceptional finesse and elegance.

Not Ready   Still evolving   Prime of its life   Drink soon   Missed the boat

1995 ★★★★★ *October 1996*

Medium yellow–green; clearly one of the best ever Petaluma Chardonnays, if not the best; the bouquet is stylish and elegant with gentle nutmeg/spice oak woven through ripe fig, pear and peach fruit. The palate is long, restrained and elegant yet intense; the fruit flavours track those of the bouquet, with similar spicy nutmeg oak wafting in the background. Excellent fruit/acid balance.

1994 ★★★★★ *October 1995*

Brilliant green–yellow; a fresh bouquet with discrete melon and fig fruit and marvellously subtle but evident spicy oak. The palate is lively, with melon, fig and a touch of citrus; one can see a touch of the malolactic influence, but not aggressively so; the oak influence, too, is restrained. Harmonious and classy.

1993 ★★★★☆ *January 1995*

Medium to full yellow–green; a complex array of aromas with almost honeyed/meady fruit, spicy nutmeg oak and some creamier notes from the malolactic-ferment component. The palate is very textured, with grilled nut, melon and fig flavours interwoven, again with the contribution of the malolactic component quite evident.

1992 ★★★★★ *November 1994*

Light to medium green–yellow; similar in style to the '90, with very elegant melon fruit and subtly integrated and balanced spicy, nutmeg oak. A long palate with melon fruit predominating, a subliminal hint of malolactic fermentation structure, and fine, spicy French oak in the background. 100 per cent Piccadilly Valley. (7/7)

1991 ★★★★☆ *November 1994*

Bright light to medium green–yellow; seemingly more restrained oak than the '90, and perhaps not with the same full fruit power, but elegant. The palate works well and has length; it seems to have been relatively early picked to combat the warm vintage, but is well constructed. 100 per cent Piccadilly Valley. (6/7)

1990 ★★★★★ *November 1994*

Glowing yellow–green; highly aromatic melon and fig fruit with wonderful nutmeg and spice oak woven throughout. The palate shows a radically different fruit structure and flavour from the older wines in the line-up, with a very long, fine flavour in the melon spectrum with perfect oak balance and integration. 100 per cent Piccadilly Valley. (7/7)

1989 ★★★☆ *November 1994*

Full yellow, showing distinct colour change to the younger wines. There are rather dusty, almost marmalade-like characters on the bouquet which seems to be showing signs of drying out. The palate, too, is showing accelerated development; the wine should be drunk soon. 60 per cent Piccadilly Valley, 40 per cent Clare Valley. (6/7)

1988 ★★★☆ *November 1994*

Deep yellow; a soft, ripe butterscotch, nutty/buttery bouquet which is quite advanced. A pleasant, mouthfilling wine on the palate which does not seem to have a prolonged future. 50 per cent Clare Valley, 50 per cent Piccadilly Valley. (5/7)

classic wines

★★★★★ Perfect	★★★★☆ Close to perfect	★★★★ Very good	★★★☆ Expected
★★★ Short of standard	★★☆ Undeserving	★★ Decayed relic	NR No rating

1987 ★★★★   *November 1994*

Medium yellow–green; a clean, smooth bouquet with well-balanced and integrated oak, and quite discrete fruit. The palate is complex, with good structure and length; there are citrus and melon flavours on the back palate, finishing with good acidity and just a touch of oak. 50 per cent Clare Valley, 50 per cent Piccadilly Valley. (5/7)

1986 ★★★☆   *November 1994*

Deep yellow; a soft, attractive, peachy bouquet showing attractive development. The palate is soft and round in the mouth, with very rich and ripe peach and butter fruit flavours. 40 per cent Coonawarra, 20 per cent Clare Valley, 20 per cent Piccadilly Valley. (4/7)

1985 ★★★   *November 1994*

Medium to full yellow–green; smooth, rounded, gently sweet white peach fruit but disfigured by a hint of green oak. The palate is elegant, in a lighter style with disappointing oak, quite different from that of the younger vintages. 45 per cent Coonawarra, 45 per cent Clare Valley, 10 per cent Piccadilly Valley. (3/7)

1984 ★★★   *November 1994*

Full yellow; a strange, rather dusty/watery aroma, again with some green oak overtones. The palate shows fine base material rather let down by indifferent oak; a pity; might have been very interesting. 50 per cent Coonawarra, 50 per cent Clare Valley. (3/7)

1983 ★★☆   *November 1994*

Deep yellow; aged, very ripe slightly burnt toffee/marmalade aromas on the bouquet; the palate is drying out and clearly past its best. 80 per cent Coonawarra, 20 per cent Clare Valley. (2/7)

1982 ★★★   *November 1994*

Glowing yellow–green; the bouquet shows some of the characters of the '78 vintage, with French-accented complexity. A complex but strange wine on the palate, uncharacteristic for Petaluma, with some French/hot solids characters. 70 per cent Coonawarra, 30 per cent Cowra. (4/7)

1981 ★★★☆   *November 1994*

Medium to full yellow; rich, ripe and full peachy/buttery aromas in archetypal Australian style. There is good fruit and complexity on the palate, with fig, melon and yellow clingstone peach all there. A success for the vintage. 50 per cent Cowra, 50 per cent Coonawarra. (3/7)

1980 ★★★   *November 1994*

Deep yellow–green; there is some lift to the bouquet with solid, peachy fruit. A nice wine with the palate, smooth, with plenty of peachy flavour in ripe traditional style; not particularly complex. 80 per cent Cowra, 20 per cent Coonawarra. (3/7)

1979 ★★☆   *November 1994*

Medium yellow–green; tending rather plain and simple, with sweet fruit and a hint of volatility. The palate shows fairly pronounced lift, with plenty of soft peachy flavour. 100 per cent Cowra. (3/7)

◄ Not Ready   ◣ Still evolving   ◗ Prime of its life   ◢ Drink soon   ⬜ Missed the boat

1978 ★★☆   *November 1994*

Medium to full yellow; smelly French sulphides/hot solids, the works. A totally aberrational wine on the palate which some will like better than I do. 100 per cent Cowra. (3/7)

1977 ★★★★   *November 1994*

Medium yellow–green; complex yet fresh with fruit and oak components both there. The palate still shows attractive ripe peachy fruit and vanillin oak; holding well. 100 per cent Cowra. (3/7)

★★★★★ Perfect   ★★★★☆ Close to perfect   ★★★★ Very good   ★★★☆ Expected
★★★ Short of standard   ★★☆ Undeserving   ★★ Decayed relic   NR No rating

petaluma coonawarra

PETALUMA

1993 COONAWARRA

750ml

PRODUCE OF AUSTRALIA BOTTLED AT PICCADILLY SA

the make-up — and the making — of the Cabernet Sauvignon-dominant Petaluma Coonawarra has evolved over the years. Up to 1982 Shiraz made varying contributions to the blend, but from 1984 onwards was displaced by Merlot. Initially the Merlot came from the Evans Vineyard, but since 1990 Merlot from the Sharefarmers Vineyard (together with some Cabernet from the same vineyard) has been used in making the wine. Thus, depending on the outcome of the seeming endless dispute regarding the boundaries of Coonawarra, there may be profound implications for the name of the wine.

The change in the varietal base, and the sourcing of the grapes, has been accompanied by a reduction in crop levels and an ongoing quest for fruit with full sensory ripeness. Leaf plucking has replaced the innovative aluminium-foil strips laid under the vines, and increasing attention has been paid to the ripeness of the seeds.

Apart from a brief and totally unsuccessful flirtation with a zero sulphur dioxide régime (in 1984 and 1985) there have only been fine-tuning changes to the making of the wine. It is fermented at moderate temperatures and is matured for two years in predominantly new Nevers oak barriques held in cooled barrel storage sheds. There are no tannin additions, there is no juice run off, the wine is only lightly fined, and it is not filtered. Further political correctness is ensured by the fact that there is no irrigation, and acid additions are required only one year in three.

With the exception of the 1979, the wines made before 1986 have failed to age satisfactorily, particularly given the high standards Petaluma sets for itself (and its customers expect). However, from that point on you see the real Petaluma.

All except the 1999 were tasted in April 2000.

1999 ★★★★☆ *June 2001*

Medium to full red–purple; even by the standards of Petaluma, a particularly complex bouquet of blackberry and plum fruit with outstanding oak balance and integration. The palate is very concentrated, with quite surprising tannins enfolding the core of sweet fruit; demands patience.

1998 ★★★★★ *April 2000*

Very youthful purple–red; sweet, smooth and luscious cassis/blackberry/plum fruit together with subtle oak on the bouquet leads into a medium to full-bodied palate, very concentrated yet perfectly balanced, with cassis and chocolate flavours supported by ripe, soft, yet persistent, tannins. Without any question, the best Petaluma Coonawarra so far.

◀ Not Ready ⟋ Still evolving ⟊ Prime of its life ⟍ Drink soon ⟎ Missed the boat

1997 ★★★★★ *April 2000*

Medium to full purple–red, much brighter than the '96. The bouquet is spotlessly clean and youthful, with surprisingly ripe plum and cassis fruit. The same sweet, ripe plum/cassis/berry fruit on the palate gains structure from the fine-grained tannins which run throughout.

1996 ★★★★☆ *April 2000*

Medium purple–red; the bouquet is quite lifted, with a mix of spice, berry, leaf and mint aromas. An attractive and well-balanced medium-bodied wine with supple, spicy fruit which will mature relatively quickly, and is already fully accessible.

1995 ★★★★★ *April 2000*

Medium to full purple–red; the bouquet is intense and rich, very classic Petaluma, with a mix of blackberry, cassis and earth. Mouthfilling, complex and rich, with tannins running through the length of the wine, and a lovely web of spice and vanilla oak.

1994 ★★★★★ *April 2000*

Medium to full purple–red; a very interesting bouquet, initially showing aromas of shoe leather and spice, then unlocking intense blackberry fruit aromas. Mouthfilling and rich on entry, concentrated and tight, then moves into a more austere finish.

1993 ★★★★☆ *April 2000*

Medium purple–red; intense aromas of spice, cedar and cassis are welded together, aided by stylish oak. A powerful wine in the mouth, initially showing fruit and spice, then with tannins which appear to be intensifying rather than diminishing as the wine ages, but I am certain this is simply a phase in development.

1992 ★★★★★ *April 2000*

Medium purple–red; a great bouquet, which evolved and changed considerably as the wine sat in the glass, with very pure blackcurrant primary fruit and some more spicy earthy characters underneath. A powerful palate, with tannins running right through its length; cedar and bitter chocolate join the blackcurrant fruit.

1991 ★★★★☆ *April 2000*

Medium red–purple; the bouquet is quite fragrant, with a mix of spice, blackcurrant and plum, and secondary earth and cedar notes starting to appear. The palate is rich, ripe and sweet with a mix of chocolate and blackcurrant fruit finishing with fine-grained tannins. Delicious now.

1990 ★★★★★ *April 2000*

Excellent, strong purple–red colour; wonderful berry/cassis fruit aromas are still in full flower, almost verging on liquorice. The palate has a level of concentration and richness way beyond any of the older wines; outstanding though the wine may be now, it has an almost indefinite cellaring future.

1989

Not made.

classic wines

★★★★★ Perfect   ★★★★☆ Close to perfect   ★★★★ Very good   ★★★☆ Expected
★★★ Short of standard   ★★☆ Undeserving   ★★ Decayed relic   NR No rating

1988 ★★★★☆ *April 2000*

Medium to full red–purple; berry, spice, cedar and a touch of sweet leather provide savoury overtones to the bouquet. The palate has ripe, plummy/blackcurrant fruit, finishing with soft tannins. The oak has entirely integrated over the past six years.

1987 ★★★ *April 2000*

Light to medium red–purple; the bouquet has pronounced earthy/dusty/charry aromas; the palate is quite assertive, but green, earthy, astringent notes will become more, not less, evident with age.

1986 ★★★★☆ *April 2000*

Medium red–purple, a radical colour change from the wines which precede it. The moderately intense bouquet has attractive, sweet, ripe cassis and blackberry fruit supported by evident but subtle oak. An elegant wine on the palate, very much alive, with fresh, red berry fruits, fine tannins and good length.

1985 ★★★ *April 2000*

Medium red–tawny; the aged, foresty/leafy bouquet is slightly musty; there are flickers of cedar and cigar box on the palate which has unequivocally moved towards the end of its secondary phase. For immediate consumption before the wheels fall off.

1984 ★★☆ *April 2000*

Light to medium red–tawny; there are strange caramel/tea-leaf aromas on the bouquet, and the fruit has largely gone from the palate, which is marginally sustained by some acidity on the finish.

1983

Not made.

1982 ★★★☆ *April 2000*

Medium red–tawny; the bouquet is clean and quite fresh, with a mix of earth, berry and leaf aromas; minimal oak. The palate has distinct elegance, with a mix of cigar box, earth and dark chocolate flavours. The tannins have largely faded from the scene.

1981 ★★☆ *April 2000*

Medium tawny–red; there are gamey echoes of dimethyl sulphide on the bouquet, with some redeeming spice. The palate has a mix of gamey, leafy and bitter chocolate flavours which give it sour edges.

1980 ★★ *April 2000*

Medium tawny–red; slightly astringent earthy/leafy/tobacco aromas are followed by a palate in which the meaty/leafy dimethyl sulphide character has ballooned over the past six years. It is a character I detest; it afflicted most Coonawarra wines of its time, most notably the Jimmy Watson trophy-winning Lindemans St George Cabernet Sauvignon.

1979 ★★★★★ *April 2000*

Medium red, headed to tawny–brick; the bouquet has an array of fragrant cedar, earth, spice and berry aromas, and has evolved remarkably well over the past six years. The palate is likewise fully mature, with a complex mix of savoury, chocolate, spice, earth and berry flavours; the tannins are fading.

━ Not Ready ＼ Still evolving ▮ Prime of its life ↗ Drink soon ⛶ Missed the boat

petaluma riesling 1979-2000

PETALUMA

1995 RIESLING

750ml
PRODUCE OF AUSTRALIA BOTTLED AT PICCADILLY SA

Winemakers in Australia have long since opted for a style of Riesling entirely different from that of either Germany or Alsace — this quite independently of the imperatives of climate. The wines are much drier than most German Rieslings and significantly less phenolic than those of Alsace.

Thus the wines are made from star-bright juice (either cold-settled or filtered) fermented at low temperatures. The best rely neither on added enzymes nor aromatic yeasts for their character. Delicate and crisp when young, they age wonderfully well in bottle.

Few would argue that Petaluma Riesling is a benchmark example of Australian Riesling style. It is made from grapes grown on the Hanlin Hill Vineyard, which was planted to riesling in the early 1970s and acquired by Petaluma in 1978. At 500 metres, it is the highest vineyard in the Clare Valley, generally regarded as Australia's greatest region of the variety. Petaluma tends to pick its riesling later than most; the low-yielding, small vines on this rugged vineyard produce grapes with above-average flavour intensity.

The striking feature of this tasting was the similarity many of the older wines had compared to the previous tasting in November 1994: they have a long plateau of drinkability, even when on the downslope. Yet by some sleight of hand, the wines are unusually full of flavour when young, and reach the start of the plateau relatively quickly.

Tasted in April 2000.

2000 ★★★★★   *October 2000*
The bouquet is quite powerful, ranging through spice, apple, passionfruit, mineral and even a hint of toast starting to appear, the crisp, long palate more disciplined, its best before it.

1999 ★★★★★   *April 2000*
Light yellow–green; a highly floral and striking bouquet with herb, grass, spice and lime aromas erupting from the glass. The palate is similarly intense and striking, with herb, grass, mineral and spice flavours. One to watch as it develops.

1998 ★★★★☆   *April 2000*
Medium yellow–green; a mix of mineral/chalk with lime and ripe apple at the other end of the spectrum. The palate is quite tight, with lime, herb and mineral flavours; has considerable grip notwithstanding the high yield.

1997 ★★★★★   *April 2000*
Light to medium yellow–green; the bouquet is clean, with a mix of lime and passionfruit aromas. The palate is fine, yet extremely long and intense, the power under absolute control.

classic wines

★★★★★ Perfect   ★★★★☆ Close to perfect   ★★★★ Very good   ★★★☆ Expected
★★★ Short of standard   ★★☆ Undeserving   ★★ Decayed relic   NR No rating

1996 ★★★★★   *April 2000*

Light to medium yellow–green; another brilliantly clean and pure bouquet with lime and apple fruit. The palate has gorgeous weight, feel and style with lime juice flavour and perfect acidity; excellent now or later.

1995 ★★★★☆   *April 2000*

Light to medium yellow–green; a spotlessly clean bouquet with an interesting mix of fresh lime, ripe apple and mineral aromas all intermingling. The medium-bodied palate is firm, crisp and tight, with a bone-dry finish.

1994 ★★★★★   *April 2000*

Medium green–yellow; the bouquet is clean and firm, with a mix of fresh, floral herb, lime, mineral and toast aromas. An excellent palate, with tight, firm lime flavours and a bone-dry finish. Still evolving.

1993 ★★★★   *April 2000*

Medium yellow–green; toasty brioche aromas dominate the bouquet, with a light touch of honey coming through in second place. The palate is quite tight, again showing pronounced toast and mineral flavours; well balanced; elegant but cerebral.

1992 ★★★★   *April 2000*

Medium yellow–green; the complex, lifted, aromatic bouquet has lime, honey and beeswax aromas signalling the presence of some botrytis influence. The fruit flavours still have some sharp edges, accented by limey acidity; a difficult wine to accurately call.

1991 ★★★★   *April 2000*

Medium yellow–green; the aromas have a distinct lift, with minerally/tinny edges and then wafts of honey. The palate starts with soft honey and baked apple flavours, but then moves through to a rather hard finish.

1990 ★★★★   *April 2000*

Medium to full yellow–green; the bouquet is complex, with distinct softness to the lime/tropical fruit. The palate is multiflavoured and complex, but doesn't have the focus or the brilliance of the best wines, and is showing the first signs of drying out. Some botrytis at work here. Very consistent with the 1994 tasting.

1989 ★★★   *April 2000*

Medium to full yellow–green; there are pronounced toast/hay/honey characters on the bouquet; the palate is rich, full and soft, but lacks continuity, and is on the way down.

1988 ★★★★   *April 2000*

Medium to full yellow–green; the bouquet is quite lively, yet smooth with lime, honey and apple aromas. There is greater sweetness and depth to the fruit on the palate than expected, although overall it is slightly soft, lacking the sharp edge of the best wines.

1987 ★★★★☆   *April 2000*

Rather more green evident in the colour; fragrant lime, herb, lemon, honey aromas with little or no toast aromas to the bouquet are followed by a fresh, zippy palate with a mix of crisp apple and a hint of kerosene flavours. Overall, excellent mouthfeel and finish.

◄ Not Ready ➤ Still evolving ▮ Prime of its life ✍ Drink soon ▯ Missed the boat

1986 ★★★★★   *April 2000*

Medium to full yellow with a touch of green. The lime and honey aromas of the bouquet have an interesting edge, part herb, part earth, characters which dissipated quite quickly. A classic, aged Riesling on the palate, with intense lime, citrus fruit; good acidity and length.

1985 ★★★   *April 2000*

Medium to full yellow–green; the bouquet is rich, again showing some lifted aromatic characters, with sweet fruit running into stone fruit and honey aromas. The palate is disappointing, rather heavy and broad, lacking focus and not developing well. Perhaps a lesser bottle.

1984 ★★★★   *April 2000*

Medium to full yellow–green; the aromatic bouquet shows some traces of volatility, with a mix of honey, citrus and herb; the palate offers clean, fresh and lively citrus flavours, but not much mid-palate complexity. An easy-drinking style from a cool vintage.

1983 ★★☆   *April 2000*

The colour is very advanced, ominously golden brown. The bouquet is surprisingly complex, with maderised, dried fruit aromas and a touch of cinnamon, but there is a lack of mid-palate fruit and intensity, giving a slightly hard/shelly impression. Frost and hail decimated the Clare Valley vineyards, so for the first and only time this wine included components from the Eden Valley and Margaret River.

1982 ★★★★☆   *April 2000*

Full yellow, but with green flecks still evident. Toast, honey and butter are the first impression on the bouquet, followed by sweet lime aromas. The palate opens with juicy lime, apple and stone fruit flavours; only on the very finish do you see the signs of age starting to catch up.

1981 ★★★   *April 2000*

The colour is still a healthy, full yellow, with just a touch of green; the sweet, rich bouquet offers a mix of honey, brioche and crystallised lemon peel, yet your sixth sense tells that the fruit is starting to dry out, and as soon as the wine is tasted, that impression is confirmed. Still enjoyable, but don't delay.

1980 ★★★★★   *April 2000*

Deep yellow–green, but quite brilliant. The clean and sweet bouquet runs through lime, spice and honey, with only the barest hint of toast. The rich, full, round mouthfilling flavours of lime and honey are showing no signs of drying out or breaking up. The sweetness is strictly fruit-derived, and not from residual sugar.

1979 ★★★★☆   *April 2000*

Bright, full yellow; toast, honey, sweet lime, mandarin and spice aromas flow into a palate with great mouth flavour and feel, balance and acidity. May well have been a freakishly good bottle, but the wine seems to have gained another lease of life, with a quite special purity.

★★★★★ Perfect	★★★★☆ Close to perfect	★★★★ Very good	★★★☆ Expected
★★★ Short of standard	★★☆ Undeserving	★★ Decayed relic	NR No rating

classic wines

205

pipers brook vineyard estate
riesling 1979-2000

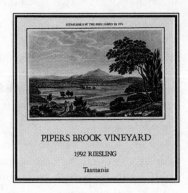

PIPERS BROOK VINEYARD
1992 RIESLING
Tasmania

andrew Pirie selected the Pipers Brook region in 1972 after an exhaustive study of the Australian climate, but whether he would make the same choice 30 years later is an interesting question: Pipers Brook produces excellent Chardonnay and Gewurztraminer and superb Riesling, but is a far more difficult proposition when it comes to red table wine.

However that may be, the 3.5 hectares of ultra-close planting produce between 2000 and 2500 cases of quite beautiful Riesling, which ages wonderfully well.

It is normally picked around the middle of April at the start of leaf fall. Botrytis is a more or less constant companion: Andrew Pirie welcomes a 10 to 15 per cent infection, which he believes adds to complexity without unduly modifying varietal flavour. But he doesn't like intervention, and in particular seeks to avoid the need for de-acidification.

German winemakers would find the alcohol levels quite amazing, and significantly higher than they would work with, but these wines do not show any heaviness or hot alcohol characters. Conversely, Marlborough's (New Zealand) makers would be surprised at the low levels of residual sugar, ranging from a low of 2 grams per litre to a high of 11 grams, but typically around 5 to 7 grams. These are exceptionally well-balanced wines, with the phenolic content, the acid and the alcohol determining the amount of residual sugar left in the wine.

First tasted in February 1996, updated, and later vintages added.

2000 ★★★★★ *October 2000*

Pristine, spotless passionfruit and lime fruit runs through a delicate but intense and long palate, with fine minerally acidity. Great Tasmanian vintage, great wine.

1999 ★★★★★ *October 1999*

Whatever second thoughts Andrew Pirie has had about the suitability of Pipers Brook's foundation vineyard to certain varieties, he has none about Riesling. Fresh and zesty lime, apple and spice aromas are replicated in the delicious flavours of the palate. Will build complexity and richness as it slowly matures.

1998 ★★★★★ *October 1998*

Light to medium yellow–green; there is fine, lime/tropical fruit in abundance on the bouquet; the elegant, tightly structured and long palate presents quite lovely lime-accented flavours, and guaranteeing a long life. One of the best Pipers Brook Rieslings for years.

1997 ★★★★☆ February 1998

Light yellow–green; a crisp, aromatic bouquet with a mix of herb, lime blossom and orange peel aromas is followed by a pungent palate with green lime flavours and high acidity. Aggressive now, but should mellow with time.

1996 ★★★★☆ May 1997

Glowing medium to full yellow–green, advanced but bright in hue; a strikingly rich bouquet, with ultra-tropical honeyed fruit aromas. The palate is rich, high-flavoured, with tropical characters predominant, and some lime and herb underneath. Given the very difficult vintage, a triumph, although the flavours and the 13 per cent alcohol suggest considerable botrytis influence.

1995 ★★★★☆ February 1996

Bright light yellow–green; as a young wine, every bit as classic as the '88, with very attractive, tangy lime fruit aromas on the bouquet; the botrytis influence seems more of a help than a hindrance. Slightly less exuberant on the palate, in a dry toasty style, spotlessly clean, and well-balanced; still coming out of its shell, with nice acidity. The only question mark is whether it is a fraction dilute. 12.1 per cent alcohol.

1994 ★★★★☆ February 1996

Light to medium yellow–green; radically different from all of the older wines, with tangy/herbal aromas and a degree of bite; no honey, toast or any of those softer fruit aromas have yet emerged. The palate is powerful, with many things going on; the fruit flavours hit right on the tip of the tongue and carry through to the finish; the exceptionally high alcohol of 13.7 per cent invests the wine with an impression of slightly sweetness.

1993 ★★★★★ February 1996

Medium yellow–green; a full, aromatic bouquet with an array of lime, honey and white peach aromas attesting to a degree of botrytis. A youthful wine on the palate, with an exuberant array of fruit flavours, and that hallmark weight and length to the carry of the fruit. 13.2 per cent alcohol.

1992 ★★★★★ February 1996

Medium to full yellow–straw; there is an abundance of complex fruit aromas in the tropical/citrus spectrum, tinged with honey. Powerful, rich and concentrated, with sweet lime flavours running right through the length of the palate. Despite all that flavour, not phenolic. 12.3 per cent alcohol.

1991 ★★★★ February 1996

Medium to full yellow, with just a touch of green, the deepest of the younger wines; the bouquet is full, soft and noticeably honeyed, though not particularly fruity. The palate is rich and full flavoured, with lots of weight and extract, but some cork/bottling problems cast a shadow over the wine. Three bottles were opened for the tasting, with considerable bottle variation. 13 per cent alcohol.

1990 ★★★☆ February 1996

Light to medium yellow–green; a clean, but distinctly lighter and less opulently fruity bouquet leads on to a fresh, light wine with pleasant fruit flavours, but lacking the concentration and complexity of most in the line-up. Does not look as if it will go on from here. 12.5 per cent alcohol, which is in fact relatively high, and more than the flavour would suggest.

★★★★★ Perfect	★★★★☆ Close to perfect	★★★★ Very good	★★★☆ Expected
★★★ Short of standard	★★☆ Undeserving	★★ Decayed relic	NR No rating

1989 ★★★★☆   *February 1996*

Medium yellow–green; a ripe, smooth, honeyed bouquet, markedly soft and initially less intense than others in the line-up, although it gained with time in the glass. A multiflavoured palate with citrus and honey, retaining good fruit, with attractive mouthfeel and fruit/acid balance. Surprisingly, only 11 per cent alcohol.

1988 ★★★★   *February 1996*

Medium green–yellow; in (mainland) Australian terms, the most classic bouquet of the wines spanning '79 to '88, with gently toasty aromas with just a touch of citrus; gentle but fine. On the palate, distinctly toasty, reflecting the warmest vintage experienced at Pipers Brook. A very good wine, although the palate does come as a qualified disappointment after the bouquet, with a touch of hardness. 13 per cent alcohol.

1987 ★★★★☆   *February 1996*

Medium green–yellow; a firm bouquet with citrus and lime together with some slightly curious coconut/beeswax edges. The palate is clean and firm, with considerable presence and length, yet has a delicacy to the back palate and finish. Could be enjoyed anywhere, any time, with or without food. A triumph for a very cool vintage which required de-acidification and was a struggle from start to finish. 11 per cent alcohol.

1986 ★★★   *February 1996*

Fresh green–yellow; a distinctly herbaceous, tart bouquet with kerosene and vegetable overtones; the only wine in the tasting to show any errant fruit characters (other than botrytis). The palate is nearly identical, with slightly green/bitter flavours and a slightly hard finish. Simply lacks the compelling charm of the other wines. The product of another very cool and difficult growing season. 11.5 per cent alcohol.

1985 ★★★★★   *February 1996*

Wonderful bright yellow–green hue; the bouquet is of medium to full intensity, at once firm yet smooth, with aromas of lime and gentle toast. A quite lovely wine on the palate, fleshy yet crisp, and still tightly structured. The most elegant of the older wines, remarkably vibrant and fresh. An easy vintage; first in the new winery. 11.5 per cent alcohol.

1984 Northern and Upper ★★★★★   *February 1996*

Glowing yellow–green; a firm bouquet with classic citrus and toast aromas and a touch of honey; in a quite different style from the older wines in the line-up. Delicious flavour, weight and texture; there is abundant lime and honey fruit balanced by crisp acid, resulting in a full but firm palate. A good vintage; not a lot of botrytis. 11 per cent alcohol.

1983 Upper Slopes ★★★   *February 1996*

Full yellow–orange; opulent lime and marmalade aromas, full-on in every respect. A big, full, somewhat heavy and phenolic style, with more of those marmalade and honeycomb characters. Hangs around and does not leave the mouth fresh. Botrytis dominated.

1983 Northern Slopes ★★★☆ *February 1996*

Full yellow; a solid, full bouquet, with just a subliminal hint of decay, and certainly major impact from botrytis. A powerful wine in the mouth which would go well with food; the botrytis influence inevitably leads to some phenolic heaviness, but the wine works well and shows no sign of break-up on the palate. High botrytis infection from a wet vintage.

1982 ★★★★★ *February 1996*

Medium to full yellow; opulent, sweet citrus peel aromas to a rich bouquet in which the botrytis influence is evident, but not unpleasantly so; smells like a mature German Auslese of high quality. There is masses of mid-palate fruit reinforcing the impression of a (dry) Auslese, with candied orange peel flavours together with citrus. Dry year, very small crop, some botrytis; basket-pressed.

1981 ★★★☆ *February 1996*

Very pale; a firm, dusty/herbaceous bouquet with hints of lime pastille fruit. The palate is firm, and slightly hollow and hard, as if stripped by some agency or other. Still very drinkable, however.

1980 ★★★★☆ *February 1996*

Medium yellow–green; a firm, toasty bouquet with hints of herb, honey and citrus, though less extravagant than the '79. Relatively light-bodied, but quite firm and racy, finishing with crisp acidity. No hint of break-up, though made in a dry, austere style which makes it slightly less instantly attractive than some of the other wines. First commercial release.

1979 ★★★★★ *February 1996*

Full yellow; lovely developed toast and lime aromas, rich, sweet and harmonious; in superb condition. The palate does not disappoint, almost unctuously soft, with lime, marmalade and honey flavours, and not drying out on the finish. Young vines, remote control winemaking, basket pressed and only 100 dozen made! Quite remarkable.

★★★★★ Perfect ★★★★☆ Close to perfect ★★★★ Very good ★★★☆ Expected
★★★ Short of standard ★★☆ Undeserving ★★ Decayed relic NR No rating

classic wines

209

plantagenet cabernet
sauvignon 1974-1998

the first and most distinguished of the Great Southern/Mount Barker Cabernets, made in a very consistent style since its introduction in 1974. Each of the winemakers — up to 1977 David McNamara, then Rob Bowen to 1987, followed by John Wade until 1992 and now Gavin Berry — has been content to allow the grapes and the terroir to speak loudest. There have been some changes in the approach to fermentation

techniques, and also in the minor blend components, but the overall style has been one of elegance, with new oak (in particular) playing only a minor role.

The core of the wine has come from the Bouverie cabernet sauvignon planted in 1968 and from Wyjup Vineyard plantings (commenced in 1971) of cabernet sauvignon and malbec. Until the end of the 1980s Malbec was typically included as a minor blend component (up to 20 per cent in some years), but since 1990 the focus has switched to Cabernet Franc and Merlot — normally 5 to 6 per cent of each, although there is no predetermined formula.

As one would expect, vintage conditions have a considerable impact on what is basically a single-variety, estate-grown wine. But if one ignores the experimental beginnings in 1974 and 1975, the wine is not only consistent in style but ages superbly in bottle for a decade or more. And unlike some other tastings for this work, the highest points were not grouped among the youngest wines.

The 1974 to 1992 vintages were tasted in October 1994; subsequent vintages upon release.

◄ 1998 ★★★★☆   *February 2001*
Medium red–purple; clean berry and blackcurrant aromas, together with a touch of oak, are followed by a delicious palate, with pristine cassis/blackcurrant fruit, a touch of chocolate, ripe tannins and subtle oak.

◥ 1997 ★★★★   *October 1999*
Medium red, with some purple hues remaining. The moderately intense bouquet is clean, with earthy berry cabernet fruit and subtle oak. Some slightly green edges to the fruit appear on the palate, which finishes with firm tannins.

▮ 1996 ★★★☆   *February 1999*
Medium red–purple; the bouquet is fairly light and relatively earthy, with not overmuch berry or cassis fruit. The palate lacks flesh, although the soft tannin balance for the light, red berry fruit is on the mark.

1995 ★★★★☆   *October 1997*

Medium purple–red; there is quite pronounced vanillin oak on the bouquet, with soft chocolatey/earthy fruit to follow. However, on the palate, sweet cassis and currant fruit is more evident than the bouquet suggests, finishing with delicate tannins and cedary oak.

1994 ★★★★★   *January 1997*

Dark red–purple; the bouquet shows perfectly ripened fruit, neither herbal at the one end nor jammy at the other, allied with subtle oak. In the mouth, a quite wonderful wine with dark berry fruits with a long, lingering finish supported by fine tannins.

1993 ★★★★★   *October 1995*

Full purple–red; marvellously balanced and integrated fruit and oak with blackcurrant aromas; a sweetly flavoursome yet elegant palate which combines depth and extract with finesse. Deservedly a gold medal winner.

1992 ★★★★★   *October 1994*

Medium to full purple–red; wonderfully bright and fresh red berry fruit with subtle oak as befits the line. The palate is already balanced, with powerful dark berry fruit flavours, finely-grained tannins, and just a hint of oak. The product of a near-perfect growing season.

1991 ★★★★☆   *October 1994*

Medium to full purple–red; a spotlessly clean bouquet with pristine cabernet varietal character together with well-balanced although not as yet entirely integrated new oak. A beautifully balanced and composed palate, with spotlessly clean cherry/berry fruit interwoven with soft, spicy Troncais-like oak. A warm to hot vintage with a dry summer and autumn, interspersed with periods of very hot weather.

1990 ★★★★★   *October 1994*

Marvellously full and deep purple–red; a concentrated, ripe bouquet showing abundant dark chocolate/briary/berry fruit. The palate again shows rich, berry fruit, riper than the '89 or '91, although not overripe; there are hints of chocolate and a touch of mint in a totally beguiling wine. A textbook growing season with a mild summer and a dry autumn.

1989 ★★★★   *October 1994*

Medium to full red–purple; initially rather subdued, with some dusty notes, but opened up in the glass, with an attractive touch of charry/spicy oak. The palate is richer than the bouquet promises, with some dark/bitter chocolate flavours, and obvious but not excessive tannins. Subtle but discernible oak. A mixed growing season, with a wet January followed by a mild, warm autumn with some rain; heavy rain the day after picking.

1988 ★★★★   *October 1994*

The colour is virtually the same as the younger wines in the group, medium to full red–purple. The bouquet is fragrant and lifted, with the faintest whisper of gravelly bitterness. An interesting wine on the palate, with distinctly minerally characters, and more structure than the older wines, perhaps due to the extended fermentation introduced by John Wade. A warm and very dry growing season with only one fall of rain in the last four months.

★★★★★ Perfect   ★★★★☆ Close to perfect   ★★★★ Very good   ★★★☆ Expected
★★★ Short of standard   ★★☆ Undeserving   ★★ Decayed relic   NR No rating

classic wines

1987 ★★★ *October 1994*

The colour is lighter, the bouquet firm and elegant, with a touch of the gravelly/minerally characters of the '88. The palate is on the austere side, lacking the flesh of the best of the wines, but has reasonable length. The product of a difficult vintage with rain throughout the latter part of the growing and harvest season.

1986 ★★★★★ *October 1994*

Medium red–purple; a wonderfully classy and elegant wine with pure cabernet fruit aromas in an obvious cool-climate mould. A beautifully flavoured and balanced wine on the palate, deceptively ready to drink; may well have entered its plateau, but will go on indefinitely as a near-perfect rendition of moderately cool-grown cabernet, and no one fruit flavour dominating. Good rainfall in February was followed by a dry and warm March and April, with a trouble-free vintage.

1985 ★★★★★ *October 1994*

The colour is still strong, showing no sign of losing its red–purple hue; another extraordinarily youthful wine on the bouquet, with delicious pristine cabernet fruit. Slightly lighter on the palate than the '86 perhaps, but with utterly delicious cassis, redcurrant fruit, perfectly balanced by tannin and acid. In the same superb class as the '86. A very mixed growing season with alternating hot weather and heavy rain, including 100 millimetres in the second week of April. Picked in fine conditions, however.

1984 ★★★★ *October 1994*

The first wine to show any significant change in hue, even though slight, and likewise the first wine to show any real sign of development on the bouquet, but still very attractive with sweet (rather than bitter) chocolate aromas. The palate follows the bouquet, seductively soft and sweet; out of the more austerely elegant mainstream style, but eminently enjoyable. The product of a cool and sometimes wet growing season.

1983 ★★★★☆ *October 1994*

Dark red–purple, strong and concentrated; the bouquet is as the colour promises, deep and concentrated, with distinct earthy/gravelly characters. The palate is extremely full bodied and rich, yet neither as ripe nor tannic as one might expect. The excellent balance of the wine will ensure it lives for another ten years. A basically dry and warm growing season with picking in ideal conditions.

1982

No wine produced, not up to standard.

1981 ★★★★★ *October 1994*

The colour is still retaining its strong red base, with no browning; a potent, masculine bouquet with gravelly/earthy/spicy/minerally characters all interwoven. A most intriguing wine on the palate, with spicy/peppery characters strongly reminiscent of Shiraz, although none is included in the wine — just malbec. A dry and warm to hot growing season with only brief periods of rain to alleviate stress. •

↤ Not Ready   ↘ Still evolving   ▮ Prime of its life   ✍ Drink soon   ⬓ Missed the boat

1980 ★★★ *October 1994*

Medium to full red; a rather developed, leafy/cedary bouquet with echoes of mint. The palate shows the flavours promised by the bouquet, predominantly leaf and mint, followed by a rather drying, tannic finish. A basically fine, hot summer with two periods of rain in early April, though picking in fine weather.

1979 ★★☆ *October 1994*

The colour is excellent, still holding its hue, but the bouquet has a distinct gravelly/smelly overtone which goes beyond regional character. Two bottles were tasted, one better than the other, but neither outstanding, the better still tending to be rather gravelly, tough and bitter. An average growing season with some periods of rain throughout, but not enough to cause major problems.

1978 ★★★☆ *October 1994*

Medium to full red; the bouquet is showing obvious cedary/leafy/briary development, now definitely into the secondary phase of its development, but is clean. An attractive wine on the palate with fine tannins and good structure; leafy and capsicum flavours are reminiscent of a wine from Bordeaux in an intermediate year in which the cabernet didn't quite ripen. A hot summer with picking delayed by heavy rainfall in April.

1977 ★★★★☆ *October 1994*

The colour is still deep and strong, quite amazing; a delicious bouquet with solidly ripe berry and chocolate fruit. The palate is precisely as promised by the bouquet, still sweet with dark chocolate and red berry flavours, finishing with strong, lingering tannins. Years in front of it. A hot summer followed by a cool autumn, and the latest vintage on record, with the cabernet not picked until the second week of May, and 100 millimetres of rain the day after picking.

1976 ★★★☆ *October 1994*

Good colour still, holding depth. The bouquet is fairly ripe with some chocolate and a whisper of gaminess, the latter closing the fruit up somewhat. A generous wine on the palate still, in some ways reminiscent of the '83, with lots of dark chocolate, dark berry and tannins. A rustic style, but none the worse for that. Good rainfall in January and February; March and April were fine and warm.

1975 ★★ *October 1994*

Tawny coloured; rather smelly, thin and leafy on both bouquet and palate. A wet, cool and difficult vintage. •

1974 ★★☆ *October 1994*

Light red, with a light, faintly petrolly bouquet and a light astringent palate. Made at Sandalford. A very cool growing season; the grapes did not ripen properly.

★★★★★ Perfect ★★★★☆ Close to perfect ★★★★ Very good ★★★☆ Expected
★★★ Short of standard ★★☆ Undeserving ★★ Decayed relic NR No rating

classic wines

213

primo estate joseph cabernet sauvignon merlot 1987-1998

Joe Grilli graduated from Roseworthy in 1980, taking with him the gold medal as dux of his class. He came back to the 19-hectare vineyard his father Primo had planted in 1973 at Virginia on the flat and distinctly unfashionable Adelaide Plains region. So unfashionable, indeed, that no other small winery has attempted to open for business there, and the only other significant winery is Barossa Valley Estate, the name of which says it all.

From a standing start more than 20 years ago (the first Primo Estate wine was made in 1979) the winery has moved into the top echelon of premium quality boutiques. It has achieved this in part through Joe Grilli's winemaking skills, but more importantly, because of his lateral thinking, his refusal to be bound by the constraints of site and climate.

One of several innovations was to borrow from Italy's Amarone technique and, after hand-picking, leave the grapes lying for two weeks in the shade while they partially desiccate. (In Italy botrytis can play an active role, and the drying period is longer.) Subtly altering the parameters, Joe Grilli has also sourced 10 per cent merlot from Coonawarra since 1992.

The grapes are then crushed, and warm-fermented in open vats; since 1993 they have been pressed at 2° baumé to finish their fermentation in a mix of French, German and American puncheons in which the wine stays for almost two years.

In Joe Grilli's words: 'A great red wine is a sublime paradox: power and concentration versus finesse; character versus subtlety; longevity versus approachability.' And indeed a vertical tasting in July 1999 of all 11 Joseph Cabernet Sauvignons released to date — 1987 to 1998 — showed all these characters.

Like any parent, Grilli sees different features, different habits, different nuances in the wines, and says between 1987 and 1992 the wines were prototypes, settling down from 1993 onwards. Yet for my taste, the family resemblances far outweighed the differences.

All except the 1998 were tasted in August 1999.

◀ *1998* ★★★★★   *March 2000*

Full red–purple; the bouquet offers a subtle interplay of ripe plum, prune, cassis and oak; mouthfilling plum, prune, blackberry and bitter chocolate fruit flavours are surrounded by a web of silky tannins and subtle oak.

◀ Not Ready   ╲ Still evolving   ▮ Prime of its life   ⌀ Drink soon   ▯ Missed the boat

1997 ★★★★ *August 1999*

Youthful purple; a clean bouquet, of moderate to full intensity, with sweet, dark berry and chocolate aromas and flavours, supported by soft, rippling tannins. Recently bottled, and the star rating may prove parsimonious.

1996 ★★★★★ *August 1999*

Yet more proof of the overall quality of the '96 vintage. The palate is beautifully rich and clean, with deep fruit, the palate exceptionally expansive, though intriguingly with depth of flavour rather than length. Balanced tannins; already seductive.

1995 ★★★☆ *August 1999*

Medium red–purple; there is a distinct new oak influence with spicy/smoky vanilla characters; overall, the wine seems to lack the depth and richness, and to have different fruit flavours, finishing shorter.

1994 ★★★★★ *August 1999*

Very strong colour; masses of concentrated prune, plum and the family chocolate flood from the glass. Predictably, the palate is stacked with very ripe, luscious prune, chocolate and plum fruit, the tannins soft but persistent.

1993 ★★★☆ *August 1999*

The aromas are slightly lighter, with fresher berry fruit, some vanilla notes and, of course, a touch of that chocolate. The wine is commensurately lighter in body, the tannins (appropriately) less evident.

1992 ★★★★☆ *August 1999*

A striking consistency is starting to emerge with the chocolate/dark plum/prune aromas and flavours, the chocolate perhaps a little stronger on the palate than the bouquet. Lashings of ripe tannin sustain the wine without in any way overwhelming it.

1991 ★★★★★ *August 1999*

Another exceptionally complex, layered and powerful bouquet redolent of prunes and plums, yet not stewy. The V8 engine which drives the palate throbs away quietly, the tannins evident but balanced. Seemingly has an indefinite life.

1990 ★★★★★ *August 1999*

A rich and complex bouquet with a distinct touch of new oak not evident in the older wines. Layer upon layer of flavour unfolds on the glorious palate, a perfect example of the best features of Amarone style. Some tar is present, but in the nicest way.

1989 ★★★★ *August 1999*

Strong colour; the core of rich, dark, berry/prune/plum/chocolate fruit which is the hallmark of the style is immediately apparent on both bouquet and palate. A wine with plenty of muscle and character (abundant tannins) but not having the mid-palate core of luscious fruit which the best wines have, leading to a slightly short finish.

classic wines

★★★★★ Perfect   ★★★★☆ Close to perfect   ★★★★ Very good   ★★★☆ Expected
★★★ Short of standard   ★★☆ Undeserving   ★★ Decayed relic   NR No rating

1988 ★★★   *August 1999*

Against the odds (of a better vintage), lighter both in colour and aroma than the '87, clean and firm but not appealing. The palate shows some green flavours, and is quite tart. In the final analysis the least of the wines in the line-up. Joe Grilli admits he overreacted to what he initially saw as excessive ripeness in the '87.

1987 ★★★★★   *August 1999*

Strong colour; the bouquet is deep, clean and rich with layered dark berry and chocolate aromas. The palate has great balance and length, with tremendous richness, yet not over the top. The tannin level seemed to recede and then intensify over a two-hour tasting period.

Not Ready   Still evolving   Prime of its life   Drink soon   Missed the boat

rosemount roxburgh chardonnay

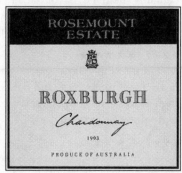

roxburgh Chardonnay can be seen as many things: as a tribute to the winemaking skills and intuitive feel of winemaker Philip Shaw; as a testimonial to the marketing genius of the Rosemount team of Bob Oatley and Chris Hancock; as a prime example of being at the right place at the right time; or as a product of a particularly distinguished site. As ever, the truth lies in the middle, or as a combination of all those things.

It comes from two 4-hectare blocks in a 120-hectare vineyard — blocks which were identified by Philip Shaw as special in the early 1980s. The particular aspect — towards the top of the hill — and the terra rossa over limestone soils are obviously important. So are the lower-than-average yields produced from the conventionally-trellised, sparse-canopied vines.

If the laconic Philip Shaw is to be believed — and I do — there is likewise no secret ingredient in the winemaking. After rough overnight settling, the juice is inoculated with a seat-of-the-pants cocktail of yeast. It is transferred to a varying mix of new and used barrels. After 11 months maturation, the wine is fined (if necessary) filtered and bottled. Hey, presto: Roxburgh.

Then comes the tasting; a roller-coaster in the early years, but with a degree of predictability — even conventionality — coming with the later vintages. Do *Wine Spectator* and Parker approve? Of course they do; half the 4000- to 5000-case production is exported each year.

First tasted in November 1994, updated, and later vintages added.

1998 ★★★   *January 2001*
Light to medium yellow–green; the bouquet shows strong barrel-ferment oak characters, the oak being slightly pencilly, and the palate, while undoubtedly having good fruit, once again shows a surprising lack of oak integration. The wine spent 18 months in bottle prior to release, and I am unable to understand why the oak is as it is. A major disappointment after the excellent 1997 vintage of this wine.

1997 ★★★★★   *October 1999*
As ever, in its own idiom with nutty, creamy aromas and plenty of oak. Has good power, length and grip with ripe nectarine/peach fruit on the mid-palate.

1995 ★★★★☆   *February 1998*
Full yellow; the bouquet has voluminous ripe peach fruit and lots of toasty, charry barrel-ferment oak. The palate is mouthfilling, with unashamedly ripe peachy/buttery fruit, and again that slice of toasty oak. Made in a tried and true fashion, and also reflecting its terroir.

classic wines

★★★★★ Perfect   ★★★★☆ Close to perfect   ★★★★ Very good   ★★★☆ Expected
★★★ Short of standard   ★★☆ Undeserving   ★★ Decayed relic   NR No rating

1994 ★★★★ *October 1996*

Advanced, full yellow; all of a sudden seems old-fashioned with a pronounced oak influence and seemingly some botrytis at work on the bouquet. The palate is certainly massively flavoured and constructed, once again in a slightly old-fashioned buttery/oaky style — or perhaps I am misinterpreting aged Hunter Chardonnay. Either way, I fancy the wine would have been better 12 months ago.

1993 ★★★★★ *November 1994*

Medium to full yellow–green; a complex and rich bouquet with good oak handling in terms of integration and balance. The palate is similarly rich and textured, with high-class barrel-ferment spicy oak running through ripe peach and fig fruit; the best wine of the tasting.

1992 ★★★★☆ *November 1994*

Medium yellow–green; the bouquet is clean and quite firm, of medium to full intensity with melon and citrus fruit aromas and a hint of oak. The palate is quite firm, indeed elegant, with herb, lime and melon flavours, interwoven with pleasant oak.

1991 ★★★★★ *November 1994*

Medium yellow–green; the aromas are complex with a toasty/honeyed overlay over some peach. As with all these wines, the oak influence is subtle and gently spicy. A very generous wine on the palate with sweet peach and vanilla fruit, well-integrated oak, and a slightly heavy finish.

1990 ★★★☆ *November 1994*

Medium to full yellow; the bouquet is somewhat closed with hints of mandarin and apricot, possibly due to botrytis. There are a range of complex secondary characters on the palate; the fruit is somewhat thin and dries out slightly on the finish.

1989 ★★★★☆ *November 1994*

There is still a hint of green to the colour; the bouquet is a total contrast to the '88, with clean, smooth white peach and honey aromas. In the mouth, much the most elegant of the wines between '83 and '89; fruit, rather than oak-driven, and should hold.

1988 ★★★ *November 1994*

Medium to full yellow; distinct matchstick/hot solids/French aromas, out of the Australian mainstream. A similarly wholly idiosyncratic wine on the palate, quite complex, but overall with an array of bitter flavours. Some may like it better.

1987 ★★★★☆ *November 1994*

Medium to full yellow with just a hint of green; a complex and potent bouquet with hints of herbaceous fruit and just a trace of matchstick aromas. The palate is quite different, with lemon and vanilla flavours, quite herbaceous, almost into mature semillon. An interesting, long-lived style.

1986 ★★★★★ *November 1994*

Deep yellow–gold; a rich, honeyed, sweet yellow peach bouquet with some volatile lift. On the palate unctuous peaches and cream with lashings of honey; the ultimate Dolly Parton style; alluring.

◂■ Not Ready ＼ Still evolving ▮ Prime of its life ✎ Drink soon ⬙ Missed the boat

1985 ★★★☆ 　　　　　　　　　　　　　　　　　　*November 1994*

The colour is good, still shot with a touch of green; however the nutty/toasty complex bouquet is starting to lose its primary fruit. The palate is fully aged, with echoes of cumquat and more herbaceous characters, drying out slightly on the finish, and with the acid poking through.

1984 NR 　　　　　　　　　　　　　　　　　　　　*November 1994*

Not rated — atrociously corked.

1983 NR

Not tasted.

★★★★★ Perfect　　★★★★☆ Close to perfect　　★★★★ Very good　　★★★☆ Expected
★★★ Short of standard　　★★☆ Undeserving　　★★ Decayed relic　　NR No rating

classic wines

219

rothbury estate semillon

When Rothbury commenced winemaking (in the appalling Hunter vintage of 1971) Len Evans envisioned just two wines, one white (Semillon) and one red (Shiraz). The varieties were not even mentioned on the front label; this was to be an estate in the most classic sense, and its wines would require no explanation or justification.

The market — and in particular the rise of Chardonnay and Cabernet Sauvignon — decreed otherwise. First back labels, then a proliferation of Rothbury Estate labels, and then a bewildering number of second labels appeared. Semillon, once intended to be the Queen — Shiraz the King — was progressively relegated down the marketing and production totem pole.

But the quality of the wine did not suffer. It wavered after the departure of Gary Sissingh (responsible for the '72 to '79 vintages) but regained its quality thereafter. The most remarkable feature is that those early vintages were made from young vines, and at least some from vineyard blocks which have either gone out of production or been sold to others.

The few remaining semillon vineyards are now fully mature and established on some of the best soil. Yields are not high (they never are in the Lower Hunter) and neither are the alcohol levels. These are wines which are a pure expression of the variety, the terroir and the climate, fermented in steel and bottled early. It is time in the bottle which works the magic; most flowering after a decade, the best living for 20 years or more.

The acquisition of Rothbury Estate by what is now Beringer Blass in 1996 has not done much for the profile of the wine, which — while hardly a surprise — is a pity.

The 1972 to 1994 vintages were tasted in November 1994; the others upon release.

2000 ★★★★☆   *February 2001*
Light green–yellow; the bouquet ranges through citrus, herb, earth, mineral and lemon, the powerful and long palate tangy and quite rich, with ripe citrussy/lemony characters and flavours.

1998 ★★★★   *March 1999*
Light green–yellow; light, crisp, mineral and herb aromas lead into a very correct varietal palate with good length, and the certainty of developing well. From the first of four very good Hunter vintages.

◄ Not Ready   ◣ Still evolving   ◀ Prime of its life   ◞ Drink soon   ▯ Missed the boat

1997 ★★★★☆   *January 1998*

Medium yellow–green; the bouquet is clean, showing an attractive lemony citrus aroma to the clearly accented varietal fruit. The palate, like the bouquet, is of medium intensity and weight, but does have good feel on the tongue and grip and power on the finish.

1996 Black Label ★★★★★   *August 1996*

Bright green–yellow; spotlessly clean, lively and tangy bouquet with crisp grassy varietal fruit introduces a similarly crisp and firm palate with bright, lemony varietal fruit. The wine has good length and excellent balance.

1995 ★★★☆   *October 1995*

Light straw–green; very discrete and withdrawn early in its life, with faintly dusty overtones. A typical young Semillon on the palate, light and crisp, giving no hint of its future, except that it is without fault.

1994 ★★★★★   *November 1994*

Brilliant green–yellow; the bouquet is crisp and lively with excellent tangy lemon/herbaceous varietal fruit of medium intensity. The palate is lively, fresh, crisp and tangy, with a touch more varietal bite than the '93 but in similar mould. Should develop into a classic.

1993 ★★★★☆   *November 1994*

Bright, light green–yellow; a crisp, clean and lively bouquet with pleasant herbaceous varietal fruit. On the palate a tight but promising young Semillon which has good length and acidity, moderately intense varietal character, and will develop well.

1992 ★★★   *November 1994*

Medium to full yellow; a peculiar bouquet with echoes of New Zealand; the aromas run from tropical to vegetal. A curious wine on the palate, too, with hay/straw/vegetal characters, out of the mainstream.

1991 ★★★★   *November 1994*

Brilliant green–yellow; there is intense lemony varietal fruit which is not blowsy or fat, with a slight fermentation/yeast toasty character detectable. Some of those medicinal fermentation characters appear on the palate, but it does have plenty of lemony tang and punch, and is much tighter than many other '91s from the Hunter.

1990 ★★★   *November 1994*

Bright green–yellow; the bouquet is fresh, tangy and lemony with varietal herbal fruit, but the palate rather hard with slightly dusty/soapy edges.

1989 ★★★★☆   *November 1994*

Glowing yellow–green; a complex bouquet, rich, powerful and honeyed. The palate, too, is soft and rich with peach and honey flavours, and far better mouthfeel than some of the wines which preceded it, contrary to what one might have expected.

1988

Not tasted.

★★★★★ Perfect   ★★★★☆ Close to perfect   ★★★★ Very good   ★★★☆ Expected
★★★ Short of standard   ★★☆ Undeserving   ★★ Decayed relic   NR No rating

classic wines

221

1987 ★★★☆   *November 1994*

Medium to full yellow–green; a somewhat soft and blowsy bouquet with hints of mandarin. The palate is soft, light and plain with hints of hay and straw; a wine without much intensity, though no fault.

1986 ★★★☆   *November 1994*

Deep yellow; a ripe, voluminous and lifted aroma with touches of cumquat. The palate is soft and ripe, almost peachy chardonnay-like; early developing.

1985 ★★★   *November 1994*

A touch of straw to the colour; the bouquet is soft and gentle with lemon, honey and a hint of toast. The palate is soft, light and rather diffuse, with gentle hay/straw characters; will not be long-lived.

1984 ★★★★☆   *November 1994*

Medium yellow–green; an interesting and complex bouquet with lively, lemony fruit and a background hint of burnt match. A powerful wine on the palate with complex flavours and many things going on; has good mouthfeel, weight and texture.

1983 ★★★☆   *November 1994*

Medium to full yellow, even with a touch of orange; a ripe, honeyed and somewhat blowsy bouquet shows the hot vintage. The palate is very developed, but quite attractive nonetheless, with soft honey/hay/straw flavours.

1982 ★★★☆   *November 1994*

Glowing yellow–green; penetrating bouquet with quite marked volatility, although not beyond the bounds of acceptability. The flavours are powerful, lifted by the volatility, which sharpens and gives length to the fruit.

1981 ★★★☆   *November 1994*

Deep yellow; rich, ripe almost peachy, reminiscent of the Tyrrell's Vat 1 of the same year. On the palate there are ripe, peachy nutmeg and spice flavours; a striking and unusual wine, very much a product of its drought year.

1980 ★★★   *November 1994*

Brilliant light green–yellow; a rather subdued and restrained bouquet with some green, camphor notes and a hint of burnt match. The palate, too, has some strange camphor and herbal characters, a letdown after the great wines of the 1970s, but does have flavour and is holding.

1979 ★★★★★   *November 1994*

Glowing yellow–green; rich, soft honeyed/buttery aromas of perfectly ripened semillon. The palate is generous and soft with honeyed/buttery fruit, a touch of grilled nuts; a lovely wine at its peak.

1978 ★★★☆   *November 1994*

Medium to full yellow; the bouquet is soft, sweet and honeyed with a slight touch of volatile lift. The palate is clean and soft, tending a little light, but still pleasant and holding its fruit well.

◄ Not Ready   ＼ Still evolving   ▮ Prime of its life   ✎ Drink soon   ▯ Missed the boat

1977 Brokenback Block H Black Label ★★★★ *November 1994*
Medium to full yellow; a riper style with hay/straw edges to the aroma. The palate is soft, ripe and slightly blowsy with some tropical flavours together with hay and straw of the bouquet.

1976 ★★★★★ *November 1994*
Brilliant, glowing yellow–green; clean, firm, fresh and youthful, with lemony aromas, and just a hint of honey. A glorious wine in the mouth, at the peak of its power; there are flavours of lemon, hazelnut and vanilla, finishing with perfectly balanced acidity.

1975 Private Bin (Mundurra Label) ★★★★★ *November 1994*
Medium yellow–green; a firm, fresh and lemony bouquet still holding tight varietal fruit. The palate, too, is tangy, fresh and lively, with clear varietal fruit definition, finishing with crisp acidity.

1974 Black Label Blocks C&E ★★★★★ *November 1994*
Full yellow, with hints of orange; a potent, rich botrytis-influenced bouquet with edges of cumquat, but totally delicious. The palate is crammed with flavour like an Ygrec, but is holding together very well with no phenolic break-up.

1973 Black Label Director's Reserve ★★★★☆ *November 1994*
Deep yellow; the bouquet is honeyed and ever so slightly maderised, but very complex, due to ageing in Limousin oak for nine months. The palate is toasty, nutty, soft and generous, though starting to dry out a little. The bottle was ullaged and may not be entirely typical.

1972 White Label ★★★★★ *November 1994*
Glowing yellow–green; a glorious bouquet as fresh as a daisy, with honey cut by lemon. The palate is as delicious as the bouquet suggests, still fresh and elegant, with a long harmonious lemon and faintly honeyed palate, and a crisp finish.

★★★★★ Perfect   ★★★★☆ Close to perfect   ★★★★ Very good   ★★★☆ Expected
★★★ Short of standard   ★★☆ Undeserving   ★★ Decayed relic   NR No rating

classic wines

223

saltram dry reds

Saltram has over 140 years of rich winemaking history, and — in celebration of its 140th birthday — staged a remarkable tasting at Saltram's winery in the Barossa Valley in February 1999. It was that event which gave rise to this classic tasting, an event made all the more remarkable by the fact that three of the winemakers who have served Saltram at various times since 1859 were present: Brian Dolan, Peter Lehmann and present incumbent Nigel Dolan (Brian's son).

It would be idle to deny that Saltram totally lost its way in the 1980s and early '90s in the time it was owned by multinational spirits and wine giant Seagram. There was a time indeed, when it seemed Seagram had entirely forgotten it owned an Australian winery.

Ironically, when Brian Dolan arrived in 1949 Saltram was in eclipse to much the same extent as it was when Nigel arrived in 1992. Brian Dolan found Shiraz from the 1946 and 1948 vintages sitting in 2250 litre old wooden vats awaiting export orders which had not arrived. The wines were ultimately sold in bulk, but not before Dolan had bottled 35 dozen of each — not for sale, but (with extraordinary prescience) for posterity.

When Nigel Dolan arrived in 1992 there were no great wines lying undiscovered in barrel (although there was the precious museum of old wines which provided the base for this tasting). The name Saltram was little more than a flag of convenience for wines sourced here, there and everywhere. Nigel's mission was to return Saltram's wines to the Barossa Valley, except for Stonyfell Metala, which has always been made from Langhorne Creek grapes. Not only has he succeeded in this, but is now making wines which will be the flagbearers in the year 2020 and beyond.

It would be unfair to pass over the role of Peter Lehmann in this evolution. More than any other single living person, he has passionately protected the Barossa Valley and its grape growers who provide its life's blood.

Postscript: the vintage conditions (shown in brackets) are derived from the excellent book Barossa Vintage Classification 1947–1998, available from the Barossa Wine and Tourism Association.

First tasted in February 1999, updated.

◄ Not Ready   ╲ Still evolving   ⌁ Prime of its life   ⌁ Drink soon   ⎕ Missed the boat

1978 Mamre Brook Cabernet Shiraz ★★★☆ *February 1999*

Youthful medium red–purple; leafy, green aromas are not a promising start, but the palate has surprisingly bright, fresh cherry fruit, fine tannins and no bitterness. Just a little light in structure. (A drier than average vintage, followed by good April rains, produced average yields and good, solid reds. Average yield 4.3 tonnes per hectare.)

1975 Show Dry Red ★★★★★ *February 1999*

Full red with a tinge of purple; an exceptionally rich, sweet and luxurious bouquet is followed by a similarly sumptuous, smooth, ripe blackberry and mint-flavoured palate. Oak is there but well balanced and integrated; quite superb. 100 per cent Cabernet Sauvignon. (A wet winter, a cool January followed by a hot, dry February then rain in March produced good white wines and medium-weight reds (although there was some outstanding exceptions, including this wine). Average yield 4.8 tonnes per hectare.)

1973 Show Dry Red ★★★ *February 1999*

The colour is excellent, still bright red without any tawny or brick hues. The bouquet is still firm and tight with some earthy notes, and a hint of new American oak. The palate is likewise youthful, with sweeter chocolate notes on entry into the mouth, then slightly higher tannins on the finish and an aftertaste which moved into aloe bitterness. While I found this greatly diminished the flavour of an otherwise excellent wine, other tasters liked the wine much more. (A dry spring was followed by a wet and cool February, March and April. A great Riesling year but not so good for red wines. Average yield 5.9 tonnes per hectare.)

1973 Bin 53 Claret (Hydraulic Pressings) ★★★☆ *February 1999*

Dark brick–red; a deep, powerful and earthy bouquet comes as no surprise. The palate provides lots of richness on the middle, but is followed by slightly prickly tannins on the finish which break up the flow of the wine. Nonetheless, a particular favourite of Peter Lehmann. (Vintage conditions as above.)

1972 Mamre Brook Cabernet Shiraz ★★★☆ *February 1999*

Medium brick–red; a turncoat, with a mix of sweet berry and bitter chocolate fruit on the bouquet. The bouquet is not deceiving, for the palate is much riper; berry and dark bitter chocolate flavours followed by pleasant tannins on the finish. (Average rainfall during the growing season was followed by mild and dry March providing ideal vintage conditions. Average yield 5.5 tonnes per hectare.)

1971 Selected Vintage Claret Bin 71/86 ★★★★★ *February 1999*

Medium to full brick–red; a solid bouquet with ripe berry and chocolate aromas together with a hint of earth is followed by a palate with excellent structure. Sweet berry and chocolate fruit is surrounded with persistent but ripe and soft tannins. (Below-average growing season rainfall and a dry January and February, extending into early March, produced ripe, strong reds. Average yield 4.8 tonnes per hectare.)

classic wines

★★★★★ Perfect ★★★★☆ Close to perfect ★★★★ Very good ★★★☆ Expected
★★★ Short of standard ★★☆ Undeserving ★★ Decayed relic NR No rating

1967 Mamre Brook Cabernet Shiraz ★★☆   *February 1999*
Light to medium red, with tawny tinges. The bouquet is light, with that mix of leaf, gravel and earth which, for better or worse, is the hallmark of the style; the palate runs through the precise taste spectrum of the bouquet. (The growing season was reasonably dry with the exception of December; an ideal warm, dry and late vintage produced medium-weight, fruit-driven reds. Average yield 4.2 tonnes per hectare.)

1965 Selected Vintage Claret Bin 41 ★★★☆   *February 1999*
Light to medium brick–red; the bouquet is clean, but much lighter and simpler than the preceding wines. The palate, however, has much more flavour than the bouquet promises, with lovely, soft, sweet berry fruit finishing with fine tannins. A surprise packet. (Excellent spring rain was followed by a warm, dry vintage which simultaneously produced good yields and high-quality wine — especially reds, which were a lighter, more elegant style. Average yield 5 tonnes per hectare.)

1964 Mamre Brook Cabernet Shiraz ★★★★   *February 1999*
Medium brick–red; while there are some leafy overtones, the bouquet is distinctly better than that of the '63; the medium-weight palate is smooth, with touches of leaf and mint, finishing with soft tannins. (Although growing season rainfall was well below average, the previously wet winter together with some rain in April contributed to above-average yields and an excellent red vintage. Average yield 5 tonnes per hectare.)

1964 Show Shiraz ★★★★★   *February 1999*
Strong red; an explosively rich and ripe bouquet with sweet chocolate, berry and liquorice fruit. A commensurately huge and concentrated wine on the palate, sweet, with powerful tannins to balance that sweetness. Even now only partially tamed. The wine spent three years in wood, and was put in a super-heavyweight bottle. Made from pressings. 100 per cent Shiraz. (Vintage conditions as above.)

1963 Bin 36 ★★★   *February 1999*
Medium to full brick–red; there are distinctly green, astringent, earthy overtones in the bouquet, and similar raspy flavours on the palate. The cabernet component seems to have been underripe. It is also possible there was some cork taint at work. 60 per cent Shiraz, 40 per cent Cabernet Sauvignon. (A warm year with above-average rainfall including a wet January and April produced good red wines tending lighter in style.)

1963 Stonyfell Angaston Burgundy ★★★★★   *February 1999*
Dense red; the bouquet is clean and full, with lovely sweet, ripe fruit. The palate fulfils the promise of the bouquet with masses of sweet cherry, berry and chocolate fruit, finishing with soft, ripe, chewy tannins. In many ways, the standout wine of the tasting. 100 per cent Shiraz. (Vintage conditions as above.)

1963 Mamre Brook Shiraz ★★★   *February 1999*
Medium brick–red; the aromas are in a leafy/minty/gravelly spectrum, strongly suggesting slightly underripe cabernet. The structure of the wine on the mid-palate is good, although slightly green tannins come again on the finish. It seems that attitudes to cabernet ripeness have changed significantly over the years. (Vintage conditions as above.)

Not Ready   Still evolving   Prime of its life   Drink soon   Missed the boat

1962 Claret Bin 33 ★★★★★   *February 1999*

Medium brick–red; the moderately intense bouquet is sweet, with attractive, fresh chocolate and earth fruit aromas. The palate is similarly attractive and of medium weight, with the sweet fruit holding up wonderfully, a lovely wine to drink. (A year of below-average growing season rainfall, although bursts of rain in January and again in March reduced vine stress and resulted in an exceptional year for outstanding red wines. Average yield 4.5 tonnes per hectare.)

1961 Dry Red Shiraz ★★★☆   *February 1999*

Light to medium brick–red; the bouquet is distinctly earthy, and showing signs of fading. The palate, likewise, has lost its fruit richness, and is rather earthy, although a touch of acid on the finish does assist in giving it length. 100 per cent Shiraz. (A hot, dry year with little rain falling at the right time during the growing season; very low yields. Average yield 2.6 tonnes per hectare.)

1960 Selected Vintage Burgundy Bin 28 ★★★★   *February 1999*

Light to medium brick–red; the bouquet has a mix of chocolate and slightly baggy/leafy notes; the palate is light, but much sweeter than the bouquet suggests, with smooth, fine tannins. 80 per cent Shiraz, 20 per cent Grenache. (Drought conditions prevailed right through the winter, spring and summer, leading to very low yields and particularly good red wines. Average yield 2.6 tonnes per hectare.)

1959 Claret Bin 25 ★★★☆   *February 1999*

Light to medium tawny–red; some soapy/gravelly overtones to the rather leafier fruit of the bouquet is followed by a palate with a touch of green to the earthy fruit. The contrast between this wine and the incredibly rich, sweet older wines is, perhaps, unfair. 65 per cent Shiraz, 25 per cent Dolcetto, 10 per cent Tokay. (A cool, dry growing season with below-average rainfall was followed by wet spells in February and March, posing some challenges. Average yield 4 tonnes per hectare.)

1958 Claret Bin 20 ★★★☆   *February 1999*

Medium to full brick–red; the bouquet is complex, with some leafy/briary notes, not as sweetly rich as the wines which preceded it. The palate, likewise, has a mix of leafy/earthy/gamey notes, followed by a fairly tannic and somewhat astringent finish. 80 per cent Shiraz, 20 per cent Dolcetto. (A dry winter and a dry vintage right through to March produced drought conditions, with yields reduced in consequence.)

1958 Claret Bin 21 ★★★★★   *February 1999*

Strong, dark brick–red, though slightly lighter on the rim. The bouquet is marvellously complex, with aromas of earth, cedar, lush, sweet chocolate, dark berry and liquorice. The palate completely fulfils the promise of the bouquet, powerful and profound, with excellent tannins on the finish contributing to the overall length. 100 per cent Shiraz. (Vintage conditions as above.)

classic wines

★★★★★ Perfect   ★★★★☆ Close to perfect   ★★★★ Very good   ★★★☆ Expected
★★★ Short of standard   ★★☆ Undeserving   ★★ Decayed relic   NR No rating

227

1957 Shiraz Bin 18 ★★★★★   *February 1999*

Medium brick–red; a sweet, particularly fresh and clean bouquet with floral fragrance overlying soft chocolate and earth. The palate is similarly sweet and fresh, with entrancing delicate cherry fruit; the first wine to show the retention of some primary fruit flavours; relatively speaking in such a powerful line-up, a wine of delicacy and length. 100 per cent Shiraz. (A year of below-average growing season rainfall, which nonetheless fell at precisely the right time; dry, trouble-free vintage with good yields. Average yield 4.8 tonnes per hectare.)

1956 Selected Vintage Burgundy Bin 19 ★★★★☆   *February 1999*

Medium tawny–red; the bouquet is fragrant and lifted, with a mix of sweet earthy and chocolate aromas. While lighter in body than the older wines, has a nicely balanced and structured palate, still holding the core of sweetness which runs through all of these wines. 100 per cent Shiraz. (Above-average growing season rainfall in spring and early summer was followed by a particularly dry and hot February which led to low yields. Average yield 3.2 tonnes per hectare.)

1954 Selected Vintage Claret Bin 5 ★★★★☆   *February 1999*

Medium red–tawny, though slightly lighter than the '52. There is a distinct lift to the bouquet with quite pronounced earthy fruit characters; the palate veers into quite fascinating, virtually pure chocolate flavours, finishing with soft, fine, silky tannins. (A year of high yields, the second-coldest year on record yet had the second-highest hours of sunlight; for the first time in 61 years there was no rain at all in February. Vintage was late and was followed by a very wet April. Five tonnes per hectare average.)

1954 Leo Buring Vintage Claret ★★★★★   *February 1999*

Medium to full red–tawny; a wonderfully rich, ripe and sweet/chocolatey bouquet is followed by a palate stacked with layers of Swiss chocolate, earth, more chocolate and red berry. Soft tannins round off an outstanding wine, giving it structure as well as flavour. (Made by Saltram and sold to Leo Buring, the sale reflecting wine surpluses generated by the large vintage.)

1952 Dry Red Bin 4 ★★★★   *February 1999*

Medium to full red, similar to the '50. The wine opened with a slightly baggy, bottle stink, with hay/straw/hessian aromas, but dissipated as the wine breathed. The palate is solid, with dark chocolate and earth flavours, followed by substantial tannin on the finish. (Above-average growing season rainfall was followed by dry ripening conditions in February and March. Average yield 3.2 tonnes per hectare.)

1950 Dry Red ★★★★★   *February 1999*

Medium to full red, slightly lighter than the '46 and '48. The palate, likewise, has a slightly lighter touch and some lift, with an edge of Swiss chocolate. The seductive palate is exceptionally elegant, still having touches of cherry and chocolate fruit. (A dry winter meant spring rain was welcome; a dry growing season until rain in February caused some downy mildew. Average yield 3.4 tonnes per hectare.)

◄■ Not Ready   ◥ Still evolving   ◗ Prime of its life   ◞ Drink soon   ▯ Missed the boat

1948 Dry Red ★★★★★ *February 1999*

Medium to full red, with just a touch of tawny. The fragrant, full, ripe and rich bouquet leads into a wine with great length and balance; not quite as rich as the '46, but every bit as good in its own way, and holding tannins on the finish. (A very dry vintage followed average rainfall through spring, the rain coming in April after the conclusion of vintage. Average yield 3.8 tonnes per hectare.)

1947

No vintage records.

1946 Dry Red ★★★★★ *February 1999*

Medium to full red, with a tawny rim; the bouquet is sweet, with a mix of earthy and rich chocolate aromas. The palate is wonderfully sweet, the sweetness coming from fruit and alcohol, and in no sense from residual sugar. Ripe and full, with soft, lingering tannins. Has years in front of it yet. 35 dozen made.

★★★★★ Perfect   ★★★★☆ Close to perfect   ★★★★ Very good   ★★★☆ Expected
★★★ Short of standard   ★★☆ Undeserving   ★★ Decayed relic   NR No rating

seppelt great western
colin preece dry reds 1925-1962

It is simply not possible to prove which of Colin Preece or Maurice O'Shea was the greater winemaker. Both were masters of their art, practising at a time when it gained scant recognition, but leaving sufficient legacies for posterity to see at first-hand the extent of the genius.

Preece became winemaker at Great Western in 1932, a position he held until his retirement in 1963. During that time he produced a seemingly endless array of dry white, dry red and sparkling wines of exceptional complexity and equally exceptional quality.

Like O'Shea he was a great blender. Not content with an array of red varieties which encompassed shiraz, cabernet sauvignon, malbec, mourvedre (known locally as Esparte), pinot meuniere (called Miller's Burgundy) and unidentified grapes simply called mixed black, Preece also unashamedly cross-blended vintages. Thus a given wine might be called 1958, but would contain — for example — components from both 1956 and 1957.

Another practice was to allow the grapes to hang on the vine until they had ripened to the point of shrivelling, and then to reduce the potentially excessive alcohol by adding water to the must. Even then technically illegal, it was a procedure strictly driven by a desire to produce wines of the highest quality: Preece believed he could not obtain the flavours he sought by any other means.

The tasting notes, incidentally, come mainly from four dinners: two in 1983, one in 1993 (variously called Single Bottle 1983, Halverson 1983 and Preece 1993), and one in 2001.

1962 Bin S115/1 Cabernet Malbec ★★★★★
Medium to full red, with a firm bouquet with strong dark fruits and a touch of prune. The palate shows similar strength with prune and dark chocolate flavours, with ample tannins on the finish. An excellent wine with plenty of life left. Preece 1993.

1962 CH20 Burgundy ★★★★★
A wine which took almost 30 years to come into full flower, consistently tasting superbly in the early 1990s. Medium to full red, with sweet, rich, ripe red berry fruit aromas, and a marvellously supple palate, lush and full of dark berries and soft dark chocolate flavours. Preece 1993.

1961 Bin MY17 Claret ★★★★
Changed little between 1982 and 1993. Medium to full red, with a sweet and full bouquet showing ripe fruits and hints of toffee and chocolate. The palate is sweet, soft and ripe, with chocolatey flavours; is of medium weight with a long finish. Preece 1993.

— Not Ready ＼ Still evolving ｆ Prime of its life ⚲ Drink soon ▯ Missed the boat

1960 Bin Q58–61 Cabernet ★★☆ — April 1983

Distinct brown tones, with very ripe and slightly porty fruit, and some minty overtones. A very ripe, sweet wine with low tannins levels. At the Preece Dinner, 1960 Bin Q60 showed unpleasant, overripe, musty characters in both bottles opened.

1958 Moyston Claret ★★★ — February 1983

Brick–red; the bouquet is smooth, showing obvious bottle development, with fairly high alcohol and some camphor characters. The wine is rich, ripe and soft, on the mid-palate, but slightly bitter on the finish.

1958 Bin O66–61 Cabernet ★★☆

Full red; both the bouquet and the palate are invested with a touch of astringency from some residual mercaptans. The palate is still relatively youthful, but toughened by those sulphides. Preece 1993.

1958 Bin O68–69 Burgundy ★★★★★

Marvellous colour, still bright and strong red, leading logically on to a wonderfully firm and fresh red berry, fractionally raisined bouquet. The palate is outrageously rich and ripe, with smooth red berry fruits, a hint of chocolate, and soft, lingering tannins. Quite extraordinary. Preece 1993.

1957 Moyston Claret ★★★

Brick–red; the bouquet has nice fruit, but both it and the palate were marred by a touch of volatility. Halverson 1983.

1956 Bin M61 Claret Type Hermitage Esparte ★★★★★

Bright red of medium depth; a very fragrant, fruity aroma with hints of cherry and mint, with lifted cedary oak. A superb palate, with a totally seductive amalgam of cherry, mint and cedar; the texture is supple and the finish fresh. Preece 1993.

1955 Bin L34 Great Western Burgundy ★★★★★

Strong red; a crystal clear bouquet, vibrant with fresh ripe fruit. In the mouth, in superb condition, with some camphor-mint flavours; a marvellously complex balance of fruit and tannin. Halverson 1983.

1954 Bin K81 Great Western Claret ★★★★☆

Dark red, still with purple–blue tinges. The bouquet is complex, with firm fruit, and just a few echoes of tobacco/leather and fresh mushroom in the background. In the mouth, enormously rich fruit on the palate leading to a surprisingly soft finish. Single bottle 1983. Significant bottle variation.

1954 Bin K72 Hermitage ★★★★

Light to medium red; sweet coffee, chocolate and toffee aromas to a smooth bouquet. The palate shows similar soft, ripe chocolatey fruit, with hints of cedary oak and soft tannins, with lemony acid on the finish. Preece 1993.

1953 Bin J13 Great Western Burgundy ★★★★

Dark colour, with a suggestion of very ripe, slightly high pH fruit. A complex bouquet, with ripe aromas and traces of tobacco, mint and bottle-developed camphor. In the mouth, a very complex amalgam of minty fruit, oak and just a hint of pencil shavings. Single bottle 1983.

classic wines

★★★★★ Perfect ★★★★☆ Close to perfect ★★★★ Very good ★★★☆ Expected
★★★ Short of standard ★★☆ Undeserving ★★ Decayed relic NR No rating

1953 Bin J34 Claret ★★★★★
Consistently the greatest of all of the Colin Preece wines made between 1940 and 1963. Still vibrantly coloured, with a fine, elegant scented bouquet with an entrancing mix of raspberry and blackberry aromas. The palate is classically constructed and balanced, still long and fresh, rich yet elegant. Preece 1993 and others.

1952 Bin I69–70 Hermitage Espa0rte ★★★★☆
Medium red; a wonderfully clean, soft and sweet bouquet in superb condition. In the mouth, clean, velvety, gently aged sweet fruit with soft tannins and then some lemony notes, possibly deriving from new wood. Preece 1993.

1951 Bin H66–68 Great Western Claret ★★★
The blend which was to be the first Moyston Claret. Deep red with just a touch of amber. The bouquet had some peculiar garlic aromas, with some of the same character coming through on to a meaty, fleshy wine. Single bottle 1983.

1950 Bin G51 Burgundy ★★★★★
Strong red tinged with garnet; a beautiful, clean wine with fresh, minty overtones to the bouquet. A big, rich, fruity wine in the mouth, still holding structure and style. Halverson 1983.

1949 Bin 80–84 Great Western Burgundy ★★★★★
Deep red; smooth, strong minty fruit on the bouquet with some camphor bottle-developed aromas. The palate shows ample, rich, minty fruit, still fresh. Considerable bottle development. September 1982 and elsewhere.

1932 K Burgundy ★★★★   *July 2001*
Pale but bright colour; the bouquet has aromas of strawberry and cherry which come through on the uncompromisingly light palate. Tasted at the 150th anniversary celebrations of Seppelt, and caused much discussion; the belief is that it is almost certainly 100 per cent Pinot Meunier, which was known at Great Western as Millers Burgundy.

1925 Bin DH18 Hermitage ★★★★★
Bright, light medium red. The bouquet is still clean and fresh, showing no decay whatsoever, no mushroom characters, still gently sweet. The palate is not complex but is spotlessly clean, incredibly fresh with cherry fruit flavours and noticeable acid. Made from a bizarre blend of hermitage and a table grape called 'black prince'. Preece 1993.

◀ Not Ready   ＼ Still evolving   ▮ Prime of its life   ◢ Drink soon   ▯ Missed the boat

seppelt great western shiraz

t he Great Western region of Central Victoria is particularly well suited to shiraz (or hermitage, as it used to be called there). Nevertheless, both site climate and vintage variation play important roles in determining the flavour and style of the individual wines.

Thus the flavours may range from pepper and spice through to dark cherry and mint, with liquorice, chocolate and earth often developing with age. In the core region around the town of Great Western the wines tend to be elegant and smooth (Seppelt and Best's) while those further away at Ararat (Mount Langi Ghiran) are often more powerful.

Seppelt's Great Western Shiraz has appeared and disappeared over the years. Colin Preece's love for and mastery of blending meant he produced only the occasional Shiraz. Then between 1975 and 1983 the wine again disappeared, blended into various Seppelt products. (As a side comment, it is hard to understand how such ordinary wines were produced between 1972 and 1974.)

Since 1984 there has been a renaissance. The wine's heart beats in the block of very old vines adjacent to the winery (never yielding more than 5.5. tonnes per hectare, sometimes much less), and there is a very real desire on the part of the Seppelt winemakers to make the best possible wine in necessarily limited quantities. They are succeeding admirably, aided by the sensible use of new French oak.

To avoid confusion, I call the wine Shiraz, although through most of its life it was called (and labelled) Hermitage.

First tasted in November 1994, updated, and later vintages added.

1997 ★★★★★   *May 2001*
Deep red–purple; deep dark berry fruit and charry/toasty French oak dominate the bouquet; the hot, dry vintage has resulted in an extremely dense palate flooded with black fruit flavours and evenly distributed tannins.

1996 ★★★★★   *October 2000*
Medium to full red–purple; a voluminous, complex and rich bouquet with cascades of liquorice, berry and blackberry flows into a powerful, rich, complex palate with a mix of the berry fruit of the bouquet and some savoury/earthy edges. Powerful but balanced tannins give the wine great structure.

classic wines

★★★★★ Perfect   ★★★★☆ Close to perfect   ★★★★ Very good   ★★★☆ Expected
★★★ Short of standard   ★★☆ Undeserving   ★★ Decayed relic   NR No rating

1995 ★★★★☆   *October 1999*
Medium purple–red; high-toned black cherry fruit marries with soft French oak on the bouquet; the palate offers cherry, mint and berry fruit flavours with those utterly distinctive, hallmark tannins of Great Western. Microscopic yields.

1993 ★★★★★   *November 1994*
Vivid purple–red; a wonderfully rich bouquet with berry and spice aromas intermingling with high-quality French oak. The palate is elegantly structured for a young wine, with fine tannins and good acidity. A classic in the making.

1992 ★★★★☆   *November 1994*
Medium to full red–purple; the bouquet is smooth, with cherry fruit and fairly pronounced sweet vanillin oak. A lighter style on the palate, well structured, and with well-balanced cherry and vanilla fruit and oak flavours, finishing with soft, fine-grained tannins.

1991 ★★★★★   *November 1994*
Medium to full red–purple; a powerful, concentrated bouquet with briary/berry/gamey aromas. The palate is as concentrated and powerful as the bouquet promises, yet is not the least bit extractive or heavy. There are abundant briary/berry fruit flavours which have swallowed up the oak.

1990 ★★★★   *November 1994*
Medium red–purple; an earthy/spicy bouquet, rather less concentrated than the '91. The palate is elegant with earthy/spicy fruit; overall a fraction on the light side, and in some ways reminiscent of Yarra Valley Shiraz.

1988 ★★★☆   *November 1994*
Medium red–purple; the bouquet is fragrant and fresh, with mint and leaf aromas, and subtle oak. The palate is very minty, a character which I personally do not enjoy when it is as dominant as it is here; vanillin oak does provide some counterbalance. From a cool vintage and imperfectly ripened fruit.

1987 ★★★☆   *November 1994*
Light to medium red–purple; there are hints of spice and leaf on the bouquet, suggesting some canopy/ripening problems. The palate, too, is in a gamey/spicy/leafy mould, and is a fraction thin in the mouth.

1986 ★★★★★   *November 1994*
Dense red–purple; a wonderfully concentrated bouquet with luscious dark chocolate, mint, earth and berry aromas. The palate, too, is massively powerful and concentrated; at this stage verging on a vinous black hole in space. Will be superb with age.

1985 ★★★★★   *November 1994*
Medium red; a complex and intense bouquet with gamey/chocolate aromas. The mouthfeel is outstanding, with chocolate and earth flavours, and wonderfully supple fine-grained tannins.

◄ Not Ready   ❧ Still evolving   ♠ Prime of its life   ✐ Drink soon   ⛾ Missed the boat

1984 ★★★★☆ *November 1994*

Medium red–purple; a smooth and sweet bouquet with vanilla and cherry fruit, and just a faint touch of mint. The palate is smooth, with dark cherry fruit, a touch of earth, finishing with moderate tannins. Subtle oak.

1974 ★★ *November 1994*

Medium red; a rather astringent, earthy and seemingly sulphidic bouquet, leading on to an astringent, earthy palate. The one redeeming feature of the wine is that it is still youthful.

1973 ★★★ *November 1994*

Medium red; the bouquet is of light to medium intensity with earthy/chocolatey aromas and some volatility apparent. The palate is earthy, sharpish and tannic, lacking sweet fruit.

1972 ★★★ *November 1994*

Medium red with a touch of tawny; the bouquet is clean, tending plain, with some typical chocolate and earth aromas. The palate too is light, lacking flesh though it does have reasonable mouthfeel.

1971 ★★★★☆ *November 1994*

Medium red; the bouquet is clean and sweet, with attractive berry and earth fruit aromas. The palate is fresh and youthful, with good concentration; there are dark chocolate and black cherry flavours on the mid-palate, finishing with quite pronounced tannins.

1968 ★★★☆ *November 1994*

Medium red; a clean, fairly light bouquet with sweet mint and berry aromas. The palate is light with chocolate, earth and mint flavours intermingling, finishing with soft tannins.

1964 ★★★★ *November 1994*

Medium to full red; the bouquet is rich and sweet, with touches of chocolate and earth, leading on to a fragrant, multiflavoured palate with truffle and chocolate flavours, finishing with fine tannins. Jimmy Watson Trophy winner 1975 and 11 gold medals. This particular bottle was not, perhaps, as good as it should have been.

1963 Bin T114/115 ★★★★★ *November 1994*

Medium to full red–purple; gamey, complex secondary fruit characters developing on the bouquet, strongly reminiscent of the Rhône. A wine still possessed of great freshness, life and lift, with hints of mint to go along with the game on the mid-palate, finishing with soft tannins and perfectly balanced acid.

1960 Bin Q97 St Ethel ★★★★★ *November 1994*

Medium red; an almost ethereal amalgam of mint, leather, coffee and dark chocolate aromas on the bouquet. The palate is rich with abundant dark chocolate and black cherry fruit; slightly burnt notes give a hint of bitterness on the finish, but the bouquet of the wine is so entrancing it has to get top points.

classic wines

★★★★★ Perfect   ★★★★☆ Close to perfect   ★★★★ Very good   ★★★☆ Expected
★★★ Short of standard   ★★☆ Undeserving   ★★ Decayed relic   NR No rating

1956 Bin M37 ★★★★★   *November 1994*

Deep red–purple, astonishing for age. A perfumed yet pure and totally fresh bouquet with hints of liquorice which carry through to an elegant, long palate, finishing with fine tannins. A superb wine.

1954 Bin K72 ★★★★   *November 1994*

Light to medium red; sweet coffee, chocolate and toffee aromas to a smooth bouquet. The palate shows similar soft, ripe, chocolatey fruit, with hints of cedary oak and soft tannins, and lemony acid on the finish.

◄ Not Ready   ＼ Still evolving   Prime of its life   Drink soon   Missed the boat

seppelt 100 year old para liqueur
ports 1878-1900

these 100-year-old wines are awesome in the power and concentration of their flavour. Consider the analysis of the 1894 vintage: 16.25° baumé, 25.2 per cent alcohol, 10.8 grams per litre of acid, and a pH of 3.68.

Then look at the consistency and colour of the wine; so dense and syrupy that it actually paints the inside of the glass brown when you swirl it. The bouquet is so heady and penetrating that a range of glasses fills the room with liquorous aromas of spice and alcohol, bringing back childhood memories of my mother making her Christmas puddings laced with brandy.

Then the flavour of the Para: so intense that a tiny sip causes every taste receptor in the mouth to react as if electrically stimulated, lingering for many minutes after it is swallowed.

The first barrel was laid down in 1878 by Benno Seppelt, and a barrel has been laid down ever since. In fact two or three are laid down, and are gradually combined into one 500 litre puncheon when wine is finally drawn off for bottling, only part is taken: the remainder is transferred to a smaller barrel, and so on and so forth.

So Seppelt not only has an uncompromised cask (i.e. 100 per cent) of the same vintage stretching from 1900 to the present day (and into the future), but also has wine remaining in perfect condition back to the original release of 1878. The 100-year-old name, incidentally, derives from the fact that these wines are released on their 100th anniversary.

First tasted in November 1994, updated, and later vintages added.

1900 ★★★★★   *October 1999*

Dark olive–brown; the bouquet moves to another dimension, with significantly more luscious raisin cake/pudding fruit and a shaft of intensity which lances the air. The palate tracks the bouquet, gorgeously supple and mouthfilling, with lingering flavours which seem to increase, rather than decrease, after the wine is swallowed and you take your first few breaths. James Godrey believes it to be the best balanced and richest of all of the Paras, and I can but humbly agree.

1899 ★★★★★   *October 1999*

Deep olive–brown; the bouquet is powerful, raisiny and rich, with caramelised toffee aromas. The palate is intense and complex; it gives the illusion of some citrussy flavours inside the toffee exterior, flavours which lengthen the palate.

classic wines

| ★★★★★ Perfect | ★★★★☆ Close to perfect | ★★★★ Very good | ★★★☆ Expected |
| ★★★ Short of standard | ★★☆ Undeserving | ★★ Decayed relic | NR No rating |

1898 ★★★★☆   *October 1999*

Dark brown, tinged with olive; the bouquet has slightly less powerful aromatics than the 1897, but takes in the usual coffee, toffee and raisin characters. These are the flavours of the palate, although it corresponds to the bouquet by having marginally less fruit power and intensity. It really is an exercise in splitting hairs to knock half a star off the wine.

1897 ★★★★★   *May 1997*

Dark olive–brown, tinged with green, and pours like viscous oil; the bouquet leaps out of the glass, with cascades of aroma; plum pudding, toffee and the works lifted by the touch of volatility one always encounters. The tiniest sip is overwhelming, drawing saliva from every corner of the mouth; incredibly concentrated and essencey.

1896 ★★★★★   *April 1997*

Dark dense brown, merging into olive; a penetrating, intense bouquet with typical rancio and a degree of volatility. Toffee, crème brûlée, plum pudding and spice aromas and flavours run through both bouquet and palate. An overwhelmingly powerful, rich and pungently long wine to 'be sipped' and savoured in minute quantities.

1895 ★★★★★   *November 1994*

Dark brown with an olive rim; the bouquet is intense and harmonious with raisiny fruit, toffee, brandysnap and a touch of caramel backed by high spirit and rancio. The palate is as harmonious as the bouquet promises, with similar brandysnap, toffee and chocolate flavours, finishing with cleansing acidity.

1894 ★★★★★   *November 1994*

Dark olive–brown; a powerful bouquet in the mainstream of the 100-year-old style, with briary/chocolate/earthy/plum pudding aromas. The palate is hugely powerful with dark briary/berry/toffee flavours and slightly more tannin than others in the line-up.

1893 ★★★★☆   *November 1994*

The colour is distinctly lighter than many, the bouquet softer and sweet with fragrant toffee and caramel aromas. The palate is similar, almost tending to tokay malt-like flavours on the mid-palate, but then firming up on the finish.

1892 ★★★★★   *November 1994*

Dark brown–olive; a sweet bouquet with toffee and brandysnap aromas predominant, but with hints of earth and chocolate there too. The palate is attractive, rich, well balanced and harmonious with toffee and plum pudding flavours giving a fleshy overall feel.

1891 ★★★★   *November 1994*

Dark olive–brown; the bouquet is somewhat spirity, lacking the richer fruit of the best wines in the line-up, but does have some pleasant chocolatey characters. The palate, too, is less rich than many, with earthy/spirity/chocolatey flavours, and fairly high, fractionally hard, acid on the finish. A hypercritical tasting note; in any normal circumstances, this is a great wine.

1890 ★★★★★   *November 1994*

The colour of the wines from this point on is so similar that I shall not comment further on it; all were dark brown, with an olive rim. The bouquet is much softer, with plum pudding aromas, touched with briar and earth. The palate is easier on the mouth than many, with most attractive soft, chewy fruit, and a lingering, yet wonderfully soft, finish.

1889 ★★★★☆   *November 1994*

The bouquet is intense, with strong rancio and a penetrating volatile lift, underpinned by briary/woody characters. The palate has more dark chocolate flavours, with good mid-palate fruit, then rancio and a degree of volatile acidity coming again on the finish. Impressively potent and powerful.

1888 ★★★★☆   *November 1994*

The aromas are very much in the dark chocolate spectrum with a hint of earthy spirit. The palate is less luscious than some, with quite firm, earthy notes, finishing with pronounced acidity.

1887 ★★★★★   *November 1994*

A wonderfully complex bouquet with toffee, brandysnap and earth aromas, shot through by moderately intense spirit. In the mouth, viscous and concentrated, particularly on the mid to back palate, with wonderful toffee and plum pudding flavours.

1886 ★★★★★   *November 1994*

The aromas are sweet and smooth chocolate and toffee intermingling, and lower rancio/volatile acidity. The palate is rich, full and sweet, with plum pudding flavours, lots of alcohol and lower apparent acid.

1885 ★★★★★   *November 1994*

A richly complex bouquet with toffee, chocolate and dark earth aromas lead on to a palate with sweet, plum pudding/chocolate/coffee flavours, with lower acidity and volatile acidity than some of the other wines in the line-up.

1884 ★★★★★   *November 1994*

There is fairly high-toned spirit on a powerful, fractionally edgy bouquet with aromas of bitter chocolate and earth. The palate is powerful and potent, with some of the same edgy earth and chocolate characters of the bouquet, and not as richly sweet as the best of the wines.

1883 ★★★★★   *November 1994*

At once having high-toned, lifted yet harmonious aromas with smooth brandysnap and dark briary earthy fruit on the bouquet. The palate is extremely rich and complex with brandysnap/chocolate flavours, with a powerful, lingering finish.

1882 ★★★★☆   *November 1994*

The bouquet is extraordinarily concentrated with masses of briary/dark chocolate fruit lifted by strong, volatile rancio characters. The palate is powerful, with penetrating rancio and volatile characters which Michael Broadbent, noted English writer, would describe as 'swingeing'.

★★★★★ Perfect   ★★★★☆ Close to perfect   ★★★★ Very good   ★★★☆ Expected
★★★ Short of standard   ★★☆ Undeserving   ★★ Decayed relic   NR No rating

classic wines

239

1881 ★★★★☆   *November 1994*

A classic, penetrating spirit and rancio bouquet with dried biscuit and toffee aromas. The palate is slightly less weighty and concentrated than some of the other vintages around this time, but has tremendous power and length, with toffee and brandysnap flavours, and strong rancio.

1880 ★★★★★   *November 1994*

The bouquet is smooth, with abundant burnt toffee/dark chocolate fruit, and moderate rancio and volatility. The palate, too, is marvellously fruity and rich, with toffee, plum pudding and raisin flavours; the acid is well balanced.

1879 ★★★★★   *November 1994*

The bouquet is much sweeter than many of the oldest wines, rounder with chocolatey/biscuity aromas and a hint of earthy spirit. The palate is slightly sweeter and slightly less aggressively intense than the 1878, with tastes of plum pudding, dark chocolate, toffee and spices; the tannins are soft, the acidity balanced.

1878 ★★★★★   *November 1994*

The bouquet is powerful and concentrated with strong rancio but volatility under control, with hints of dried leaf and wood. The palate is, like all of these old wines, mouth puckering in its concentration, but with superb sweet fruit on the mid-palate in that infinitely complex spectrum of flavours, finishing with lingering acidity.

seppelt para liqueur port

If the tasting of the 100-year-old Para Ports was the most challenging, that of the ten-year progression of the wines from 1904 to 1994 was the most fascinating tasting of all.

Research has shown that the baumé (sugar concentration) peaks when the wines reach 50 to 75 years of age, between 12° and 17° baumé; that acid peaks at 50 years, between 6 and 11 grams per litre, and like the baumé, then stabilises; and that the alcoholic strength will vary according to the humidity and atmospheric conditions of storage. This concentration takes place as over two-thirds of the original volume of wine is lost by evaporation — the so-called Angel's Share. A pretty big share.

This process of concentration was abundantly obvious in the tasting. The 1994 was there to demonstrate one thing: this just-born infant is perfectly formed and balanced, delicious now. Development continues apace with the '84, '74 and '64; with the last wine you hit the first real indication of what lies in store. Indeed, unless you knew better, you could not imagine a more concentrated wine than the '64.

In fact the '54, '44 and '34 are further stepping stones until you reach the '24. From this point backwards all the way to 1878 the differences are minuscule: as James Godfrey, senior Seppelt winemaker at Seppeltsfield whose task it is to make the young wines and guard the old wines, says, 'You taste by exception'.

First tasted in November 1994, updated.

1994 NR   *November 1994*

Bright red; a lively, fresh, spotlessly clean bouquet with spicy/nutmeg varietal fruit aromas. The palate is fresh and as perfectly balanced as any table wine I have ever tasted; the sweetness is not particularly obvious, and the wine could be drunk with total enjoyment before its first birthday.

1984 ★★★★☆   *November 1994*

The colour is still red, but starting to develop tawny aspects; the bouquet is complex, with fine spirit, and what appears to be a touch of oak (it will remain in this barrel for more than 50 years, and will reabsorb the oak over this time). The palate shows a wine in transition, not yet a true tawny, yet not a young wine either. However, the all-important balance is there.

classic wines

★★★★★ Perfect   ★★★★☆ Close to perfect   ★★★★ Very good   ★★★☆ Expected
★★★ Short of standard   ★★☆ Undeserving   ★★ Decayed relic   NR No rating

241

1981 ★★★★★ *April 1997*

Medium tawny–red; the bouquet has a well-balanced mix of spicy fruit and pleasantly earthy spirit; the exceptional harmonious palate shows ripples of gently spicy fruit interwoven with soft tannins, a touch of rancio lift and perfectly balanced acidity.

1979 ★★★★★ *November 1994*

Medium to full tawny; the bouquet is penetrating, with fine, faintly earthy spirity notes and pronounced rancio; there are the usual complex array of spicy, nutty aromas also present. A harmonious wine on the palate, with a fine, lingering raisin, toffee and biscuit palate with a cleansing finish.

1977 ★★★★☆ *November 1994*

Medium tawny; the bouquet seems to be rather softer than the '79 with a complex array of toffee, nut, biscuit and tea-leaf aromas. The palate, too, is distinctly soft, and although very complex has some tea-leaf and sweet orange flavours which seem to put it a little to one side of the mainstream, but which are very attractive.

1974 ★★★★☆ *November 1994*

Medium to full tawny, with a hint of olive on the rim; strong rancio characters are starting to develop on the bouquet; while the wine is very long on the palate, with a cleansing finish, remarkable for what was an appalling vintage in the Barossa Valley. It seems to be going through a phase of its development where the alcohol is relatively aggressive in comparison to the fruit development.

1964 ★★★★★ *November 1994*

A further dramatic shift in the colour is evident, now dark, deep brown with an olive rim; the bouquet is very concentrated with earthy, pungent rancio aromas. The palate is much richer, with dark chocolate and toffee flavours, finishing with balancing acidity.

1954 ★★★★☆ *November 1994*

Deep olive–brown; the bouquet shows rather lighter and less luscious fruit than the '64, perhaps reflecting the further development of the wine as caramel and toffee aromas intermingle with more woody/spirity characters. The palate, however, shows extreme concentration and power with a rich toffee and caramel mid-palate, finishing with pronounced acidity. Some volatile acidity is starting to make its presence felt, which is only appropriate.

1944 ★★★★★ *November 1994*

Deep olive–brown; the bouquet is smooth, with hints of chocolate, earth, raisin and toffee all cut by the now fully-developed rancio and volatile acidity. The palate is powerful, with chocolate, toffee, woody, briary flavours intermingling, balanced by acidity which prevents the finish from cloying.

1934 ★★★★★ *November 1994*

The colour has many hues, basically deep olive, but shot with some unexpected red–brown hints. The bouquet is rich, sweet and very concentrated with almost voluptuous chocolate and toffee fruit aromas, seemingly with significantly higher alcohol. The palate, too, has tremendous sweetness and richness on entry to the mouth with a range of toffee, chocolate and caramel flavours, then running into pronounced rancio, and acidity in various forms.

◄■ Not Ready   ＼ Still evolving   ▮ Prime of its life   ✎ Drink soon   ☐ Missed the boat

1925 ★★★★★ *November 1994*

Impenetrable, dark colour, the texture of the wine in the glass viscous. The bouquet is unbelievably concentrated and complex, rich and woody, with strong rancio characters. In the mouth, another quantum leap in concentration, gloriously rich, textured and sweet on the mid-palate, with perfect acid balance on the finish. A superb wine.

1914 ★★★★☆ *November 1994*

Deep, dark olive–brown; the bouquet shows pronounced rancio and volatility, giving extraordinary complexity. On the palate, the rancio and volatile characters are the first impression, then rich chocolate, toffee and plum pudding flavours come through progressively.

1904 ★★★★★ *November 1994*

Impenetrable olive–brown; a deep, concentrated bouquet with wood, earth, briar and chocolate aromas intermingling. The palate is tremendously rich and chewy with dark chocolate, toffee and plum pudding flavours, followed by that omnipresent (and very necessary) acidity on the finish.

★★★★★ Perfect ★★★★☆ Close to perfect ★★★★ Very good ★★★☆ Expected
★★★ Short of standard ★★☆ Undeserving ★★ Decayed relic NR No rating

seppelt show sparkling burgundies

Some of you will barely stop to read the heading, and pass on wondering why anyone should waste time with such strange wines. Others will be as jealous of this tasting as any other, and I suppose it is to those I speak.

As will be seen, up to 1967 the base wine varied between 100 per cent Great Western Shiraz and a veritable cocktail; from 1972 onwards all the wines have been made entirely from Great Western Shiraz — more particularly, from the block of very old vines adjacent to the winery. A battle royal is waged between the team responsible for the Shiraz (dry red) and that responsible for the Sparkling Burgundy, each wanting the lion's share of the grapes.

That tug-of-war underlines the fact that Sparkling Burgundies are far closer to conventional red wines than are their white counterparts. This similarity becomes more and more pronounced as the wines age and lose their gas: indeed many bottles of the '44 and '46 have next to no visible carbon dioxide, and it is only a faint prickle on the tongue. Yet the gas has played an essential role in preserving fruit freshness: these are glorious renditions of old Shiraz.

It follows that I would not hesitate to cellar the new show reserve wines which are disgorged after ten years on yeast lees and released at that age. They will only get better and better. Incidentally, the notes are from a single tasting in November 1994, but occasionally make reference to an earlier (similar) tasting in 1984.

◄■ 1991 ★★★★☆   *November 1994*
Medium to full red–purple; an exceptionally complex bouquet with very similar characters to the '85, with a strong varietal gamey overlay. The palate is complex, with abundant game and mint flavours to a big, rich wine with enormous potential, particularly if you like the style of the '85. Not for release until 2001.

◄■ 1990 ★★★★☆   *November 1994*
Full purple–red; complex dark berry, chocolate and spicy fruit aromas with the faintest whisper of aldehyde. The palate has layer upon layer of flavour in the dark chocolate and berry spectrum. Another great wine in the making.

❧ 1987 ★★★★☆   *November 1994*
Medium to full red–purple; the bouquet has a wide spectrum of aromas, with dark berry, spice and earth intermingling, with a fraction of liquorice. The palate shows a similar amalgam of leaf, liquorice and berry flavours reflecting a cooler, but very dry, vintage. Potent and youthful.

◄■ Not Ready   ❧ Still evolving   ♟ Prime of its life   ✑ Drink soon   ⌻ Missed the boat

1986 ★★★★★ October 1997

Medium to full red; a complex mix spice, plum, game and earth claim the varietal origin of the wine. A marvellously balanced palate with spice, liquorice, game and earth flavours, with a dash of dark chocolate thrown in for good measure, and most impressively of all, without undue sweetness. Winner of 16 gold medals.

1985 ★★★★★ November 1994

Medium to full red; an ultra-distinctive bouquet with strong gamey shiraz varietal character. The palate has identical gamey flavours, which, taken with the dosage, give a quite sweet overall impression. A wine with a tremendous show record.

1984 ★★★★★ November 1994

Medium to full red; a distinctly peppery/spicy bouquet with clear-cut and spotlessly clean cool-grown varietal shiraz aroma. The palate is lively and fresh, again with pronounced peppery/spicy flavours and a crisp finish. Idiosyncratic, but I personally like the style.

1983 ★★★★☆ November 1994

Medium to full red, with just a touch of purple remaining; the bouquet is clean and smooth, with sweet berry fruit, and just a hint of mint. The palate shows rather more minty characters, but not to the point of exaggeration or domination, with red berry fruits also present, a hint of oak, and likewise earth. An elegant wine, maturing nicely.

1982 ★★★★ November 1994

Light to medium red; a hint of vanillin oak can be detected, along with minty/earthy varietal shiraz fruit on the bouquet. The palate is complex, with a range of flavours through sweet berry to mint and earth. The dosage is nicely balanced, giving a pleasantly dry (or, at least, not sweet) finish.

1972 ★★★★☆ November 1994

Medium red, amazingly holding a touch of purple. The aromas are complex with mint, leaf, chocolate and earth all present, and then an intriguing aroma of something akin to soapsuds, though not the least unpleasant. Spicy characters progressively came up on the palate which has touches of chocolate and earth, finishing with fine tannins, and — again — well-balanced dosage.

1967 Bin 7A Dry Red ★★★★★ November 1994

40 per cent South Australia Dry Red, 27 per cent Rutherglen Dry Red and 33 per cent Great Western Shiraz. Medium to full red; some leafy/gamey notes on the bouquet, but a potent, rich and powerful wine on the palate with lots of chocolate, leaf and berry flavours, reminiscent of the '87.

1965 Bin 94A ★★★☆ November 1994

100 per cent Great Western Shiraz. Medium to full red with no gas evident at all. The bouquet has a curious varnishy/woody edge, the palate tending hard. In the 1984 tasting, the wine did not show especially well, but on that occasion had mushroomy characters. There is obvious bottle variation, and this bottle, too, was quite possibly not representative.

classic wines

★★★★★ Perfect	★★★★☆ Close to perfect	★★★★ Very good	★★★☆ Expected
★★★ Short of standard	★★☆ Undeserving	★★ Decayed relic	NR No rating

245

1965 Bin 93A ★★★★ *November 1994*

No region of origin given. The colour is medium red, with the gas largely dissipated. The bouquet is sweet, clean and attractive with chocolate, berry and spice aromas, promising much more than the palate in fact delivers, which is rather lighter and rather more earthy — even bitter — than the bouquet suggests it will be.

1964 Bin 85C ★★★★★ *November 1994*

46 per cent Rutherglen, 39 per cent Barossa Valley, 15 per cent Great Western Shiraz. Youthful red–purple; lives up to the colour, with clean youthful but rich dark chocolate and cherry aromas. The palate is rich and fuller than the Bin 87A, likewise slightly sweeter. Like the 87A, finishes with fine tannins and good acid.

1964 Bin 87A ★★★★★ *November 1994*

100 per cent Great Western Shiraz. Medium red; the bouquet has wonderful character with abundant sweet chocolate aromas and a touch of shiraz varietal earth. A beautifully balanced and flavoured wine on the palate, with a mix of chocolate flavours, finishing with fine, soft tannins on a long farewell. In perfect condition.

1963 ★★★★☆ *November 1994*

Medium red, with just a touch of tawny starting to develop. The bouquet is fragrant, with clean spicy/earthy varietal fruit. The palate shows similar characters ranging from spice to tobacco to cedar/cigar box, all denoting secondary flavour development. (No bin number.)

1963 Bin 81A ★★★★☆ *November 1994*

71 per cent Great Western Shiraz, 20 per cent Great Western Dry Red, 9 per cent Great Western Malbec. Light to medium red, holding its gas well. A very complex bouquet with some of those gamey characters reminiscent of the '85 and '91. The palate, likewise, is very complex with flavours ranging from gamey to spicy; in the 1984 tasting, was magnificent, with Burgundian-like characters.

1963 Bin 80B ★★★★ *November 1994*

66 per cent Rutherglen Dry Red, 24 per cent Great Western Shiraz, 6 per cent Great Western Shiraz and Black Prince, 4 per cent Great Western Malbec. Medium red; aromas of spice, earth and chocolate appeared first, followed by a faint hint of mushroom which progressively developed in the glass. The palate shows a similar blend of wood, earth, berry and mushroom flavours of medium weight but considerable flavour complexity.

1961 Bin 74A ★★★★★ *November 1994*

100 per cent Great Western Shiraz. Medium to full red; strong berry and chocolate aromas dominate a fresh and powerful bouquet. The palate is everything the bouquet promises, still with strong berry chocolate and earth flavours; not the least bit sweet, and will be long lived.

Not Ready   Still evolving   Prime of its life   Drink soon   Missed the boat

1957 Bin 58C NR

November 1994

35 per cent Great Western Dry Red, 29 per cent Rutherglen Dry Red, 27 per cent Great Western Hermitage, 9 per cent Barooga Shiraz/Cabernet. In the 1994 tasting, totally dominated by the aroma and taste of fresh mushrooms, and impossible to see any other aromas or flavours. In the 1984 tasting, showed some aggressive tar/Marmite aromas, but the palate was much better with considerable lift, length and pleasant acidity on the finish.

1954 Bin 46A ★★★★★

November 1994

74 per cent Hermitage, 5 per cent Pinot Meuniere, 3 per cent grey Pinot, all from Great Western; 12 per cent South Australian Dry Red and 6 per cent Rutherglen Shiraz. Light to medium red, with a touch of tawny. The bouquet is clean and soft, of light to medium intensity, with gently sweet berry and chocolate aromas. In the mouth, a superb aged wine, beautifully balanced, with gentle chocolate and earth flavours, yet fresh as a daisy. Perfect acid/dosage. Disgorged 1984, and magnificent in that tasting too. The best in this tasting.

1946 ★★★★★

November 1994

No blend details available, but the label states Great Western Hermitage. Light to medium tawny; there is a faint hint of mushroom, allied with sweet chocolate and earth fruit which is still surprisingly powerful. The palate is potent, with more mushroom characters than the wine normally shows, but not detracting from it. The finish is still long and powerful. This remains a remarkable wine.

1944 ★★★★★

November 1994

No blend details. Light to medium tawny, with just a touch of red. There is lovely chocolatey fruit, as fresh as a daisy on the bouquet with hints of liquorice also adding to the appeal. Wonderfully rounded, sweet, mouthfilling chocolate and liquorice flavours; great balance and elegance. Together with the '54, quite magnificent wines.

★★★★★ Perfect　　★★★★☆ Close to perfect　　★★★★ Very good　　★★★☆ Expected
★★★ Short of standard　　★★☆ Undeserving　　★★ Decayed relic　　NR No rating

classic wines

247

seville estate shiraz 1976-1997

Unlike Guill de Pury of Yeringberg (who pulled out his shiraz after the 1981 vintage, simply because no one wanted the wine at the time notwithstanding its exceptional quality), Dr Peter McMahon persevered with his shiraz at Seville Estate. Indeed, in order to protect it from the depradations of botrytis, he removed the neighbouring riesling and ceased making his great late harvest beerenauslese and trockenbeerenauslese wines.

It was a far-sighted decision, and was doubtless a contributing factor in Brokenwood's decision to acquire a controlling interest in Seville Estate in 1997 — after a lengthy courtship during which Iain Riggs (of Brokenwood) assisted in the making of Seville Estate wines in 1996 and 1997.

Another turning point came with the retention of Dr Richard Smart as viticultural consultant in 1990. This led to radical changes in the trellis design and canopy management, changes which had the effect of providing far riper grapes, with better colour, better pH and better acidity. The red volcanic soils of this southern side of the valley, coupled with higher rainfall and slightly lower temperatures, contribute to vigorous growth, and the original vine training systems caused excessive shading.

Between 1993 and 1996 the Yarra Valley had a series of difficult vintages, in particular those of '95 and '96, each marked by heavy rainfall in the latter part of vintage. They were not kind years for late-ripening varieties such as shiraz, and with a return to normal conditions Seville Estate will undoubtedly produce many more wines with the quality of the '91 and '93 vintages.

All except the 1997 were tasted in August 1997.

1997 ★★★★ *February 1999*

Full red–purple; the bouquet is rich and powerful, with abundant dark berry/cherry fruit, with oak in support. The high-flavoured palate shows rather more oak extract, but the fruit is there as are chewy tannins. A striking example from a warm, low-yielding Yarra vintage. Gold medal 1999 Sydney Royal Wine Show.

1996 ★★★☆ *August 1997*

Excellent purple–red colour; the bouquet is clean, with that mix of black cherry, earth and spice in abundance; the palate shows a similar range of cherry, spice and strongly earthy fruit, supported by subtle oak and moderate tannins. In retrospect, the rating may be a little on the harsh side.

◄━ Not Ready　　❮ Still evolving　　❰ Prime of its life　　⚲ Drink soon　　▯ Missed the boat

1995 ★★★★ *August 1997*

Strong purple–red; dark cherry aromas, together with hints of liquorice and boot polish on the bouquet, are followed by smooth, well-balanced tannins with supple red cherry fruit, integrated oak and soft tannins.

1994 ★★★★☆ *August 1997*

Medium purple–red; an aromatic and complex bouquet with Rhône Valley overtones and hints of forest and leather is followed by a wine which already shows a range of secondary fruit characters, forerunners of those to be found in the wines of the 1980s.

1993 ★★★★★ *August 1997*

Medium purple–red; a fragrant bouquet with a mix of black cherry and spice fruit leads into an arresting and powerful palate, long and intense, with pronounced spicy fruit flavours.

1992 ★★★★★ *August 1997*

Medium to full red–purple; a complex and fragrant bouquet with sweet leathery characters of the vineyard just starting to emerge; a lovely wine on the palate, with smooth, sweet cherry fruit; very good fine tannins and mouthfeel.

1991 ★★★★★ *August 1997*

Bright and strong purple–red; a dramatic shift in the aroma and flavour, with a concentrated and powerful bouquet heralding a ripe palate flooded with black cherry fruit and complexing touches of liquorice and spice. Has authority; the structure is good, as is the mouthfeel. Will age very well.

1990 ★★★★ *August 1997*

The purple–red hue is good, though light in density; the palate is light, with distinct spice, and some hints of leather and earth starting to develop. The palate is still quite fresh, in a light spicy mode, but does show some of those dilute 1990 characters evident in many (though not all) Yarra Valley reds of this vintage.

1989 ★★★☆ *August 1997*

Light to medium red; the bouquet is radically different from the wines from '91 and younger, like an old Hunter Shiraz, yet not unattractive. The palate shows a mix of the earth, leaf, leather and spice characters which run through so many of the older wines, finishing with sharpish acid. A satisfactory outcome for one of the most difficult Yarra vintages.

1988 ★★★★ *August 1997*

Medium red–purple; a relatively youthful bouquet of medium intensity, with that mainstream vineyard/varietal earthy character dominating both the bouquet and palate, allied with some forest/woody characters on the mid-palate. The wine does have power and good structure.

1987 ★★★☆ *August 1997*

Medium red–purple; shows a relatively cool vintage with somewhat aged leafy overtones, although there are some spicy characters on the bouquet. The palate shows the impact of the vintage, too, with slightly sharp edges.

classic wines

★★★★★ Perfect ★★★★☆ Close to perfect ★★★★ Very good ★★★☆ Expected
★★★ Short of standard ★★☆ Undeserving ★★ Decayed relic NR No rating

249

1986 ★★★★ *August 1997*

Medium red–purple; a fragrant bouquet with earthy/spicy/leather characters, very much in the vineyard style, leads into a palate with penetrating flavours of spice, earth and leather, still fresh and lively.

1985 ★★★★★ *August 1997*

Excellent, bright purple–red; the bouquet is complex, with a mix of liquorice and leather/boot polish varietal aromas, the palate rich and complex, with mouthfilling sweet liquorice and black cherry fruit; long finish.

1984

Not made.

1983 ★★★ *August 1997*

Once again, the colour is tending to brick–brown, the bouquet distinctly leafy/spicy, and the palate showing an array of flavours all suggesting imperfectly ripened fruit, probably the result of extreme stress and leaf-drop during a drought vintage.

1982 ★★★ *August 1997*

Slightly browner in colour than the '81; light leaf, spice and earth aromas are followed by a rather gamey palate with dimethyl sulphide characters and slightly medicinal overtones.

1981 ★★☆ *August 1997*

Reasonably good medium red hue; the leafy/earthy bouquet is of light to medium intensity, with some old leather aromas, and the wine is starting to fade on the palate, with the acid poking through the remnants of fruit.

1980 ★★★☆ *August 1997*

Medium brick–red; the aromas are quite complex, with a mix of gentle leather, liquorice and spice, and just a hint of dimethyl sulphide characters. The flavours, too, run in the spice/medicine/liquorice spectrum, but the wine does have some flesh and is hanging in there well.

1978 ★★★☆ *August 1997*

Medium red, quite bright; the bouquet has some Hunter Valley-like notes in an earthy/spicy/charry range, leading into a palate which is quite firm and fresh with a mix of leathery/earthy flavours, legitimate reflections of aged Shiraz, and finishing with moderate acid.

1977 ★★ *August 1997*

Volatile acidity on both bouquet and palate, together with some stewed fruit characters, make the wine unacceptable.

1976 ★★★★ *August 1997*

Amazing depth to its colour; the bouquet is still concentrated and powerful, ripe berry fruit tinged with dark chocolate. The palate shows similar ripeness, with prune and dark chocolate flavours, strikingly different from the immediately following vintages, and a quite remarkable first-crop wine.

➛ Not Ready   ❯ Still evolving   ❙ Prime of its life   ⌀ Drink soon   ▯ Missed the boat

st hallett old block shiraz

there are those who would see the national and international reputation of Old Block as nothing more than a reflection of the marketing skills of former Managing Director Bob McLean. And since McLean did not become a shareholder (and director) of St Hallett until 1988, this would suggest Old Block is a kind of vinous nouveau riche, here today and gone tomorrow.

The truth is otherwise. For a start, the wine is made from vines grown on 18 very small, carefully selected vineyards, most of which are over 100 years old, and no new vineyard source is used unless wine has been made from it in previous vintages.

What is more, the wine had been made — and its quality recognised — well before Bob McLean joined St Hallett. Indeed, it is a fair assumption that he recognised it as one of St Hallett's substantial, if intangible assets. In turn, both sides of the equation were ahead of the field in identifying Shiraz made from old, unirrigated, low-yielding vines as a precious, indeed, unique, Australian asset which would inevitably gain international recognition.

In conjunction with long-time friend and winemaker, Stuart Blackwell, McLean has both protected the wine while judiciously increasing volumes. There are some who see the introduction of an element of new American oak as a plus, others who do not. But no one disputes the integrity of the quality of the wine. The rapid ownership changes in 2001, culminating with the Lion Nathan ownership, herald a new order.

Tasted in November 1994, updated, later vintages added.

◀ *1997* ★★★★☆   *March 2000*
Medium red–purple; the bouquet is complex, with a mix of cedar, vanilla and chocolate over the red berry fruit; the flavours are quite intense though far from heavy, offering cherry and the faintest hint of mint, closing with fine tannins.

◀ *1996* ★★★★☆   *October 1994*
Medium red–purple; there are distinct minty notes to the fruit which come and go in ripe Barossa shiraz. The palate has soft, easy cherry/mint fruit, nicely handled oak and fine tannins. Elegant, but once again, I would have hoped for a touch more concentration.

classic wines

★★★★★ Perfect   ★★★★☆ Close to perfect   ★★★★ Very good   ★★★☆ Expected
★★★ Short of standard   ★★☆ Undeserving   ★★ Decayed relic   NR No rating

1995 ★★★★☆   *January 1998*

Medium red–purple; a clean, smooth bouquet of medium intensity with cherry and vanilla aromas interwoven announces an ultra-smooth palate with a mix of dark plum and black cherry fruit supported by soft vanilla oak and fine tannins. An understatement, rather than an overstatement.

1994 ★★★★☆   *May 1997*

Medium to full red–purple; the bouquet is smooth, with earthy shiraz varietal character set in fairly obvious American oak in the modern style. On the palate there is ample fruit to support the generous helpings of American oak; a well crafted and sculpted wine.

1993 ★★★★★   *January 1996*

Medium to full red–purple; clean, moderately intense bouquet of dark cherry and plum fruit, with oak evident but in restraint. As ever, a marvellously stylish wine on the palate, spotlessly clean and very well crafted, with that black cherry fruit and a vanilla cream texture and flavour coming from the judicious use of good American oak. Right up to form.

1992 ★★★★★   *November 1994*

Medium to full red–purple; fragrant, spicy varietal fruit with an abundant sweet cherry core and a hint of vanillin/coconut oak. The palate shows lovely cherry fruit with a hint of liquorice and more spice than either the '91 or '90 vintages.

1991 ★★★★☆   *November 1994*

Medium red–purple; a clean bouquet of medium to full intensity with smooth minty berry and vanillin oak aromas. That vanillin oak is quite pronounced on the palate, which has a chewy texture and plenty of weighty, ripe fruit, with a hint of spice lurking in the background. A big wine which should mature well.

1990 ★★★★★   *November 1994*

Full red–purple; a most attractive bouquet with a pronounced varietal spicy edge to dark berry fruit and well-integrated oak. The palate is at once concentrated and classy, with lots of red berry/dark cherry fruits and vanillin oak which is obvious, but well handled and integrated. The structure of the wine is particularly impressive.

1989 ★★★★   *November 1994*

Medium to full red–purple; a smooth bouquet with generous, dark berry fruits and a hint of varietal earth; the oak is evident, but in restraint. A nicely rounded wine on the palate with soft dark berry and chocolate fruit flavours, finishing with soft tannins. Will be relatively early maturing, but an unqualified success for the vintage.

1988 ★★★★☆   *November 1994*

Medium red–purple; smooth, clean berry fruit with the first obvious vanillin notes from the introduction of new American oak. A lighter wine on the palate, which is still quite fresh, again showing cedary oak input; has finer structure and tannins than the older wines.

━◄ Not Ready   ╲ Still evolving   ▮ Prime of its life   ✓ Drink soon   ☐ Missed the boat

1987 ★★★★☆ *November 1994*

Medium red–purple; a far riper and more luscious bouquet and palate than one might expect from the vintage, indeed one of the richest of all South Australian '87 red wines I have tasted. There are earthy/chocolatey notes, rounded off by soft, lingering tannins.

1986 ★★★★☆ *November 1994*

Medium to full red–purple; concentrated, ripe but not jammy, dark berry fruit aromas lead on to a solid, youthful palate with dark briary/berry fruit flavours, finishing with well-balanced tannins.

1985 ★★★☆ *November 1994*

Medium red–purple; a lighter style, quite complex but with gamey/leafy/ earthy notes dominating. The palate, too, is in a lighter mould, with gamey/ leafy characters suggesting less ripe fruit.

1984 ★★★★★ *November 1994*

Strong red–purple; the bouquet is clean, smooth and full, with no oak influence, just chocolate and earth Shiraz. In the mouth, an exceptionally rich and ripe wine for a cool year, with masses of chocolatey fruit, finishing with soft, mouthfilling tannins. (Under the old Gothic label.)

1983 ★★★★☆ *November 1994*

Medium to full red; firmer and distinctly more youthful than the '80; rich and ripe with plenty of fruit depth and a touch of volatility. The palate has abundant dark berry and chocolate fruit flavours, finishing with fine, lingering tannins.

1982

Not tasted.

1981

None made.

1980 ★★★★★ *November 1994*

Dark red with just a hint of tawny. A scented, layered bouquet with ripe, sumptuous chocolate aromas leads on to a super-rich, essence of dark chocolate flavoured palate, rich and mouthfilling, with fine tannins.

★★★★★ Perfect   ★★★★☆ Close to perfect   ★★★★ Very good   ★★★☆ Expected
★★★ Short of standard   ★★☆ Undeserving   ★★ Decayed relic   NR No rating

classic wines

253

tahbilk 1860 vines shiraz

phylloxera is the singularly destructive insect that laid waste to the vineyards of most of the world in the last quarter of the nineteenth century. Victoria was the most affected Australian State, and the Goulburn Valley did not escape.

How, then, does a single small block of shiraz vines planted at Tahbilk in 1860 survive, an island surrounded by phylloxera? Part of the answer may lie in the sandy soil of the small knoll upon which the vines are planted. Phylloxera travels underground through the cracks which open up in soils with a significant clay content, so sand forms a barrier. But why does it not move the short distance (less than 100 metres) from the infected blocks by air?

In any event, it has not done so, and the frail, gnarled old vines survive, their trunks twisted into surreal shapes often hollow in the middle and with only the odd vein of functioning wood to carry nutrients from the roots.

Until 1979, the grapes were used in Tahbilk Shiraz (providing the core of the Special Bin wines in the years in which Shiraz was chosen in preference to Cabernet Sauvignon) but in that year the decision was taken to keep the wine separate.

Between 250 and 500 cases are made each year, the vines yielding between half and one and a half tonnes per acre. Since 1991, 10 per cent new oak has been used, but other than this the wine receives no special treatment, the magic lying with those ancient vines.

All except the 1997 were tasted in Octber 1995.

◀ 1995 ★★★★★   *October 2000*

Medium red–purple; the solid bouquet is stacked with ripe plum fruit together with touches of chocolate and vanilla flowing into a powerful, concentrated, rich and sweet palate with a mix of plum, berry and mint, supported by lingering tannins through the mid to back palate. The best 1860s Vines wine for years. 290 dozen made.

◀ 1992 ★★★★★   *October 1995*

Extremely deep red–purple; there is potent, plum and earth fruit on the bouquet with just a hint of oak. Not surprisingly, a powerful and concentrated wine in the mouth with lots of dark berry fruit flavours and excellently balanced tannins. A slightly cooler vintage than '91.

1991 ★★★★★ *October 1995*

Strong red–purple; sweet, smooth red berry fruit aromas with much more fleshy berry character than the older vintages. A glorious wine on the palate, with a mix of plum, black cherry and dark berry fruits, and immaculately balanced fine, lingering tannins.

1990 ★★★☆ *October 1995*

Medium red, with some purple hues. The bouquet is harmonious with gently earthy notes; a much lighter with slightly jammy plum-accented fruit and soft tannins, tailing away a little on the finish. A year in which the vines gave up at the end of the growing season.

1989 ★★★ *October 1995*

Medium red, still with vestiges of purple. An unusual bouquet with sweet minty notes intermingling with more herbaceous characters. Much lighter structure in the mouth, with pronounced minty flavours, showing the effects of a cool year, and low baumé and alcohol.

1988 ★★★ *October 1995*

Medium red; the bouquet is of medium intensity, with a mix of earthy and red berry varietal shiraz aromas, leading on to a faintly stemmy/woody palate lacking richness.

1987 ★★☆ *October 1995*

Quite strong red; a leafy/minty, faintly stemmy bouquet; the palate is another Cabernet look-alike, tending towards soapiness and stemminess. I simply don't like the wine, but it is very much the product of a cool year.

1986 ★★★★★ *October 1995*

Strong red; a complex bouquet, rich and intense, with charry/cedary notes from secondary bottle development, together with the faintly gamey farmyard characters one often finds in Shiraz. A very powerful and complex palate with dark briary flavours and marvellous tannins; superb structure.

1985 ★★★ *October 1995*

Distinctly lighter colour, with some red hues; a faintly dusty/stalky bouquet which is quite herbaceous; an elegant wine on the palate, but (like the '87) one could easily think it was made from Cabernet; atypical.

1984 ★★★★★ *October 1995*

Strong red; a spotlessly clean bouquet with most attractive sweet red berry fruit. A marvellous example of the iron fist in a velvet glove; powerful red berry fruit flavours are surrounded by taut but balanced tannins. Total harmony.

1982 ★★★★☆ *October 1995*

Full red; a sweet, almost flowery bouquet with an array of aromas ranging through berry to mint to earth. As the wine enters the mouth the first flavour is mint, followed by red berry fruits; quite pronounced tannins then come as something of a surprise towards the end of the palate, but don't overwhelm the wine.

classic wines

★★★★★ Perfect   ★★★★☆ Close to perfect   ★★★★ Very good   ★★★☆ Expected

★★★ Short of standard   ★★☆ Undeserving   ★★ Decayed relic   NR No rating

1981 ★★★★ *October 1995*

Medium to full red; a solid, complex bouquet with earthy/chocolatey aromas showing warm-grown shiraz varietal character at its best. The palate has more of that attractive earthy Shiraz, with quite pronounced tannins; the ripeness and the high alcohol become progressively more apparent as the wine is retasted. Needs a rich steak.

1979 ★★★ *October 1995*

Light brick–red; surprisingly aged with gently earthy and faintly bitter notes to the bouquet; as the bouquet promises, lacks intensity on the palate, earthy and faded, with very soft tannins.

tahbilk marsanne 1953-1999

Just how rare the marsanne grape is can be gauged from the fact that Tahbilk's 35 hectares was until recently the largest single planting in the world (and reputedly the oldest, with the vines almost 70 years old).

Tahbilk has always adopted a classic approach to making Marsanne, and in particular has eschewed the use of oak. But there have been four changes in its production. Up until 1978 it was made in the old red wine cellars without any refrigeration or temperature control; in 1979 the new white wine cellar was opened, and the wine was given 12 to 18 hours skin contact; in 1987 gas cover was introduced; and finally since 1994 the period of skin contact has been significantly reduced.

These changes can be seen quite clearly in the wines, but of course increasing bottle age also exerts a major influence. Thus Alister Purbrick sees three ages for Marsanne: nought to five years the development phase; six to ten years the period of maximum manifestation of varietal character; and over ten years the potential for maximum complexity.

I chose the word 'potential' deliberately, for it does not automatically follow that Marsanne will improve with bottle age in the same way as a Riesling or a Semillon. But it shares with both — and Semillon in particular — a shy delicacy in its youth, needing at least a few years to begin to flower. At its best, it is a superb wine; at its least, coarse and devoid of distinction.

First tasted in October 1995, updated, and later vintages added.

1999 ★★★★   October 2000
Light to medium yellow–green; the complex bouquet opens with minerally/earthy aromas, followed by a touch of toast, and then herb, grass and lemon; the palate has crisp lemon and grass flavours, complemented by an attractive acid cut on the finish; all it needs is time.

1998 ★★★★   December 1998
Light green–yellow; a clean, crisp lemony bouquet is accompanied by a palate with excellent length and early flavour, all pointing to great development potential. It is very difficult to give appropriate points to a wine barely out of its nappies.

1997 ★★★★   November 1997
Light to medium yellow–green; the bouquet is clean, of medium intensity with classic faint honeysuckle aromas. The palate needs time to bring out its latent varietal character, but has plenty of fruit weight, and is almost certain to develop very well with age.

classic wines

1996 ★★★★ *October 1996*

Medium yellow–green; considerable depth to the bouquet with that ever so typical faintly chalky, faintly honeysuckle aroma. The palate is still discrete and closed; bloodlines suggest the wine will develop very well indeed given time.

1995 ★★★★☆ *October 1995*

Very light yellow–green; youthful and crisp with a distinct hint of that varietal chalkiness on the bouquet; tight and fine with citric/herbaceous flavours to the palate; a polar opposite to the '94 in style, but is very likely to develop extremely well.

1994 ★★★☆ *October 1995*

Very light yellow–green, almost watery pale; the bouquet still showing young wine/fermentation characters, and the palate seemingly much sweeter than the others, although technically it isn't. The sweetness raises the question about the future direction of the wine, although it does need time.

1993 ★★★★☆ *October 1995*

Light yellow–green; there are fragrant, lifted, almost Riesling-like limey overtones to the bouquet; on the palate, a young wine with excellent though undeveloped fruit; very good acidity, and looks likely to age superbly.

1992 ★★★★ *December 1998*

The promise of a wonderful, glowing, golden–green colour is immediately fulfilled by the very expressive, gently honeyed bouquet and a lovely array of floral honey/honeysuckle flavours which flood the mouth. Truly, a miracle.

1991 ★★★★ *October 1995*

Medium yellow–green, signalling an abrupt colour change from the '92 and younger wines. The bouquet is firm, quite discrete, but with a tangy undertone; there are some interesting flavours on the palate with pronounced honeysuckle varietal character and again an echo of that tangy character evident on the bouquet. Still opening up, but has length.

1990 ★★★ *October 1995*

Deep yellow; the bouquet is developing as quickly as the colour suggests, and seems a fraction dilute. In the mouth, a pleasant, forward wine with some honeyed aspects. Already there and will not repay cellaring.

1989 ★★★★★ *October 1995*

Medium yellow–green; a smooth, complex and concentrated bouquet with citrus and honey fruit aromas. There is lots of flavour and concentration on the palate which is smooth and perfectly balanced, again showing a range of citrus and honey flavours. Some botrytis, but picked before the rain.

1988 ★★★★★ *October 1995*

Medium to full yellow–green; a very complex bouquet reminiscent of the '79, surprisingly concentrated and rich. The palate provides more of the same, once again eerily like the '79, with tangy honeyed/honeysuckle fruit, complex and concentrated.

◄━ Not Ready   ❧ Still evolving   ❘ Prime of its life   ✎ Drink soon   ◻ Missed the boat

1987 ★★★★☆
October 1995

Glowing yellow–green; strong honeysuckle aromas with that indefinable slightly vegetal tang which comes up in a number of these wines. There is abundant tightly structured varietal fruit on the palate; harmonious and long.

1986 ★★★☆
October 1995

Bright medium to full yellow; a toasty, honeyed rich bouquet of medium intensity which is showing obvious development. There is considerable weight to the initial impact, but the wine dips fractionally on the mid-palate, with a firm, relatively dry finish.

1985 ★★★★
October 1995

Medium to full yellow–green; the bouquet is soft, with mainstream honeysuckle varietal character. An attractive palate which, while relatively soft, is rather drier in feel than the other wines from the late '70s and early '80s. Does have good length, though.

1984 ★★★★★
October 1995

Glowing medium to full yellow–green; a clean, smooth bouquet of moderate intensity which has an almost Semillon-like touch of honey and butter. The palate is most attractive, with a tangy/lemony bite again harking to Semillon; has exceptional length.

1983 ★★★☆
October 1995

Deep bronze, as developed as any in the entire line-up. The bouquet is rich, with some botrytis-like apricot overtones, in fact simply deriving from a very hot vintage. The palate is very sweet and concentrated, with slight maderisation. All in all, very much the product of a hot vintage.

1982 ★★★
October 1995

Bronze–yellow; the bouquet is of moderate intensity, but lacks the definition and intensity of the older wines which precede it. The flavours are attractive enough, in a honey/caramel/toast spectrum but — like the bouquet — tending to lack structure and concentration.

1981 ★★★☆
October 1995

Deep yellow–bronze; a solid wine, with some dried tropical fruit aromas leads on to a fleshy, solid palate, though tending a little heavy and phenolic.

1980 ★★★★☆
October 1995

Medium to full yellow; sweet, almost buttery fruit to a solid bouquet. The palate, too, is substantial, with sweet fleshy fruit filling out the mid-palate and holding well; simply lacks the extraordinary complexity of the '79, but is a very, very good wine.

1979 ★★★★★
October 1995

Deep but bright glowing yellow–green; a marvellously complex and intense bouquet, much more concentrated than any of the other old wines. There are many flavours to the palate with almost freakish concentration, running through honey, lime and a hint of bottle-developed camphor.

classic wines

★★★★★ Perfect   ★★★★☆ Close to perfect   ★★★★ Very good   ★★★☆ Expected
★★★ Short of standard   ★★☆ Undeserving   ★★ Decayed relic   NR No rating

1978 ★★   *October 1995*

Straw–bronze; the bouquet shows the signs of oxidation, and is somewhat dilute, the palate likewise weak and now quite oxidised.

1976 ★★☆   *October 1995*

Light to medium yellow–green; there are sharp edges to the aromas, possibly yeast-derived, possibly volatility, possibly sulphur dioxide, or a blend of all three. There is plenty of flavour to the palate, but those sharp edges once again intrude and detract.

1975 ★★☆   *October 1995*

Bronze colour; a wine showing distinct oxidation and lacking fruit intensity on the bouquet, although the palate is marginally better. Simply lacking intensity.

1974 ★★★★   *October 1995*

Light green–gold; an attractive, lively and crisp tangy/citrussy bouquet leads on to an incredibly tight and youthful wine on the palate, preserved by high sulphur dioxide additions. The sulphur dioxide inevitably invests the wine with a fraction of hardness, but it is a price worth paying.

1973 ★★★   *October 1995*

Medium to full yellow–green; distinct solids/warm fermentation characters give a slightly hessiany/baggy character to the bouquet. The wine has some of the slightly caramelised flavours of the '72, and falls away somewhat on the finish, but is sound enough.

1972 ★★★☆   *October 1995*

Bronze colour; a soft, somewhat blowsy bouquet, with a hint of caramel; those caramel, even butterscotch, characters of the bouquet are even more pronounced on an interesting, although not classic, palate, which intriguingly finishes with quite good acid.

1970 ★★★   *October 1995*

Pale green–yellow, very undeveloped; the bouquet showing the effects of high sulphur dioxide additions, crisp and undeveloped. A pointy wine on the palate, sharpened by that high sulphur dioxide; there are some citrus flavours underneath and, if the cork holds, will live forever — but will never be great.

1953 ★★★★   *October 1995*

Full yellow–gold; a marvellous old wine bouquet with inevitable hints of maderisation, but still nutty and sweet, holding well and showing no outright decay. The palate is drying out a fraction, together with a trace of maderisation, but still a remarkable old wine and a privilege to taste.

━◖ Not Ready   ◣ Still evolving   ◢ Prime of its life   ◢ Drink soon   ◗ Missed the boat

tahbilk special bin dry reds

the history of the Special Bin Dry Red of Tahbilk — traditionally the best 500-gallon (2250-litre) vat of wine made each year — goes back a long way. Max Lake writes reverentially of the 1938 Claret Bin 5X in *Classic Wines of Australia*, Len Evans in not dissimilar terms of Bin 11 of 1948. Both singled out the '60, '61 and '62 vintages, and it was the '60 vintage which started this particular tasting in October 1995.

Over the years, the Special Bin oscillated between Shiraz and Cabernet Sauvignon, but between 1975 (and the decision thereafter to release the 1860 Vines Shiraz as a single wine) and 1994 had settled on Cabernet Sauvignon. Since 1994 a new Reserve label has been used, with both Shiraz (from 1930 plantings) and Cabernet Sauvignon released each year.

Pressings to one side, these wines simply speak of the vineyard (and the vintage). New oak has never been used, and is not likely to be; pressing and fermentation are ultra-traditional, and post-fermentation handling is kept to a minimum.

The tasting showed several things: first, that there was remarkable consistency and uniformity among the wines thanks to the constancy of the winemaking and vineyard sources (which largely though not entirely overrode the varietal shifts between Shiraz and Cabernet); and second, that you have to work hard to capture the fruit flavours before the tannins take over. Finally, and most importantly, these are wines which will be best enjoyed with substantial red meat dishes.

First tasted in October 1995, updated, and later vintages added.

1994 Reserve Cabernet ★★★★☆   *October 2000*
Medium to full red–purple; there are pronounced earthy bottle-developed cabernet aromas on the bouquet, with slightly dusty oak. In the mouth, powerful tannins run through an austere, savoury wine in traditional style. I would just like to see a touch more sweet berry fruit.

1991 Special Reserve ★★★★☆   *December 1998*
Medium to full red, still with touches of purple remaining. The bouquet is clean and rich, with abundant red berry, chocolate and earth aromas. The palate is very powerful, pitting strong tannins against dark chocolatey/berry fruit. It is impossible to tell which force will prevail.

classic wines

★★★★★ Perfect   ★★★★☆ Close to perfect   ★★★★ Very good   ★★★☆ Expected
★★★ Short of standard   ★★☆ Undeserving   ★★ Decayed relic   NR No rating

261

1986 Cabernet Sauvignon Bin 73 ★★★☆   *October 1995*

Medium red; the bouquet is of medium intensity with some faintly gamey notes and touches of chocolate. A somewhat disjointed palate with faintly musty/gamey flavours; the question is whether the wine is still coming together or about to crack up; hopefully the former.

1985 Cabernet Sauvignon Bin 72 ★★★★★   *October 1995*

Strong red; lots of power to a clean bouquet with an array of briary/chocolatey/earthy aromas. An attractively powerful wine on the palate, with plush chocolate and berry fruit flavours, and lingering, chewy — but not aggressive — tannins.

1984 Cabernet Sauvignon Bin 71 ★★★★☆   *October 1995*

Medium to full red, with a touch of purple; a strong, powerful and ripe bouquet with a mix of earthy (predominant) and berry fruits. Powerfully structured and very long on the palate, with faintly herbaceous, earthy cabernet fruit flavours.

1983 Cabernet Sauvignon Bin 70 ★★★☆   *October 1995*

Dark red; two bottles opened, both faintly porty/oxidised on the bouquet, although the palate was much better, with big, rich berry chocolate flavours and lingering tannins. Despite the bouquet, seems highly likely to have considerable improvement in front of it, if soundly corked, and rated accordingly.

1982 Cabernet Sauvignon Bin 69 ★★★★★   *October 1995*

Light to medium red–purple; there are fragrant and strongly varietal fruit aromas in the cedary/dusty/fractionally minty spectrum. An altogether elegant wine on the palate, smooth and supple, with flavours of mint and a little chocolate; well balanced and structured, with lingering but gentle tannins.

1981 Cabernet Sauvignon Bin 68 ★★★★★   *October 1995*

Medium to full red–purple; a powerful bouquet with abundant dark chocolate and red berry fruit. Another very good wine on the palate with berry, cedar and chocolate flavours; the tannins are, of course, there, but are well balanced.

1980 Cabernet Sauvignon Bin 67 ★★★★★   *October 1995*

Medium red–purple; a wonderfully clean, smooth bouquet with nicely ripened fruit flavours and a faint hint of mint. Caresses the mouth with lovely red berry fruit and almost silky tannins. One of the all-time greats, and part of a marvellous run of wines between 1980 and 1985.

1979 Cabernet Sauvignon Bin 66 ★★★   *October 1995*

Medium to full red–purple; a complex bouquet, but with a strange array of gamey/vegetal/slightly feral notes. A strongly styled wine on the palate with more of those slightly gamey characters, and finishing with lots of tannins. Indubitably has character, but not the sort I would seek.

1978 Cabernet Sauvignon Bin 65 ★★★☆   *October 1995*

Dark opaque red; seemingly very ripe with a faintly oxidised bouquet. In the mouth, big, robust, tannic and concentrated; while very substantial, the bouquet raised the question whether this was a particularly good bottle. Might deserve an even higher rating.

◄━ Not Ready   ❭ Still evolving   ❘ Prime of its life   ✐ Drink soon   ⛾ Missed the boat

1977 Cabernet Sauvignon Bin 64 ★★★☆ *October 1995*

Full brick–red; very pronounced eucalypt/mint aromas showing much more youthful fruit than any of the older vintages with the exception of the '76. The palate, too, is fruity, though surprisingly light on the mid to back palate, and has relatively soft tannins. Something of an odd-man-out in the range, though far from unattractive.

1976 Cabernet Sauvignon Bin 63 ★★★★★ *October 1995*

Full brick–red; a much riper bouquet than any of the older wines, with a hint of hay/straw suggesting a whisper of oxidation. A magnificently rich and full wine on the palate, much riper and with more pronounced fruit than any of the older wines; the tannins are strong but are adequately supported by that fruit.

1975 Cabernet Sauvignon Bin 62 ★★★★☆ *October 1995*

Medium brick–red; an interesting bouquet with faintly dusty/minty/piney aromas of light to medium intensity; youthful. The palate starts with dusty flavours, moves to dark dried berries and prunes, and then finishes with hallmark tannins. Altogether interesting.

1974 Shiraz Bin 60 ★★★ *October 1995*

Medium red; the initial impression is of condensed milk/milk chocolate, with lactic overtones; then briary/woody notes come up, then a hint of linoleum. A strange wine on the palate; notwithstanding all the characters on the bouquet, slightly hollow and shelly; the tannins tend to take over.

1973 Cabernet Sauvignon Bin 59 ★★★★ *October 1995*

Medium red; a moderately sweet bouquet with a range of cedary/chocolatey, berry fruit; strangely, does not show a huge difference in the varietal base. A fine wine on the fore to mid-palate, but then the tannins do tend to take over; the product of a cooler year.

1972 Shiraz Bin 58 ★★★☆ *October 1995*

Medium red; shows rich, chocolatey shiraz varietal fruit on the pleasantly sweet bouquet; lacks the power and richness of the '71 on the palate, but does have some intriguing flavours.

1971 Shiraz Bin 57 ★★★★★ *October 1995*

Medium to full red; a surprisingly elegant bouquet of medium intensity, with touches of liquorice and dark chocolate. The palate is ample and rich, with plenty of extract, again showing the liquorice and bitter chocolate flavours promised by the bouquet; the tannins are powerful but balanced. Lives up to the reputation of one of the greatest vintages for Chateau Tahbilk.

1970 Cabernet Sauvignon Bin 55 ★★★ *October 1995*

Relatively light but still quite bright red; there are distinctly unripe characteristics to the bouquet with slightly vegetal overtones, but that lack of ripeness seems to preserve some of the fruit on the palate; a wine similar in style to the '69, and far lighter than the younger wines which followed it.

classic wines

★★★★★ Perfect ★★★★☆ Close to perfect ★★★★ Very good ★★★☆ Expected
★★★ Short of standard ★★☆ Undeserving ★★ Decayed relic NR No rating

(263)

1969 Cabernet Sauvignon Bin 52 ★★★★★   *October 1995*
Light brick–red; the aromas are minty, sappy, almost running into pine; the palate shows similar minty/sappy flavours with a strong impression of fruit which has been unduly shaded during the growing season. The tannins are softer than in many of the wines, but the fruit ripeness is not there either.

1968 Cabernet Sauvignon Bin 51 ★★★★★   *October 1995*
Brick–red; the bouquet is soft, complex, with cedary overtones to perfectly aged Cabernet Sauvignon. There are attractive cedar, chocolate, briar and earth flavours on a perfectly structured and balanced palate with tannins certainly evident but balanced. Motoring along very nicely.

1967 Cabernet Sauvignon Bin 27 ★★★☆   *October 1995*
Light to medium brick–red; the bouquet shows quite pronounced varietal character with a range of vegetal/herbaceous/minty aspects. On the mid-palate there is attractive, relatively sweet, chocolatey fruit followed fairly smartly by those Tahbilk tannins.

1966 Cabernet Sauvignon Bin 19 ★★★★   *October 1995*
Medium brick–red; a complex bouquet with sweet red berry/cassis fruit to the fore, with hints of pine and mint in the background. The same flavours manifest themselves on the palate until pervasive tannins take over. Just a little less tannin would have made a truly wonderful wine.

1965 Cabernet Sauvignon Bin 14 ★★★★★   *October 1995*
Brick–red; a fine, clean bouquet with a mix of sweet berry and earth aromas leads on to a marvellously elegant and well-balanced palate, flooded with softly sweet fruit woven through equally soft tannins.

1964 Cabernet Sauvignon Bin 28 ★★★★   *October 1995*
Aged brick–red; the bouquet is clean, of medium intensity with quite smooth and earthy/berry aromas; a fully mature wine on the palate with those almost indefinable aged earthy/cedary characters with just a hint of berry fruit in the background. The tannins are holding but not overly aggressive.

1962 Cabernet Sauvignon Bin 26 ★★★★★   *October 1995*
One of the all-time great Tahbilk Cabernets which I drank with Alister Purbrick, Len Evans and others after the memorial service for Eric Purbrick some years ago. It was as vital as Eric in his prime, and a testament to the Special Bin line.

1960 Shiraz Bin 28 ★★☆   *October 1995*
Medium brick–red; flowered ever so briefly in the glass with gently earthy sweet fruit aromas and a touch of chocolate. Then decay rapidly manifested itself as the wine breathed, and there was not a great deal on the palate left other than the remnants of the Tahbilk tannins. Obviously, at this age, bottle variation must be expected, and other bottles may well drink far better.

Not Ready   Still evolving   Prime of its life   Drink soon   Missed the boat

tyrrell's vat 47 chardonnay

t he label used to read Pinot Chardonnay, an old-fashioned (and technically incorrect) name for the grape variety used by the late Murray Tyrrell when he made the first vintage in 1971. While Craigmoor (in Mudgee) made a Chardonnay the same year, it was Vat 47 which was to take the variety from obscurity to virtually a generic term for white wine.

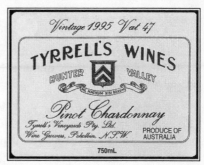

The grape had existed in Australia in minute quantities since the early nineteenth century, and it was an old clone which Tyrrell accessed in the late 1960s. The wine set new standards, pointed a new direction for Australian white wine. Tyrrell had to do much of the pioneering work, for oak matured white wines of any description had not previously existed. He moved to barrel fermentation well before his competitors, using French oak and constantly experimenting with oak types and toasts.

The style has evolved over the years, as one would expect. The '71 came from the worst Hunter vintage in living memory, and was in some ways an inauspicious start; but the '72 and '73 were, and still are, great wines, way ahead of their time. The intervening years show the varying impact of vintage conditions, changes in fruit sources and some changes in winemaking style: particularly through the 1980s and up to 1991 the wine became richer and more complex, but not necessarily longer lived or more elegant. The '92 seemed to mark a turning point back to a finer, more elegant and somewhat longer-lived style.

First tasted in November 1994, updated, and later vintages added.

2000 ★★★★★   *May 2001*

Medium yellow–green; a silky smooth bouquet offers stonefruit, melon and oak; the palate is likewise spotlessly clean and immaculately balanced, the fruit and oak seamlessly interwoven.

1999 ★★★★★   *March 2000*

Light to medium yellow–green; the bouquet is elegant yet complex, with particularly harmonious oak integration through the melon and nectarine fruit. The palate has that extra dimension and length which immediately sets this wine apart from all of its peers.

classic wines

★★★★★ Perfect	★★★★☆ Close to perfect	★★★★ Very good	★★★☆ Expected
★★★ Short of standard	★★☆ Undeserving	★★ Decayed relic	NR No rating

1998 ★★★★☆ *October 1999*

Medium yellow–green; quite obvious charry barrel-ferment oak is followed by gentle, white peach fruit on the bouquet. A stylish wine, cleverly made, even if the oak component needs time to settle down; has good length and acidity.

1997 ★★★★★ *October 1998*

Glowing yellow–green; melon and nectarine fruit is balanced by the very clever use of barrel ferment and toasty oak on the bouquet. The palate emphasis is on the nectarine and melon fruit, running through to a long finish. The oak is ever present but never dominant.

1996 ★★★★☆ *April 1997*

Glowing yellow–green, already quite advanced for its age. A bigger style on the bouquet, with smooth peachy fruit and good oak balance and integration. The wine is even richer and fuller again on the palate with peachy fruit and lots of spicy, charry oak, all filling out on the back palate. Fast-developing style.

1995 ★★★★★ *February 1996*

Medium yellow–green. Obvious French barrel-ferment oak gives the wine its initial impact on both bouquet and palate, but there is tangy citrus/melon fruit and crisp acid under that oak. Very much in the style established by Vat 47 over the past few years.

1994 ★★★★★ *October 1995*

Medium to full yellow–green; as sophisticated as ever with tangy melon/citrus fruit and wonderful oak. On the palate, a stylish wine with clever oak use counterbalanced by long, fresh citrus and melon flavoured fruit.

1993 ★★★★☆ *November 1994*

Glowing yellow–green; finely structured with 'cool', tangy peach and melon fruit, and excellent oak handling. A lively, fresh wine on the palate, with attractive spicy oak, and superb length, acidity and balance.

1992 ★★★★★ *November 1994*

Marks the turning point in style continued with the '93. Fine, scented citrus-tinged fruit with toasty barrel-ferment oak on the bouquet leads on to a lovely wine of light to medium weight, with a fine, long finish. By rights should prove to be long lived.

1991 ★★★☆ *November 1994*

Medium yellow–green; a big, forward style with heavy aromas. A rich wine on the palate, helped by good acidity, but less so by fractionally oily oak.

1990 ★★★★☆ *November 1994*

Medium yellow–green; smooth, bottle-developed, honeyed/buttery aromas. The palate is particularly smooth, with rounded, soft, gently honeyed fruit, well-judged acidity and good length to the finish.

1989 ★★★★★ *November 1994*

Medium full yellow–green; the bouquet is very complex and stylish, with Burgundian overtones to buttery/honeyed fruit. In the mouth the wine is extremely rich, almost viscous, with honey and toffee fruit and oak flavours now at their peak.

◂ Not Ready   ↘ Still evolving   ▮ Prime of its life   ✦ Drink soon   ▯ Missed the boat

1988 ★★★ *November 1994*

Medium to full yellow–green; a complex aroma with many things going on, not all pleasant, with a particular question mark about the oak aroma. The flavour is, however, generous and chewy, even if fractionally rough on the finish.

1987 ★★★☆ *November 1994*

Full yellow; rich and developed, with some caramel and toffee aromas; viscous/honeyed palate, but apparently slightly corked, and difficult to judge.

1986 ★★★ *November 1994*

Full yellow; honeyed/buttery bouquet followed by a big, forward, mouthfilling wine marred by a fraction of bitterness/roughness on the finish.

1985 ★★★★☆ *November 1994*

Medium to full yellow; a smooth, clean and stylish bouquet of medium intensity; the palate is very smooth with peachy fruit, subtle oak and great body and length, excellent acid and intensity on the finish.

1984 ★★★★★ *November 1994*

Glowing yellow, with an extremely complex bouquet marked by strong charry/toasty oak. The palate is similarly complex, strongly oak influenced, but carrying that oak very well; a wine of style and length, ageing superbly.

1983 ★★★ *November 1994*

Full yellow–orange; very full-bodied, honeyed bouquet with hints of coffee and mandarin. The palate, too, is extremely rich with candied fruit, iced coffee and dried leaf flavours all evident.

1982 ★★★★☆ *November 1994*

The very developed, full yellow–orange colour suggests the wine is past its best, but it is not; the bouquet is very rich with candied cumquat peel and honey aromas, while the palate is exceedingly luscious with mouthfilling tropical fruits; in a particular style, but nonetheless showing very well.

1981 ★★☆ *November 1994*

Full yellow–orange; the bouquet is rather rough, showing some hot solids fermentation characters which are also evident on a rather coarse palate; I simply do not like the wine.

1980 ★★★☆ *November 1994*

Excellent, bright, medium to full yellow–green colour; the bouquet has an edge of the hot fermentation characters of the '81, but is far more stylish. The palate is very complex with a touch of citrus; all in all, the wine is not entirely clean but has some real character and style, and finishes particularly well.

1979 ★★★★★ *November 1994*

Deep, bright golden–yellow; an exceptionally smooth, clean, honeyed bouquet with attractive oak; honeyed/peachy fruit, smooth and well balanced, dominates the palate which has a long finish with good acidity. A complete, mature wine.

classic wines

★★★★★ Perfect   ★★★★☆ Close to perfect   ★★★★ Very good   ★★★☆ Expected
★★★ Short of standard   ★★☆ Undeserving   ★★ Decayed relic   NR No rating

(267)

1978 ★★☆   *November 1994*

Reasonably bright full yellow, with just a touch of orange; both the bouquet and palate are rough and coarse; not certain whether this was an 'off' bottle, or whether hot solids fermentation characters have marked the wine.

1977 ★★★☆   *November 1994*

Full yellow–orange; the bouquet is full and rich with cumquat and honey, the palate fairly sweet with quite strong oak leading on to a finish which has just a hint of bitterness.

1976 ★★★★★   *November 1994*

Glowing yellow; a very full, rounded, buttery/peachy bouquet with strong vanillin oak which one would swear was American, although it is French. Those vanillin flavours carry through on a palate which is still holding its fruit exceptionally well. This bottle was consumed over two days; on the second day it was as attractive as it was on the first.

1975 ★★★★   *November 1994*

Bright, deep yellow–green; a complex, toasty, honeyed bouquet with just a hint of what appears to be fermentation roughness. The palate has lots of toasty, honeyed fruit, regional more than varietal, but with good structure and weight still. Grew and improved in the glass.

1974 ★★★☆   *November 1994*

Deep orange–gold; very raisined, rich mandarin-accented bouquet showing the evidence of botrytis. The palate shows marked botrytis influence, and has started to break up, displaying strange cosmetic characters, though still a wine of complexity in some respects.

1973 ★★★★★   *November 1994*

Incredibly bright and fresh yellow–green colour with a very youthful, crisp bouquet, utterly unlike the wines which followed. The palate is equally extraordinarily fresh and crisp, with wonderful texture, and showing absolutely no sign of decay. Undoubtedly helped by a percentage of Semillon in the blend.

1972 NR

Not tasted on this occasion.

1971 ★★★★   *November 1994*

Bright yellow–gold; an initially slightly musty bouquet (the bottle was ullaged) blew off to show toasty/honeyed fruit. The palate is toasty, still with hints of sweet fruit, showing the first signs of maderisation. For all that, holding on the finish, and a remarkable old wine given the ullage.

◄━ Not Ready   ❯ Still evolving   ❰ Prime of its life   ✎ Drink soon   ☐ Missed the boat

tyrrell's vat 9 shiraz 1980-1997

If you visit Tyrrell's historic winery in the Hunter Valley, be sure to look at the vines on the right-hand side of the drive as you go up the hill. There you will see vines planted in 1879 (the Four Acre Block) and just prior to the turn of the century (the Eight Acre Block). Actually, you will see half the vines: in the mid-1960s every second row was pulled out to permit a tractor to gain access. Prior to that time all the work was done by horse (and hand) in the close-planted rows.

These two blocks provide the core of the grapes used in Vat 9, supplemented by high-quality grapes from other old, unirrigated Lower Hunter vineyards. The wine is made in ultra-traditional fashion in open wax-lined concrete fermenters, hand-plunged every five hours, with malolactic fermentation completed more or less at the end of the primary fermentation.

The wine is pressed at that stage, and transferred to old 2250-litre French casks, where it matures for 12 months. In recent years a small percentage has been given limited small new French oak ageing. The late Murray Tyrrell said it 'has not altered the style, but has lifted and freshened the wine', and he was right.

This is a first class Hunter Shiraz, which has an illustrious show record, and which ages magnificently, gaining complexity without losing richness and generosity.

First tasted in November 1994, updated, and later vintages added.

1997 ★★★★☆   *April 2001*
Medium red–purple; the bouquet is distinctly riper than the '96, with strong, plummy fruit, and even a touch of prune. Spice, plum and prune fruit on the palate is complemented by an attractive touch of sweet oak and ripe tannins. An excellent outcome for a less than perfect vintage.

1996 ★★★★   *April 2001*
Light to medium red–purple; a moderately intense bouquet has typically savoury/earthy regional varietal character, with some dark cherry/red berry fruit. The palate is somewhat sweeter than the bouquet suggests it will be, with dark cherry/plum fruit supported by soft and ripe tannins.

1995 ★★★★   *April 1997*
Medium red–purple; the bouquet is of light to medium intensity with quite fragrant aromas of liquorice and spice and the typically restrained oak usage of Tyrrell's. There are interesting Rhône-like flavours on the deceptively light palate, with liquorice, spice and black cherry fruit; soft tannins to close.

★★★★★ Perfect   ★★★★☆ Close to perfect   ★★★★ Very good   ★★★☆ Expected
★★★ Short of standard   ★★☆ Undeserving   ★★ Decayed relic   NR No rating

classic wines

269

1994 ★★★★☆   *November 1995*

Medium red–purple; a clean, lifted bouquet with an amalgam of dark cherry, mint and spice aromas. A lively and attractive wine on the palate with pronounced spicy characters; while in a lighter style, has good balance and length.

1993 ★★★★☆   *November 1994*

Medium purple–red; fresh and clean dark cherry/red berry aromas, slightly lighter than the '92, lead on to a palate with lots of juicy berry fruit, but rather less extract. Appears it will be fairly quick maturing.

1992 ★★★★★   *November 1994*

Medium to full purple–red; a lifted, lively fragrant bouquet with exemplary spice and liquorice varietal fruit aromas. An absolutely delicious wine in the mouth with similar spice and liquorice varietal fruit, even a touch of cassis. Soft tannins, subtle oak and good acidity.

1991 ★★★★★   *November 1994*

Startling depth of red–purple colour; a deep, concentrated plum, briar and berry bouquet, entirely fruit-driven. The palate is full and ripe, with plum, raspberry and chocolate flavours; perfectly balanced tannins and extract. A 30-year classic.

1990 ★★★★☆   *November 1994*

Medium to full red–purple; the bouquet is youthful, of light to medium intensity with slightly squashy red berry fruit aromas, not surprising given that there were 450 millimetres of rain in vintage. What is surprising is the concentration of the palate, with earth, berry and chocolate fruit flavours, finishing with nicely balanced tannins. A triumph for a very difficult year.

1989 ★★★★☆   *November 1994*

Medium to full red, with a touch of purple remaining. The bouquet is clean, with red berry fruits and fairly marked volatility. The palate is fresh and of medium weight, with liquorice and berry fruit flavours, rounded off by fine-grained tannins.

1988 ★★★   *November 1994*

Light to medium red; a rather light, plain and somewhat earthy bouquet leads on to a wine with similarly light, plain, leafy/earthy flavours which lack fruit richness.

1987 ★★★★★   *November 1994*

Medium to full red–purple; a firm but complex bouquet with briar, leaf, spice and liquorice aromas all intermingling. A lovely wine on the palate, with lots of berry, spice and liquorice fruit, yet also having elegance and style.

1986 ★★☆   *November 1994*

Medium to full red, with a touch of purple. The bouquet is complex, but the sweaty/gamey/animal characters which run through both the aroma and through the palate spoil the wine, leading to bitterness on the finish.

1985 ★★★★☆   *November 1994*

Medium to full red; a concentrated, powerful bouquet with earth, berry and mint aromas. The palate is similarly powerful, with chocolate and dark berry fruit flavours, finishing with lingering tannins.

   ◄ Not Ready   ➘ Still evolving   🍾 Prime of its life   ⟋ Drink soon   ▯ Missed the boat

1984 ★★★ *November 1994*

Medium red; an array of aromas running from sappy/spicy through to leafy/gamey. The palate shows similar leafy/sappy/gamey fruit, in stark contrast to the '83.

1983 ★★★★★ *November 1994*

Medium to full red, with a hint of purple. A wonderfully concentrated bouquet with aromas of dark berries, briar, earth and bark. The palate delivers that which the bouquet promises, with briary/dark berry fruit, echoes of new oak, and lots of tannin on the finish.

1982

Not tasted.

1981 ★★★★★ *November 1994*

Medium to full red; rich, full and ripe with lots of sweet berry and earth aromas, even a hint of spice, the latter surprising given the hot vintage. The palate is as concentrated as the bouquet promises, with masses of chocolate, berry and earth flavours, finishing with appropriate tannins. While powerful, it is not extractive, just as the bouquet is not porty.

1980 ★★★★☆ *November 1994*

Medium to full red; a fragrant, complex bouquet with classic Hunter barnyard and earth aromas. The palate shows rather more fruit and berry concentration than the bouquet suggests, with some chocolate flavours there too, finishing with well-balanced tannins. Ageing slowly but surely.

★★★★★ Perfect ★★★★☆ Close to perfect ★★★★ Very good ★★★☆ Expected
★★★ Short of standard ★★☆ Undeserving ★★ Decayed relic NR No rating

eight different capsule designs, four label changes and three different bottle shapes and sizes between 1973 and 2000 is a not dissimilar story to that of McWilliam's Elizabeth. Here, likewise, such changes should not be allowed to obscure the great history of the wine, first made (as Vat 1) in 1964 and which has handsomely answered the test of time.

The wine is sourced primarily from the so-called Short Flat Vineyard, supplemented by grapes from the sandy flats of De Beyers Vineyard and older vines from the Long Flat (Tyrrell's really does own a vineyard of that name). The Short Flat contains 4 per cent of old roussanne vines — perhaps a secret ingredient in the wine. The vines are now between 30 and 100 years old.

In the 1960s and 1970s the grapes were picked early to mid season, but Murray Tyrrell moved to later picking for a period during the 1980s in a quest for more flavour. In retrospect, it was not a success, and these days the primary emphasis is placed on natural acidity and pH — and hence a reversion to slightly earlier picking.

Other than this, the making techniques have remained largely unchanged: cold fermentation (now in stainless steel, though originally in old oak casks) and early bottling in June or July of the year of vintage. Time does the rest. Since 1963 Vat 1 has won 45 trophies and 167 gold medals. The vintage weather notes in brackets are those of Tyrrell's.

Most tasted April 2001; the remainder October 1997 or November 1994.

2000 ★★★★★   *April 2001*

Pale straw–green; an exceptionally fragrant bouquet offers crisp, lemon/citrus and mineral aromas. The palate has equivalently abundant flavour, fine, tight and lemony, with good length and acidity. So precocious that it seems almost certain the wine will be relatively quick-maturing. (Good winter rain was followed by mild growing conditions until mid-January, then fine and warm to hot through to the end of vintage. Very good white year, great red year.)

1999 ★★★★★   *April 2001*

Bright, pale straw–green; intense lemon and citrus aromas, together with a touch of nashi pear, lead into a palate with lots of richness and flavour for such a young wine, with classic lemony acidity to close. (Picked in the first two weeks of February in almost perfect conditions, dry and warm. 10.4 degrees alcohol.)

◄━ Not Ready   ❖ Still evolving   ❦ Prime of its life   ✎ Drink soon   ☐ Missed the boat

1998 ★★★★☆ April 2001

Bright straw–green; the bouquet is clean, absolutely in its transition phase from young to mature, and closed down. The palate has considerable weight and roundness on entry, then tightens up with crisp, tangy acidity on the finish. (Picked in the last week of January and first week of February, said to be not dissimilar to the 1991 as a young wine, but with better fruit and acidity.)

1997 ★★★★☆ April 2001

Medium yellow–green; a clean bouquet, with some minerally notes, like the 1998, still in transition. The palate is tightly structured, with more of the minerally notes of the bouquet appearing on the mid-palate, but also the first signs of softening and the building of the sweeter, honey characters. (Good rain and conditions throughout the growing season. A mixture of extremes through February of heat, cold nights and rain. Picked early, with a touch of botrytis, described as 'ideal conditions for classic ageing Hunter Semillon'.)

1996 ★★★★★ April 2001

Glowing yellow–green; the bouquet is fresh and clean, with lots of ripe, tangy, citrus fruit. The palate is outstanding; great length, grip and concentration, with multifaceted citrus/lemon/stonefruit flavours, and a long finish. (A mixture of hot and cold weather throughout the growing season. A touch of rain in late January. Fine vintage, cold snap in mid-February.)

1995 ★★★★★ April 2001

Developed but bright yellow–green; a rich but smooth bouquet with distinct toasty notes starting to develop, surrounded by honey. The palate provides more of the same, rich and mouthfilling, with honey, nuts and toast. Moderate length, and fleshier than most in the line-up. (Picked mid to late February with higher sugar levels than usual, second only to the 1992. A drought year. Crop reduced by 40 per cent. Cool dry vintage.)

1994 ★★★★★ April 2001

Glowing, deep yellow–green; a complex and intense array of lime, citrus, honey and toast aromas are captured in a bouquet which is still quite tight. The palate has great concentration and texture, with a powerful array of flavours running right through its length and into its long, fine finish. (Late budburst. Extreme heat and bushfires early January. Fine through the rest of vintage.)

1993 ★★★★★ October 1997

Full, glowing yellow–green; a complex bouquet, toasty with hints of spice; a supple and delicate array of flavours on the palate which are starting to sing. Between the time it was first tasted in 1995 and late 1997 had developed and will go on from there. (A good growing season until a fiercely hot harvest period.)

1992 ★★★★ April 2001

Yellow–gold; the bouquet is rich and full, complex, but showing what appears to be botrytis influence. The palate is luscious and rich, again with those suggestions of botrytis, and is soft; was always seen as a quick-developing wine, an assessment which has now caught up with it. (Drought conditions but cool growing period. (Heavy rainfall early vintage.)

classic wines

★★★★★ Perfect ★★★★☆ Close to perfect ★★★★ Very good ★★★☆ Expected
★★★ Short of standard ★★☆ Undeserving ★★ Decayed relic NR No rating

1991 ★★★★ *April 2001*

Medium green–yellow; rich, buttered toast and honey together with ripe citrus aromas lead into a palate which is showing lots of development on entry and through to the middle, then bound together on the finish by slightly grippy acidity. Marks the move from the old Riesling bottle to the Burgundy shape. (Ideal growing conditions. No rain during vintage. Big full whites with great acid balance.)

1990 ★★★★☆ *April 1997*

Medium to full yellow–green; another complex bouquet with intense citrus varietal fruit and some of those French characters of the '89. The palate is very lively, zesty and youthful, and has built considerable complexity over the past few years, with the appropriate balance and structure to continue that development. (Ideal growing conditions, heavy rain mid-February. Whites picked early. Lighter but great acid.)

1989 ★★★★☆ *April 2001*

Medium to full yellow–green; as ever, that challenging French bouquet, showing both a touch of volatility and of botrytis, but with tremendous individuality. A lively, highly-pointed, intense and complex palate, well to the left of centre, with the volatile acidity starting to assert itself a little more. On the evidence of this bottle, at least, has seen better days. (Long, cool growing period, some rain late January. Extended fermentation time. Whites with excellent middle-palate and fine acid.)

1988 ★★★ *April 1997*

Glowing yellow–green; the bouquet is soft and toasty initially, but then throws up some rather baggy hay/straw aromas. The palate shows pronounced vegetal characters, and is slightly thin in the mouth. Unsuccessfully centrifuged. (Hail October. Cooler, wetter growing season. Rain mid-January and February. Lighter, delicate whites lacking complexity.)

1987 ★★★★★ *April 1997*

Absolutely brilliant green–yellow; an extraordinarily potent and powerful bouquet, with intense tangy/herbal/citrus aromas of enormous concen-tration and distinctly French character. The palate is quite special, with length and vinosity rarely encountered in even the greatest semillons. Penetrating and long, yet balanced and harmonious. Deserved a sixth star. (Perfect weather conditions. Only one day's rain during vintage. Whites of great character and flavour.)

1986 ★★★★★ *April 2001*

Deep, glowing gold; a fragrantly sweet bouquet oozing rich lime-marmalade and honey is followed by a palate with great structure, crammed with fully-developed fruit flavour in a citrus and toast mode; it is hard to say precisely why, but I fancy this wine will start to show its age in another three or four years, and is at its peak now. (Rain early vintage. Great white year.)

1985 ★★★☆ *April 1997*

Medium yellow–green; a crisp, lemony/tangy bouquet followed by a fresh, youthful and clean wine on the palate, although it is slightly short and hollow on the finish. Several bottles tasted, with radical differences between them. This is a note of the best at the '97 tasting. (Good rain October, November. Hot dry vintage. Big but good acid.)

◄ Not Ready ＼ Still evolving 🍷 Prime of its life ⌇ Drink soon ⬚ Missed the boat

1984 ★★★☆   *April 1997*

Glowing yellow–green; a rather dry, toasty bouquet with a hint of leafiness and a touch of lime. The palate is better, with some depth, though the finish is a fraction phenolic, and there is a suggestion of a hint of residual sugar. (Softer, cooler summer. Some rain in vintage. Whites lighter in colour but with fruit and elegance.)

1983 ★★★   *November 1994*

Medium to full yellow–green; the bouquet is complex but errant, with a range of hot solids/wild yeast and other strange characters. The palate is complex, but doesn't really work or hang together; structurally disjointed, and again a suspicion of unfermented sugar. (Yield down on 1982. Initially wines of full colour and fine flavour, but developed ahead of many of the vintages.)

1982 ★★★   *April 2001*

Brassy–gold; the bouquet is soft, with slightly blurred fruit aromatics, suggesting some fermentation idiosyncracies. The palate is moderately rich, slightly maderised and edgy but has enough character to make it drinkable with food. (Good growing conditions. Rain at vintage. Wines lighter in colour, high glycerol and flavour.)

1981 ★★★   *April 2001*

Glowing gold; very ripe fruit in a honeyed/peachy/citrussy spectrum is followed by a big, full-blown palate with some phenolics but looking marginally better than it did four years ago. (Very hot vintage, labour strike, too big to be great.)

1980 ★★★   *April 2001*

Full yellow–gold; the aromas have some hay/straw/oatmeal overtones, the palate less aberrant, with honeyed/maderised fruit then a slightly tough finish. Very consistent with the 1997 tasting. A wine with a once-only label. (Very dry summer. Hot dry vintage, big white wines, initially slow developers.)

1979 ★★★   *April 1997*

Full yellow; the bouquet is attractive, with smooth, gently honeyed, toasty/nutty fruit. Very aggressive acid on the finish unbalances the wine, a pity after the excellent bouquet. pH 2.89. Dry vintage, big crop. (Perfect climate, rain early vintage. Top white year, fuller wines with good acid balance.)

1978 ★★★★   *April 1997*

Bright but full yellow–green; started full of promise, with aromas of citrus, mineral and toast tinged with greener characters. A somewhat schizophrenic palate, with herbaceous citrus/lemon fruit and moderately high acid giving an initial impression of crispness and elegance, but there is an echo of those green, almost mouldy characters of the bouquet. The late Murray Tyrrell hated the wine. (Very dry summer, heavy rain late January. Early vintage.)

1977 ★★★★★   *April 2001*

Deep gold; a rich, full and complex bouquet with ultra-classic honey and toast aromas flows through into the rich, full-bodied palate. Here honey and toast, with a touch of peach, floods the mouth; good structure and balance. An even worse cork than that of the 1975, but the wine confirms its classic rating, having tasted much the same in 1994, 1997 and now 2001. (Very dry summer, followed by a very wet vintage. Good white year, softer acid than 1976.)

★★★★★ Perfect   ★★★★☆ Close to perfect   ★★★★ Very good   ★★★☆ Expected
★★★ Short of standard   ★★☆ Undeserving   ★★ Decayed relic   NR No rating

1976 ★★★★★   *November 1994*

The colour still has a hint of green, heralding a wine with a wonderfully fresh bouquet, the fruit still in superb condition. The palate is lively and fresh, with the tangy lemon/citrus flavours promised by the bouquet. Has a long, cleansing finish; will live for decades. (A wet vintage which, in typical fashion, produced excellent white wines.)

1975 ★★★★★   *November 1994*

Glowing yellow; a complex bouquet with a great mix of honeycomb, savoury herb and toast aromas. The palate has excellent mouthfeel and weight, softly honeyed on the mid-palate, followed by good acidity on the finish. (Excellent growing conditions. Warm dry summer.)

1973 ★★★★★   *April 2001*

Bright, deep gold; the bouquet is holding remarkably well, with smooth honey, toast and butter aromas. Despite the fact that the bottle was significantly ullaged, and the cork in the last stages of decay, an amazingly fresh palate, with great mouthfeel and structure. It is hard to imagine what a bottle in top condition would provide. (An excellent growing season until heavy rain in the first two weeks of February, but by that time most of the semillon had been picked.)

1970 ★★   *April 1997*

Orange hues to the colour warn of what is to follow; a tired, maderised bouquet, and pretty much a relic on the palate, finishing with hard acid. Signs of inadequate sulphur dioxide protection. (Good summer. Fair rain. Excellent white year. Some outstanding wines made.)

◄ Not Ready   ↘ Still evolving   ▮ Prime of its life   ⌀ Drink soon   ⎕ Missed the boat

vintage ports — australian

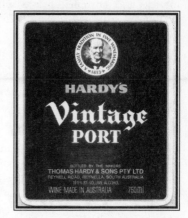

It is exceedingly unlikely that a tasting of the magnitude of that organised by James Godfrey, Seppelt's chief fortified winemaker, will ever be staged again. The 100 or so tasting notes which follow were but half of the tasting, the other 100 being Portuguese vintage ports spanning the same 70 years.

Australia's vintage ports emerged badly beaten by their Portuguese counterparts, notwithstanding that the Australian wines made between 1927 and the end of the 1950s have aged magnificently. These were the best of the best of their era, an era when 90 per cent of all Australian wine was fortified. They were made from old, low-yielding, dry-grown bush-pruned vines, hand-pruned and hand-picked.

That they were — and are — Australian fortified red wines having nothing to do stylistically with their Portuguese counterparts does not matter: I have judged and pointed them for what they are. But after 1960 the wheels started to fall off as Australia's winemakers sought to make wines which did not need 30 or 40 years to become drinkable.

The problems came with a continued dependence on ultra-ripe shiraz, grenache and mourvedre (with the curious anomaly of Lindemans with its now-defunct Corowa Vineyard) and on the use of high-toned fortification spirit to give complexity. It is all very well to have an Australian-style wine, but it has to be pleasant to drink.

The future direction seems to lie with Portuguese varieties, notably touriga nacional; with the use of neutral fortifying spirit; and with lower baumé levels. There has been a strong revival in interest in Portuguese vintage ports in the United States and elsewhere. Time will tell whether that interest rubs off on these Australian wines.

Tasted in August 2000.

classic wines

★★★★★ Perfect   ★★★★☆ Close to perfect   ★★★★ Very good   ★★★☆ Expected
★★★ Short of standard   ★★☆ Undeserving   ★★ Decayed relic   NR No rating

277

1995 Seppelt ★★★★☆
August 2000

Medium red–purple; a most interesting wine, with very careful style delineation and balance between the tangy fruit and spirit of the bouquet. A very powerful, intense and complex palate with great length and good balance. Made from 100 per cent touriga.

1995 Lehmann AD2016 ★★★★☆
August 2000

Medium to full red–purple; a big, powerful wine with the spirit in line with the 1990 vintage rather than the 1988 or 1987. Much the same goes on in the mouth, with abundant fruit but also lots of brandy spirit. A blend of 65 per cent shiraz and 35 per cent touriga.

1994 Chateau Reynella ★★★★
August 2000

Medium purple–red; quite fragrant fruit and spirit, the latter once again slightly toned down. That high-toned spirit is a little more assertive on the palate, but nice tannins run through vibrant red fruit flavours and provide balance.

1990 Lehmann AD2011 ★★★★
August 2000

Medium to full red–purple; the brandy spirit is high-toned, but less aggressive than on the AD2009. The spirit and fruit are coming back into balance on the palate, albeit still very pointed.

1988 Lehmann AD2009 ★★★★
August 2000

Medium to full purple–red; very much in the same style as the AD2008, although the bouquet is slightly less intense. The palate races in the opposite direction, with very strong spirit in an individual style.

1988 Hardy ★★★★☆
August 2000

Medium to full red–purple; the bouquet is solid, quite deep with a mix of earth and berry and clean, relatively neutral, spirit. The palate is in the same spectrum, with restrained, slightly earthy spirit, and strong regional chocolate-tinged shiraz fruit.

1987 Seppelt GR124 ★★★★☆
August 2000

Light to medium red–purple; a much lighter style than many, with distinctly savoury fruit aromas and pleasantly neutral spirit. The palate is lighter and drier, and perhaps less complex, but has a distinct touch of class. Made from touriga.

1987 Lehmann AD2008 ★★★★
August 2000

Dense purple–red; a huge wine on the bouquet, with strong brandy spirit; spirit which is simply too aggressive on the palate, taking it into a style which was once very fashionable.

1985 Seppelt GR55/41 ★★★★
August 2000

Medium to full red; the bouquet is more savoury and slightly more woody/foresty than the GR123. High-toned, hot spirit dominates the palate, which lacks the fruit power and complexity of GR123.

1985 Lehmann AD2006 ★★★★
August 2000

Excellent red–purple colour is a promising start, as is the stylish brandy spirit. However, a slightly rubbery edge to the bouquet is followed by a palate with minty characters; not in the class of the '83 vintage wine.

◄ Not Ready   ↘ Still evolving   ▮ Prime of its life   ✎ Drink soon   ▯ Missed the boat

1985 Yalumba Bounding Away ★★☆   *August 2000*
Light red–brown; the aroma and palate are appropriate to a tawny port, perhaps, but not to a vintage port. •E•

1984 Seppelt GR123 ★★★★☆   *August 2000*
Dark, dense red; a powerful, fruit-driven bouquet, complexed by a subtle touch of earthy spirit. The palate is complex and powerful with spicy liquorice fruit and good structure. Perhaps I am optimistic, but this might develop into something special.

1984 Yalumba Red Anchor ★★★   *August 2000*
Red–brown; continues a reliable run of spirity but weak wines.

1983 Lehmann AD2004 ★★★★☆   *August 2000*
Medium to full red–purple; complex bouquet is partially driven by slightly hot but tangy brandy spirit. The palate is likewise complex, rich and tangy; all in all, a very successful imitation of the Chateau Reynella style.

1983 Yalumba Strawberry Road ★★★☆   *August 2000*
Medium red, with brick–brown on the rim. The bouquet is clean, rather plain, with some earthy spirit; a traditional, sweet Australian style, braced by some tannin on the finish.

1982 Seppelt GR72/73 ★★★★☆   *August 2000*
Medium red–purple; the bouquet is quite complex and rich, with dark, charry fruit; nicely balanced and integrated spirit. There is lots of flavour on the quite sweet mid to back palate, before the wine dries off pleasingly on the finish.

1982 Penfolds ★★★☆   *August 2000*
Medium to full red–purple; a clean, smooth bouquet with well-balanced and integrated neutral spirit; a rich, traditional Australian dry red port style with no semblance of complexity.

1982 Yalumba Gurners Lane ★★★   *August 2000*
The colour is quite brown, the aromas similar to the 1980, in a tangy/citrussy spectrum. Potent Chateau Reynella brandy spirit dominates the palate, which finishes weakly.

1981 Seppelt GR119/120 ★★★★   *August 2000*
Medium red; the aromas are light and a fraction simple, but the spirit is delicate. The palate has good structure, with a mix of chocolate and earthy/savoury flavours, balanced by fine tannins, all of which come together on a good finish.

1981 Yalumba Manikato ★★★   *August 2000*
A brownish rim to the colour introduces a plain and simple wine which is dominated by spirit.

1980 Yalumba Kingston Town ★★★   *August 2000*
Medium red; there is quite tangy, lifted spirit on the bouquet, but the palate descends rapidly into mediocrity.

★★★★★ Perfect   ★★★★☆ Close to perfect   ★★★★ Very good   ★★★☆ Expected
★★★ Short of standard   ★★☆ Undeserving   ★★ Decayed relic   NR No rating

1980 Lindemans Bin 5737 ★★★★ *August 2000*

Very deep, dark and youthful colour; the bouquet is clean and fragrant, with fine fruit but also some volatility which seemed to become more apparent over time. A most interesting wine on the palate with powerful tannins and remarkably youthful fruit.

1980 Chateau Reynella ★★★★ *August 2000*

Medium red–purple; strong lantana brandy spirit dominates both the bouquet and palate. An extreme example of an aberrational style which was once very fashionable. Almost impossible to give rational points to; four stars is halfway between love it and hate it.

1980 Hardy Bin D555 ★★★☆ *August 2000*

Medium red; the moderately intense bouquet is clean and quite youthful, but not especially complex. The palate, likewise, tends plain and slightly earthy/dull. Would quite possibly look better if not confronted by a class of wines such as this.

1979 Lehmann AD2000 ★★★★ *August 2000*

Bright red with a touch of purple. The bouquet is very earthy and leathery, like a fugitive from the Hunter Valley. The spirit-dominated palate veers off into citrussy flavours; the prophecy of maturity was spot on, but it is improbable this was a typical bottle.

1979 Seppelt GR151/153 ★★★☆ *August 2000*

Dark brick–red; the powerful bouquet has slightly earthy overtones to the fruit and slightly unusual high-toned brandy spirit. The Achilles Heel of the wine is the excessively sweet palate.

1979 Yalumba Dulcify ★★ *August 2000*

Distinctly brown colour introduces a completely and unpleasantly oxidised wine.

1979 Chateau Reynella ★★★★ *August 2000*

Medium to full red; high-toned, tangy lantana brandy spirit leads into a palate in that inimitable style. The texture and structure are good; simply a pity about the warped blackberry nip flavour.

1978 Chateau Reynella ★★★★ *August 2000*

Medium to full red–purple. A firm, deep bouquet with ribena and black fruit aromas supported by spirit which are not exaggerated. The palate is rich, with strongly chocolatey regional fruit flavours, good spirit and soft tannins. All in all, a pretty nice wine.

1978 Lindemans Bin 5532 ★★★★☆ *August 2000*

Medium to full red; a clean, firm bouquet is not particularly aromatic, but the spirit is nicely integrated. The palate has good style, with persistent but not aggressive fruit and tannin flavours, possibly with improvement in front of it. •C•

1978 Yalumba Family of Man ★★★ *August 2000*

Medium red; the bouquet is clean, plain and not aromatic. Quite hard spirit rules the palate, with some peculiar minty/lemony notes on the finish. •D•

◄━ Not Ready   Still evolving   Prime of its life   Drink soon   Missed the boat

1978 Leo Buring ★★★★ *August 2000*

Medium red touched with purple; the moderately intense bouquet has some earthy notes, but is not particularly aromatic. The full-bodied palate is chewy, but the fruit and tannins are quite well balanced. Produced from Modbury shiraz.

1978 Seppelt GR71/51 ★★★★☆ *August 2000*

Impressive, deep red, with some purple hues remaining. The quite powerful and direct bouquet has an array of dark red fruits complemented by slightly earthy spirit. The palate is undeniably complex, strongly structured, with dark berry and chocolate fruit.

1977 Hardy Bin D439 ★★★★ *August 2000*

Medium red–purple; the expected spicy ribena aromas are present, with less expected and slightly hard earthy notes. The palate, likewise, is a conundrum, youthful and drier, with slightly green edges to the spicy, savoury fruit. Not at all what I anticipated on the basis of prior tastings.

1977 Lindemans Bin 5432 ★★★★ *August 2000*

Light to medium red, with a hint of purple. The aromas are quite different from the other wines in the tasting, with leafy/minty characters in a ruby port style. The wine changed significantly on the palate, initially plain, pleasant and faintly spicy, but with some persistence.

1977 Yalumba ★★ *August 2000*

Brown and completely oxidised; presumably a very poor bottle.

1976 Chateau Reynella ★★★★☆ *August 2000*

Medium to full red; a complex bouquet with lifted, high-toned brandy spirit and a big, powerful and sweet palate. A good example of the Australian style if this is what you want.

1976 Seppelt GR80 ★★★☆ *August 2000*

Medium red; distinctly earthy spirit on the bouquet introduces a palate which is quite savoury, with dry, earthy characters and faintly bitter marzipan on the finish.

1976 Yalumba Without Fear ★★★★ *August 2000*

Medium to full red; the bouquet is solid, smooth, quite ripe and not especially complex, but well balanced. The palate is well structured and balanced, with supple dark fruit flavours, nice tannins and harmonious spirit. One can see why the race horse series flew from the barrier.

1975 Quelltaler Wyatt Earp ★★★ *August 2000*

Medium to full red, with a touch of purple; volatile acidity is quite evident on the bouquet, and utterly dominates the palate.

1975 Hardy Museum ★★★★☆ *August 2000*

Medium to full red–purple; the bouquet is full, quite rich and complex, but with a curious and probably not typical fish oil character. The potent and powerful palate has complex spice and liquorice flavours woven through brandy spirit.

1975 Hardy Bin D332 ★★★ *August 2000*

Light to medium red; a plain and rather leafy wine, possibly not typical.

classic wines

★★★★★ Perfect ★★★★☆ Close to perfect ★★★★ Very good ★★★☆ Expected
★★★ Short of standard ★★☆ Undeserving ★★ Decayed relic NR No rating

1975 Chateau Reynella ★★★★★   *August 2000*
Strong red–purple; powerful and complex liquorice-accented fruit easily carries the brandy spirit. The palate has most attractive texture and structure, the flavours less extreme than in some of the Reynella and Hardy wines of the last 25 years. •C•

1975 Seppelt GR123 ★★★☆   *August 2000*
A powerful and complex wine with liquorice, prune, chocolate and spice, but corked. The wine might equally well have been given a much higher rating, but marked as tasted.

1975 Seppelt Bin RR701/75 ★★★★   *August 2000*
The colour is still quite purple; a moderately complex wine with quite distinct spirit which was distilled at Rutherglen. Still quite fresh and young, with smooth berry fruit and a pleasantly dry finish. Another quite successful attempt at greater elegance.

1975 Lindemans Bin 5634 ★★★☆   *August 2000*
Medium to full red; a different spectrum of aromas running through leaf, mint and earth, the palate coffee and mocha with six teaspoons of sugar.

1973 Yalumba ★★★☆   *August 2000*
Full red; there are slightly dusty overtones to the bouquet suggesting 'off' characters from old oak; on the plus side some chocolatey fruit. The palate regresses, heavy and very tannic.

1973 Stonyfell Metala ★★★   *August 2000*
Medium red; an odd assembly of aromas ranging through hay, straw, coffee cake and coconut followed by an odd, oaky/milky palate, finishing with high acidity.

1973 Saltram Mamre Brook ★★★☆   *August 2000*
Medium red; the bouquet is clean and light, with a hint of chocolate. The sweet berry palate is simple and lacks structure, but at least the wine has clean flavour.

1972 Seppelt GR72 ★★★★☆   *August 2000*
Medium to full red colour with a touch of purple; the bouquet is smooth and harmonious with black fruits, chocolate and subtle spirit. In the mouth a big, rich and quite sweet wine, with complexity and some lift on the finish. Unequivocally Australian in style.

1972 Stonyfell Metala ★★★★   *August 2000*
Medium to full red; smooth chocolate aromas intermingle with clean, well–balanced and integrated spirit. The palate opens most attractively with chocolate and fine tannins before drying out on the finish.

1972 Yalumba ★★★☆   *August 2000*
Medium to full brick–red; the bouquet is clean, somewhat simple, but does have a considerable volume of fruit. The palate is quite raisiny, but one of the better Yalumba ports.

Not Ready   Still evolving   Prime of its life   Drink soon   Missed the boat

1972 Seppelt Rutherglen ★★★★   *August 2000*

Medium red; a fragrant, lifted and complex bouquet with hints of tea leaf is followed by a palate which is quite fascinating, in very different style, and with some elegance. Has only 2.5 baumé of residual sugar; the tea leaf makes me wonder whether a small amount of muscadelle (tokay) found its way into the wine.

1972 Hardy Bin D61 ★★★   *August 2000*

Light to medium red; the bouquet is very light, simple and with the slightest suggestion of some fungal or bacterial activity, possibly deriving from the cork. The palate is a little better than the bouquet, with good balance, but at the end of the day rather simple.

1971 Yalumba ★★★☆   *August 2000*

Quite dark red; the bouquet is concentrated, with earthy/dark berry aromas and fairly neutral spirit. A big, rustic style, with heaps of tannin on the finish.

1971 Stonyfell Metala ★★★   *August 2000*

Medium to full red, with a touch of purple; the bouquet is firm with slightly charry/earthy overtones to dark chocolate fruit; an extractive, rustic and tannic palate is inherently unlikely to soften.

1971 Saltram Mamre Brook ★★★☆   *August 2000*

Medium red–purple; solid dark chocolate aromas with plenty of depth are followed by a moderately complex palate, with chocolate-accented fruit, strong brandy spirit, and strong tannins on the finish.

1971 Hardy Bin C873 ★★★   *August 2000*

Light to medium red; a plain, light and slightly burnt bouquet is not redeemed by the palate.

1971 Chateau Reynella ★★★☆   *August 2000*

Light to medium red; the bouquet is light, quite elegant, but simple, the palate likewise. Those who know the wine well said it was a poor example.

1970 Yalumba ★★★   *August 2000*

Light to medium red–brick; a very sweet, slightly burnt bouquet otherwise lacks complexity, the palate no more, no less.

1970 Seppelt GR139 ★★★   *August 2000*

Medium to full red, with some brick on the rim; a strange, savoury/earthy bouquet with slightly aldehydic characters. The palate is dry, and off on a track all of its own. The base wine was Cabernet Sauvignon from Barooga in the Riverland.

1970 Saltram Mamre Brook ★★★   *August 2000*

Quite brown, suggesting high pH; a dusty, barky oxidised bouquet leads into a dusty, slightly oxidised and very aged palate.

1970 Chateau Reynella ★★★☆   *August 2000*

Medium to full red; ultra-typical, extreme, warped brandy spirit in the style I describe as lantana-like dominates both the bouquet and palate; still bounding along if these are characters you enjoy.

classic wines

★★★★★ Perfect   ★★★★☆ Close to perfect   ★★★★ Very good   ★★★☆ Expected
★★★ Short of standard   ★★☆ Undeserving   ★★ Decayed relic   NR No rating

283

1969 Leo Buring P129 ★★★   *August 2000*

Medium to full red; takes the lantana brandy spirit of the '67 another stage further, into a weird, distorted spectrum which carries through onto the over-the-top palate.

1968 Lindemans Bin 3740 ★★★★   *August 2000*

Dark red–brown; voluminous raisin, prune and plum fruit aromas are followed by a big, dense and rather extractive dark prune and plum-flavoured palate, which finishes with slightly dry, dusty tannins. Lots of cheese and walnuts required here.

1968 Reynella ★★★★   *August 2000*

The colour is dramatically different from the others of its era, light red–brown; the fragrant and spirity bouquet has a mix of leafy/savoury/cigar box aromas, while the palate shows another clear attempt at a Portuguese style, far lighter, more lively and more savoury.

1967 Yalumba ★★★☆   *August 2000*

Medium to full red; the solid, earth and chocolate aromas of the bouquet have a hint of astringency, the palate with strong dark, bitter chocolate flavours, and altogether different fortifying spirit character.

1967 Lindemans Bin 3642 ★★★★   *August 2000*

Dense red; an ultra-rich, ripe, chocolate and berry bouquet is followed by a huge, dense chocolate and prune-flavoured palate, with lingering, soft tannins. A blend of 75 per cent touriga and 25 per cent shiraz, which must have been picked when the grapes were virtually raisins.

1967 Leo Buring Bin P35 ★★★★   *August 2000*

Medium to full red; the complex bouquet shows strong brandy spirit characters together with spice, earth and Christmas cake. The strongly styled palate is quite fascinating, pre-dating the famous Hardy/Reynella wines of 1975 and 1977.

1967 Reynella ★★★★☆   *August 2000*

Medium red; a more refined style, with lighter fruit and gentle brandy spirit to the bouquet. The palate has more richness and substance, although it does have a slightly hot spirit finish.

1966 Yalumba ★★★   *August 2000*

Medium red; the bouquet has more complexity and style than the previous Yalumba vintages, although there is a touch of wet bandaid character. The palate is an alcoholic form of sweet milk chocolate, far too sweet for good balance.

1965 Lindemans Bin 3111 ★★★★   *August 2000*

Dense, dark red; big, earthy berry aromas with relatively subdued spirit on the bouquet are followed by a big, soft, cheerful palate with berry and chocolate flavours supported by soft tannins.

1965 Seppelt DP13 ★★★★   *August 2000*

Medium to full red–brick; the complex bouquet shows aromatic brandy spirit and spicy fruit, characters which follow through on the palate, the polar opposite in style to the Lindemans of the same vintage.

1965 Yalumba ★★★
August 2000

Medium red; a slightly smelly/rubbery bouquet is followed by a fairly plain palate lacking complexity.

1965 Leo Buring VP32 ★★★
August 2000

A bizarre, completely impenetrable, colour; the bouquet is akin to a black hole in space, the palate incredibly extractive. To reach this point after 35 years suggests no amount of time will fix it.

1965 Seppelt DP32 ★★★☆
August 2000

Medium brick–red; the slightly leafy/earthy bouquet is a complete contrast to DP13 of the same vintage; the same savoury/earthy characters carry through on the light palate.

1964 Chateau Reynella ★★★★
August 2000

Medium red; another wine with much lighter, more floral/herbaceous fruit aromas; the palate is certainly elegant, reflecting a deliberate change in style, but arguably taken a little bit too far.

1964 Yalumba ★★★☆
August 2000

Medium red; the bouquet is clean, not especially complex, earthy spirit the driver. The palate is pleasant, simple, well balanced but lacks complexity.

1964 Hardy Bin C464 ★★★☆
August 2000

Light to medium red–brick; the bouquet is very light, lacking fruit richness and/or complexity, the palate having gone too far in the search for delicacy.

1964 Penfolds ★★★
August 2000

Medium red; sweet minty fruit on the bouquet is followed by minty/earthy flavours on the palate, which simply don't work.

1964 Saltram Museum Release ★★★☆
August 2000

Dense colour; an immensely concentrated bouquet of chocolate and prune is followed by a huge palate, massively extractive, and lacking vinosity; a tyrannosaurus; from one extreme to the other.

1963 Quelltaler Wyatt Earp ★★★☆
August 2000

Light to medium brick–red; the bouquet is much lighter and more fragrant than the other wines in the line-up, with some cedar and cigar box, together with a degree of volatile lift. I simply cannot relate to the herbaceous fruit on the palate, no matter how famous the wine is or was (and it was very famous)

1962 Seppelt DP3 ★★★★
August 2000

Dense red; the bouquet has quite complex fruit and spirit, although there was a suggestion of mustiness. A powerful, bold style, not overly sweet, and with slight astringency on the finish.

1962 Lindemans Bin 2520 ★★☆
August 2000

Medium red; overall, volatile and tired.

classic wines

★★★★★ Perfect   ★★★★☆ Close to perfect   ★★★★ Very good   ★★★☆ Expected
★★★ Short of standard   ★★☆ Undeserving   ★★ Decayed relic   NR No rating

1962 Penfolds Bin 621 ★★★★   *August 2000*

Medium to full brick–red; aromas of sweet chocolate, earth and mint are followed by a palate which is literally loaded with chocolate, finishing with soft tannins. Has late-bottled vintage port character in a wholly Australian idiom.

1960 Penfolds Bin 479 ★★★☆   *August 2000*

Medium brick–red. The moderately intense bouquet is relatively simple other than for a very slight baggy character. A simple, sweet wine on the palate, still holding much of its fruit but going nowhere.

1958 Penfolds Bin 480 ★★★☆   *August 2000*

Light to medium red; the bouquet has sweet vanilla notes, but lacks fruit intensity and richness. The palate tends simple and sweet, neither fish nor fowl.

1958 Hardy Bin C134 ★★★★   *August 2000*

Medium to full red; strong, earthy brandy spirit mixes with bitter chocolate on the bouquet. The palate has nice grip; I particularly like the balance of tannin, spirit and fruit, which help both the length and finish of the wine. I must admit that others liked this wine less than I.

1957 Lindemans Bin 1280 ★★★★☆   *August 2000*

Virtually impenetrable colour, so dark is it. Very dense, rich, sweet dark plum and prune fruit aromas and distinctly different fortifying spirit are mirrored in the very different palate with its plummy fruit and soft, fine tannins.

1957 Chateau Reynella ★★★★★   *August 2000*

There is a radical colour change to light medium red; the aromas are in the flowery, herbal spicy spectrum, hinting of the palate which has elegance and length; a definite and quite successful attempt at Portuguese style.

1956 Hardy ★★★★★   *August 2000*

Dark red–brown; an intensely rich and complex bouquet with strong liquorice, spice and chocolate augmented by sweet brandy spirit. An extraordinary wine on the palate, rich, full and complex, with chocolate, liquorice and spice bound together with soft, sweet tannins. The bottle in this tasting was slightly off-song; the note is a blend of this tasting and that of November 1994.

1956 Seppelt DP17 ★★★★☆   *August 2000*

Very dense red–brown colour. The powerful and concentrated bouquet has ripe fruit, chocolate and sweet earth aromas; there is enormous concentration on the palate, with an almost soupy richness; good spirit, but this is a little too much of a good thing.

1954 Hardy Bin M169 ★★★★★   *August 2000*

Dark brick–red; the potent aromas of the bouquet are fuelled by strong brandy spirit, and have much greater complexity than many of the wines. The palate, too, is powerful and complex, rich and layered, with some cherry fruit and perfect tannins.

1954 Lindemans Bin 1285 ★★★★   *August 2000*

Full brick–red; there is a rainbow of aromas with liquorice, spice, date and Christmas cake contrasting with earthy spirit. Once again, there is a very different fruit character to the palate, with liquorice, cake and chocolate.

1953 Stonyfell ★★★★☆
August 2000

Strong, full brick–red colour; a clean, powerful bouquet with earthy spirit and dried prune/date aromas. The palate is crammed with masses of chocolate, prune and plum fruit, the finish long. Just a little over the top.

1952 Seppelt DP8 GR28 ★★★★☆
August 2000

Medium mahogany colour; sweet plum jam fruit, chocolate and spice aromas on the bouquet lead into a very complex, luscious and rich palate. Needs a touch more authority in the structure to gain maximum points.

1950 Stonyfell ★★★★
August 2000

Full brick–red; rich, ripe dark berry and prune fruit intermingles with earthy spirit on the bouquet. A big, solid, ultra–Australian style, with a slightly chunky finish, quite tannic and extractive.

1949 Lindemans Bin 1087 ★★★★★
August 2000

Medium to full brown, with some brick on the rim. The bouquet is fragrant and stylish, with spice, a hint of liquorice and good spirit. The palate has excellent structure, weight and balance; harmonious and elegant. A blend of alvarelhao, bastardo and touriga.

1949 Hardy Tintara Bin 418 ★★★★☆
August 2000

Medium brick–red; the bouquet is clean and firm, with slightly earthy spirit and fractionally repressed fruit aromatics. Any shortcomings on the bouquet are made up for by the long, intense palate which progressively builds towards the finish. Quite sweet.

1948 Seppelt DP136 ★★★★☆
August 2000

Medium tawny colour; the sweet bouquet has a touch of Christmas cake, but is otherwise relatively simple. The palate, however, is radically different, with sweet, intense fruit and a tangy, lifted finish. Poles apart from the '47 Seppelt.

1947 Seppelt DP2A GR5 ★★★★
August 2000

Dark brick–red; powerful, earthy, chocolately savoury aromas introduce a wine which is distinctly drier in terms of both its fruit and its finish than any of the older wines, with slightly muddy characters.

1946 Hardy ★★★★★
August 2000

Deep brown, with touches of brick on the rim; the powerful, rich bouquet has an array of plum, prune and chocolate aromas, the magnificently rich palate loaded with dark chocolate. A freak wine which will live for decades.

1946 Lindemans ★★★★★
August 2000

Deep amber–brown; a very aromatic, essencey bouquet with striking raisin fruit. There is similar raisiny fruit on the palate with distinctly different fruit character, presumably coming from the touriga and alvarelhao varieties used to make the wine.

classic wines

★★★★★ Perfect   ★★★★☆ Close to perfect   ★★★★ Very good   ★★★☆ Expected
★★★ Short of standard   ★★☆ Undeserving   ★★ Decayed relic   NR No rating

1945 Stonyfell ★★★★★   *August 2000*

The colour is light brown, with some orange hues; the fragrant, spicy and highly aromatic bouquet immediately sets this wine apart from all others. The palate, likewise, is utterly different, with long, spicy flavours, well-balanced spirit and subliminal tannins. A freak wine resulting from the accidental fortification of high-quality cabernet sauvignon, an extreme rarity at that time.

1942 Seppelt DP150 ★★★★★   *August 2000*

Dark brown colour, with some olive on the rim; powerful plum and raisin aromas intermingle with touches of char and earth on the bouquet. The palate is similarly powerful, with rich, raisin fruit; still has grip to the long, lingering finish.

1940 Chateau Reynella ★★★   *August 2000*

Slightly cloudy, pale orange hue; the caramel and toffee aromas of the bouquet are pretty much a remnant; the palate still has flavour, toffee with a citrus twist, but the varietal character and vintage port style have long since gone.

1936 Chateau Reynella ★★★★★   *August 2000*

Robust, clear red–brown colour; the bouquet is ripe, with some raisin fruit and very good spirit. The palate has plenty of substance and weight, with sweet, dark raisin fruit, powerful spirit and some remnants of tannin.

1927 Hardy ★★★★   *August 2000*

Light tawny colour long past any primary hues; sweet caramel and raisin aromas hint at the soft, rich and incredibly sweet raisiny fruit on the palate; there is good acidity, but the tannins have gone.

a s a stand-alone estate, Virgin Hills always defied the odds and the gods alike. When Melbourne restaurateur Tom Lazar established it in 1968, he was told by all and sundry that the grapes would never ripen, and his already formidable reputation as an eccentric was significantly enhanced.

Well, in some years the grapes didn't fully ripen, but in 1974, 1976 and 1980 he made quite superb wines which are still a pleasure to drink, and he didn't do too badly in many of the other vintages. In the end, it was not the climate which defeated him, but the microscopic yields (and some unrelated financial misadventures).

When Marcel Gilbert (and his family) purchased Virgin Hills from Lazar in 1980, he was well aware of the climatic razor's edge on which this property is perched at an altitude of 600 metres near Kyneton in the Macedon Ranges. He also knew that the extremely low yields, averaging a tonne to the acre but sometimes as little as one-third of a tonne per acre, and the resulting crush of less than 30 tonnes, would likely preclude the winery from making a commercial profit.

His aspirations were simply to protect, and wherever possible enhance, the great reputation Virgin Hills had already acquired. He didn't touch the stark, minimalist gold on white labels, nor abandon the 60 mm long corks — longer than any other cork to be found in Australia (or elsewhere).

Mark Sheppard became his winemaker, and in 1982, 1985 and 1992 wines on the same plane as the best of Tom Lazar's were made. Not content with this, in 1988 Virgin Hills embarked on what seemed to be a romantic folly even greater than Lazar could have conceived: from that time on the wines were made organically, without the use of sulphur dioxide.

Typically, the publicity-shy Marcel Gilbert did not make a big thing of this, eschewing the claim to be the greatest producer of sulphur-free red wines in the world, which in my book they are. Nor, on the other side of the coin, did Gilbert or Sheppard make much of the fact that no 1989 wine was released under the Virgin Hills label. This was not due to the new organic winemaking techniques, but simply the result of the climatic gods finally catching up with the vineyard in a vintage many wineries in less marginal sites would prefer to forget.

Against this background a vertical tasting was staged in Melbourne in early July 1998, covering all the vintages from 1974 to 1997, although only Marcel Gilbert (and family) had any inkling of the negotiations then underway for the sale of Virgin Hills to Vincorp. Since then, Vincorp has been dismantled, and Virgin Hills is now part of Michael Hope's (of Hope Estate) empire.

Note: the tasting notes also make reference to (and occasionally incorporate notes from) earlier tastings for the purposes of comparison. Occasionally, the prior note from 1993 has been used where the wine in question was not present at the 1998 tasting.

★★★★★ Perfect   ★★★★☆ Close to perfect   ★★★★ Very good   ★★★☆ Expected
★★★ Short of standard   ★★☆ Undeserving   ★★ Decayed relic   NR No rating

classic wines

289

1998 ★★★★☆ February 2001

Medium red–purple, the hue reassuringly bright; the clean and smooth bouquet shows a pleasantly ripe and complex mix of berry fruits. The elegant, bright and lively palate has a slight minty backdrop to the predominant red berries, finishing with fine tannins and subtle oak.

1997 ★★★☆ August 1999

Medium red–purple; the fragrant bouquet offers spicy fruit with a touch of mint together with smoky/cigar box oak. The palate has red berry, cherry and mint flavours which are much less dense than the barrel sample previously tasted. All in all, shows the low alcohol of 11.3 degrees.

1996 ★★★☆ July 1998

Medium purple–red; a wine which shows some of the sweet characters of the '93, but is less confection and more concentrated. The palate follows the bouquet, sweet and ripe, with moderate to full tannins. Very nearly rated four stars. (Not previously tasted.)

1995 ★★★★ July 1998

Medium to full red–purple; the bouquet is fragrant, of moderate intensity, with cedar, cigar box, leaf and spice aromas. The palate is fine and elegant, with leaf, mint and spice flavours underlying the red cherry/berry fruit; fine-grained tannins on a delicate but long finish.

1994 ★★★☆ July 1998

Medium purple–red; the bouquet has touches of game, liquorice, spice, leaf and leather, all of which are to be found on the palate. Another cool vintage (like 1993) and very likely at the peak right now, notwithstanding the fairly high acid. (1997 4 stars.)

1993 ★★★☆ July 1998

Light to medium red–purple; the bouquet shows sweet, almost confectionery rhubarb fruit characters, the palate following suit but adding touches of mint. By no means unpleasant, but it is hard to see how this wine will have a long life, particularly if the '86 and '87 vintages are a guide. (Previous 3.5 stars.)

1992 ★★★★★ July 1998

The colour is much denser than the '91 or '90 vintages; the ripe, powerful bouquet offers earth, aniseed and blackcurrant aromas, while the palate is holding all the life and fruit one could hope for, perfectly ripened and seemingly assured of a long life. (1993 4 stars.)

1991 ★★★★☆ July 1998

Medium purple–red; there is very good fruit concentration on the bouquet, with a mix of spice and berry aromas. The palate has excellent structure, with soft but evident tannins attesting to the warm vintage. A lively and delicious wine. (1993 5 stars.)

1990 ★★★★ July 1998

Light to medium red–purple; the bouquet is clean, relatively light, with hints of charry oak and touches of spice. The supple and delicate palate shows cherry, cherry pip and spice, all attesting to the unusually high percentage of shiraz (44 per cent) in the blend. (Not tasted previously.)

Not Ready   Still evolving   Prime of its life   Drink soon   Missed the boat

1990 Reserve ★★★★★   *1993*

Vivid purple–red; fresh, elegant and fragrant with strong spicy notes from the shiraz component; good acidity and low tannins; very long finish. (1993 5 stars.) (Not retasted.)

1989

No wine made.

1988 ★★★★☆   *July 1998*

Strong red; the complex aromas chase each other around the glass, variously showing red berries, earth, touches of spice and sweet leather. A wine which retains the delicacy and freshness it showed when much younger, with delicious raspberry fruit and gentle tannins. I would be inclined to drink it sooner rather than later, however. (1993 5 stars.)

1987 ★★☆   *July 1998*

Light red; the green vegetal/dimethyl sulphide fruit characters have led to a precipitous decline in the flavour and character of the wine, proving once and for all that cool vintages are the nemesis of Virgin Hills. (1993 4 stars.)

1986 ★★★   *July 1998*

Light red, with a touch of purple. The opposite of the '85, essentially thin and unripe, with a mix of leaf, mint and spice flavours which were briefly attractive in their youth — but no longer. (1993 4 stars.)

1985 ★★★★★   *July 1998*

What a brilliant wine. Deeply coloured, it has an abundance of concentrated, rich and ripe dark berry/black cherry fruit on the bouquet, and a sensuous palate, crammed full of delicious plummy/cherry fruit. Will live for decades to come. (1993 5 stars.)

1984 ★★★   *July 1998*

The colour is vibrant, and everything about the wine attests to a cool vintage producing a high acid, low pH wine with light peppery/spicy aromas and flavours and an acidic finish. Will never throw off the constraints of the vintage. (1993 2.5 stars.)

1983 Gold Hill (Magnum) ★★★★☆   *July 1998*

Strong colour; the bouquet has a particular aroma with a mix of cassis, sweet leather and that earthy edge of mature cabernet one encounters in Coonawarra. The palate is powerful and quite tannic, attesting to the low crop and dry, hot summer. An El Niño year like 1998. (Not tasted previously.)

1983 ★★★☆   *July 1998*

Medium purple–red; there is a touch of volatility running through a solidly concentrated bouquet, and that volatility kicks again at the end of the palate. There is, however, ample dark berry fruit, cedary oak and good tannin balance. (1993 3.5 stars.)

1982 ★★★★★   *July 1998*

The colour is still bright and appealing, the sweet fruit of the bouquet smooth and fresh, supported by a nice touch of oak. The palate follows on logically, sweet, smooth and long, with supple, soft tannins rippling through on the finish. The vintage conditions were like those of 1997, quite ideal. (1993 5 stars.) •C•

classic wines

★★★★★ Perfect   ★★★★☆ Close to perfect   ★★★★ Very good   ★★★☆ Expected
★★★ Short of standard   ★★☆ Undeserving   ★★ Decayed relic   NR No rating

291

1981 ★★★★★   *July 1998*

Good colour; very sweet, ripe red berry fruit aromas are followed by a palate still oozing ripe, sweet berry fruit complemented by a touch of new oak. Just a hint of drying tannin on the finish. Utterly at odds with the tired bottle tasted in 1991; the crop was around one-third of a tonne per acre. (1993 3 stars.)

1980 ★★★★   *July 1998*

Less deep than the '79; the bouquet is clean, with pleasant fruit, and the wine really shines in the mouth, with soft spicy fruit offset by perfectly balanced tannins on the finish. (1993 4.5 stars.)

1980 Veronique ★★★☆   *July 1998*

(A special bottling of 100 per cent Cabernet Sauvignon from the Gold Hill block.) Strong colour; there is abundant sweet fruit surrounded by volatility, seemingly induced by a longer time in oak. A powerful and rich palate, yet somewhat disjointed, finishing with pronounced tannins. (Not tasted previously.)

1979 ★★★☆   *July 1998*

Noticeably deeper colour, quite dense. The potent, powerful earthy bouquet has concentrated fruit characters quite different from all of the older wines, the palate unexpectedly massive and quite tannic. (1993 4 stars.)

1978 ★★★☆   *July 1998*

Slightly darker hues, perhaps blackish, perhaps purple. Floral, sweet berry notes and a dash of green canopy characters come through on the bouquet, leading to a jumble of charry oak, some earth, mint and slightly boiled sweet fruit flavours. Left field, but far from unattractive. (1993 4 stars.)

1977 ★★★   *July 1998*

Fair red; the bouquet shows a mix of herbaceous dimethyl sulphide aromas and boiled fruit. There is a similar unusual mix of leaf, spice and slightly boiled fruit — and again those dimethyl sulphide characters. (1993 3 stars.)

1976 ★★★★★   *July 1998*

Outstanding colour for age. The bouquet, too, is rich with berry, spice, leaf and mint aromas and no 'off' characters of any description. Great texture and structure in the mouth, with delicious spice, red berry fruit and nuances of chocolate; soft, fine tannins on the finish. (1993 5 stars.)

1975 ★★★   *July 1998*

Slightly lighter in colour; a more complex bouquet which, however, became more and more earthy as the wine sat in the glass. The fruit is dropping away, the palate thinning out and inexorably tasting more acidic. (Not tasted previously.)

1975 Pressings ★★★★   *July 1998*

The colour is incredibly deep purple–red; the bouquet huge and extractive, with some minty characters and some volatility. The palate is likewise enormous, with chewy minty/meaty fruit which, all in all, is somewhat over the top, although this is a style greatly appreciated by some. (Not tasted since 1993; it is most likely this wine will have declined since 1991.)

   ◄ Not Ready   ◣ Still evolving   ◈ Prime of its life   ◢ Drink soon   ◻ Missed the boat

1974 ★★★★★   *July 1998*

For such a mature wine, still with a healthy bright red colour. The aromas range through cedar, spice, tobacco and leaf, with that patina of age yet no decay. A truly excellent palate, still holding gently sweet, spicy fruit; soft tannins run through a quite lovely old wine. (1993 5 stars.)

1973 ★★★★★   *July 1998*

As with the '74, still bright red with no browning. A deliciously fragrant and pure bouquet, with redcurrant and cedar notes. The palate is every bit as good, a classic aged wine, with silky tannins and crisp acidity on the finish. Far better than the bottle tasted in 1991. (1993 4 stars.)

★★★★★ Perfect   ★★★★☆ Close to perfect   ★★★★ Very good   ★★★☆ Expected
★★★ Short of standard   ★★☆ Undeserving   ★★ Decayed relic   NR No rating

classic wines

293

wendouree cellars dry reds

1975-1998

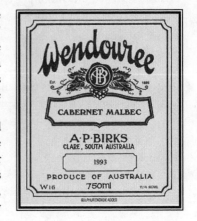

the vineyards, dating back to 1893, the winery (to 1894), the memory of 'Roly' Birks, the quiet but fiercely passionate stewardship of present owners Tony and Lita Brady, and the wines: all should be regarded as part of the National Heritage, what the Japanese would call a 'Living Treasure'.

Throughout the latter part of the 1980s and early 1990s the vineyards were re-trellised (some given a proper trellis for the first time in their lives), 'on the theory that when we die the trellis will be so good they won't remove the vines', quips Tony Brady. For it is indeed the truly unique Wendouree terroir — the combination of soil, site and site climate — and the age of the vines which are primarily responsible for wines which cannot be compared to any others in Australia, or for that matter in the world.

The self-effacing Bradys and their sympathetically quiet consultant winemaker Stephen George play an essential midwives' role of course, but these wines essentially spring from the womb of the earth. Tucked away in a side valley, nature works magic on the vineyard, producing grapes with a chemical composition, colour and flavour which others can only dream of.

It is as useless to put them in a masked line-up of conventional red wines, as it is to apply conventional ageing yardsticks. These wines move on another plane of power and concentration, yet magically avoid coarseness or over-extraction. They are not only unique; they are magnificent.

The 1975 to 1992 vintages were tasted in October 1994; the others upon release.

◄■ **1998 Cabernet Malbec ★★★★★**   *March 2001*
Medium to full purple–red; the bouquet has high-toned edges to the blackberry, earth and spice; the massive, mouthfilling blackberry/blackcurrant palate has all-pervasive tannins running through its length, yet is still in balance.

◄■ **1997 Shiraz ★★★★☆**   *December 1999*
Youthful, vivid crimson–purple. The bouquet is clean but still closed; you can sense the fruit with flecks of cherry, leather and earth escaping from the black hole. The palate is very youthful; the components are still disjointed, but are balanced; demands at least a decade before any realistic rating of its quality can be given.

1996 Cabernet Malbec ★★★★★ *February 1998*

Medium to full red–purple; a stupendously concentrated and powerful bouquet, bursting with ripe blackberry fruit; the palate is opulently rich, ripe and round, with the Malbec influence very evident. Luscious and mouthfilling.

1996 Shiraz ★★★★★ *December 1999*

Deep, bright, full purple–red; the bouquet is highly fragrant, redolent of spice and cherry pips. There is quite lovely multiflavoured cherry, plum and spice fruit on the palate, with excellent tannin balance in the context of the style. A quite marvellous wine which fully lives up to the reputation of the vintage.

1995 Cabernet Malbec ★★★★★ *May 1997*

Dark, deep purple–red; a concentrated, dense and powerful bouquet with brooding, dark fruits leads to a massively concentrated palate with a complex array of fruit flavours in the mint/blackberry/briar spectrum, finishing with persistent tannins. Notwithstanding all the power and concentration, is immaculately balanced.

1995 Shiraz ★★★★ *December 1999*

Strong, deep purple–red; there is concentrated dark berry, liquorice and leather on the bouquet, with an underlying touch of astringency. An extremely powerful and aggressive palate; there is no point in arguing with or about it. Only in ten years will the true quality of the wine, good or not, become apparent.

1994 Shiraz ★★★★★ *December 1999*

Has the wonderful deep purple–red of young Wendouree wines; the bouquet has a cascade of liquorice, leather, black cherry and spice aromas, followed by a palate with fantastic fruit concentration; here intense liquorice and berry flavours are surrounded by tannins which are under perfect control. Twenty years will see a supreme wine.

1994 Shiraz Malbec ★★★★ *December 1999*

Again, strong, deep but brilliant purple–red colour. The bouquet is fragrant and juicy, with the impact from the malbec immediately obvious. The palate has strong, juicy/berry flavours, but the fruit dips slightly on the back palate before tannins come through strongly on the finish. The rating may prove to be harsh, but, either way, the wine needs time to make up its mind.

1993 Cabernet Malbec ★★★★★ *October 1995*

Full red–purple; voluptuous, sweetly ripe blackcurrant and blackberry fruit aromas leap from the glass; there is marvellously full, deep and concentrated fruit of identical flavours on the palate, surrounded by balanced but persistent tannins. The oak input throughout is under restraint.

1993 Shiraz ★★★★ *December 1999*

Medium to full red–purple; the moderately intense bouquet has a mix of berry, earth and that typical sweet shoe leather seen in a number of the wines. A slightly disjointed palate, with earthy/leathery/berry fruit which is a little sloppy on the mid-palate, although the tannins bolster the finish.

classic wines

★★★★★ Perfect   ★★★★☆ Close to perfect   ★★★★ Very good   ★★★☆ Expected
★★★ Short of standard   ★★☆ Undeserving   ★★ Decayed relic   NR No rating

295

◀■ *1992 Cabernet Malbec* ★★★★☆   *October 1994*

As one would expect, dense, youthful purple–red colour, with a ripely potent bouquet with briary/berry aromas complexed by an obvious contribution of plummy malbec fruit. Formidably massive in the mouth, with powerful, potent, earth/briary/berry fruit flavours, nowhere near approachable.

◀■ *1991 Shiraz* ★★★★★   *December 1999*

The colour has lightened off somewhat over the past five years, but is still strong by normal standards. The bouquet is fragrant and complex, with wonderfully sweet dark cherry, plum, spice and shoe leather. The palate opens with masses of sweet, ripe spicy cherry fruit then moves through to persistent, dusty tannins which, while powerful, are not abrasive. A wine which is just starting to unfold, and suggests it will ultimately have a touch of elegance.

◀■ *1991 Malbec* ★★★★★   *October 1994*

A special bottling which will only appear in exceptional vintages. Impenetrable purple hue, with a huge volume of fruit on the bouquet, the very essence of jammy varietal character, but jammy in the positive sense; not at all porty, and incredibly fragrant. The flavours follow the aromas, with essence of fruit. The wine has wonderful acidity and tannins in balance.

◀■ *1990 Shiraz* ★★★★★   *October 1994*

A glorious wine with spotless, pure dark cherry fruit and perfectly integrated oak. The palate has abundant cherry/berry fruit with noticeable but balanced charry oak and good tannin balance.

◀■ *1989 Shiraz* ★★★★☆   *December 1999*

Medium to full purple–red; the aromas range through sweet berry/cherry, earth and mint. The palate is rich, full and concentrated, with abundant dark cherry and plum fruit before the Wendouree tannins come towards the back palate and finish. I strongly suspect this wine may be going through a disjointed phase of its development, and has every prospect of coming together again by 2005.

🍷 *1988 Cabernet Sauvignon* ★★★★☆   *October 1994*

Deep, youthful purple giving no hint of colour change. The bouquet is high-toned and fragrant with earth, mint and berry aromas; the palate is powerful, with lots of fruit, and tannins still to resolve themselves. Needs 20 years.

🍷 *1987 Cabernet Sauvignon* ★★★☆   *October 1994*

Slightly out of the mainstream of the Wendouree style, although sharing the same exceptional colour of the other wines. There are complex briary/leafy/berry aromas, and similar slightly minty/leafy/gamey fruit flavours. A product of a very cool vintage, and a question mark as to whether the tannins will outlive the fruit.

🍷 *1986 Cabernet Sauvignon* ★★★★★   *October 1994*

Nigh on perfect, with potent, spotlessly clean cassis and red berry fruit aromas leading on to a concentrated, long and smooth palate. The flavours are primarily in the cassis/berry range, with just a hint of mint; the oak is subtle and the tannins well balanced on a long finish.

◀■ Not Ready   🍷 Still evolving   ▮ Prime of its life   ⌇ Drink soon   ⟁ Missed the boat

1985 Shiraz ★★★★   *October 1994*

Medium to full red–purple, with initial hints of hay and straw reminiscent of Hunter Shiraz from a warm year, then riper, earthy notes came up. A strongly varietal wine in flavour, with complex earthy/briary/chocolatey fruit; the tannins are a fraction hard.

1984 Cabernet Sauvignon ★★★★   *October 1994*

All in all, the product of a cooler vintage. The colour is still strong; the bouquet equivalently youthful, with distinct herbaceous cabernet sauvignon varietal fruit. The same strongly varietal/herbaceous fruit comes through on the palate, giving the wine a certain austerity when contrasted with the layered plushness of the other wines.

1983 Shiraz ★★★★★   *October 1994*

Deeply coloured and very concentrated, reflecting the exceptionally low yields of the drought year. Redolent of ripe, sweet mint and berry fruit, and a touch of spice which may be fruit, or oak–derived. A complex, rich and concentrated palate with ripe cherry fruit which is complexed by a touch of new oak and the expected tannins. A great success.

1982 Cabernet Sauvignon ★★★★★   *October 1994*

Still retains its youthful deep purple–red colour, with concentrated, ripe dark berry and currant fruit with a hint of chocolate to the bouquet. There is subtle new oak influence throughout the wine, which has exceptionally ripe, juicy, sweet blackcurrant fruit, finishing with beautifully balanced tannins. So good it can be enjoyed now, even though it has a long way to go.

1982 Malbec Cabernet ★★★★★   *December 1999*

Medium red–purple; a complete change of pace, being fragrant with some leafy aromas, and reminiscent of the Penfolds wines of the same vintage. The palate is very smooth and elegant, with attractive berry, chocolate and mint flavours, replete with fine tannins on a long palate and finish.

1981 Cabernet Malbec ★★★★☆   *October 1994*

Dark coloured, but showing the faintest hint of development. The bouquet is complex, with an array of berry, chocolate, leaf and mint aromas. The palate is very full-bodied, with ripe berry fruit, some dark chocolate and a hint of mint.

1980 Cabernet Malbec ★★★★☆   *October 1994*

Even by the standards of Wendouree, an exceptionally youthful wine, still with a brilliant full purple–red hue, and voluminous blackcurrant fruit aromas, with just a hint of chocolate. In the mouth there are bright edges to the juicy, minty, berry fruit flavours, and the tannins are still firm.

1980 Pressings ★★★★   *December 1999*

Dense red–purple; the bouquet is clean, with a mix of savoury/earthy aromas and sweeter blackberry fruit. As expected, the wine is ultra-full-bodied, with ripe, minty fruit, finishing with strong but not overly aggressive tannins.

classic wines

★★★★★ Perfect   ★★★★☆ Close to perfect   ★★★★ Very good   ★★★☆ Expected
★★★ Short of standard   ★★☆ Undeserving   ★★ Decayed relic   NR No rating

1979 Cabernet Malbec Shiraz ★★★★☆   *October 1994*

The colour shows a hint of development; the bouquet is (relatively speaking) lighter and sweeter, with fragrant red berry, caramel and chocolate aromas. There is a panoply of sweet flavours on the palate ranging from chocolate, liquorice through to red berry fruits, with tannins starting to soften on a lingering finish.

1978 Shiraz ★★★★★   *October 1994*

Still strongly coloured in the red–purple range, with concentrated sweet berry, liquorice and dark cherry fruit aromas. A wonderful wine in the mouth, which is starting to open up ever so slightly, showing multi-layered flavours of cherry, chocolate and liquorice; the tannins are balanced.

1978 Shiraz Mataro ★★★★★   *December 1999*

Full brick–red; a sweet, fragrant, aromatic bouquet with a range of berry, liquorice and sweet leather aromas. A beautifully rich and soft palate with chocolate and berry flavours supported by soft tannins. Has reached its peak, which it will almost certainly hold for another decade at least.

1977 Pressings ★★★★☆   *October 1994*

Although the label does not say so, in fact made from a blend of Shiraz and Mourvedre (called Mataro by Wendouree). Deeply coloured, with a very concentrated sweet berry bouquet which is not, however, extractive. The palate is hugely powerful and concentrated, and is tannic as one would expect, but not aggressively so. There are plenty of red berry, cherry and mint fruit flavours there for the long haul — which the wine needs.

1976 Shiraz Mataro ★★★★★   *October 1994*

Deeply coloured, with very different aromas, briary and initially with a hint of varietal straw which seemed to blow off with time. A very powerful rich and complex wine on the palate, with some minty flavours which did not show on the bouquet; powerful tannins on the finish.

1976 Shiraz ★★★★★   *October 1994*

Incredibly deep colour, still purple–red. The bouquet is clean, firm, deep and concentrated, with liquorice and spice fruit. A wonderfully structured and concentrated wine in the mouth with dark cherry fruit predominant and just a touch of mint. Powerful tannins run throughout. Will seemingly live forever.

1975 Malbec Shiraz ★★★★☆   *October 1994*

Deep red, still with some purple hues. Voluptuous and complex aromas ranging through fragrant, ripe berry fruit to more liquorice/briary characters which seemed to change and evolve as the wine breathed. A complex, rich and complete palate with coffee, berry and spice fruit and tannins perfectly in balance. No sign of fading, and years in front of it.

woodley coonawarra reds

t his tasting was held at Len Evans's Bulletin Place Restaurant in 1970 or 1971; while I have the notes (they first appeared in my book *Coonawarra*, published in 1983) I neglected to record the precise tasting date, hence the uncertainty. In any event, it predated the shorter Treasure Chest tasting in Sydney by over 20 years. Comparing the two sets of notes emphasises two things: first, there is no such thing as great old wines, only great old bottles. Second, it was indeed true that the '55 needed more time when tasted in 1970/71.

The wines in this tasting all came from Tony Nelson's private cellar. Austrian-born and trained (his name was anglicised), Nelson had joined Woodley Wines as technical manager in 1940, and in 1945 first acquired control of Woodley Wines and then later in the same year purchased Chateau Comaum (now known as Wynns Coonawarra Estate) from brandy makers Milne & Co.

Woodley's had sourced much of its best red wine from Coonawarra via the Redman family — notably Bill Redman — since 1920, when Bill Redman had entered into a long-term arrangement with Woodley's founder, Colonel Fulton. Particularly famous were the Woodley St Adele Clarets of 1933 and 1935; the former was placed first in a wine exhibition in London, while the latter is said to be partly responsible for Samuel and David Wynn's decision to buy Chateau Comaum in 1951.

So while the tasting is an old one, the wines have great historic significance, and I know of no subsequent showing or tasting of the wines from 1948 and previous. For the record, all were made from Shiraz.

1956 ★★★★☆
Colour: medium to deep red; touch of amber on rim. Bouquet: very fine and clean with strong cigar box aroma. Palate: beautifully balanced, with fresh lively fruit and an excellent clean crisp acid finish.

1955 ★★★
Colour: similar to the '56; very good for age. Bouquet: slightly more aggressive, bordering on being coarse. Palate: very firm, full fruit. Still developing; needs more time.

classic wines

★★★★★ Perfect   ★★★★☆ Close to perfect   ★★★★ Very good   ★★★☆ Expected
★★★ Short of standard   ★★☆ Undeserving   ★★ Decayed relic   NR No rating

299

1954 ★★☆
Colour: brown–amber. Bouquet: objectionable 'bottle stink' showing both hydrogen sulphide and volatility, but which improved as the wine lay in the glass. Palate: showing its age; rather thin and light.

1953 ★★★★★
Colour: good deep red. Bouquet: clean and fine. Palate: a very similar wine to the '56; beautifully balanced fresh fruit and fine crisp acid.

1952 ★★★★☆
Colour: superb red–purple. Bouquet: very firm, very clean. Palate: another beautifully balanced wine at its peak, and extraordinarily similar in structure and finesse to many of the other wines in the line-up.

1951 ★★★★☆
Colour: deep red. Bouquet: an extra depth and dimension to the fruit. Palate: one of the few wines in the line-up to show significant tannin, which resulted in a slightly hard finish. A robust wine with years in front of it.

1950 ★★☆
Colour: touch of amber on rim. Bouquet: trace of acetic/lactic aroma. Palate: smooth but light fruit on forepalate and a slightly sour finish.

1949 ★★★★
Colour: dark and deep. Bouquet: immense ripe fruit. Palate: an enormous, giant of a wine, more akin to vintage port and with years and years in front of it. Radically different from the other wines and consequently difficult to judge with them.

1948 ★★☆
Colour: medium red with amber rim. Bouquet: slightly oily aroma. Palate: again shows a slight 'off' character, although there is sound fruit underneath.

1945 ★★★★★
Colour: medium to full red. Bouquet: nigh on perfection. Palate: superb fruit; glorious balance and an equally superb finish.

1943 ★★★★★
A carbon copy of the '45, but just a fraction fuller and firmer.

1942 ★★★★
Colour: exceptionally deep and dark. Bouquet: clean firm fruit, rich and deep. Palate: falls away somewhat, with an astringent acid finish.

1941 ★★★★★
Colour: good vibrant red. Bouquet: muted cigar box and good fruit. Palate: marvellously complex flavour and in great condition. Showing no signs of age whatsoever.

1935 ★★☆
Colour: some amber tints. Bouquet: marked volatility. Palate: age has at last caught up with one of these wines, but obvious volatility does not completely spoil the fruit.

➟ Not Ready ＼ Still evolving ▲ Prime of its life ✎ Drink soon ⏻ Missed the boat

1932 ★★★☆
Colour: very good for age. Bouquet: essencey/estery with a suspicion of volatility. Palate: suffers in comparison with the '30 but on its own would probably be considered remarkable.

1930 ★★★★★
Colour: almost unbelievable; dark purple–red with only a slightest trace of amber on the rim. Bouquet: rich, firm and complex; no sign of age. Palate: an extraordinary Peter Pan wine, with youthful fruit and tannin coupled with lively acid on the finish.

★★★★★ Perfect   ★★★★☆ Close to perfect   ★★★★ Very good   ★★★☆ Expected
★★★ Short of standard   ★★☆ Undeserving   ★★ Decayed relic   NR No rating

woodley coonawarra treasure chest
claret 1949-1956

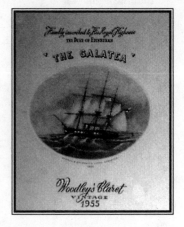

t hese are legendary wines, and deservedly so. Sets come up for auction every now and then, usually selling for around $1800 if the labels are in good condition. For while the wines are remarkable in their own right, the labels are even more so. In real money terms, they were (and remain) the most expensive ever printed in Australia, engraved and printed (in sets of eight) on a single sheet of near parchment quality paper, each featuring a painting or sketch originally painted or created in the nineteenth century.

The wines were made for the then owner of Woodley's, Austrian-born Tony Nelson, by Bill Redman. During part of this time Nelson owned what is now Wynns Coonawarra Estate, selling it to the Wynn family in July 1951. But he retained Woodley Wines, his Adelaide-based wine business, and what is more had the foresight to hold back significant quantities of these wines in Woodley's underground cellars in the drives of an old silver mine on the outskirts of Adelaide.

In the mid-1960s a decision was taken to sell these old vintages, and the beautiful labels which adorn them were commissioned. The wines, made in the simplest possible fashion from 50-year-old shiraz vines, are a priceless legacy of the Coonawarra of yesterday. I have tasted them on many occasions; the notes for this tasting come from a Legends of Coonawarra dinner held in Sydney in September 1994.

1956 ★★★☆
Medium red, with some slightly porty/earthy characters on the bouquet with a touch of volatility, and the fruit just starting to fade. On the palate a hint of volatility again evident, but there is still sweet, liquorice-accented fruit remaining. The only wine to show any real signs of bottle decay.

1955 ★★★★★
Excellent red colour with a clean, ripe, full bouquet with a hint of sweet caramel, fruit, rather than oak-derived. The palate is incredibly fresh, holding marvellously well, with generous, round, sweet berry fruit, finishing with soft tannins.

1954 ★★★★
Light to medium red, with a fine, fragrant bouquet with classic, gently earthy shiraz aromas. The palate is lighter than the bouquet suggests, with almost ethereal flavours, and the tannins long gone. For all that, holding remarkably well.

➡ Not Ready   ❰ Still evolving   ❙ Prime of its life   ✐ Drink soon   ⬓ Missed the boat

1953 ★★★☆
Medium red; the bouquet is of light to medium intensity with complex minty/charry aromas, with an almost riesling-like kerosene edge. The palate initially showed delicate sweet fruit, but the tannins seemed to become rather more bitter as the wine sat in the glass. For all that, still a remarkable drink.

1952 ★★★★
Even better colour than the '53, with a very complex bouquet running from sweet caramel, toffee and earth characters through to the more fragrant petrolly/kerosene edge noted in the '53. In the mouth, a relatively light-bodied wine, not especially structurally complex, but with quite a long finish and some lingering sweetness.

1951 ★★★★☆
Exceptionally deep colour, with a voluminous, ripe chocolatey/dusty bouquet. An amazingly powerful wine for its age in the mouth, with ripe fruit and some slightly tough, drying tannins.

1950 ★★★
Light to medium red; the bouquet is quite fragrant, of light to medium intensity, clean and with gently earthy varietal fruit. The palate is not unlike an old Hunter, with a hint of spice, but some astringency on the finish. Much less generous and sweet than the '49.

1949 ★★★★★
An extraordinary wine from start to finish, still with a deep red, even purple-tinged hue, and abundant sweet red cherry and plum fruit aromas. The palate has similarly abundant sweet fruit with some minty notes, finishing with perfectly balanced soft tannins. As close to perfection as a wine of this age can be.

★★★★★ Perfect   ★★★★☆ Close to perfect   ★★★★ Very good   ★★★☆ Expected
★★★ Short of standard   ★★☆ Undeserving   ★★ Decayed relic   NR No rating

wynns coonawarra estate black label cabernet sauvignon 1952-1998

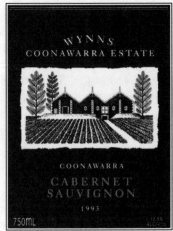

the Black Label version of the classic Wynns woodcut label graces the best known commercial Cabernet Sauvignon in Australia. It is produced entirely from Wynns estate-grown grapes, in awesome quantities given its quality.

It was not always thus. Initially, production was minuscule, as there were only nominal plantings of cabernet sauvignon in Coonawarra before the mid-1960s. Indeed, it is reasonable to assume that the vintages of the '50s and early '60s had a significant percentage of Shiraz — the laws and the practices of those times were very different from those of today.

Whatever be the case, those early wines were of exceptional quality, the best still drinking well to this day. Volatility then became intrusive, starting in 1960 and increasing through to 1966 — although the '60 and '62 are wines of considerable character.

While the volatile acidity came back under control, the quality of the wines between 1966 and 1981 was uninspiring to say the least. It was the time of the red wine boom, of corporate changes in ownership and redneck marketing strategies. But with a few vintage wobbles, the quality since 1982 has been exemplary, and since 1987 has been quite outstanding given the price of the wine.

The wine is made entirely from cabernet sauvignon, and is matured in a mix of new and used American oak hogsheads for 18 months.

First tasted in March 1993, updated, and later vintages added.

1998 ★★★★★   *November 2000*
Medium to full red–purple; sweet and ripe cassis/blackberry/raspberry fruit aromas are followed by a full-bodied, fruit-driven style, with oak and tannins playing a nicely judged support role; smooth and supple; every bit as good as the vintage reputation would suggest.

1997 ★★★★☆   *October 1999*
Medium red–purple; the bouquet is quite fragrant with cassis berry fruit, a touch of mint and subtle oak. The palate offers nicely ripened black and redcurrant fruit, neatly handled oak, and soft tannins. Not a '96, but a useful wine nonetheless.

◄■ Not Ready   ❧ Still evolving   ♪ Prime of its life   ✎ Drink soon   ⬮ Missed the boat

1996 ★★★★★   *December 1998*

Medium to full red–purple; the bouquet is extremely attractive, with an array of cassis, blackberry and mint fruit characters, the palate elegant and stylish. Instead of succumbing to the temptation of extracting every bit of character from the wine, it has been allowed to express itself in an unforced fashion.

1995 ★★★★☆   *January 1998*

Medium to full red–purple; there is a classic mix of cassis, olive/herb and earth on the strong bouquet, with just a hint of oak. The palate is complex, with strong varietal character (olive and cassis) and exhibiting quite pronounced tannins which build on the second half of the palate. Gentle oak throughout.

1994 ★★★★☆   *April 1997*

Deep colour; sweet cassis fruit, mixed with seductive albeit gentle vanillin oak on the bouquet leads on to a palate with excellent structure, showing classic cabernet varietal fruit, with touches of chocolate, olive and earth, and sustained length.

1993 ★★★★   *March 1996*

Full red–purple; a high-quality example of pristine cabernet sauvignon varietal character, with a mix of ripe blackcurrant/cassis fruit and that particular regional earthy undertone. The palate is powerful, with a mix of blackcurrant and a touch of dark chocolate and briar, and the oak largely, but not entirely, swallowed up by the fruit.

1992 ★★★★☆   *March 1997*

Medium to full red–purple; the bouquet is of medium intensity, clean and smooth, with fresh red and blackcurrant fruit aromas. Somewhat lighter than the '91, which is hardly surprising; very smooth on entry to the mouth, with touches of mint to go with the blackcurrant fruit, then quite firm tannins come on the finish.

1991 ★★★★★   *March 1993*

Deep purple–red; concentrated, warm, ripe fruit with sweet oak and some dusty cabernet aromas; a powerful wine with dark berry/plum/blackcurrant fruit and ample balancing tannins. Winner of three trophies.

1990 ★★★★★   *March 1993*

Dark red–purple; complex, sweet fruit with an attractive hint of gaminess, and subtle oak. In the mouth, a wine of outstanding weight, structure and balance, as concentrated as one could wish for. There are abundant dark berry fruit flavours, finishing with fine tannins. Will be very long lived.

1989 ★★★☆   *March 1993*

Dark red; the bouquet shows an amalgam of briary/berry fruit backed by a touch of stalkiness which is not unattractive. The palate shows more gamey/leafy '89 vintage characters but is presently quite attractive. Definitely a wine to be drunk rather than cellared.

1988 ★★★★☆   *March 1993*

Medium to full red–purple; a full, solid and ripe bouquet with sweet blackcurrant and mulberry fruit. The palate is elegant and smooth, with good fruit ripeness and nicely weighted and balanced oak.

classic wines

★★★★★ Perfect   ★★★★☆ Close to perfect   ★★★★ Very good   ★★★☆ Expected
★★★ Short of standard   ★★☆ Undeserving   ★★ Decayed relic   NR No rating

1987 ★★★ *March 1993*
Medium red; leafy/sappy/soapy dimethyl sulphide characters are reflected in both bouquet and palate. Does have flavour, but may not appeal to all.

1986 ★★★☆ *March 1993*
Dark red; a very ripe, almost porty bouquet of considerable complexity. The entry to the mouth shows abundant ripe fruit, but is still fractionally hard on the finish, and should soften and open up with age, even if always in a fairly opulent style.

1985 ★★★☆ *March 1993*
Medium red; while the bouquet is noticeably less rich and ripe than others in the line-up, does have attractive leafy/spicy notes; the palate, too, has cedary/leafy/spicy flavours which, while different, are far from unattractive.

1984 ★★☆ *March 1993*
Medium red; strong ripe style, bordering on overripe in its aromas. In the mouth, a curious melange of ripe and green fruit flavours, with a fractionally soapy edge, all pointing to some problems in the vineyard.

1983 ★★☆ *March 1993*
Medium red; a rather plain, slightly soapy/leafy bouquet which improves somewhat on the palate, although those leafy notes continue.

1982 ★★★★☆ *March 1993*
Medium red; soft, cedary, cigar box nuances to attractively ripened and weighted fruit on the bouquet. The palate is fine, elegant and harmonious with a hint of blackcurrant fruit still lingering, complexed by cedar and cigar box overtones.

1981 ★★ *March 1993*
Medium red with some tawny aspects; tobacco/hay/straw aromas, lacking style and intensity; similar straw/green/soapy notes are evident on the palate which will not improve. •E•

1980 ★★☆ *March 1993*
Light red; an extremely herbaceous aroma with leafy and tobacco characters predominating. Similarly herbaceous on the palate, almost into a Chinon style.

1979 ★★☆ *March 1993*
Light red; the bouquet is clean, but rather plain and lacking substance, the palate similarly plain, light and inoffensive.

1978 ★★☆ *March 1993*
Light to medium red; the bouquet is adequate, but does not show a great deal of varietal character or style. The flavour is rather better, with pleasant leafy/tobacco characters and pleasant mouthfeel.

1976 ★★☆ *March 1993*
A green, leafy astringent bouquet leads on to a very green, soapy/herbaceous palate. A Jimmy Watson Trophy winner which is well past its best, but was very much a product of changing tastes in any event.

◄ Not Ready ◄ Still evolving ▌Prime of its life ✦ Drink soon ⊔ Missed the boat

1975 ★★ *March 1993*

Medium red; slightly boiled fruit characters to the bouquet, also showing a touch of volatility. The palate veers more to the soapy/green spectrum, lacking concentration and ripeness.

1973 ★★☆ *March 1993*

Distinctly brown hued, with aged, oxidised aromas, but a far better wine on the palate, with pleasant ripe chocolatey flavours still lingering.

1972 NR *March 1993*

Not rated; corked sample.

1970 ★★★ *March 1993*

Medium red; reasonably complex cedary/leafy aromas lead on to a pleasantly aged medium-bodied wine with similar cedar and leaf flavours, finishing with appropriate tannins.

1969

Not made.

1968 ★★★ *March 1993*

Medium red with a tawny edge to the hue; the bouquet clean, but somewhat plain, with slightly roasted fruit characters. Tasted from a magnum, there was pleasant sweet fruit, even if slightly dilute. A conventionally-sized bottle might be a more chancy business.

1966 ★★★ *March 1993*

Medium to full red; ripe fruit aromas with hints of dark chocolate and some volatility evident. In the mouth, high levels of volatility intrude, although the wine does have some substance.

1965 ★★★ *March 1993*

Strong red; there are solidly ripe dark fruit characters still evident on the bouquet which are more or less precisely repeated in a generously proportioned, if slightly flawed (by volatility) palate.

1964 ★★ *March 1983*

Brown red; dull bouquet showing little or no varietal character. Fruit fading on the palate with a light finish.

1963 NR *March 1993*

Poor year; wet vintage.

1962 ★★★★ *March, 1993*

Medium red, tending tawny. The bouquet opened up in the glass, initially showing aged, leafy aromas, but subsequently showing more truffle and earth-accented fruit. The palate, too, shows some volatility, though it is far from unattractive; all in all, not unlike a very old Bordeaux.

1961

Not made.

★★★★★ Perfect   ★★★★☆ Close to perfect   ★★★★ Very good   ★★★☆ Expected
★★★ Short of standard   ★★☆ Undeserving   ★★ Decayed relic   NR No rating

classic wines

307

1960 ★★★☆   *March 1993*

Medium red; a complex bouquet with obvious volatility, a touch of mushroom and some of those aged Bordeaux characters evident in the '62. In the mouth, a powerful, high-toned wine; it all depends on one's acceptance (or otherwise) of volatility. Some cedary/earthy flavours also developed.

1959 ★★★☆   *March 1993*

Medium red; aged aromas with obvious volatility and hints of fresh earth. The palate is very consistent with the wines between 1959 and 1962, with aged, leafy, cedary flavours.

1958 ★★★★   *March 1993*

Medium tawny–red; the aromas are now all well into secondary characters showing cedar, cigar box and camphor, but are really quite attractive. The palate has similar flavours, but still retains quite firm tannins; an interesting old wine which is far from dead.

1957 ★★★★   *March 1993*

Medium to full red; developed, stylish cedary/cigar box aromas lead on to a high-toned leafy/minty/cedary palate, still showing varietal character lifted by a whisker of volatility.

1956

Not made.

1954 ★★★   *March 1983*

brick–red; marked coffee-essence aromas, but rather better fruit on the palate, with a quite crisp, clean finish.

1953 NR

Great vintage; no extant tasting note.

1952 NR   *March 1993*

Poor year; light and fairly acid wine.

wynns coonawarra estate shiraz
(hermitage) 1953-1999

Wynns Coonawarra Estate Hermitage (now called Shiraz) was first made in 1952, the year following the acquisition by Samuel Wynn of the historic winery and vineyards which had been built by John Riddoch in 1891.

Ian Hickinbotham made the first two vintages, establishing a simple discipline for making the wine which has changed little in the intervening 40 plus years. It is a fruit-driven style, with varietal spice sometimes evident in young wines, but usually subsiding with age; new oak plays no part in shaping the wine.

Apart from the usual variations in vintage conditions, a number of vertical tastings have pointed to a significant dip in quality over the '60s and '70s. Quality has improved greatly since 1984, and currently the wine ranks as one of the best value reds in Australia.

Most of the notes of the old vintages come from a tasting at the winery in March 1993, supplemented in a few instances by references to tastings in March 1982 (again at the winery) and in August 1982.

Finally, tasting notes of the legendary Michael Hermitage are given throughout the main notes. A freak wine made in 1955 (250 dozen) from a particular 2250-litre barrel purchased secondhand; all attempts to repeat the wine failed. In 1990 Wynns reintroduced the brand as a super-premium brother to John Riddoch Cabernet Sauvignon using the same fruit selection and new oak making techniques as those employed with John Riddoch.

1999 ★★★★   *November 2000*

Medium to full red–purple; clean, smooth, cherry and plum fruit with a touch of vanilla oak is followed by a medium-bodied palate with good balance, weight and extract. A very good outcome for the vintage.

1998 Michael ★★★★★   *March 2001*

Dark red–purple; the bouquet exudes oak from every pore as only Michael can; powerful, sweet black cherry and plum fruit on the palate demands to be heard behind the fanfare of oak trumpets; prior history makes it a near certainty the wine will sort itself out, however improbable that may seem right now.

1998 ★★★★☆   *December 1999*

Medium purple–red; the moderately intense bouquet is clean and smooth, with excellent mulberry fruit and oak integration and balance. There is plenty of sweet, dark berry/cherry fruit on the palate with soft tannins contributing to a well-structured wine.

classic wines

★★★★★ Perfect   ★★★★☆ Close to perfect   ★★★★ Very good   ★★★☆ Expected
★★★ Short of standard   ★★☆ Undeserving   ★★ Decayed relic   NR No rating

309

◀■ *1997 Michael* ★★★★☆   *October 2000*

Medium red–purple; that satin-smooth and sweet bouquet with abundant berry fruit and plenty of sexy oak leads into a palate with a similarly silky, smooth texture; here liquorice and chocolate join the sweet berry, encased in sweet oak and lingering, faintly milky, tannins.

1997 ★★★★   *December 1998*

Medium red–purple, but showing a little more development than one would expect. The bouquet has a distinct touch of cinnamon spice, together with subtle oak. The palate is pleasant, with gently spicy fruit, but lacks the concentration of the '96 and '95 vintage wines.

◀■ *1996 Michael* ★★★★★   *December 1998*

Dense purple–red; the bouquet is typically super-concentrated, oozing ripe black cherry fruit and heaps of oak. The palate is at once profound, yet smooth, almost glossy, with black cherry fruit and cedar/vanilla oak. The tannins are ample but round and soft.

◥ *1996* ★★★★★   *January 1998*

Strong purple–red; and exceptionally smooth and intense bouquet, with abundant rich and sweet dark cherry and plum fruit swells into a round, mouth-filling palate, showing more of the same fruit flavours tinged with spice and subtle oak, closing with soft tannins.

1995 ★★★★   *October 1997*

Medium to full red–purple; there is far more concentration and weight to the bouquet than most wines in its price category, with abundant dark berry, spice and briary fruit. Has developed extremely well since release, with plenty of briary/dark berry fruit flavours, good tannins and subtle oak. No doubt benefits from the inclusion of the portion normally destined for Michael Shiraz.

◀■ *1994 Michael* ★★★★★   *April 1997*

Dense purple–red; extremely rich, ripe and concentrated mulberry and spice fruit is supported by toasty vanillin oak. The palate is every bit as concentrated and chewy as the bouquet suggests it will be, with abundant spicy berry fruit and even more abundant oak.

1994 ★★★★☆   *March 1996*

Medium to full red–purple, bright and clear; the bouquet shows an array of spicy black cherry fruit aromas with oak barely perceptible. A strongly fruit-driven wine in the mouth, with intense earthy/spicy dark cherry fruit; the oak has been used as a medium for maturation and not as a flavour modifier. Less opulently ripe than some of the prior vintages, but none the worse for that.

◥ *1993 Michael* ★★★★★   *March 1996*

Medium to full red–purple; a show-stopper of a wine, or as Robert Parker might put it, a gob-stopper. The bouquet is potent, with slightly resinous oak; the palate is massive and powerful, needing much time, with an extraordinary array of minty/cherry fruit and oak and fruit tannins all intermingling.

1992 ★★★★☆   *March 1993*

Medium red; attractive clean spicy/peppery varietal fruit with subtle oak. There are pronounced pepper/spice varietal flavours on the palate, yet the wine has adequate weight and extract, finishing with good acidity and subtle oak.

1991 *Michael* ★★★★★   *March 1993*

The bright purple–red colour leads on to a fragrant, scented bouquet with voluptuous sweet berry fruit and balanced oak. The palate is very complex and stylish with red berry/cassis/raspberry fruit flavours with hints of spice in the background. Will be approachable earlier than the 1990, but still needs great patience to allow it to show its best.

1991 ★★★★★   *March 1993*

A wine in radically different style from the '90, with fresh pepper, spice, red berry and cherry aromas and a fresh, vibrant well-balanced palate with soft tannins and minimal oak influence.

1990 *Michael* ★★★★★   *March 1993*

Dense purple–red in colour; the bouquet is nearly overwhelming with lush berry, mint and eucalypt aromas married with strong oak. In the mouth the wine is exceptionally powerful, concentrated and rich with minty/berry fruits and powerful tannins. A 30-year cellaring special, i.e. to 2020.

1990 ★★★★★   *March 1993*

The colour is still a strong red–purple, with a complex, solid ripe and dense aroma. In the mouth the wine is very rich and structured, promising a very long life; the balance cannot be faulted. Has already entered what will be a long plateau.

1989 ★★★☆   *March 1993*

A fairly impressive effort for an indifferent year, even if the colour shows the difference between the excellent vintages either side of it. There are some sweet coconut vanillin overtones to the bouquet, with echoes of spice; the palate shows no errant fruit characters, and finishes with soft tannins, simply lacking mid-palate vinosity. Not to be cellared.

1988 ★★★★   *March 1993*

The colour is very good, medium to full red–purple; the bouquet has abundant depth with strong liquorice and crushed ant fruit aromas, but a rather elegant yet firm palate, with good structure, acidity and freshness.

1987 ★★★☆   *March 1993*

While at its peak, is certainly not going to hold for much longer; the colour is very developed, and overall the wine shows the effects of a cool vintage with herbaceous notes running through.

1986 ★★★★   *March 1993*

A wine with life in front of it, made in a generous, ripe style with plenty of varietal spice and earth edges to the sweet fruit on the bouquet. The palate has depth and sweetness, with well-balanced tannins.

classic wines

★★★★★ Perfect   ★★★★☆ Close to perfect   ★★★★ Very good   ★★★☆ Expected
★★★ Short of standard   ★★☆ Undeserving   ★★ Decayed relic   NR No rating

1985 ★★★☆   *March 1993*

The medium red colour shows some development, but the bouquet is complex and fragrant with hints of tobacco and cigar leading on to an attractively harmonious palate with cedar, mint and leaf flavours, finishing with soft tannins.

1984 ★★★☆   *March 1993*

The solid medium to full red colour heralds a wine with very ripe, lush berry fruit aromas which on the palate verge on being porty, but redeemed with hints of liquorice and pepper.

1983 ★★★☆   *March 1993*

A wine which is holding up well in a somewhat sweet slightly jammy style, with abundant ripe berry and earth aromas and lots of flesh on the palate.

1982 ★★★☆   *March 1993*

Effectively marks the start of the renaissance of the wine, with a very slightly decadent but complex bouquet with gamey characters; the palate, too, is complex with a mix of gamey/animal, earthy characters under the fruit, but with quite good length to the flavour.

1981 ★★☆   *March 1993*

Distinctly brown in colour, faintly stemmy/bitter notes on both bouquet and palate detract somewhat, although there are some vestiges of fruit remaining.

1980 ★★   *March 1993*

A very light, developed colour betokens a leafy, thin, herbaceous wine which lacks distinction.

1979 ★★   *March 1993*

Was very light when tasted in 1982, and will almost certainly have collapsed by now.

1978 ★★☆   *March 1993*

Was quite attractive as a young wine (in 1982) but I suspect it is now faded. The rating is guesswork.

1977

Not tasted.

1976 ★★★   *March 1993*

A distinctly aged and slightly roasted bouquet is partially redeemed by the palate, which while a little on the jammy side, does have plenty of flavour.

1975 ★★☆   *March 1993*

Had some pepper/spice varietal fruit but was very light when tasted in 1982, and has almost certainly faded away since.

1974 ★★☆   *March 1993*

Somewhat porty, oxidised fruit aromas, with a very ripe mulberry-accented palate.

1973 ★★★   *March 1993*

Far from disgraced in the 1993 tasting, with touches of mushroom and spice in the sweet fruit aroma, and a light but pleasant leafy/minty/spicy palate. •D•

Not Ready   Still evolving   Prime of its life   Drink soon   Missed the boat

1972 ★★   *March 1993*

Always a poor and disappointing wine, now verging on the undrinkable.

1971 ★★★☆   *March 1982*

Drank very well in 1982 with full, sweet berry aromas touched with fresh earth, leading on to a medium to full weight palate with sweet, solid fruit.

1970 ★★★★   *March 1993*

Showed infinitely better in the 1993 tasting than in 1982; another wine to show as much Hunter as Coonawarra regional character, with a gently sweet and very attractive bouquet leading on to a multiflavoured, cedary palate with considerable style.

1969

Not tasted.

1968 ★★   *March 1993*

Very light red–brown in colour, the wine has long passed its best with tired, aged tobacco aromas and broken, sweet fruit on the palate.

1967 ★★   *March 1993*

Volatility dominates the wine to an unacceptable level; at least it marks the end of an era.

1966 ★★★☆   *March 1993*

The colour is holding well, perhaps assisted by the volatility, which runs through both bouquet and palate in a lively wine.

1965 ★★★★★   *March 1993*

An absolutely classic aged Shiraz in which developed varietal character has overtaken the region, making it almost Hunter-like, with gently sweet, earthy aromas swelling out on the palate, which is complex, chewy and holding marvellously well.

1964 ★★★   *March 1993*

An aged wine, medium red in colour, with earthy, truffle and mushroom aromas, and with volatility trembling on the brink of acceptability.

1963 ★★★☆   *March 1993*

There is striking similarity between the 1982 and 1993 tastings: the volatility is there on both bouquet and palate, but there are masses of underlying sweet fruit. A striking wine if you are prepared to look past the volatility.

1962 ★★★★   *March 1993*

Curiously, not tasted since 1982 when the wine was in fine fettle with plenty of rich flavour, particularly on the middle palate on the finish, and giving the appearance that it would hold for many years. Rated on the basis of that tasting.

1961 NR

Not tasted.

1960 ★★★☆   *March 1993*

Medium tawny–red in colour, the wine has a complex array of aromas ranging from animal scents to cedary, to sweet leather with some volatility woven throughout. The taste repeats the aromas; tannins intrude slightly on the end.

★★★★★ Perfect   ★★★★☆ Close to perfect   ★★★★ Very good   ★★★☆ Expected
★★★ Short of standard   ★★☆ Undeserving   ★★ Decayed relic   NR No rating

classic wines

313

1959 ★★★★   *March 1993*

A wine which showed surprisingly well in the 1993 tasting; initially showing some volatility on the bouquet, gently sweet fruit progressively appeared as the wine sat in the glass. The flavours are quite complex with reasonable bite to the finish.

1958 ★★★   *March 1993*

A wine which marks the onset of a period during which many of the wines suffered from high levels of volatile acidity. There has always been speculation as to how much volatility was introduced deliberately, and how much was accidental. Even ten years ago the wine was suffering from a degree of volatility, with some sweet cherry flavours to redeem it.

1957 ★★★☆   *March 1982*

Fresher and brighter in colour, and a wine with considerable depth and complexity, but with some burnt/medicinal characters running through both the bouquet and palate.

1956 ★★★★   *March 1982*

The tawny colour and clean but fading bouquet lead on to a wine which is light, almost ethereal but, if the cork is sound, without any 'off' characters whatsoever.

1955 Michael ★★★★★   *March 1993*

At once classic and unique, a freakish wine which has always been of sublime quality unless the cork (or storage conditions) have failed it. Ethereal yet intense aromas of cedar, sweet fruits and a whisper of chocolate and earth lead on to an exquisitely-balanced palate, still with gently sweet, velvety/earthy fruit, with a surprisingly long finish.

1955 ★★★★★   *March 1993*

The colour is still dark red, with just a touch of brown on the rim; the bouquet is very complex with an amalgam of cedary/leafy/briary and earthy aromas. In the mouth, an extraordinary wine still, crammed with flavour, tasting of leather, liquorice and cigar box, and with balanced tannins.

1954 ★★★★★   *March 1993*

Still clear, bright red; the bouquet is utterly delicious, a wonderful tapestry of aromas which lead on to a sweetly elegant palate with aged cedary flavours, great mouthfeel and balance. I was moved to write 'like a treasured grandmother' in the 1993 tasting.

1953 ★★★★★   *March 1993*

Still a remarkable old wine, truly great for its age, but even allowing for inevitable bottle variation, slightly behind the '54 and '55 in quality. The bouquet typically needs 30 minutes aeration to open up; palate has much more life than the bouquet suggests, still holding sweet fruit, with toffee and vanilla overtones, yet no suggestion of overripeness.

◄ Not Ready   ➘ Still evolving   ▮ Prime of its life   ⚲ Drink soon   ⬮ Missed the boat

wynns john riddoch cabernet sauvignon 1982-1998

it is no coincidence that the renaissance in the quality of Wynns Black Label Cabernet Sauvignon came in 1982, for this was the year of the birth of the now famous John Riddoch deluxe cuvée. John Riddoch, of course, was the founder of Coonawarra (and in 1891 built the winery now owned by Wynns) and his name is used — confusingly — by four Coonawarra producers: Wynns, Katnook Estate, Riddoch Estate and Rymill R i d d o c h Run (the last owned by Peter Rymill, a direct descendant of John Riddoch).

To confuse the issue further, Katnook uses the Riddoch name as a second (of lesser quality) label. The same cannot be said of Rymill nor, of course, Wynns. Nor is there the least question that the John Riddoch really is in the super-league of Australian red wine.

Indeed, if there is a question about John Riddoch it is whether it is just too much of a good thing. It is hard to visualise how more colour, flavour (in terms of both fruit and oak) and extract could be crammed into a premium quality wine — for do not misunderstand me, this is premium wine. It will live for decades, and provide a great match for the best Australian rump steak or lamb. But it is not for the faint of heart, nor those whose tastes run more (say) to fine Burgundies. Which is why wine is such fun. For the record, matured in new French oak hogsheads for 24 months.

All vintages up to and including 1991 tasted in March 1993. A subsequent tasting in March 1996 showed that the wines of the 1980s had in fact opened up more rapidly than I had originally expected, but without compromising their likely end-point.

First tasted in March 1993, updated, and later vintages added.

1998 ★★★★★   *March 2001*

Impenetrable purple–red; blackberry/cassis/blackcurrant fruit has largely soaked up the oak on the bouquet; likewise, intense and powerful cassis/blackcurrant/blackberry fruit drives the palate, with oak well integrated and balanced. An exceptionally powerful wine, but the balance is already there to be seen. A major success for John Riddoch.

classic wines

★★★★★ Perfect   ★★★★☆ Close to perfect   ★★★★ Very good   ★★★☆ Expected
★★★ Short of standard   ★★☆ Undeserving   ★★ Decayed relic   NR No rating

315

◄■ *1997* ★★★★☆   *October 1999*

Deep purple–red; sweet cassis fruit and powerful but integrated oak on the bouquet lead into a power-packed palate, rich and deep, with tannins providing a sledgehammer finish. History shows that the tannins will in fact soften.

◄■ *1996* ★★★★★   *December 1998*

Dark, deep red–purple; the bouquet is as concentrated and rich as one would expect, with a mix of blackberry and blackcurrant fruit; ample but not excessive oak. The palate is immensely powerful and concentrated, precisely as one would expect from Riddoch in a vintage such as '96, with a full panoply of dark, black fruit flavours, tannin and oak.

1995

Not made.

◥ *1994* ★★★★★   *April 1997*

Strong red–purple; a fragrant bouquet with the first signs of that earthy character, which is the hallmark of Coonawarra cabernet starting to appear. A powerful mature palate, arguably the most classic for many years. There is layer upon layer of fruit flavour perfectly matched by vanillin oak, and supported by long, lingering tannins. A multiple trophy and gold medal winner at major Australian wine shows.

◥ *1993* ★★★★☆   *March 1996*

Full purple–red; slightly deeper than the '92 vintage; the bouquet shows a complex mix of sweet, ripe fruit, charry oak and that family/regional hint of earth. The powerful palate has many layers of flavour, with sweetly ripe dark berry fruits intermingling with more briary/foresty/earthy characters and appreciable vanilla and cedar oak.

◢ *1992* ★★★★   *December 1994*

Deep red–purple, chocolate, briar and cassis aromas mingle with strong vanillin oak on the bouquet, in a slightly less forceful mode than either the '90 or '91 vintages. The palate, too, is ever so slightly more accessible at this early stage of its development, no doubt a factor contributing to its three gold medals.

◢ *1991* ★★★★☆   *March 1993*

Impenetrable colour; extremely complex, briary dark fruits with a hint of dark chocolate. The palate is extremely potent, full to the brim with dark berry fruits, a touch of bitter chocolate, and abundant tannins.

◢ *1990* ★★★★★   *March 1993*

Dense purple–red; the bouquet shows massive power and extract, with supple, dark berry fruit and sumptuous oak. The palate is similarly driven by very rich, scented oak, but there is layer upon layer of cassis fruit and substantial tannins.

1989

Not made.

1988 ★★★★★ *March 1993*

Typically dense, almost opaque red–purple. The bouquet is concentrated, dense, and quite similar to the '90, with strong oak and richly ripe chocolate-accented fruit. The palate is redolent of dark chocolate and blackcurrant fruit in a luscious, ripe mould; the oak is evident but well balanced.

1987 ★★★★ *March 1993*

Medium to full red–purple; a typically complex bouquet with some ripe berry fruit aromas but also some more resinous/leafy characters, suggesting a touch of dimethyl sulphide. The palate shows similar faintly resinous characters, but does have masses of flavour and structure.

1986 ★★★★☆ *March 1993*

Impenetrable red colour announces an extraordinarily immature wine with dense, ripe, chocolate-accented fruit on the bouquet followed by a huge palate — an amalgam of ripe fruit and faint herbaceous notes, with abundant tannins on the finish.

1985 ★★★★★ *March 1993*

Medium to full red–purple; the bouquet is firm, slightly greener in style, and with well-balanced oak. The first of the wines in the line-up to show any real signs of bottle development, with attractive cedary notes and the tannins starting to soften as the wine tentatively moves towards opening up. Trophy winner 1994 Australian National Wine Show.

1984 ★★★★ *March 1993*

Full red–purple; a very concentrated bouquet with ripe fruit and some vanillin notes to the oak. The flavours are in many ways reminiscent of those of the '86, with tannins which need to soften, and ever so faintly green characters. Still a massively powerful and potent wine.

1983

Not made.

1982 ★★★★★ *March 1993*

Medium to full red–purple; the bouquet is very clean and stylish, with aromas of dark chocolate and red berry. The palate is smooth, with briary/berry fruit, cedary oak and soft tannins; just entering the prime of its life.

★★★★★ Perfect ★★★★☆ Close to perfect ★★★★ Very good ★★★☆ Expected
★★★ Short of standard ★★☆ Undeserving ★★ Decayed relic NR No rating

wynns ovens valley shiraz
(burgundy) 1955-1992

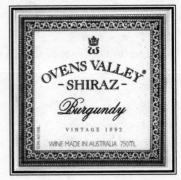

t his wine remains one of Australia's best kept secrets; it is almost as if Wynns is embarrassed about its existence, which is not altogether surprising. For one thing, the quantity produced does not go close to meeting existing (let alone potential) demand; for another, it has had a somewhat chequered existence at various stages of its career, as its regional source and its quality both wandered off-course for a while.

The first vintages (commencing in 1955) were based on Shiraz made by Cliff Booth at Taminick in the Ovens Valley of North East Victoria, purchased in bulk and blended with 10 per cent or so of wine from elsewhere. By 1967 the Booth component had fallen to 10 per cent, and thereafter his contract with Wynns came to an end.

Other sources around Glenrowan in North East Victoria were substituted, and are now said to provide the major component, supported by wine of similar richness from McLaren Vale and the Barossa Valley — a distracting contribution from Coonawarra and/or Padthaway having been discontinued.

The word Burgundy has been reduced to a small typeface on the label, but the best of these wines (and there have been many) were indeed Burgundies in the best and most luscious Australian mould. The accent has been on rounded, ripe fruit rather than oak, and the top wines have aged splendidly.

Postscript: production was suspended after 1992, and — unhappily — will not be recommenced.

Tasted in March 1993.

1992 ★★★★☆
Medium to full purple–red; has a clean and smooth bouquet with attractive dark plum and dark liquorice fruit. The palate is immaculately balanced, with flavours of plum, and no oak forcing.

1991 ★★★★☆
Dense red–purple; rich and full aromas of dark chocolate, liquorice and berry. A powerful wine with good structure and texture showing the hallmark liquorice and dark berry flavours of all of the young Ovens Valley wines.

1990 ★★★★★
Full purple–red; very rich, dense liquorice and prune fruit aromas. A similarly rich, dense and chewy palate with lots of stuffing and style; sweet liquorice and prune fruit is balanced by good tannins; will be extremely long lived.

Not Ready   Still evolving   Prime of its life   Drink soon   Missed the boat

1989 ★★★★
Full red–purple; solid, clean, dark berry fruit aromas with an ever so slightly jammy edge. The palate has abundant clean and smooth sweet, dark berry fruits, showing no hint of the errant characters of so many of the Australian 1989 red wines.

1988 ★★★★☆
Bright, full purple–red; very fresh and clean red berry fruits drive the bouquet; the palate is every bit as stylish as the bouquet promises, with fine-grained tannins running throughout dark currant fruit flavours.

1987 ★★☆
Medium red; a rather plain and closed bouquet; the palate lacks richness and weight; workmanlike at best.

1986 ★★★★☆
Medium red–purple; a clean, solid bouquet with hints of dark chocolate. The palate has abundant dark fruits with cherry notes, a nice touch of oak and fine-grained tannins on the finish.

1985 ★★★☆
Medium red; noticeably ripe and sweet fruit aromas with berry and liquorice notes; the bouquet is likewise solid and ripe, with lots of dark, briary, berry fruit flavours.

1984 ★★
Developed medium red; a gamey/leafy bouquet which lacks concentration, and a similarly relatively thin palate.

1983 ★★☆
Dark red; the bouquet is of medium intensity with minty/leafy overtones, leading on to a palate which is not especially complex, but does have some sweet minty fruit which will hold the wine in the short term.

1982 ★★★
Medium red; secondary, bottle-developed characters are starting to build on the bouquet, which is in transition. There is abundant fruit on a chunky palate with relatively strong tannins. More power than elegance.

1981 ★★
Medium red; some rather vegetal/skinny/stemmy aromas with a hint of gluepaste, and a similarly disappointing plain and skinny palate.

1980 ★★★☆
Medium red with just a touch of purple. A strikingly different bouquet with distinct peppery/spicy shiraz varietal character. The palate shows similarly vibrant peppery/spicy fruit flavours in a modern cool-climate style, which comes out of nowhere in the line-up.

1979 ★★★
Medium red, with just a touch of tawny; an initially rather plain bouquet which did, however, develop in the glass, bringing up touches of both liquorice and spice. The palate shows good, ripe shiraz varietal character with touches of chocolate and liquorice, and a faintly roasted edge.

★★★★★ Perfect ★★★★☆ Close to perfect ★★★★ Very good ★★★☆ Expected
★★★ Short of standard ★★☆ Undeserving ★★ Decayed relic NR No rating

1978 ★★☆

Medium red; the bouquet is quite pleasant, with hints of chocolate, but the palate decidedly less attractive, with leafy/soapy fruit.

1976 ★★

Tawny–red; a plain, soapy, leafy bouquet and a rather strange, thin, leafy palate, right out of style.

1975 ★★

While the colour is quite strong and good, the wine shows overripe hay/straw/oxidation characters throughout; possibly a poor bottle.

1974 ★★★★

Dark red; the aromas are complex with excellent ripe fruit balanced by cedary/cigar box bottle-developed aromas. The palate is strong and robust, with remarkably firm fruit; once again those cedar and cigar box characters come through to add complexity and underline the bottle age.

1973 ★★★☆

Youthful colour for its age, with fresh, leafy/spicy aromas and fresh fruit flavours on the palate, with touches of spice; all in all, strongly reminiscent of the '80.

1972 NR

Not tasted.

1971 ★★★★

Medium red; a gently ripe bouquet with quite deliciously sweet and earthy shiraz varietal character. The palate is very complex, full and sweet, with faintly earthy farmyard characters and strong tannins.

1970 ★★★★

Medium tawny–red; the bouquet is full, sweet and ripe, with attractive hints of earth and mushroom. The palate is full-blown, with some volatile lift and sweetly ripe fruit; a complex wine with attractive, slightly decayed fruit.

1969 ★★★

Medium tawny; a very ripe, indeed jammy bouquet, but a less rich and weighty palate which is pleasant rather than great.

1968 ★★★★

The promise of the bright colour is fulfilled by both the bouquet and palate, both of which are remarkably fresh and youthful. There are gently sweet aromas with a range of green hay through to toffee aromas, and similar flavours with herbaceous notes, more suggestive of Cabernet Sauvignon than Shiraz.

1967 NR

Not rated. A bottle destroyed by extremely volatile acidity.

1963 NR

Not rated. Sour, lactic and volatile characters make for an unpleasant wine.

◀ Not Ready　　　❯ Still evolving　　　▮ Prime of its life　　　◢ Drink soon　　　▯ Missed the boat

1962 ★★★
Medium red; the bouquet is very youthful with lifted volatility which, in the end, add to rather than detract from the wine. That volatility lifts the finish and adds a certain brightness.

1961 ★★☆
Medium red; rather overripe hay/straw aromas to the bouquet are reflected in the rather squashy flavours of the palate. Going nowhere from this point onwards.

1960 ★★★☆
Medium red, with a touch of tawny; the bouquet is smooth, still retaining some sweet fruit, but with edges of hay and straw. In the mouth, an archetypal aged Australian Burgundy, ripe, soft, gently sweet and full bodied.

1959 ★★★★☆
Strong red; a very stylish and complex bouquet with aged sweet fruit and cigar box aromas. The palate fulfils the promise of the bouquet, with sweet dark cherry, chocolate and cigar box flavours, balanced by good tannins. A lovely old wine.

1956 ★★★★★
Dark red; an exceptionally complex bouquet with many characters emerging, faintly roasted and with liquorice overtones. A wine of extraordinary richness and depth of flavour on the palate, velvety sweet and sumptuously soft, yet full on the finish.

1955 ★★★
Dark brown; extreme bottle-aged camphor/menthol aromas which come through on the palate. These very old wine characters do have their place.

★★★★★ Perfect   ★★★★☆ Close to perfect   ★★★★ Very good   ★★★☆ Expected
★★★ Short of standard   ★★☆ Undeserving   ★★ Decayed relic   NR No rating

classic wines

321

yalumba signature series

the story has been told many times. At a luncheon held in Adelaide for Members of the Royal Stock Exchange of South Australia the guest speaker rose after lunch holding a glass of Yalumba's 1961 Special Reserve Stock Galway Claret in his hand. 'Gentlemen. This is the finest Australian wine I have ever tasted.' The speaker was R G Menzies, Prime Minister of Australia, not a breed noted for its vinous knowledge, but then Menzies was no ordinary Prime Minister.

The wine became known as 'The Menzies' and indirectly gave birth to the Signature Series — although it was to be almost 30 years before a Yalumba wine bore the Menzies name, and then was not part of the Signature Series. The latter was inaugurated in 1962 as the best red wine of the vintage, named Samuels Blend in honour of the founder of Yalumba. Since then 31 members of the Hill-Smith family and of the Yalumba corporate family have been recognised in this fashion.

But there has also been a high-quality requirement: thus there was no Signature Series in '65, '69, '72, '79, '80 or '82; while in '64, '66, '67, '68, '70, '71 and '76 each produced more than one Signature wine.

The wine has always been a blend of Cabernet and Shiraz, although the percentage contribution of each has fluctuated widely over the years. The geographic contributions have varied even more, but since '88 there has been a constant mix of Barossa and Coonawarra cabernet sauvignon and Barossa shiraz.

First tasted November 1994, updated, and later vintages added.

◀ 1997 Vittorio 'Vic' Di Biase ★★★★☆   *February 2001*
Medium to full red–purple; rich, ripe, dark berry fruit is accompanied by strongly accented vanilla oak on the complex bouquet. The palate carries on in much the same vein, with rich, luscious dark berry and dark chocolate fruit supported by ripe tannins. An outstanding achievement for the '97 vintage.

1996 James Wark ★★★★   *March 2000*
Medium to full red–purple; the bouquet opens with sweet, rich dark chocolate and plum, then moves through to plentiful American oak. The palate has red berry, dark plum and vanilla flavours in abundance, neatly cradled by soft tannins.

1995 Every Man and Woman ★★★★   *March 1999*
Medium red–purple; a fragrant bouquet with dark berry and plum fruit married with scented oak; the flavours of the palate run through berry, plum, cedar and earth, with the sweet oak evident but not overdone.

1994 Peter Graugh ★★★★ *January 1998*

Strong red; an excellently rich and complex bouquet with blackberry, chocolate and earth supported by harmonious and sweet oak, and a substantial, chewy palate with an identical range of flavours. Will reach a peak around 2004, but will hold that peak almost indefinitely.

1993 Bill Wilksch ★★★★☆ *April 1997*

Medium red–purple; a fine mix of earth, cedar, vanilla and gentle red fruits on the bouquet leads on to a palate with surprisingly charry/earthy notes to go with blackberry and cedar flavours; persistent tannins on the finish. First tasted April 1997. Retasted October 1997 and, if anything, seemed even younger, with powerful, penetrating fruit and those persistent tannins still very much evidence.

1992 Eddy Waechter ★★★★☆ *October 1996*

Medium to full red–purple; gently ripe but intense chocolate and earth fruit aromas are surrounded by positive but not excessive vanillin American oak on a fragrant bouquet; overall, the wine is quite tangy with lemony/smoky oak and red fruits merged on the mid-palate, finishing with quite pronounced tannins. A high-class wine which will age well.

1991 Mark Hill Smith ★★★★★ *October 1995*

Medium to full red–purple; a complex bouquet of medium to full intensity, with smoothly interwoven dark berry fruits and high-quality American oak. The palate is exceptionally elegant and well structured, with near-perfect oak balance and integration of ripe chocolatey fruit and cedary oak.

1990 Peter Wall ★★★★★ *November 1994*

An outstanding wine fully reflecting the great vintage. The bouquet shows concentrated briary/berry fruits with good oak integration and balance. The palate, too, is powerful yet balanced, with dark berry, cassis and plum fruit flavours backed by opulent oak.

1989 Graeme McDonough ★★★★ *November 1994*

A modern style of wine, with medium to full purple–red colour, spotlessly clean bouquet with lots of oak, although there is abundant fruit on the palate in the blackcurrant and black cherry spectrum, complexed by a touch of mint. Good tannin structure, and plenty of extract; a great success for a difficult year.

1988 Colin Gerhardy ★★★★★ *November 1994*

Still holding its red–purple hues; a very stylish, concentrated bouquet with lots of berry fruit and well-handled oak. The palate is driven by a stylish, high-quality cabernet, with cedary notes and fine tannins. Excellent structure.

1987 Dudley Ward ★★★ *November 1994*

Medium red–purple; the aromas are lifted and complex, with a hint of gaminess, even farmyard. The palate, too, is gamey and complex, and quite tannic.

1986 Helen Hill Smith ★★★☆ *November 1994*

A lighter style altogether, but fresh, with sensitively-handled oak on both the bouquet and palate. There are flavours of berry and mint, finishing with soft tannins.

classic wines

★★★★★ Perfect   ★★★★☆ Close to perfect   ★★★★ Very good   ★★★☆ Expected
★★★ Short of standard   ★★☆ Undeserving   ★★ Decayed relic   NR No rating

1985 Dennis Ryman ★★★★☆   *November 1994*

The strong colour is an indication of a wine with plenty of depth and concentration, showing mainstream dark berry and chocolate fruit aromas. In the mouth a strong wine, with lots of dark berry fruit, well balanced and structured, finishing with good tannins.

1984 John Gillespie ★★★   *November 1994*

A very different style, with the Coonawarra component quite dominant. The bouquet is quite youthful, with primary fruit aromas still evident, and on the palate there are slightly squashy/minty berry fruit flavours, but not a great deal of structure. A lighter style to be drunk before the fresh fruit fades.

1983 Ross Bradbury ★★★   *November 1994*

Medium red; another lighter style, with distinct minty aromas, and mint and chocolate flavours on the palate. Not much depth; the product of a very difficult year.

1981 Joe Stevens ★★★★   *November 1994*

Amazingly, the colour still retains a hint of purple; the bouquet is concentrated with ripe, sweet chocolate and earth aromas. The palate has strong, dark berry fruits, still sweet, finishing with well-structured tannins.

1978 Colin Hayes ★★★   *November 1994*

Potent, indeed pungent, cigar box aromas and a curious mixture of sweet and sour, young and old characters on the palate, again seemingly looking as much to Coonawarra as to the Barossa.

1977 Harry Mahlo ★★☆   *November 1994*

Developed red colour, with a bouquet of cedar, tobacco and earth. A light wine in the mouth, earthy and drying, lacking the fruit richness of many of the wines on either side.

1976 Sid Hill Smith ★★★   *November 1994*

Medium developed red; the bouquet shows fresh earth and a hint of spice, the palate earth, spice and chocolate flavours, but finishing rather sharp and hard.

1976 Ron Skate ★★★   *November 1994*

Medium to full red; a quite oaky bouquet with a fractionally milky/lactic overlay. The palate is substantial, with lots of tannin and extract, and some black cherry fruit. Powerful rather than elegant.

1975 Walters ★★★★   *November 1994*

Full, healthy red; the aromas are complex and very much in the style of the best of the older wines in the line, with earth and chocolate dominant. In the mouth, a rich, dense wine with abundant chocolate, ripe berry and prune fruit flavours with strong tannins. Very much alive.

1974 Christobels ★★★★   *November 1994*

A total contrast to Walters, light to medium red in colour, with an elegant cedary/leafy bouquet and a similarly light and elegant leaf, mushroom and mint flavoured palate. A famous wine at the end of its life.

◄━ Not Ready   ❯ Still evolving   ▮ Prime of its life   ✓ Drink soon   ⬯ Missed the boat

1973 Wyndhams ★★★☆   *November 1994*

Medium red with some tawny hues. The bouquet is distinctive, with sweet caramel and toffee fruit and oak aromas combined. In the mouth, a ripe style with vanilla and caramel flavours again apparent; the oldest wine in the line-up to show obvious oak influence.

1971 Alf Madder ★★★   *November 1994*

The colour is quite good, but the bouquet shows distinct volatility, with similar lifted mint and ripe berry fruit flavours on the palate, finishing with quite pronounced tannins.

1971 Bruce Coulter ★★★☆   *November 1994*

Strong red colour, with a soft, ripe sweet chocolate and earth bouquet. The palate has lots of flesh, with ripe to overripe dark berry and dark chocolate fruits, with a chewy, lingering finish.

1970 Paddy Fitzgerald ★★☆   *November 1994*

Light to medium tawny–red; the bouquet is light and earthy, with the fruit starting to fade, doing the same on the rather simple palate on which the tannins linger on.

1970 Les Falkenberg ★★★☆   *November 1994*

Holding its hue well, with a generous and solid bouquet, with sweet, pruney fruit. The palate has lots of ripe mint, plum and prune fruit, but even more tannins which seem likely to outlive the wine.

1968 Eric Mackenzie ★★☆   *November 1994*

Medium to full tawny–red, with a quite rich earthy bouquet leading on to a distinctly earthy/dried berry palate.

1968 Mich Hungerford ★★☆   *November 1994*

Medium tawny–red, with a light, lifted fragrant bouquet with hints of sweet chocolate. The palate is disappointing, the fruit now being very delicate, and the tannins drying out on the finish.

1967 Claire Chinner ★★   *November 1994*

Possibly not a good bottle, but very aged and faded with slightly musty overtones.

1967 Rudi Kronberger ★★★☆   *November 1994*

Quite strong tawny–red colour, with a stylish, lifted earth and chocolate aroma. Volatility is quite evident on the palate, but within the bounds of acceptability; all in all, an elegant old wine.

1966 Harold Yates ★★★★   *November 1994*

Medium tawny–red; sweet, ripe fruit aromas on the bouquet with soft, chocolate flavours on the mid-palate and pleasant tannins on the finish. Hanging in there wonderfully well.

1966 Harold Obst ★★☆   *November 1994*

The bouquet is rather better than the palate, fine and clean, with lifted family chocolate aromas. In the mouth the volatility intrudes to a marked degree, particularly on the finish.

classic wines

★★★★★ Perfect   ★★★★☆ Close to perfect   ★★★★ Very good   ★★★☆ Expected
★★★ Short of standard   ★★☆ Undeserving   ★★ Decayed relic   NR No rating

325

1966 Alfred Wark ★★★★   *November 1994*

A remarkable old wine, with good developed colour, a solid, chunky, earthy bouquet, and a powerful palate, with some minty notes and pronounced but balanced tannins.

1964 Percys ★★☆   *November 1994*

Very similar to the Olivers, with chocolatey fruit on both bouquet and palate sharpened by the volatility.

1964 Olivers ★★☆   *November 1994*

Strong dark chocolate and cedar aromas are lifted by the volatility which dominates the palate, giving an aggressive finish.

1963 Sydneys ★★★☆   *November 1994*

Medium brick–red, with a fully developed chocolate and coffee-accented bouquet. The palate is quite rich, with tobacco, chocolate and sweet earth flavours, and there is little or no volatility evident. Lovely old wine.

1962 Samuels ★★★★★   *November 1994*

A glorious start to the Signature series, with a complex coffee, chocolate and sweet berry bouquet with minimal oak influence. The palate is holding together superbly, with ripe fruit, chocolate and tobacco flavours finishing with generous but soft tannins.

◀━ Not Ready   ◣ Still evolving   ▲ Prime of its life   ✒ Drink soon   ⛴ Missed the boat

the 2-hectare Yarra Yarra Vineyard established by Ian and Anne Maclean between 1979 and 1980 was very much a love child: Ian Maclean was a busy CEO in Melbourne and the vineyard was a weekend and holiday affair.

'I suppose you can say I started Yarra Yarra, and chose its site, because of Graeme Miller,' (of Chateau Yarrinya, now De Bortoli's) says Maclean. 'I used to help him pick his grapes, including the year he won the Jimmy Watson Trophy. He grew superb quality fruit.'

So the Macleans found a northeast-facing, low vigour site at Steels Creek in the same part of the Yarra Valley as Chateau Yarrinya, and (consistently with Miller's practices) established it without the aid of irrigation.

Vines planted this way take a significantly longer time to come into production, so the first wines were not made until 1984: a single barrel of Semillon, and a red, then and now called Cabernets (a term conjured up by another of Maclean's mentors, Dr John Middleton of Mount Mary).

It was sold through a word-of-mouth mailing list, and to a steadily growing number of the finest restaurants in Melbourne and Sydney. Although Ian Maclean did little or nothing to gain publicity, word got around that the wines were of exceptional quality.

Just how exceptional became apparent at vertical tastings of each wine held in 1999. The common bond of the Cabernets is the mid-palate softness and fruit sweetness which only comes from fully ripened grapes, initially showing as cassis, plum and red berry fruit and then, as the wine ages, acquiring the slightly more savoury/ earthy/leathery/cedary characters of mature Cabernet Sauvignon.

First tasted in July 1999, and a later vintage added.

◀ **1998** ★★★★☆   *April 2001*

Medium purple–red; the immediate impression of the bouquet is strongly reminiscent of Bordeaux, with savoury, dark berry/blackcurrant fruit and subtle oak. The palate is finely structured and styled, neither over, nor under-ripe, and slightly leaner and more racy than so many Australian Cabernets. Sweet French oak on the finish is an excellent counter-poise.

◀ **1997** ★★★★★   *July 1999*

Excellent full red–purple; a clean and concentrated bouquet with blackcurrant fruit and a touch of well-integrated spicy oak is followed by a powerful, concentrated palate with lots of blackcurrant/cassis fruit and ripe but potent tannins which are quite different from those of any other wine in the line-up. Like a big Bordeaux from a ripe year.

classic wines

★★★★★ Perfect	★★★★☆ Close to perfect	★★★★ Very good	★★★☆ Expected
★★★ Short of standard	★★☆ Undeserving	★★ Decayed relic	NR No rating

1996 ★★★☆ *July 1999*

Medium red–purple; the bouquet is quite fragrant but distinctly lighter, with touches of spice and leaf as well as red berry. The palate has fresh, crisp berry fruit flavours, lacking the opulence of the better wines and will mature quickly.

1995 ★★★★★ *July 1999*

Medium to full red–purple; back in the mainstream of the line, with a mix of sweet cassis, earth and cedar aromas; no question about the ripeness here. The palate has excellent weight, flavour, texture and structure; has the hallmark sweetness and suppleness of the best wines from Yarra Yarra, and a triumph for a vintage which wasn't always easy.

1994 ★★★☆ *July 1999*

Medium red–purple; the bouquet shows some slightly herbaceous/olivaceous characters which lurk underneath the sweeter notes on the palate. Intelligent use of oak has helped, but shows the mark of a cool vintage.

1993 ★★★★☆ *July 1999*

Medium to full red–purple; a clean, polished bouquet with ripe blackcurrant and chocolate fruit together with a touch of cedary oak. The palate is still evolving, elegant but quite tight; good acidity and well-balanced and integrated oak.

1992 ★★★★ *July 1999*

Medium red–purple; the aromas are soft yet quite complex, with sweet cedar and hints of caramel. A complex wine on the palate; a hint of premature development, perhaps, which shortens and dries out the palate slightly. Two bottles opened, and neither lived up to the theoretical status of the wine, or the wine as Ian Maclean knows it can be. Marked as tasted.

1991 ★★★★☆ *July 1999*

Medium to full red–purple; a cascade of lush, ripe plum, blackcurrant, prune and spice aromas are followed logically by an opulent, lush spicy bouquet with abundant chocolate as a sauce. Decadent and appealing, but a little over the top, and perhaps missing the classic elegance of the very best Yarra Yarra Cabernets. However, has time on its side.

1990 ★★★★ *July 1999*

Medium red–purple; another stylish bouquet, initially relatively restrained and slightly lighter than the older wines, but which opened up progressively. The palate is similarly restrained, with some earthy notes, and the tannins evident though not aggressive. In the final analysis, lacks the sweet fruit of the best wines in the line-up.

1989

Not made.

1988 ★★★★★ *July 1999*

Medium to full red–purple; the bouquet is very stylish indeed, disconcertingly Bordeaux-like; fragrant, perfectly ripened cassis, berry and cedar aromas waft out of the glass. The palate lives up to the bouquet; very harmonious and by no means heavy or opulent, but has it all there: berry, cedar and those hallmark gentle tannins. A great Yarra Valley vintage.

1987 ★★★☆   *July 1999*

Light to medium red; another mature wine, with a mix of earth, leaf and leather aromas around a core of gently sweet fruit in a lighter mould. The palate is similar, elegant yet quite ripe, aided in particular by gentle but sweet tannins.

1986 ★★★★   *July 1999*

Medium red, holding its hue well although not to the extent of the '85. The bouquet has distinct touches of earth and leather, with slightly smoky overtones, all a legitimate expression of aged Cabernet. An elegant, lighter-bodied wine on the palate with considerable length bolstered by light tannins and crisp acidity.

1985 ★★★★★   *July 1999*

Quite dazzling colour for a wine of this age, still bright and with no hint of browning. The moderately intense bouquet has a complex array of cassis and plum with splashes of liquorice and chocolate. The palate is at once full-bodied yet elegant; richly ripe fruit flavours run through the spectrum from cassis to plum to chocolate; simply outstanding for a wine of its age.

1984 ★★★★☆   *July 1999*

Medium red–purple; gently aged, with hints of tobacco and sweeter/cedary caramel characters surrounding an attractive core of sweet berry fruit. The palate is harmonious and balanced, with attractively sweet fruit supported by almost invisible oak and tannins. A lovely mature wine.

classic wines

★★★★★ Perfect   ★★★★☆ Close to perfect   ★★★★ Very good   ★★★☆ Expected
★★★ Short of standard   ★★☆ Undeserving   ★★ Decayed relic   NR No rating

329

yarra yarra sauvignon semillon
1989-1999

In the New World — Australia included — Sauvignon Blanc, even when blended with Semillon, is not expected to repay cellaring. In part, this may simply reflect the truth for sauvignon blanc grown in areas which are too warm, depriving it of varietal character and natural acidity.

When you look at sauvignon blanc grown in cool areas like the Yarra Valley or Marlborough, the picture changes, particularly when Semillon comes into the blend. No better example could be given than this wine; the 1989, for example, was still full of life when 11 years old. Even more remarkable is the fact that it came from one of the worst Yarra Valley vintages in the past 25 years.

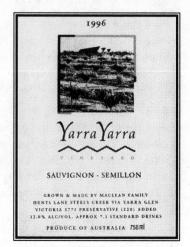

For the record, as it were, the wine is barrel-fermented in one-third new French oak barriques, two-thirds older. Ian Maclean uses different yeasts, increasingly moving towards wild (or indigenous) yeasts.

It is treated in much the same way post fermentation as barrel-fermented Chardonnay, with regular lees stirring before being cleaned up for bottling.

Tasted in July 1999, updated, and later vintages added.

1999 ★★★★☆   *April 2001*
Light green–yellow; an intensely fragrant bouquet with aromas of cut flowers, herbs and lanolin leads into a highly structured, crisp and lively palate with those distinctive characters of the bouquet repeated, and a mix of spicy and more lemony oak.

1998 ★★★★   *March 2000*
Light to medium yellow–green; that typically rich, powerful and complex mix of tangy fruit and a hint of spicy oak is followed by a quite fleshy palate, much fatter than the usual style, no doubt thanks to the relentless heat of the '98 vintage. Spicy nutmeg oak does help the finish.

1997 ★★★★★   *July 1999*
Light to medium green–yellow; once again, there is a seamless marriage of both fruit and oak on the bouquet, with hints of honey and caramel. The palate is potent, dense and concentrated, but with the same excellent balance of all constituents: fruit, oak and acidity.

◄── Not Ready   \ Still evolving   ▮ Prime of its life   ✧ Drink soon   ▯ Missed the boat

1996 ★★★★☆   *July 1999*

Light to medium yellow–green; the trademark mix of honey and citrus, and the equally consistent gentle touch of vanilla oak on the bouquet is followed by a perfectly balanced and composed palate; a silken thread of acidity runs throughout the wine through to a long finish.

1995 ★★★☆   *July 1999*

Light to medium yellow–green; the aromas are quite firm and fresh, with the first hints of honey developing. The palate is similarly firm and clean, but lacks the layered complexity of the best wines in the line-up, not surprising given the vintage.

1994 ★★★★★   *July 1999*

Medium yellow–green; fragrant, sweet, gently honeyed aromas with a twist of lemon peel are followed by a marvellous palate, which combines elegance, harmony and power with lively, zesty fruit and good acidity.

1993 ★★★★   *July 1999*

Quite developed yellow–green; the bouquet offers soft, rich, honeyed aromas which are layered and quite complex. The palate has considerable fruit sweetness and density; rich and bordering on heavy. In this instance very typical of '93 white wines from the Yarra.

1992 ★★★★☆   *July 1999*

Medium to full yellow–green, the most developed of the older wines. The bouquet is very ripe, with dried fruit aromas and slightly dusty edges. The palate likewise shows some warm vintage character, with quite high alcohol, but nevertheless has the structure evident in all the good wines in this group. 1992 was a different year from other parts of the Valley for this vintage.

1991

Not made.

1990 ★★★★★   *July 1999*

Medium to full yellow–green; the bouquet is quite complex with interesting, faintly pongy/vegetal, characters reminiscent of white Bordeauxs. The palate introduces some sweeter oaky notes which counter the fruit flavours; good structure; has presence and complexity. I changed the rating three times on this wine.

1989 ★★★★★   *July 1999*

Medium yellow–green; abundant sweet fruit with tropical overtones and minimal oak influence are followed by a remarkably youthful palate, with excellent fruit, still relatively tight and smooth. A miraculous outcome for a treacherous vintage. Did look a touch older and more developed the second time around, but still remarkable.

★★★★★ Perfect   ★★★★☆ Close to perfect   ★★★★ Very good   ★★★☆ Expected
★★★ Short of standard   ★★☆ Undeserving   ★★ Decayed relic   NR No rating

classic wines

331

yarra yering dry red no 1

i chose the location of Coldstream Hills (the winery my wife and I founded) for a mix of reasons, but the most important was its closeness (a few hundred metres) to Yarra Yering. I had encountered these wines at the end of the 1970s, and been hugely impressed; nothing I have seen since has caused me to alter my opinion one iota.

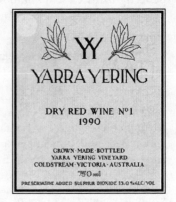

The wines made between 1973 and 1976 were, it is true, idiosyncratic, usually with higher than normal levels of volatile acidity. 1977 saw the start of a change, reinforced in 1978 when Bailey Carrodus instituted an earlier bottling program (and commenced using stalks in the ferment).

Since that time the main change was the switch to French-made barrels (in 1980) and an increase in the amount of new oak to between 85 per cent and 100 per cent as from 1985 — oak which the wine literally swallows up.

The wines are still fermented in the square, stainless steel-lined half-tonne fermenters looking for all the world like tea-chests, and hand-plunged. The varietal mix continues to be fine tuned: 80 per cent to 85 per cent Cabernet Sauvignon, 10 per cent Malbec, the remainder Merlot and a hatful of Cabernet Franc and Petit Verdot (with Merlot the one component on the increase).

Dry Red No 1 is a splendidly rich, opulent wine magically combining concentration with great elegance. I have no idea how long the best vintages will live: perhaps 50 years or more.

First tasted in March 1995, updated, and later vintages added.

1999 ★★★★★   *March 2001*

The best colour of all of the '99 wines from Yarra Yering, strong red–purple; the aromatic bouquet has distinctive earthy/leafy/olive overtones, strongly reminiscent of Bordeaux. The palate has good structure and texture, with blackberry/blackcurrant fruit, fine tannins, and positive but balanced oak. A major success for an ordinary vintage.

1998 ★★★★☆   *March 2000*

Medium to full red–purple; there is more slightly charry oak evident on the complex bouquet, with its sea of dark berry fruit. Quite firm berry fruit, and a touch of mint needs time to evolve, and the oak is more restrained on the palate.

  ◀ Not Ready   ❭ Still evolving   ❙ Prime of its life   ⌇ Drink soon   ⛶ Missed the boat

1997 ★★★★★ *March 1999*

Medium to full red–purple; red berry fruits, a touch of leaf and nicely judged, slightly charry oak make up the bouquet; the wine has the depth of structure needed for a wine built to live. Dark berry fruits and tannins run through the palate from start to finish.

1996 ★★★★★ *February 1998*

Medium to full red–purple; the bouquet is ripe and full, with strong Cabernet varietal aromas; cassis and earth. The palate is powerful and well structured, with potent blackberry and cassis fruit, the oak immaculately balanced and integrated.

1995 ★★★★☆ *April 1997*

Medium red–purple; the bouquet is of medium intensity with a gentle mix of cedar, leaf, cassis and earth surrounded by perfectly integrated French oak. The palate has very good flavour, with fully ripe fruit and no green canopy characters whatsoever; the flavours range through blackberry, blackcurrant and red berry fruits.

1994 ★★★★☆ *March 1995*

Medium purple–red; a clean, smooth and elegantly styled bouquet; as with all of the No 1 Dry Reds, an almost seamless marriage between the fruit and surprisingly subtle French oak. As befits the vintage, a concentrated wine on the palate, with the tannins starting to manifest themselves immediately the wine is taken into the mouth; there are flavours of mint and blackcurrant, and the wine will surely prove a classic once it settles down. (Tasted very shortly after bottling.)

1993 ★★★★★ *March 1995*

Youthful red–purple; a solid and dense bouquet of luscious, ripe blackcurrant fruit is almost as striking as the amazing '80 vintage. On the palate, rich, complex and intense fruit in a blackberry to cassis to mulberry range, followed by fine but persistent tannins on the finish.

1992 ★★★☆ *March 1995*

Lighter in colour than the majority of the younger No 1 Dry Reds; the bouquet, too, is slightly lighter, with some cedar and leafy notes, with a suspicion of lift. The palate only serves to confirm the impression of the colour and bouquet, being lighter and slightly sharper than the others in the line-up; however, all things are relative, and there are certainly pleasant red berry fruits running across the tongue.

1991 ★★★★☆ *March 1995*

Deep purple–red; a fragrant and complex bouquet which is not dissimilar to a pumped-up, fuller and richer version of the '89; the multifaceted aromas include hints of cedar and game. The palate, too, shows an array of cedar, game, mint and earth flavours surrounded by soft but persistent tannins.

1990 ★★★★★ *March 1995*

Dense, deep purple–red; a magnificent and ultra-concentrated and complex bouquet with layer upon layer of perfectly-ripened fruit, redolent of blackberry and chocolate. An immensely powerful and concentrated wine with deep but velvety black fruit flavours, appropriately emphatic tannins, and extraordinary length.

★★★★★ Perfect   ★★★★☆ Close to perfect   ★★★★ Very good   ★★★☆ Expected
★★★ Short of standard   ★★☆ Undeserving   ★★ Decayed relic   NR No rating

1989 ★★★★   *March 1995*

Medium red–purple; a very fresh, almost juicy berry bouquet, sweet and striking, and in very different style from most in the line-up. The flavours, too, are unusual with slightly stewed juicy berry flavours and a touch of spice. Bailey Carrodus regards this difficult vintage as a great success for Yarra Yering, and in an idiosyncratic fashion, it is not hard to see why.

1988 ★★★   *March 1995*

Medium red, showing obvious development; the bouquet is light, with some sweet caramel/vanilla bean aromas without the concentration of the other wines in the range. The palate is slightly weak and sweet; overall there are suggestions of oxidation at work. Note that this wine was withdrawn after it was released, with an offer of exchanging it for the '90 vintage (an offer which is no longer open of course).

1987

Not tasted.

1986 ★★★☆   *March 1995*

Medium to full red, rather more developed than the following (older) wines; there are distinctly leafy/gamey canopy-derived aromas, attesting to a cool ripening season. These characters reappear in the flavours of the palate, which do not flood the mouth like the others. However, it was a low-yielding vintage, and Bailey Carrodus thinks the wine will shine in the long term.

1985 ★★★★☆   *March 1995*

Dense, full red–purple; a powerful, ripe and concentrated bouquet with lots of dark chocolate, just a touch of gaminess and a hint of lift leads on to an exceedingly powerful and complex wine, with layer upon layer of flavour, relying more on power than finesse to make its point — but does so emphatically.

1984 ★★★★   *March 1995*

Medium red–purple; there are quite sweet, gently earthy aromas of dark chocolate and prune, but the palate is more in the cedary/leafy/gamey spectrum, finishing with some acid bite on the finish.

1983 ★★★★☆   *March 1995*

Medium to full purple–red; a strikingly youthful bouquet with fresh, primary red berry fruits, mint and leaf and a background whisper of the farmyard. The palate is just as fresh as the bouquet with more of those primary red and black berry fruit flavours, and a touch of mint. The tannins are soft, and the flavours clean throughout. Belies the exceedingly hot bushfire vintage.

1982 ★★★★★   *March 1995*

Medium to full red–purple; the bouquet is powerful, still youthful, with complex blackberry, blackcurrant fruit and some of those family dark chocolate and earth characters. A most attractive wine on the palate, with gently chewy tannins running right through, and giving an extra dimension to the structure; sweet earthy flavours of cabernet sauvignon at its best.

Not Ready   Still evolving   Prime of its life   Drink soon   Missed the boat

1981 ★★★★ *March 1995*

Medium to full red–purple; a clean, rich and obviously ripe bouquet with plummy/pruney, chocolate and earth characters. The palate is much more elegant and harmonious than the bouquet might lead one to suspect, in the mid-range of weight, with ripe plum, dark chocolate and mint flavours, touched by cedary oak.

1980 ★★★★★ *March 1995*

Deep red–purple; an immediately and strikingly distinctive and concentrated bouquet with a fascinating melange of spice, meat, berries and other aromas which spark like a Catherine Wheel. The palate is incredibly youthful, rich and concentrated, with idiosyncratic but compelling flavours of blackberry and spice surrounded by abundant but not harsh tannins.

1979 ★★★☆ *March 1995*

The colour is noticeably less dense than the majority in the line-up, though the hue is holding; fragrant leafy/minty aromas with hints of spice and tobacco attest to a cooler vintage. The palate is precisely as the bouquet would lead one to expect, soft, and ready now, with leafy/gamey flavours and gentle tannins. A mild, damp year.

1978 ★★★★★ *March 1995*

Still retaining distinct purple hues to its strong colour; a wine which says different things to different people, Bailey Carrodus seeing it as relatively austere in overall style, whereas I see it as much more luscious and ripe, with red berry and chocolate fruit aromas leading on to a palate with marvellous texture, mouthfeel and flavour. There are more of those ripe, dark berry fruits backed by abundant bitter chocolate flavours finishing with persistent but fine tannins. A cold year; reminiscent of a high-class Bordeaux.

1977 ★★☆ *March 1995*

Striking colour, still medium to full purple–red; the bouquet is complex, with powerful dark berry and dark chocolate fruit aromas, but the volatility present in the wine tending to become more and more pronounced as it sits in the glass. A powerful wine, certainly, but I personally find that level of volatility to be distracting.

★★★★★ Perfect   ★★★★☆ Close to perfect   ★★★★ Very good   ★★★☆ Expected
★★★ Short of standard   ★★☆ Undeserving   ★★ Decayed relic   NR No rating

classic wines

335

yeringberg dry red 1974-1999

When Guill de Pury replanted 2 hectares of vines on the slopes of Yeringberg in 1969 he followed in the footsteps of his grandfather, Baron Frederic Guillaume de Pury, 100 years earlier. For Yeringberg had become one of the three great vineyards and wineries of the Yarra Valley following its acquisition (from the pioneering Ryrie family) in 1863, and was the last to cease production (in 1921).

Yeringberg is unique in a number of ways. First, the wines of today are made in the still remarkably preserved three-storey wooden winery which was built in 1885 at the height of Yeringberg's fame, and when production was many times greater than it is today.

Second, it is the only one of the three major wineries of the last century (St Huberts and Chateau Yering being the other two) from which wines made in the later part of the nineteenth century and up to 1921 remain in existence. Lastly, it uses — with minimum change — the labels from that golden era.

I have been privileged to share a number of bottles, both white and red, from that time. Most were superb, none more so than a Cabernet from 1915 tasted on two occasions, once with Hugh Johnson and Guill de Pury. Johnson subsequently described it thus: 'Absolutely on a level with Chateau Lafite. Just incredible. It was young and delicate, full of colour and life and fruit, a most brilliant wine. A great historical moment to taste this 80-year-old wine.' Amen.

The tasting of the modern-day Yeringbergs (from 1974 to 1995) was held by the de Purys at the great Melbourne restaurant Est Est Est on 9 July 1997. It shows the evolution of Yeringberg (this particular wine is now simply called that on its front label, as it was in the nineteenth century) from 100 per cent Cabernet Sauvignon to its present blend of Cabernet Sauvignon, Cabernet Franc, Merlot and Malbec.

The vines are now between ten and 30 years of age, and vintages such as 1988, 1991, 1994 and 1997 pose the question — will they last as long as the 1915? I, for one, would like to think that they will.

1999 ★★★★☆   *March 2001*
Deep, dark red–purple; rich, blackberry, blackcurrant and mulberry fruit on the bouquet is followed by a soft, rich and full palate, with hints of plum and chocolate joining the blackberry/blackcurrant of the bouquet. The tannins are soft, the oak balanced; a particularly good outcome for the vintage.

1998 ★★★★☆   *March 2000*
Medium red–purple; the bouquet is moderately intense, clean, with gently ripe blackberry/blackcurrant fruit and a hint of spice. In typical fashion, there is far greater depth and richness to the fruit on the palate, flooded with sumptuous flavours of cassis, blackberry and blackcurrant. Every bit as good as the '97.

◄■ Not Ready   ＼ Still evolving   ▮ Prime of its life   ✎ Drink soon   ⬜ Missed the boat

1997 ★★★★★   *March 1999*

Medium red; the bouquet opens quietly, with earthy/berry fruit and subtle oak. It is in the mouth that the elegant blackcurrant/cassis fruit-driven palate comes to the fore, with a long, lingering finish woven through with fine tannins. The grapes were fully ripe, but the wine does not show its 14 degrees alcohol. The best Dry Red for some years, requiring time to flower.

1996 ★★★★   *February 1998*

Medium red; the bouquet is distinctly herbaceous, with leafy/earthy fruit, but the palate has surprisingly good mouthfeel, smooth and gentle with savoury red berry, leaf and mint flavours.

1995 ★★★☆   *July 1997*

Medium purple–red; a spotlessly clean and fragrant bouquet with a mix of gentle cassis, earth and light cedary notes. There is fair depth of flavour, with red fruit flavours attenuated by slightly leafy/squashy berry characters. Overall lacks the concentration and richness of the best wines of the group, and is the lightest of the '90s. Picked 29 April; 50 per cent Cabernet Sauvignon, 25 per cent Cabernet Franc, 15 per cent Merlot, 10 per cent Malbec, 12 degrees.

1994 ★★★★★   *July 1997*

Denser in colour than the '95, indeed slightly opaque. The bouquet is powerful and concentrated with red berry/redcurrant fruit, and — as always — subtle oak. The palate is as powerful as the bouquet promises, with touches of dark chocolate and briar; very good length and mouthfeel, finishing with silky tannins. Picked 30 April; 12 degrees; 2 tonnes to the acre.

1993 ★★★★☆   *July 1997*

Excellent colour, retaining even more purple hues than the '94. Given the reputation of the vintage, the bouquet is surprisingly ripe, plummy and rich, with more of the same on the palate: sweetly ripe fruit, gentle but sufficient tannins, and that silky feel of the Yeringberg marque. Picked 24 April; 13.5 degrees; 1.9 tonnes per acre.

1992 ★★★★☆   *July 1997*

There is no discernible colour change whatsoever, still purple–red. However, the bouquet shows a marked change to the younger vintages, with touches of leaf and mint, and some of those cool climate gamey characters. There is a similar gamut of flavours on the palate, earthy, cedary and leafy alongside the red fruit core. Picked 25 April; 59 per cent Cabernet Sauvignon; 13 degrees; 4.5 tonnes per acre.

1991 ★★★★★   *July 1997*

Again, exceptionally consistent colour in terms of depth and hue; concentrated and powerful fruit on the bouquet is still in the primary phase, albeit ripe. The palate is exactly as the bouquet promises, powerful and ripe, with dark plum fruit. Supple and sumptuous, with soft tannins on the finish. Picked 13 April; 59 per cent Cabernet Sauvignon; 13 degrees; 3.6 tonnes per acre.

★★★★★ Perfect   ★★★★☆ Close to perfect   ★★★★ Very good   ★★★☆ Expected
★★★ Short of standard   ★★☆ Undeserving   ★★ Decayed relic   NR No rating

1990 ★★★★ *July 1997*

A continuation of the strong purple–red colour, with virtually no change. The aromas are strongly varietal cabernet, but not in a particularly generous mood, especially after the '91; firm, with gravelly/earthy aspects. In the mouth the wine lacks the texture of the lower-yielding, riper years, and also some of the tannins, although it does have good length and some elegance. Picked 22 April; 60 per cent Cabernet Sauvignon; 12.6 degrees; 5.2 tonnes per acre.

1989 ★★★☆ *July 1997*

Still fresh and bright, medium purple–red; there are distinctly leafy/gamey/earthy aromas, typical of the vintage, and which follow through on a palate with a mix of spice, leaf and game flavours. However, the wine has good acidity, soft tannins and surprising length. Picked 15 April; 60 per cent Cabernet Sauvignon; 11.8 degrees; 3.1 tonnes per acre.

1988 ★★★★★ *July 1997*

Retains strong colour; the bouquet is powerful, initially showing classic cedary/earthy bottle-developed cabernet aromas, but with sweeter dark chocolate notes becoming more evident as the wine sat in the glass. The rich and powerful palate likewise evolved, with dark berry and dark chocolate flavours, and was excellent structure given its relatively modest alcohol. Picked 9 April; 58 per cent Cabernet Sauvignon; 12.4 degrees; 3.8 tonnes per acre.

1987 ★★★ *July 1997*

The wine has a lighter colour, showing the first obvious signs of development. A distinctly leafy bouquet with some slightly burnt medicinal aromas leads into a palate with a range of medicinal/cedary/leafy/minty flavours in a fairly extreme canopy-derived style. Notwithstanding the low yield, the wine seems to lack concentration. Picked 18 April; 58 per cent Cabernet Sauvignon; 12.4 degrees; 2.7 tonnes per acre.

1986 ★★★★ *July 1997*

Superb colour, still bright purple–red. The aromas are quite powerful, with a mix of briar, cedar and more vegetal notes, with that dusty character of mature cabernet. The palate is powerful, but with some green tannin or dimethyl sulphide flavours, and one wonders why it was picked at such a low baumé. Picked 12 April; 62 per cent Cabernet Sauvignon; 11.8 degrees; 4 tonnes per acre.

1985 ★★★☆ *July 1997*

Light to medium purple–red; the bouquet is light and fresh, quite surprising given its low alcohol, and with intriguing Italianate overtones. The palate has spicy/medicinal flavours presumably deriving from a shaded canopy; the wine is light in the mouth, finishing with dry tannins. Picked 6 April; 80 per cent Cabernet Sauvignon; 10.9 degrees; 2 tonnes per acre.

1984 ★★★★☆ *July 1997*

Amazingly, still showing strong purple–red hues; the bouquet is also impressively youthful, with sweet earth and cigar box aromas. A true Peter Pan on the palate, firm, fresh and crisp; you really wonder when the wine will evolve and, in a sense, where it is headed. An exceptional outcome for a wet vintage. Picked 20 April; 80 per cent Cabernet Sauvignon; 11.5 degrees; 2.4 tonnes per acre.

1983 ★★★☆ *July 1997*

While relatively light in colour, still retains excellent red–purple hue. The bouquet is spotlessly clean and youthful, with slightly leafy/minty aromas. The palate, however, betrays the very low alcohol level and, presumably, the high acidity. The product of a severe drought and stressed vines. Picked 23 April; 80 per cent Cabernet Sauvignon; 10.1 degrees; 2.8 tonnes per acre.

1982 ★★★☆ *July 1997*

Medium red–purple; the bouquet shows considerable development with cedar, cigar box, leaf and game aromas. The palate likewise shows leafy, cedary, minty flavours, but does have a remarkably long, almost slippery, finish. The mercury hit 45 degrees three weeks before vintage. Picked 10 April; 80 per cent Cabernet Sauvignon; 11.4 degrees; 3.5 tonnes per acre.

1981 ★★★★★ *July 1997*

Youthful red–purple colour; a marvellous bouquet showing concentrated, classic bottle-developed cabernet varietal character leads on to a wine with excellent flavour and texture on the palate. A mix of briar, plum, and dark chocolate fruit is followed by well-balanced tannins. Picked 21 March; 80–90 per cent Cabernet Sauvignon; 12.5 degrees; 2.2 tonnes per acre.

1980 ★★★★★ *July 1997*

The colour is quite astonishing, even by the standards of Yeringberg, still youthful purple–red. The bouquet is dense, even slightly closed, with dark blackberry/blackcurrant fruits and a substrate of earthy bottle-developed cabernet character. The palate is tightly knit and constructed, with lots of fruit and fine tannins. Picked 19 April; 100 per cent Cabernet Sauvignon; 12.3 degrees; 3.3 tonnes per acre.

1979 ★★★★☆ *July 1997*

Medium red–purple; fresh, clean and lively red berry/cherry fruit aromas lead on to an elegant wine on the palate. Not a big wine by any means, but has lingering, supple flavours and textures, and should have a long life in front of it. Picked 14 April; 100 per cent Cabernet Sauvignon; 3.2 tonnes per acre.

1976 ★★★★★ *July 1997*

Extraordinary dark red–purple colour. The bouquet is strong and concentrated, with blackberry/plum fruit and undertones of briar and cedar. The palate is rich, powerful and chunky, with far more tannins than any other wine made in the 1970s by Yeringberg. It must have been a monster when it was young. Picked 27 March; 100 per cent Cabernet Sauvignon.

classic wines

★★★★★ Perfect	★★★★☆ Close to perfect	★★★★ Very good	★★★☆ Expected
★★★ Short of standard	★★☆ Undeserving	★★ Decayed relic	NR No rating

1975 ★★★   *July 1997*

Medium red–purple; a complex earthy/charry nose, no doubt in part a residue of the excess level of sulphur dioxide inadvertently added to the wine early in its life. The palate is likewise slightly furry/charry/biscuity, but does have flavour. Because of the high sulphur dioxide levels the wine did not undergo malolactic fermentation. Picked 25 April; 100 per cent Cabernet Sauvignon.

1974 ★★★☆   *July 1997*

Medium red–purple; similar slightly earthy/charry aromas to the '75, but a much better palate, youthful, firm and fresh. It is slightly one-dimensional, but does show good cabernet varietal character, now into the earthy phase, finishing with fine tannins. Like the '75, had high sulphur dioxide additions and did not undergo malolactic fermentation. Picked 10 April; 100 per cent Cabernet Sauvignon.

new zealand

classic wines

ata rangi pinot noir 1989-1999

he team at Ata Rangi produces one of New Zealand's most celebrated and internationally known Pinot Noirs. The team are the owners Clive Paton and Phyllis Pattie, increasingly supported by winemaker Oliver Masters. In the early years Clive Paton looked after the viticulture and made the red wines, while Phyllis Pattie (with a Food Technology degree from Massey University and a prior career as a winemaker with Montana at its Blenheim winery) was in charge of the white winemaking. As the detailed vintage notes indicate, constant refinements have been sought in both vineyard and winery over the relatively short period of production.

The yields are low (around 2 tonnes to the acre) and the main core of the plantings are now 20 years old, a factor which the team believes is playing an important part in the ascending quality of the wine. The core clone is known as the 'Abel', spirited into New Zealand from France over 20 years ago. Five other clones have been added more recently, notably the so-called Pommard clone, and Clones 114, 115 and 667 from the Raymond Benard/Dijon University selections.

Winemaking is traditional, using small, closed fermenters with wide-top manholes which allow hand-plunging. Experimentation with some batches each year has helped to finetune the winemaking style. Indigenous yeasts and malolactic bacteria ferment the wine, which typically has a cool pre-fermentation maceration. About one-fifth of the ferments include whole bunches. Both pre-fermentation cold soak, and post-fermentation maceration lengthen the primary ferment of around four to five days to a total of three weeks. Twenty-five per cent of the barrels (Burgundy barriques) are new, and the wine undergoes malolactic fermentation in barrel.

Ata Rangi has had enormous success in wine competitions in New Zealand and abroad. Both the 1993 and 1994 were awarded the Bouchard Finlayson Trophy for Best Pinot Noir at the 26th and 27th International Wine & Spirit Competitions in the United Kingdom. The '90, '91, '92 and '94 each won a gold medal and trophy for Champion Pinot Noir at the annual Air New Zealand Wine Awards (New Zealand's top wine show) while the '95 won a gold medal at the National Wine Show in Canberra, Australia, and the '96 received a gold medal at the 29th International Wine & Spirit Competition.

(Vintage notes in brackets are by Phyll Pattie.)

First tasted in March 1998, updated, and later vintages added.

1999 ★★★★★   *February 2001*

Typically deeply coloured; potent plum, black cherry and spice aromas flood the bouquet; ravishly sweet but not jammy dark berry, plum, cherry and spice flavours on the palate swell to a crescendo on the finish, the tannins in much better balance than they were in 1998.

★★★★★ Perfect	★★★★☆ Close to perfect	★★★★ Very good	★★★☆ Expected
★★★ Short of standard	★★☆ Undeserving	★★ Decayed relic	NR No rating

🖌 *1998* ★★★★☆   *January 2000*

Medium to full red–purple; the bouquet is rich and sweet with complex plummy fruit; the immediate presence of long tannins mark the opening of the palate; dark berries and some savoury characters then appear, followed by slightly hot alcohol on the finish. Phyll Pattie says: 'It is one of the biggest we've made,' and I wouldn't quarrel with that.

🖌 *1996* ★★★★★   *March 1998*

Medium to full red–purple; a reversion to the concentration of the '94 and preceding vintages, awesome in the depth of its fruit. Plum, black cherry and spice run through both the bouquet and the palate, which finishes with just the right amount of tannins to sustain the wine as it matures and develops more foresty/gamey characters. (Hot and dry, crops 3 tonnes per acre, rich ripe flavours in '96 again. More trialling of Smart Dyson, and for future: looking again at VSP with closer row and plant spacings.)

🖌 *1995* ★★★★☆   *March 1998*

Medium purple–red; the bouquet is clean and firm with abundant plum, cherry and raspberry fruit. The palate is fresh, with direct cherry and plum fruit of medium weight. A very attractive wine, although not especially complex. This may well come with time given the performance of the older wines in the group. (Hot and dry, vintage marred with rain, some dilution inevitable. Good crop levels like '96. Smart Dyson trellising kicking in for 15 per cent of intake. Starting to get more backbone as older vines produce bigger and better tannins. 1980 plantings.)

🖌 *1994* ★★★★★   *March 1998*

Light to medium red–purple, with no hints of brown. The bouquet is lively, with a mix of sappy and cherry/plum notes; has elegance and verve. The palate provides the same mix of flavours, and has quite marvellous length and aftertaste which lifted it into the highest rank. (Coolish start, low yields, very good post-Christmas period, excellent settled-weather vintage. Small berries, good concentration, started to extend lees contact through malo and beyond.)

🖌 *1993* ★★★★★   *March 1998*

The lively and tangy bouquet has an attractive mix of spice, forest and earth. The palate comes up and up the more you taste it, with silky Burgundian characters which are persuasive, even if there is not an abundance of sweet fruit. (Not much better than '92, terrible yields. Whole bunch still included, but reduced to about 15 per cent.)

🖌 *1992* ★★★★☆   *March 1998*

Medium red; a wine showing the progressive evolution from primary to secondary savoury foresty characters. The palate has considerable length, not as much perhaps as the great '94, but good by any other standards. The problem is the slightly woody/stemmy astringency and fractionally green tannin. (Terribly cold summer, very low yields. Some whole bunch from 1992 onwards.)

🖌 *1991* ★★★★   *March 1998*

Light to medium red; the bouquet is light and earthy, lacking concentration. The palate is quite pleasant, with evolved earthy notes, balanced by touches of plum and spice. Mildly disappointing. (Quite a bit of young vine material in this blend. Started cold soak pre-maceration about here.)

◄ Not Ready   ＼ Still evolving   🖌 Prime of its life   ⌁ Drink soon   ⎕ Missed the boat

1990 ★★★★★ *March 1998*

Light red; the complex bouquet runs through sappy/earthy and foresty characters similar to many Martinborough Vineyard wines. The palate is very powerful, with some sappy, tomato vine characters and moderately high acidity. The overall effect is distinctly Burgundian, and one I like. Others may not be so enraptured. (Intermediate sort of year heat-wise.)

1989 ★★★★ *March 1998*

The colour is medium red, but slightly dull. The bouquet is sappy, with some soapy notes suggesting slightly high pH, together with gamey/foresty notes. The palate has some length, persistence and grip, but the fruit has definitely started to fall out of the mid-palate. Clearly, a wine which was once better. (A bit like '98? Very hot, not quite as dry.)

cloudy bay chardonnay
1986-1999

I am on record (David Hohnen forgets nothing, and forgives little) as questioning the wisdom of extending the Cloudy Bay range from its original single wine (Sauvignon Blanc) to a more conventional string of wines, now including not only a Chardonnay but also Pinot Noir and a Cabernet Merlot and an occasional Botrytis Riesling (leaving Pelorus to one side).

Well, the Cabernet Merlot did not set the world on fire as did the Sauvignon Blanc, but the Chardonnay is a more than useful wine in its own right. Cloudy Bay has over 35 hectares of chardonnay in its control; much goes to Pelorus, but the ripest blocks produce the grapes for this wine.

A mix of tank and barrel fermentation, malolactic fermentation, prolonged yeast lees contact and ageing in French oak are the technical weapons, and are more or less standard for top quality Chardonnay in this day and age. As with the Sauvignon Blanc, it is the disciplined way in which they are used — and the high quality of the base material — which makes the critical difference.

Whereas so many New Zealand Chardonnays age rapidly into an egg-yellow, oily, cosmetic/phenolic fluid barely recognisable as wine, Cloudy Bay Chardonnay ages surely and gracefully.

First tasted in October 1994, updated, and later vintages added.

1999 ★★★★☆   *February 2001*
Medium to full yellow–green; the usual complex inputs from the barrel and malolactic fermentation provide toasty/smoky/cashew overtones to the tangy melon fruit of the bouquet. The palate is rich, with melon, nectarine and white peach offset by the softening effects of the malolactic cashew characters.

1998 ★★★★★   *January 2000*
Medium to full yellow–green; rich and tangy fruit on the bouquet is supported by clear but controlled barrel-ferment characters. The palate is remarkably rich, the fruit continuing to build in waves on an intense, long finish.

1997 ★★★★★ *February 1999*

Quite full straw–yellow colour, although reassuringly pale by normal New Zealand standards. The bouquet is concentrated and complex, with distinctly Burgundian overtones, and typical of the striking fruit character of the best Chardonnays from the low-yielding vintage. The palate is exceptionally tight and intense, fruit-driven, even though malolactic fermentation (60 per cent) and oak (25 per cent new) have contributed to the complexity of the wine.

1995 ★★★★★ *February 1997*

Glowing yellow–green; a complex yet smooth bouquet showing all of the winemaking craft and skills evident in the Cloudy Bay Sauvignon Blanc; cashew, malolactic-fermentation characters are allied with subtle oak on the bouquet, with a kaleidoscopic array of similar influences on the palate. Here creamy/nutty characters, partly textural and partly flavour-oriented are married with an almost minerally, dry finish. A spectacular achievement for a difficult vintage.

1994 ★★★★☆ *February 1996*

Full yellow–green; a highly stylised wine, looking quite European when tasted in a line-up of Australian Chardonnays, with pronounced toasty/mealy aromas. The palate shows a spectrum of spicy/mealy/buttery/nutty flavours woven through subtle smoky oak, finishing with well-balanced acidity. No-holds-barred Cloudy Bay stuff.

1993 ★★★★ *October 1994*

Light to medium green–yellow; the bouquet is well balanced with very sweet fruit components ranging from melon and fig through to pineapple, reflecting some botrytis. The palate is very rich and concentrated, with sweet peach/melon/fig flavours. An extraordinary achievement given the appalling vintage.

1992 ★★★★ *October 1994*

Light to medium green–yellow; a wine still coming together when tasted, with some oak influence still to integrate, though far from aggressive; faintly herbal/green citrus aspects to the bouquet. The palate is firm, with fruit sweetness balanced by echoes of the herbal characters of the bouquet. A cool, relatively low-yielding vintage of high quality.

1991 ★★★★★ *October 1994*

Light to medium yellow–green; a complex bouquet with a touch of lift, similar fruit aromas to the '90, and subtle oak. A powerful wine in the mouth, with a long, complex, melon flavoured palate with some underlying nutty malolactic-fermentation (mlf) characters, and good structure.

1990 ★★★★☆ *October 1994*

Medium yellow–green; the bouquet is complex and tangy, with stylish citrus and melon fruit. The palate is very lively with very well-balanced barrel-ferment and malolactic-fermentation characters, providing plenty of depth and structure, yet not imperilling the ripe fruit. The chardonnay was picked before the frost.

classic wines

★★★★★ Perfect   ★★★★☆ Close to perfect   ★★★★ Very good   ★★★☆ Expected
★★★ Short of standard   ★★☆ Undeserving   ★★ Decayed relic   NR No rating

1989 ★★★★☆   *October 1994*

Medium green–yellow; lively and complex aromas, with some very interesting nutty 'dirty French' aromas, and obvious malolactic fermentation inputs. The palate is very concentrated and structured, with sweet nutty/melon fruit starting to move into its secondary phase. Has considerable length. The earliest, warmest vintage on record.

1988 ★★☆   *October 1994*

The colour shows distinct orange hints, even browning, the bouquet with strong hay/straw/apricot aromas indicating botrytis at work. The palate also shows a strong botrytis influence, with some maderised characters.

1987 ★★★★★   *October 1994*

A bright yellow–green colour introduces a wine with a smooth yet full bouquet with some slightly nutty characters. The palate is very stylish, with wonderful fruit and oak balance and integration. Ageing with grace, and will be long lived, with good acidity. Note some bottle variation does exist. A cool vintage which finished dry.

1986 ★★★★☆   *October 1994*

Medium to full yellow–green; high powered, highly aromatic fruit, intensely regional with some tropical/jungle aromas, but showing no signs of break up. A big, generously flavoured, rounded, mouthfilling wine with the illusion of sweetness, but finishing dry. Note that there was no malolactic fermentation in this wine. A relatively cool and overall fairly wet year.

◀── Not Ready   ❯ Still evolving   ⌁ Prime of its life   ✎ Drink soon   ∏ Missed the boat

cloudy bay sauvignon blanc

1985-2000

When I learned that David Hohnen was planning to stage vertical tastings of Cloudy Bay in both New Zealand and in Australia to celebrate the tenth birthday of Cloudy Bay in 1994 I was interested. When I heard that he believed the tastings would demonstrate how well Cloudy Bay Sauvignon Blanc ages I became sceptical: it had always seemed to me that Cloudy Bay was at its brilliant, zesty best in the few months following its release. After all, it is within this time-frame that 99 per cent of each year's wine is consumed.

In the event, it seems to me the result was a draw. The tasting demonstrated that while Cloudy Bay does not actually improve with age, neither does it decline — or at least, not within the ten-year perspective of that tasting. No less importantly, it underlined another Hohnen tenet: that the shape and character of each vintage of Cloudy Bay is essentially determined by the climatic conditions of the year. It is grown in what Hohnen describes as the end of the viticultural extreme, with little or no margin for nature's error.

This may be so, but no one should doubt the level of intellectual skill and discipline involved in actually making Cloudy Bay: the varying dab of semillon, the touch of barrel ferment, the judicious tempering of acidity, the eschewing of residual sugar. This is as much a winemaker's wine as a vineyard wine.

Vintage notes from Cloudy Bay in brackets.

First tasted in October 1994, updated, and later vintages added.

2000 ★★★★★   *November 2000*
Light green–yellow; the bouquet is clean but complex, with a multiplicity of aromas covering the full spectrum of varietal fruit ripeness. The palate offers more of the same, running from mineral, grass and herb through to tropical, yet without any one character or flavour dominating. Excellent dry, cleansing but persistent finish.

1999 ★★★★★   *November 1999*
Brilliant light green–yellow colour, an elegant, multifaceted bouquet with fruit aromas which refuse to be pinned down into one type, and a subliminal touch of oak. The palate positively sparkles with life, with lively citrus and gooseberry flavours running through to a very long, intense lingering finish. Just great summer drinking.

★★★★★ Perfect   ★★★★☆ Close to perfect   ★★★★ Very good   ★★★☆ Expected
★★★ Short of standard   ★★☆ Undeserving   ★★ Decayed relic   NR No rating

1998 ★★★★☆ *November 1998*

Light to medium yellow–green; a crisp, clean bouquet with a slightly subdued mix of lime, herb and gooseberry aromas. The palate is more delicate than the usual Cloudy Bay style, but, as ever, is beautifully balanced with a long, cleansing finish.

1997 ★★★★★ *January 1998*

Light to medium yellow–green; the bouquet shows a range of complex gooseberry, passionfruit and more smoky/mineral aromas, the palate lively and fresh with crisp gooseberry, apple and passionfruit. Has the usual impeccable balance and length. Simply as outstanding as ever.

1996 ★★★★★ *December 1996*

An absolutely glorious wine, one of the best yet to come out under the Cloudy Bay label. There is beautiful fruit expression on the bouquet with a mix of passionfruit and a gentle underlay of herbal notes; the palate as close to perfection as one could ever expect with gentle yet intense fruit ranging through gooseberry to herb/herbal to tropical. A wine that caresses the mouth.

1995 ★★★★ *November 1995*

Light yellow–green, with a clean, crisp bouquet with tangy fruit aromas running from grapefruit through to tropical. There is no question the palate is lighter than in most years, but the wine provides a totally delicious, harmonious mouthful that will frighten no one, and please many. A powerful testimony to the skills of the winemaking team.

1994 ★★★★★ *October 1994*

Like all the wines from the '90s, bright, light green–yellow in colour. The bouquet is intense and clean, with beautifully balanced gooseberry/tropical aromas set against more herbal characters, but not the least green or aggressive; a subliminal touch of spice. A wonderful wine on the palate, with very good acid balance and length. Has overt varietal character, yet not at all in the cut-throat razor range. (Poor flowering produced a small crop which ripened in perfect conditions.)

1993 ★★★★ *October 1994*

A firm, crisp, tangy herbal/lime bouquet leads on to a palate which has remarkably good balance for what was a very difficult year. Cloudy Bay resisted the temptation to balance the acidity with residual sugar, and, what is more, the wine is not excessively acid in any event. (Minute yields of often very acid grapes, and a nightmare from a viticultural viewpoint.)

1992 ★★★★★ *October 1994*

Gloriously lively, fresh and crisp when tasted at the end of 1994, with pristine gooseberry/herbal varietal aromas. The flavour is lively, fresh, clean and crisp, retaining primary fruit without any signs of modification. A long finish. (Nigh-on-perfect vintage from start to finish.)

1991 ★★★☆ *October 1994*

Bright in colour, with a very firm, acutely herbal bouquet which, like the palate, appears to have volatility, but in fact does not. A rather sharp wine, which could conceivably come together with age. (A schizophrenic vintage with rain, hail and snow in the middle, and sun in the finish.)

◄ Not Ready ＼ Still evolving ﹗ Prime of its life ✦ Drink soon ⛁ Missed the boat

1990 ★★★★ *October 1994*

Bright yellow–green, with a firm, crisp, direct bouquet showing pristine herbal varietal character. In the mouth, fresh, smooth, rounded lime fruit on the mid-palate, followed by a faint dry hay/straw character on the finish. (A memorable year with a black frost halfway through vintage which defoliated all the vines.)

1989 ★★★★ *October 1994*

Still bright and youthful in colour, with a smooth, fairly tight bouquet, but the palate marking the break point between the older and younger wines in terms of fruit development. Good flavour with rounded fruit starting to move into secondary characters. (A warm and early vintage, regarded by David Hohnen as dull and boring.)

1988 ★★★☆ *October 1994*

Medium to full yellow–green colour, showing development. The bouquet is soft and broad, with fairly diffuse fruit. The palate is noticeably softer than the other old wines, showing a complex array of botrytis-infected herbal/green bean/tobacco/ asparagus flavours. (The year of Cyclone Bola, heavy mid-season rains, but a dry harvest.)

1987 ★★★★ *October 1994*

Medium to full yellow–green. The bouquet is complex, with some green bean and asparagus aromas, and an aroma not unlike herbed focaccia. The palate is likewise complex, with secondary fruit characters which will appeal to some more than others. (Another difficult year with a massive storm at the end of summer, followed by a dry spell. Cloudy Bay picked hours before a further deluge arrived.)

1986 ★★★★☆ *October 1994*

Medium to full yellow–green; firm, quite clean, almost lime-accented bouquet with hints of tobacco and straw coming up as the wine breathed in the glass. The palate showing ripe, honeyed/spice/tobacco flavours, with an underlying mature White Bordeaux character; a wine which personally appealed to me. (One of the wettest summers on record was followed by a warm, dry finish.)

1985 ★★★★★ *October 1994*

Medium to full yellow–green; very complex and rich secondary green bean/asparagus/focaccia aromas. The palate has a core of strength which is holding the wine together still, with strong green bean/asparagus flavours and soft acid providing excellent balance. (A cool year, with snow falling on the nearby ranges on the first day of vintage, the grapes being picked at 2°C.)

classic wines

| ★★★★★ Perfect | ★★★★☆ Close to perfect | ★★★★ Very good | ★★★☆ Expected |
| ★★★ Short of standard | ★★☆ Undeserving | ★★ Decayed relic | NR No rating |

dry river craighall riesling

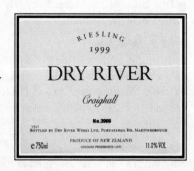

Craighall takes its name from the second of the two vineyards established by Dr Neil McCallum and wife Dawn in Martinborough — 200 metres away from the first vineyard (and winery). A thin, vertical wall of Scott-Henry-type trellis is used, and the crop is thinned down to 6.25 tonnes per hectare or less. Says Neil McCallum: 'I am aiming for a focused, reticent style which tends towards austere when young and can take four to five years to start opening up. I expect most to have a life of over ten years.'

As with all the tasting notes for Dry River (and the other New Zealand classics) my tasting notes were written before I received the vintage commentaries. In most instances there is a reasonably good correlation, and I have resisted the temptation to change my notes or my predictions, even though I would strongly suspect that Neil McCallum would have a far better idea about the future of specific vintages than I do.

The major change in the style seems to have taken place after the 1992 vintages. Prior to that time, the amount of residual sugar varied with the year, and in a vertical tasting, was slightly disconcerting. Since 1993 the Riesling has been labelled 'dry', and the Botrytis Bunch Selection wines have made their appearance. Says Neil McCallum: 'This style aims for purity of expression, ten-plus years of life, and botrytis characters which only reveal themselves with time.'

Annual production is only 300–400 cases.

(Background notes in brackets supplied by Neil McCallum.)

First tasted in March 1998, updated, and later vintages added.

◀■ *2000* ★★★★★   *May 2001*

Medium yellow–green; sweet lime, stonefruit and honey aromatics are followed a palate of daunting intensity, which floods the mouth with flavour, long and intense. While the wine has an element of sweetness, the only question is about the degree of acidity, which does tend to build up after the second glass.

◀■ *1999* ★★★★★   *January 2000*

Medium yellow–green; an exceptionally intense and powerful bouquet ranging through lime, toast and a touch of kerosene. The palate is, quite simply, imperious, long and with a near bone-dry finish.

1998 ★★★★★ *March 1999*

Full yellow–green; the bouquet is overflowing with classic lime and toast aromas, with the complexity and depth one would expect from a five- to ten-year-old wine. The palate, likewise, has tremendous depth and length, with awesomely rich lime and toast flavours; immaculately balanced, with a seemingly dry finish.

1997 ★★★★☆ *March 1998*

A wine with surprising depth to the colour already showing. The palate is soft, with full, gentle and obviously very ripe lime-accented fruit. The palate is as precocious as the colour and bouquet suggest, with lots of fruit flavour and depth nicely balanced by acidity, and with a long finish. It may get better with age, but then it may not, and — either way — a pleasure to drink now.

(No botrytis, showing nice varietal flavours from an excellent Riesling vintage.)

1996 ★★★★★ *March 1998*

Medium yellow–green; the classic bouquet provides a quite gentle mix of lime, toast and mineral aromas which are more or less precisely replicated on the beautifully structured and balanced palate. Great now, but will be even better with more bottle age. (Warmish year; nice dry autumn. Still a baby.)

1996 Botrytis Selection ★★★★★ *March 1998*

Medium yellow–green; a quite exceptional wine from start to finish, with intense, luscious lime and clingstone peach aromas, followed by a palate of extraordinary power and intensity. The lingering acidity provides a long, cleansing finish. (The year was a little warmer than average, with a nice dry autumn, but enough humidity to produce perfect botrytis.)

1995 ★★★★ *March 1998*

Light to medium yellow–green, with just a touch of straw. Fresh, floral, lifted fruit aromas suggest a hint of botrytis; an elegant, medium weight wine in the mouth, with good, fresh acidity. (Warm year, low pH. The wine will take some time to show its colours.)

1995 Botrytis Selection ★★★☆ *March 1998*

Medium yellow–green; the thumbprint of the 1995 vintage, evident in all the Dry River wines, comes through loud and clear. The palate shows obvious botrytis, with peachy fruit and relatively soft acid. It is hard to imagine this wine having a particularly long life. (Year a little warmer than average, nice dry autumn, but enough humidity to produce perfect botrytis.)

1994 ★★★★★ *March 1998*

Medium to full yellow–green; a marvellously concentrated and intense bouquet with rich lime juice aromas is followed by an equally impressive palate. Lots of flavour and concentration, with long, gently sweet lime juice flavours; harmonious and well balanced. In the context of the style, dry.

(Slightly cooler than the average year, with a classic dry autumn. The grapes ripened a little faster than I would have liked.)

★★★★★ Perfect   ★★★★☆ Close to perfect   ★★★★ Very good   ★★★☆ Expected
★★★ Short of standard   ★★☆ Undeserving   ★★ Decayed relic   NR No rating

classic wines

353

1993 ★★★☆   *March 1998*

Medium to full yellow–g°reen; it would seem that botrytis has been at work, with dusty/funky/minerally esters, yet for all that quite powerful. The palate opens with tropical fruit flavours, then is softened or weakened as a dry style by that botrytis influence. Overall, quite developed. (A cold year; small crop.)

1992 ★★★   *March 1998*

The full yellow–green colour hints at the development; the bouquet has a strong beery/toasty overlay to mature Riesling fruit aromas which are akin to those of Australian Riesling. On the palate the sweetness comes through to prop up or to unbalance the wine, depending on one's viewpoint and personal preference. (A very cold year, with a heat summation equivalent to that of Invercargil. Fruit picked very late with long ripening. Starting to drink well.)

1991 ★★★★☆   *March 1998*

Full yellow–green in colour. The bouquet is quite intense, with some lifted aromas showing toast, honey and lime in abundance. In the mouth, an uncompromisingly sweet spätlese verging on auslese style, and if this is what you are looking for in Riesling, very good indeed. (A coolish but almost perfect season. Some botrytis, ripe fruit.)

1990 ★★★★   *March 1998*

Medium straw colour, with the aromas showing a range of bottle-developed characters through toasty to a touch of kerosene. The palate is definitely starting to show age, but the residual sweetness helps more than it hinders the wine. A mix of first and second crop grapes. (A hot, dry summer, smaller canopies and a wet April. The grapes were picked in May when it had dried out.)

1989 ★★★★★   *March 1998*

The colour is still bright and green-tinged. The bouquet is at once youthful and quite intense, with quite delicious lime juice aromas. A delicate spätlese style showing no signs of drying out; all in all, a remarkable testament to the quality it is possible to obtain from the first crop, even if I must admit to giving it five rather than four and a half stars for sentimental reasons. (Warmish vintage; good canopies for most of summer; clean harvest.)

dry river gewurztraminer

1990-1999

the Dry River Gewurztraminer is presented in a bone dry style (Neil McCallum actually underlines the words 'bone dry', which, he says, gives the fruit a different expression). While McCallum allows the vines to crop at a higher level than the other varieties (around 3 tonnes to the acre) the grapes almost invariably ripen to perfection, producing a relatively high alcohol style — which in turn provides its own particular form of sweetness.

McCallum sees these wines as normally for drinking as younger wines, somewhere between two and five years old. Well, as the tasting notes indicate, in 1998 I thought the 1990, 1991 and 1992 vintages were all still on the plateau of peak drinkability, and (with the notable exception of Alsace) I am not normally a particularly vocal supporter of Gewurztraminer. It is simply McCallum's wine artistry which makes these wines so complete and appealing, plus — of course — the incomparable Wairarapa soil and climate.

The Botrytis Selection Gewurztraminers of Dry River are, likewise, in a class all of their own. Says Neil McCallum: 'The style relies on hanging the grapes out very late to produce the weight and richness of a Vendage Tardive.' All I can say is I completely agree, and that I made the direct comparison with Vendage Tardive before reading McCallum's note (shown in brackets), which was spot on.

All except the '99 were tasted in March 1998.

1999 ★★★★★   *January 2000*
Brilliant green–yellow; the bouquet is intensely aromatic, with spice almost verging on liquorice; the palate is rich, intense and luscious, with perfectly balanced sugar and acid. Takes Gewurztraminer onto another plane.

1997 ★★★★★   *March 1998*
Bright green–yellow; a voluptuous, perfumed bouquet redolent of tropical peach, spice and lychee is followed by a palate absolutely packed with flavour; unctuous, rich and finishing with soft acidity. Very much in the Zind Humbrecht style. (A top-flight aromatic white vintage; low cropped and close to Vendage Tardive — Neil McCallum.)

1996 ★★★★☆   *March 1998*
Light to medium yellow–straw; the aromas are crisp, minerally and clean, with restrained rose petal characters. The palate, by contrast, is much sweeter than the bouquet suggests, and while quite elegant really needs more fruit intensity to carry that sweetness.

classic wines

★★★★★ Perfect   ★★★★☆ Close to perfect   ★★★★ Very good   ★★★☆ Expected
★★★ Short of standard   ★★☆ Undeserving   ★★ Decayed relic   NR No rating

1995 Botrytis Selection ★★★★   *March 1998*

Full yellow colour, with a touch of pink. The aromas run through spice, lychee, rose petal and soft peach, with botrytis very evident. The palate is soft, moderately sweet with orange peel characters and that slightly ignoble rot influence.

1994 ★★★★☆   *March 1998*

Light green–straw; the clean, crisp, delicate bouquet with its tangy and mineral overtones is as far removed from the characters of the '92 as one could imagine. The palate has sweetness, but is balanced by acidity, and has considerable length.

1994 Botrytis Selection ★★★★☆   *March 1998*

Medium yellow–green; the bouquet is relatively robust, with flowery and intense lime and spice aromas. The same flavours come through on the palate which is of spätlese, rather than auslese, sweetness, offering both balance and concentration.

1992 ★★★★   *March 1998*

Full yellow; the ripe, peachy tropical fruit aromas are reminiscent of the '97 vintage, strikingly perfumed. The palate logically tracks the bouquet with abundant apricot, peach and lime fruit balanced by good acidity. I am not entirely convinced, however, that this is what Gewurztraminer should smell or taste like.

1991 ★★★★★   *March 1998*

The light green–straw colour is the first indication of an extraordinarily youthful Peter Pan style. The bouquet has hints of rose petal, mineral and citrus with spicy nuances; the palate is superb, long and subtle, yet with power and grip. A wine which will very probably be every bit as good as it is today in 20 years time.

1991 Botrytis Selection ★★★★★   *March 1998*

Medium yellow–green; the lifted and intense bouquet shows strong varietal character with a mix of spice, lime and mineral characters, the palate offering lime, spice and lychee flavours. The acidity perfectly balances the residual sugar on a long finish.

1990 ★★★★   *March 1998*

Medium to full yellow; the rich and full bouquet with tropical spicy fruit and a faintly mineral underlay. A wine with similarities to the '92 and '97 vintages, although not ascending the very heights of the '97. There is still lots of sweet spicy fruit on the palate.

1990 Botrytis Selection ★★★★   *March 1998*

Glowing yellow–green; the aromas are intriguing, with a melange of beeswax, candlewax, spice, lychee and lime. If this were not enough, some peachy notes come through on the palate, which finishes with firm acidity.

dry river pinot gris 1987-1999

If there is better Pinot Gris made anywhere else in the world outside of Alsace, I am yet to taste it. In saying this I do exclude the Pinot Grigios of northern Italy, which — while made from the same grape variety — are so different in style that direct comparison is valueless. If I had to make it, my answer would be even more emphatic, for I far prefer the Alsatian style to the Italian.

Neil McCallum says that most of the cropping for his pinot gris tends to be in the range of 1 to 2 tonnes per acre. This no doubt stems from the fact that the clone is 'tokay a petit grains' imported by Mission Estate in 1886. McCallum adds: 'It is widely accepted in Alsace that the larger-berried clones give bigger crops but cannot match the quality.'

From direct observation, it would seem that the Australian plantings are different from those of Dry River, for super-abundant crops are the norm in Australia, although the individual berry and bunch size is typically small. The one point of similarity is that on both sides of the Tasman winemakers are of the view the style gains a lot by being left out late for extra weight and richness. Thus the leading Australian exponent, T'Gallant on the Mornington Peninsula, typically picks its top pinot gris with a potential alcohol of over 14 degrees, sometimes approaching 15 degrees.

Neil McCallum suggests that cellaring for at least four years is essential to see the real class of the wine, and I would not disagree.

(Background notes in brackets supplied by Ian McCallum.)

First tasted in March 1998, updated, and later vintages added.

1999 Martinborough ★★★★★   *May 2001*
Light to medium yellow–green; the bouquet is clean but reserved, with some floral and spice aromas to be uncovered. The luscious, rounded, honeyed palate shows the 14 degrees without leading to an alcohol burn on the finish.

1998 Estate ★★★★★   *May 2001*
Glowing yellow–green; the bouquet is slightly more minerally than some, but with strong spice and citrus also evident. A massively rich, ripe and honeyed wine, absolutely in the mainstream of this challenging style.

1997 ★★★★★   *March 1998*
Bright green–yellow; the bouquet is clean with hints of honey and spice to the tropical fruit. A wonderful wine in the mouth, with viscosity which runs right through the sweet herb, lime, honey and spice flavours of the palate. Sensuous and precocious; like the '97 Gewurztraminer, strongly reminiscent of the best wines of Zind Humbrecht. (No botrytis; excellent vintage.)

classic wines

★★★★★ Perfect   ★★★★☆ Close to perfect   ★★★★ Very good   ★★★☆ Expected
★★★ Short of standard   ★★☆ Undeserving   ★★ Decayed relic   NR No rating

1996 Pinot Gris Selection ★★★★★   *March 1998*

Light green–yellow; the bouquet is fresh and clean, with gently spicy fruit, the palate powerful and strongly reminiscent of Alsace Vendage Tardive in structure. Only slightly sweet, but strongly structured, and quite certain to live for many years.

1995 ★★★★   *March 1998*

Medium yellow–straw, with the faintest hint of pink. The bouquet is quite intense, with a range of minerally tangy citrus fruits which seem to come through many of the wines, but is also ever so faintly sweaty. The palate is very powerful, intense and long, with a somewhat grippy finish. I really don't know whether these characters will resolve themselves with time, but I would be inclined to give the wine the chance. (Warm year yet low pH.)

1994 ★★★★★   *March 1998*

Medium green–yellow; a wonderfully smooth bouquet with spicy, slightly tropical and fully ripe fruit. The palate has near perfect balance, with that touch of viscosity of top Pinot Gris, and a Joseph's Coat of flavours including pear and musk. Will age superbly. (Cooler than average, but with a classic dry autumn.)

1993 ★★★★☆   *March 1998*

Light to medium yellow–green; that range of hard-to-define fruit aromas, predominantly in the dusty/herbal/mineral range. The crisp and youthful palate has a mix of citrussy, tangy and more herbal notes; also some lime. Botrytis? (A cold year.)

1992 ★★★☆   *March 1998*

Medium yellow–green; showing honeyed edges to the fruit along with bottle development. The palate seems to be heavily modified in terms of the varietal fruit flavour, and to lack the tightness of the best wines under this label. (Very low cropping level.)

1991 ★★★★   *March 1998*

Light to medium yellow–green; an extraordinarily youthful and crisp bouquet with a cross section of tangy herb, honey and mineral aromas. The palate has lots and lots of flavour, but is dominated by its sweetness, and I would have preferred a touch less residual sugar. (A coolish but almost perfect season.)

1987 ★★★   *March 1998*

Medium to full yellow–orange; the bouquet is showing signs of break-up, although mineral, herb and lime aromas are still there. The palate has similar flavour, but like the bouquet, is in decline. An interesting wine for a vertical tasting, and extremely rare. First crop. (Cool dry summer, dry ripening conditions.)

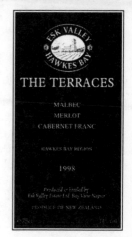

he terraces of Esk Valley are utterly different from any other New Zealand vineyard, looking more like vines one might encounter in the Douro Valley of Portugal or in some untamed part of Spain. They were carved out of the hillside behind the winery in 1950 or thereabouts by a skilled and brave bulldozer driver. The then-owner of Esk Valley, Robert Bird, planted the terraces to Albany Surprise, a decision which only makes sense in the context of that time. Even allowing for that, and notwithstanding the fact that the vines thrived, high labour costs led to their removal in 1959 and to the establishment of a pine plantation.

Thereafter the wheel turned full circle, the pines being removed and the terraces replanted with the four Bordeaux red varieties in 1988.

Grant Edmonds presided at Esk Valley from 1989 until 1993 before being appointed chief winemaker of the entire Villa Maria/Vidal/Esk Valley Wine Group. He was succeeded by Gordon Russell, who has nurtured the same passion for The Terraces as that of Grant Edmonds. Peter Saunders, the New Zealand wine writer, quotes Gordon Russell as describing The Terraces as 'a truly great wine; rain does not weary them.'

Rain may not do so, but the cool climate of Hawke's Bay and the particular characteristics of the site led to the removal of the cabernet sauvignon after the 1995 vintage. No Terraces was made in 1993, and Cabernet was excluded from the blend in 1992 and 1995 because it was not ripe, so it is not hard to see why the decision was taken. (Into the bargain, no Terraces was made in 1996 or 1997.)

The wines are made in wax-lined concrete fermenters and hand-plunged. As the detailed vintage notes indicate, the wines are typically aged in new French oak for between 22 and 24 months. They are egg-white-fined if necessary, but not filtered.

Gordon Russell comments: 'I find the malbec grown in this vineyard very distinctive for its black fruits and peppery notes, and it is nearly always our favourite cellar wine.' The Terraces is unlike any other New Zealand red wine, simply because of its sheer power, opulence and extract. Whether this makes it the best wine is another issue, and one which will very likely produce disagreement between any group of knowledgeable wine tasters. But even if it is not the best, it certainly ranks high among them. And the major lesson from the tasting is to be patient, and not consider approaching the wines when they are less than five years old. How long thereafter they will live is anyone's guess, but 20 years (like rain) should not weary them.

Background information (in brackets) supplied by Gordon Russell, Esk Valley.

First tasted in March 1998, updated, and later vintages added.

classic wines

★★★★★ Perfect	★★★★☆ Close to perfect	★★★★ Very good	★★★☆ Expected
★★★ Short of standard	★★☆ Undeserving	★★ Decayed relic	NR No rating

◄■ **1998** ★★★★★   *January 2000*

Medium to full purple–red; a very smooth and suave bouquet, concentrated but not flashy, is followed by a palate with rich, ripe, sweet and dense fruit balanced by wholly appropriate tannins. The ultimate iron fist in a velvet glove.

1997

Not made.

1996

Not made.

1995 ★★★★★   *March 1998*

Dense red–purple; a Leviathan on the bouquet, laden with luscious sweet blackberry and cassis fruit. The palate provides another truckload of the same, with massively dense fruit and lots of oak. Little or no subtlety now, but on the evidence of the prior vintages will come together with age, and could end up as an extraordinary benchmark. (40 per cent Merlot, 40 per cent Malbec, 20 per cent Cabernet Franc. Aged in 100 per cent new French oak barriques for 22 months. A very hot and dry year with picking completed in the last week of March before any rainfall. 250 cases produced.)

1994 ★★★★☆   *March 1998*

Strong red–purple; the bouquet shows some green canopy characters along with ripe fruit. The palate has some slightly minty/sappy characters evident, though not nearly as green as the bouquet might suggest. Perhaps these characters only show themselves because of the lusciously sweet character of the other wines in this tasting. (50 per cent Merlot, 25 per cent Malbec, 15 per cent Cabernet Franc, 10 per cent Cabernet Sauvignon. A dry but cool harvest resulted in a late vintage, but with the grapes in good condition. Slightly minty as are most of the 1994 Hawke's Bay reds. Opens up in the glass.)

1993

Not made.

1992 ★★★★★   *March 1998*

Medium to full red–purple; the bouquet is clean, pleasantly ripe and of medium intensity, with attractive sweet berry fruit and the first signs of secondary characters starting to appear. The palate is stylish and complex, with some Bordeaux characters; fine tannins to close. (40 per cent Merlot, 40 per cent Malbec, 20 per cent Cabernet Franc. A cool vintage, and the Cabernet Sauvignon did not achieve the required ripeness. The lightest of the line-up, with the Malbec showing through. Still needs time.)

1991 ★★★★★   *March 1998*

Full red–purple colour, outstanding for a wine of this maturity. The bouquet is quite luscious with sweet and ripe blackberry/cassis fruit pouring out of it. A lovely wine on the palate, sweet and round, almost fleshy; that blackberry/cassis fruit of the bouquet is there in abundance, and for once the tannins are soft and ripe. Well-integrated oak adds further lustre to the wine. (30 per cent Merlot, 30 per cent Cabernet Franc, 30 per cent Malbec and 10 per cent Cabernet Sauvignon. The first vintage from The Terraces; a great year for red wines, especially young vines. Aged for 24 months in new French barriques and not filtered.)

◄■ Not Ready   ➘ Still evolving   ▮ Prime of its life   ✔ Drink soon   ⬜ Missed the boat

goldwater estate 1983-1998

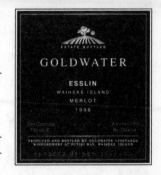

former engineer and fashion photographer Kim Goldwater and wife Jeanette were the first to plant vines on Waiheke Island when they commenced establishing their vineyard in 1978. The initial planting was of 4 hectares of the classic Bordeaux mix of cabernet sauvignon, merlot and a little cabernet franc.

The Goldwaters then proceeded to reverse the history of the prior 100 years by amalgamating small suburban-sized blocks to gradually extend the size of the 'home' vineyard to just under 10 hectares. (All of the land surrounding the Goldwater property had once been a large grazing property established by a Scottish family in the 1880s, with subsequent generations progressively selling ever smaller pieces to provide cash flow.) In 1995 they purchased what they describe as the most expensive new vineyard in the southern hemisphere, a 5-hectare block on the other side of the road, which has been planted to chardonnay.

It was the Mediterranean lifestyle which attracted the Goldwaters to the island, and to the idyllic setting looking out over the water of Putiki Bay. No one can fail to be charmed by the quietly spoken Goldwaters nor fail to be impressed by Jeanette's cooking, simple yet classical.

But I have to admit to having initially failed to properly appreciate the early vintages of Goldwater Estate. Between 1996 and 1998 I had a number of opportunities to reassess the wines, the most important being the vertical tasting in March 1998, although a visit to the winery in September 1997 had overwhelmed any previously held reservations.

I discussed this change in attitude with Bob Campbell MW, and found that he, too, had not been overwhelmed by those early wines. Yet we both agreed the older wines showed very well (and far better than we had expected) in the tasting. As for the younger wines: well, the tasting notes and the ratings will speak for themselves. This, quite simply, is one of the best producers of Bordeaux-style red wines in New Zealand.

The vintage notes (in brackets) were provided by Kim Goldwater after I had written up the tasting notes.

First tasted in March 1998, updated, and later vintages added.

◀ *1998 Esslin Merlot* ★★★★★   *May 2001*
Clear, medium red–purple; a fragrant and complex bouquet dances through a mix of cedary, savoury, leafy, olive and red berry aromatics, flowing into a light to medium-bodied palate, with sweetly savoury flavours, hints of olive, leaf and cedar, all showing good varietal character and structure. From one of the most successful vintages in New Zealand for the Bordeaux varieties.

classic wines

★★★★★ Perfect   ★★★★☆ Close to perfect   ★★★★ Very good   ★★★☆ Expected
★★★ Short of standard   ★★☆ Undeserving   ★★ Decayed relic   NR No rating

361

1997 Esslin Merlot ★★★★★   *March 1999*

Medium red–purple; the bouquet is wonderfully fragrant, with a mix of spicy oak and sweet cherry fruit. A glorious wine in the mouth, with soft, silky, supple fine tannins and what can only be described as sexy oak.

1996 Esslin Merlot ★★★★★   *March 1998*

Medium purple–red; the fragrant bouquet offers an exotic array of redcurrant, pepper, clove, plum and tobacco spice (almost snuff) aromas. The spotlessly clean palate is elegant almost to the point of delicacy, with red berry and plum fruit, the oak balanced and integrated, and nice acidity. A strangely restrained, albeit very good, landing after the wild ride of the bouquet. (First crop from specially selected clones of merlot.)

1995 Cabernet Merlot ★★★★★   *March 1998*

Medium purple–red; the fragrant bouquet offers a mix of cassis, olive and leaf aromas supported by subtle oak. A medium weight wine in the mouth, with clean, red berry fruit and the tannins just a little on the green side, hardly surprising given the vintage. (Great summer with a damp ending but fine wine.)

1994 Cabernet Merlot ★★★★★   *March 1998*

Medium to full red–purple; the bouquet is much more concentrated than that of the '95, with abundant black cherry, chocolate and a hint of game. A powerful wine with lots of authoritative tannins running through the length of the palate and for the time being slightly obscuring the dark berry fruit characters. A wine which needs time, although there is a slight question mark over the degree of extraction of those tannins. (Superb summer. Great concentration; small crop.)

1993 Cabernet Merlot ★★★★★   *March 1998*

Youthful and bright purple–red; the bouquet is redolent of fresh sweet red berry and redcurrant fruit with nicely balanced and integrated oak. The palate is powerful but particularly well balanced, with red berry fruit flavours surrounded by clearly defined tannins. Not as big or as rich as the '94, but arguably better balanced. (Fine but cool summer. Good crop, well ripened.)

1992 Cabernet Merlot ★★★★   *March 1998*

Medium red, without either purple or brown tinges. The aromas are fragrant and lifted, with quite sweet minty overtones to cedary/leafy characters underneath. A lighter style, reflecting the vintage, showing considerable development, albeit with quite attractive leafy, minty, cedary flavours. (Very cool year but very fine, giving increased herbal characters to the wine.)

1991 Cabernet Merlot ★★★★★   *March 1998*

The colour is slightly darker than the '92, solid red. The fragrant bouquet offers a multitude of aromas: cedar, earth, sap, mushroom and even hints of sweet chocolate and caramel. The substantial palate has those hallmark tannins of the riper vintages of Goldwater but with plenty of sweet berry fruit to plump up the mid-palate, and authoritative but well-balanced tannins on the finish. A class act. (Lovely vintage after a good year.)

◄ Not Ready   ╲ Still evolving   ▮ Prime of its life   ✐ Drink soon   ▯ Missed the boat

1990 Cabernet Merlot ★★★★★ March 1998

Medium to full red–purple; the bouquet is rich, with abundant dark berry, cassis and ripe plum fruit with just a touch of more briary/earthy character. A remarkably rich wine on the palate with considerable fruit weight; dark berry flavours and a touch of bitter chocolate run right through the well-balanced finish. Should hold for years. (Lovely wine from a good year. Wine showing great structure as vines start to mature.)

1990 Merlot Cabernet Franc ★★★★ March 1998

Medium red; the Merlot certainly dominates the sappy, leafy bouquet which is now well into the secondary phase of its development. Considerably less weight than the Cabernet-dominant wine of the same vintage, but does have attractive and elegant cedar, leaf and mint flavours. The tannins are well under control. (Experimental wine which I think worked well. Forerunner to the Esslin Merlot.)

1989 Cabernet Merlot ★★★★☆ March 1998

Light to medium red; the bouquet, while fairly light, is very fragrant with a mix of sweet berry fruits and touches of tobacco. The palate exhibits sweet, almost Italianate, flavours, gently ripe but with tinges of more sappy characters. An interesting wine at its peak, but not for long holding. (Twenty-nine consecutive days of rain in January, but what a lovely wine. Who cares about the weather.)

1988 Cabernet Merlot ★★★★ March 1998

Medium red; the bouquet is clean, quite firm and with some slightly green sappy aromas. The palate, too, has a certain degree of fruit austerity, and indeed a touch of astringency. All in all, a remarkable wine for a very difficult vintage. (A summer which looked like it was going to be as good as 1987, but then came Cyclone Bola.)

1987 Cabernet Merlot ★★★★☆ March 1998

Medium to full red; the bouquet is quite rich and sweet, with a mix of earthy and more plummy fruit, and touches of cedar. Overall, holding very well. The palate is every bit as rich and complex as the bouquet suggests, with sweet plum and blackberry fruit on entry, followed by formidable tannins on the mid to back palate. (The most perfect summer of all time; I wish we could have a few more like it. Biggest and best crop ever.)

1985 Cabernet Merlot/Franc ★★★★☆ March 1998

Medium purple–red; the bouquet is quite fragrant, with some lift, and holding its fruit well, like an old Bordeaux. Those characters are, if anything, even more pronounced on the palate, with lots of cedar and tobacco, but the sweet fruit is starting to drop out of the mid-palate. (First significant Bordeaux blend.)

1985 Cabernet Sauvignon ★★★★ March 1998

Medium red; the aromas are predominantly in the cedary/tobacco leaf spectrum, but there is a thin skein of sweetness still running through it. The palate has earthy characters, and also some of the Italianate notes of the '89. The acid is a little sharp on the finish. (Not enough Merlot and Cabernet Franc, so some Cabernet Sauvignon was kept separate.)

classic wines

★★★★★ Perfect   ★★★★☆ Close to perfect   ★★★★ Very good   ★★★☆ Expected
★★★ Short of standard   ★★☆ Undeserving   ★★ Decayed relic   NR No rating

363

1984 Cabernet Sauvignon ★★★☆   *March 1998*
Medium red; the aromas are leafy and herbal, with gamey overtones, yet miraculously holding together. The palate is a replay of the bouquet, distinctly green and fairly acidic, yet not decayed. The bad news is that the wine won't go anywhere much from here. (Influenced by the youth of the vines.)

1983 Cabernet Sauvignon ★★★★   *March 1998*
Medium red; the bouquet is not rich, but nonetheless surprisingly youthful, with aromas of slightly squashy berry fruit and cedar. The age is also apparent on the palate, with the tannins poking through to a degree, but still retaining some sweet fruit on the mid-palate, and by no means a shell. (A very cool, dry summer responsible for some herbal characters.)

kumeu river chardonnay

1985-2000

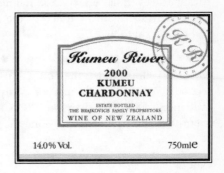

michael Brajkovich (New Zealand's first Master of Wine) studied oenology and obtained his degree at Roseworthy College (now part of Adelaide University) in Australia. He makes no bones about the fact he wished he had studied in France, for he believes the philosophies and practices there have far more relevance for grape growing and winemaking in New Zealand than do those of Australia. Vintages working within the Moueix Group (Chateau Petrus, etc.) have further refined and developed the Brajkovich approach to winemaking.

He puts it this way: 'There is very little point in reinventing the wheel when it comes to making wine, and the techniques that have successfully produced quality wines for hundreds of years in the superior wine regions of France will still perform the same today in our environment. Of course, our understanding of how this occurs is now much better than before and we are technologically better equipped to avoid the problems of the past.'

In practical terms this means reliance upon natural yeasts for both the primary and secondary fermentation; whole-bunch pressing; rough settling before transfer to barrel; and barrel fermentation at ambient temperatures, nominally no more than 20 degrees Celsius but often briefly peaking at 24 to 25 degrees Celsius.

Naturally enough, lees contact and stirring follows, during which time the malolactic fermentation takes place. The wines are kept in oak for nine months, and are then stability-fined and cold-stabilised before being bottled.

Michael Brajkovich is no stranger to controversy. In his opinion, the Chardonnays have often been misunderstood and misjudged, and it is perfectly certain this is true. However, this is par for the course when you march to the beat of such a different drum.

The second leg of controversy comes from the region itself. The Auckland area is very demanding, with the warm, humid and not infrequently wet summers making it almost impossible to keep some degree of botrytis out of the vineyard. Many keen judges have wondered how good the wines would be if the grapes were grown in Hawke's Bay or Martinborough. I believe he remains the captive of the vintage, but when it is on his side, great New Zealand Chardonnays are the result.

Vintage notes (in brackets) provided by Michael Brajkovich.

First tasted in March 1998, updated, and later vintages added.

classic wines

★★★★★ Perfect ★★★★☆ Close to perfect ★★★★ Very good ★★★☆ Expected
★★★ Short of standard ★★☆ Undeserving ★★ Decayed relic NR No rating

2000 Matés Vineyard ★★★★★   *April 2001*

Medium yellow–green; a powerful and complex bouquet, with no particular fruit aroma dominant, but rather a web of influences and winemaking philosophy. The palate, however, has unexpected richness and luscious mouthfeel, with sweet melon and stonefruit flavours, a touch of the cashew and oatmeal which one does expect, and typical subtle oak.

1999 Matés Vineyard ★★★★   *April 2001*

Medium yellow–green; the bouquet is in the mainstream Kumeu style, with subtle, secondary aromas with mix of nutty/cashew, oak and malolactic-fermentation influences. Less rich than the 2000, with some minerally notes shortening the mouthfeel and flavour, not, as one might expect, lengthening it.

1998

Not tasted.

1997 ★★★★★   *March 1998*

Light to medium yellow–green; the bouquet, like that of the '96, is discreet and elegant, with tight mineral and citrus notes. The palate is lovely, with tight citrus, melon and mineral flavours with hints of cashew and oatmeal from the malolactic fermentation. Long finish; as always, subtle oak.

1996 ★★★★★   *March 1998*

Light to medium yellow–green, a complete contrast to the '95. The bouquet is fine and discreet, with attractive mineral and citrus aromas. The palate, too, is elegant, fine and long with hazelnut malolactic characters and lingering citrus and melon fruit. Should age well, and is a fine wine by any standards.

1995 ★★★☆   *March 1998*

Medium yellow–straw, much darker than the younger vintages. Botrytis influence is quite evident in the mandarin and cumquat aromas; a touch of burnt match into the bargain. The palate initially shows complexity, but is somewhat weak in the middle, and it is probable the wine won't age well.

  (Rain during harvest; a difficult vintage.)

1994 ★★★☆   *March 1998*

Medium to full yellow–straw; a soft bouquet with some vanilla notes along with a gentle solids underlay; hints of botrytis. A pleasant, easy-drinking style with nice balance and length, though not particularly intense.

1993 ★★★★☆   *March 1998*

Medium to full yellow–green; a wine with lots of fruit on the bouquet in the overall context of the Kumeu River style, and the usual complexity. An excellent palate, with good fruit intensity and length; sweet citrus and stone fruit flavours should sustain the wine for years to come. (The product of an excellent vintage in the Auckland area.)

◄■ Not Ready   ＼ Still evolving   ❙ Prime of its life   ✎ Drink soon   ⎵ Missed the boat

1992 ★★☆   *March 1998*

Medium yellow–orange; there are truly strange aromas, with piercing, spicy/dusty/metal characters. The palate is quite sharp, with stinging nettle character, suggesting a degree of volatile acidity. (A year of incredibly low yields, and wines with great concentration of flavour. Probably a bad bottle tasted.)

1991 ★★★★★   *March 1998*

The bright yellow–green colour is an early sign that all is well with this wine. The bouquet is complex, stylish and complete, with gently Burgundian overtones. The palate is an exercise in unforced elegance, complex yet not front-end loaded; as ever with these wines, minimal oak input. (A standout vintage notwithstanding that the spring and flowering were both late, resulting in a later than usual harvest. Fine weather leading up to picking produced grapes in excellent condition and a ripeness level approaching that of the 1989 vintage.)

1990 ★★☆   *March 1998*

Full yellow–orange; the bouquet shrieks of botrytis with a mix of cumquat, mandarin and slightly spiky nettle fruit, and the palate overgrown with botrytis.(A light vintage without the power of some others; to drink now.)

1989 ★★★   *March 1998*

Medium to full yellow–orange; the bouquet is quite complex and rich, but with botrytis evident and somewhat phenolic. The palate does have flavour, with the typical complexity of Kumeu River; the flavours are of peach, mandarin and cumquat. (One of the earliest and best vintages we have seen, with a lower than normal crop level. Nonetheless, starting to fade.)

1987 ★★☆   *March 1998*

Medium to full yellow–orange; the bouquet shows distinct break-up characters, yet has complexity, with a mix of mineral and mandarin aromas. Regrettably, that is where the wine stops, with the acidity (which, contrary to commonly held beliefs, remains constant) now dominant. (A warm growing season, with the vineyards coming into full production. The grapes were picked very ripe, with botrytis present.)

1986 ★★★☆   *March 1998*

Full yellow–orange; the strikingly complex bouquet is at the far extreme of the solidsy wet dog aromas of traditional White Burgundy. The palate has masses of flavour, and delivers precisely that which the bouquet promises in an extreme Burgundian style, coupled with raw, splintery oak. (The vintage conditions were extremely good, but the wine has always been spoilt by resinous oak.)

classic wines

★★★★★ Perfect   ★★★★☆ Close to perfect   ★★★★ Very good   ★★★☆ Expected
★★★ Short of standard   ★★☆ Undeserving   ★★ Decayed relic   NR No rating

martinborough pinot noir
1985-1998

a vertical tasting of every vintage made between 1985 and 1996 — including the Reserves of 1991, 1994 and 1996 — in Auckland in March 1998 emphasised a number of things. First, by the standards of Pinot Noir, these are relatively long-lived wines. Second, although Larry McKenna had constantly refined his methods of making Pinot Noir, the terroir of Wairarapa comes through with clarion clarity, unifying the wines to a remarkable degree.

Thirdly, and contrarily, vintage conditions do impose their mark. The best vintages are the warmer, drier ones: here an extra dimension of sweet fruit comes through on the mid-palate, softening that almost intellectual rigour of the overall style.

Finally, in creating the Reserve bottling, McKenna has exercised the same restraint and integrity which marks everything else he does. These are distinctly superior wines, yet the style is not so different from the mainstream Martinborough Pinot Noirs: they are not loaded up with oak, nor forced to be something they are not.

In a final testament to Larry McKenna's skill and integrity, the creation of the Reserve wine has not robbed the standard wine of the relevant vintage of its character or quality. Time will tell whether his shoes will prove too big to fill in the wake of his departure from Martinborough Vineyards in 1999.

(Notes in brackets are by Larry McKenna.)

First tasted in March 1998, updated, and later vintages added.

1998 Reserve ★★★★★   *February 2001*
Medium to full red–purple; the bouquet has, as one would expect, very ripe plum and spice fruit, which stops well short of being overripe or pruney, and a positive but not excessive hint of smoky oak. Again as one would expect, the wine has a full mid-palate, with excellent texture and balance, finishing with soft, ripe tannins.

1996 Reserve ★★★★★   *March 1998*
Medium purple–red; the bouquet is quite sweet (in the context of the Martinborough style) with cherry and plum fruit supported by subtle oak. The palate is silky and long in the mouth with red cherry and plum fruit supported by fine, soft tannins. (All ten bar five clone. Great year — very long stable harvest period. Yet to be released. Same aims and approach as '91 and '94.)

1996 ★★★★   *March 1998*
Medium purple–red; yet another replay of so many wines in the tasting, stylish and running across the earthy/foresty/stemmy spectrum. The palate is lighter than one would expect from the '96 vintage, but has appealing cherry/berry fruit in an unforced style. As ever, subtle oak. (Great year, warm and clean. Extended use of natural ferment and cold soak. Some whole-bunch ferment.)

◄ Not Ready   ＼ Still evolving   ▮ Prime of its life   ◢ Drink soon   ▯ Missed the boat

1995 ★★★★☆ *March 1998*

Attractive red–purple colour of medium depth. The bouquet is not particularly intense, but is clean, with a nice amalgam of red fruits and more foresty characters. The palate unexpectedly shows more sweet fruit than the '96, with plum and red berry flavours. The tannins are evident, but by no means excessive, providing great structure. (Heavy selection of fruit to avoid botrytis. Warm summer. Because of year quite straightforward winemaking, wine sterile filtered because malolactic fermentation not quite finished.)

1994 Reserve ★★★★★ *March 1998*

Medium purple–red; the bouquet is complex, and distinctly richer and bigger than the varietal release of the same year. The palate is outstanding, silky, long and lingering, with the almost piercing linear flavour expanding into the peacock's tail on the finish. (UCD13. Great year. Very well-received wine, winner of six trophies in Australia and the UK. Same approach and goals as the '91.)

1994 ★★★★☆ *March 1998*

Light to medium red; yet more of the same on the bouquet, distinctly earthy, with foresty/gamey overtones. The palate is light but stylish, a cross between the Pinot Noirs of Bass Phillip and lighter Burgundies. A deceptive wine, for it has length and will particularly appeal to those who are prepared to accept the tomato vine characters. (Very good summer — not hot but very clean fruit. Some whole bunch used, large macerations. Introduction of large-scale natural/native ferment and started experiments with cold soaking.)

1993 ★★★★ *March 1998*

Near identical colour to the older wines in the line-up. A light yet stylish bouquet with pleasant forest floor characters. The palate is tangy, almost citrussy, yet the flavours are of authentic Pinot Noir. Not lush, and similar to the '88. (Very cool year, 980 degree days; somewhat herbaceous introduction of UCD6 and 13. No whole bunch but long vat times.)

1992 ★★★★☆ *March 1998*

Medium red, again with that slightly brick tinge. The bouquet is strongly earthy, with potent forest and briar overtones, very much in the heartland of the Martinborough style. The palate is certainly at the green end of the spectrum, with earth, forest, briar and mushroom characters, yet they all come together. (Very cool year, 930 degree days — 1100 is normal, so somewhat herbaceous in my opinion. Introduction of clone UCD5. No whole bunch but long post maceration.)

1991 Reserve ★★★★★ *March 1998*

A near-identical colour to the standard release. The bouquet is, of course, lighter than the '94 or '96 Reserve, but is complex, with a mix of gamey/foresty and plummy fruit. The palate is very Burgundian indeed, with forest floor, cedar and spice flavours. Like the standard release of the same year, better drunk sooner rather than later, but it is impossible to say it is over the hill. (Single clone. First wine to be 18 months in oak. Looked for greater structure and power. Start of approaches which gave more tannin and backbone to the wine.)

classic wines

★★★★★ Perfect ★★★★☆ Close to perfect ★★★★ Very good ★★★☆ Expected
★★★ Short of standard ★★☆ Undeserving ★★ Decayed relic NR No rating

369

1991 ★★★★★   *March 1998*

Medium red, with a hint of tawny on the rim. The bouquet is riper and sweeter than any of the older wines with distinctly Burgundian plummy/gamey characters and a hint of volatility. The palate is complex and soft, probably reaching the end of the plateau of its best form, but still on it. Interestingly, does not show any weakness as a consequence of the making of the first Reserve wine in this vintage. (Great summer, marred by rain during harvest — 100 mm in three days. Ferments and malolactic fermentation very slow. Very complex — and controversial — wine, mainly due to poor nutrient status of juice.)

1990 ★★★★   *March 1998*

Light to medium red; the bouquet is very light, having moved entirely into pencilly/earthy/foresty/charry secondary characters. Yet the palate, like the '94, is much better than the bouquet suggests, still holding fruit, with both intensity and length. (Cooler year, small crop, single clone, started experiments with whole-bunch fermentation and extended post maceration. Stopped sterile filtration of reds.)

1989 ★★★★★   *March 1998*

The colour is strong, dark red and with some gas on the rim. Has a mix of foresty, plummy and briary fruit; in the mouth, a powerful wine still well in its prime with a complex mix of sweet plum and forest flavours. (Great year — better than '88. Longer vat times than '88. Wine was somewhat under-oaked due to larger than expected crop. Always one of my favourites.)

1988 ★★★★   *March 1998*

Light to medium red; the bouquet is certainly light, but does have stylish sappy/foresty aromas. The palate is similar, and fairly and squarely in the Martinborough Vineyards style. Aged, yet still holding, although one wonders for how long. (Great year — very warm. Picked over a long period so some fruit was very ripe. Single clone plus simple winemaking techniques. Short vat times.)

1986 ★★★★☆   *March 1998*

Light to medium red; the fragrant bouquet exhibits a range of secondary pinot characters running through foresty, pencilly and earthy notes. The palate, however, offers unexpectedly sweet plummy fruit with hints of vanilla. A wine which came up and up in the glass as it breathed. A particularly impressive achievement. (Larry McKenna's first wine. Good vintage, very straightforward winemaking and viticultural techniques; one clone only.)

1985 ★★★☆   *March 1998*

The colour is extraordinary, youthful red–purple, seemingly impossible for Pinot Noir of this age. The bouquet shows a mix of earthy, sappy and stemmy characters with a certain degree of volatile sharpness. A strange wine on the palate, with an utterly different feel and character from all of the others in the tasting. You have to wonder whether this is 100 per cent Pinot Noir or whether a percentage of strongly coloured hybrid was added. (No comments from Larry McKenna; the wine predated his arrival at the winery.)

Not Ready   Still evolving   Prime of its life   Drink soon   Missed the boat

neudorf moutere chardonnay

It was, to put it mildly, fascinating to read the vintage notes supplied by Tim Finn, and to compare those with the tasting notes. In almost every instance you can see the vintage and winemaker influences coming through loud and clear in the wine in the glass.

My personal experience with the Neudorf Chardonnay dates back to the 1989 vintage, which — more or less coincidentally — was the oldest vintage in this tasting. There were preceding Chardonnay vintages (Neudorf's first was in 1981) but they were not considered relevant any more. The 1989 vintage caused a minor sensation at the 1991 Sydney International Wine Competition. Through some quirk, it ended up in the medium-bodied white wine class, and collected a number of trophies. Tim Finn made the journey across the Tasman partly to collect his trophies, but also curious to know what the full-bodied Chardonnays in the competition looked like. Well, of course, there weren't any wines bigger or richer than the Neudorf; it had simply found its way into the wrong class, something I have to admit partial responsibility for, as I was chairman of the show in question.

Not a great deal needs to be said about the winemaking techniques employed, for these are reflected in the individual comments for each vintage, and as the notes for the '96 disclose, Tim Finn is still seeking ways and means to refine and improve the style, as every good New World winemaker should be doing. It would be extremely unkind of me to comment, but I think 65 cases too many were made in 1995, but that is a small complaint in the grand scheme of things.

A high level of viticultural expertise and attention to detail is matched by equal zeal in the winery to produce Chardonnays which are very distinctive, but at the same time have universal appeal.

Vintage notes (in brackets) are by Tim Finn, winemaker at Neudorf. All except '98 and '99 were tasted in March 1998.

First tasted in March 1998, updated, and later vintages added.

1999 ★★★★★   *February 2001*
Light to medium yellow–green; the bouquet is more intense than the Nelson Chardonnay with citrus-edged melon fruit. The palate is substantial, yet has finesse, with cashew, fig and melon woven through spicy French oak.

classic wines

★★★★★ Perfect   ★★★★☆ Close to perfect   ★★★★ Very good   ★★★☆ Expected
★★★ Short of standard   ★★☆ Undeserving   ★★ Decayed relic   NR No rating

371

1998 ★★★★☆   *January 2000*

Medium to full yellow–green; an exceedingly complex bouquet with obvious barrel-ferment and malolactic-ferment inputs is followed by an explosion of flavour on the palate with a mix of tropical/figgy fruit, butterscotch and spicy oak.

1996 ★★★★★   *March 1998*

Medium yellow–green; there are quite lovely nectarine fruit aromas, delicate yet intense, and that hallmark subtle oak. The palate combines elegance and power, more towards Chablis than the usual Montrachet mould of the best Neudorfs. The palate is perfectly balanced, with long, fine almost silky nectarine and citrus flavours. (Picked at lower potential alcohol and taken through 100 per cent malolactic fermentation to explore less racy, more elegant style. Good conditions.)

1995 ★★☆   *March 1998*

The poor, orange colour tells you all you need to know. The bouquet is maderised and the palate completely perverted by massive botrytis. On the track to nowhere. (Good summer, wet vintage. Continued selective picking against botrytis resulted in only 65 cases produced.)

1994 ★★★★★   *March 1998*

Medium yellow–green; the bouquet oozes character and style, substantial grip and Burgundian overtones. The palate is as intense and as complex as the bouquet suggests, with citrus/grapefruit flavours, subtle oak and appropriate acidity. (Warm summer, powerful wine. Launch of Village Chardonnay label (later Nelson) to enable barrel selection for Moutere Chardonnay label.)

1993 ★★★★☆   *March 1998*

Medium to full yellow–green; a wine which, both on the bouquet and the palate, has pleasing complexity. The bouquet is reticent, but you can see the power is there, and the palate has a structured complexity with pleasing nutty characters, yet seems to envelope the fruit. (Cool spring, warm autumn. First use of Clone 2/23 — more 'fruity' less alcohol and acid — is minor part of blend.)

1992 ★★★★   *March 1998*

Medium yellow–green; from start to finish, a wine which has lots of character but is rather confrontational, and not particularly friendly. The bouquet is minerally, with pronounced solids fermentation characters and a hint of matchbox/burnt match. In the mouth, very intense with minerally/dusty overtones to the fruit, finishing with pronounced acidity and grip. Very French, albeit in austere mode. (Very cool summer, Mt Pinatubo erupts; low yield help.)

1991 ★★★★★   *March 1998*

Medium yellow–green; the powerful yet smooth bouquet has it all: ripe nectarine fruit and toasty/nutty malolactic and barrel-ferment characters, yet not overtly oaky. The palate is utterly delicious, with lovely silky nectarine and white peach fruit. Youthful, perfectly balanced and harmonious; shades of Montrachet. (Good conditions, low yield, high acid, very tight wine.)

1990 ★★★   *March 1998*

Medium to full yellow–orange; the strongly botrytised and aromatic bouquet has aromas of mandarin and cumquat, and while the palate does have flavour, is warped by botrytis and past its best. (Good conditions, higher crop.)

1989 ★★★   *March 1998*

Medium to full yellow–orange; the bouquet has ripe mandarin and peach fruit with a substrate of mineral, but the palate is largely gone, with the last embers of sweet fruit and a phenolic finish. Once a great wine, now long past its best. (Good year — some botrytis, first year of whole bunch press.)

stonyridge larose cabernets

Without having had (nor ever being likely to have) the opportunity to do extensive combined vertical/horizontal tastings of (say) the five most recent vintages of New Zealand's best red wines, it is hard to be dogmatic, but unless and until that opportunity arises, I cannot go past the Stonyridge as New Zealand's foremost producer of Cabernet-based wines. What is more, they are unquestionably among the great Bordeaux-blend styles of the world, and will maintain that position so long as Stephen White continues to own and run Stonyridge Vineyard in the way he does today. When you consider that only 14 vintages have been produced, this is an extraordinary achievement, but then Stephen White is no ordinary man, and even less is the vineyard an ordinary vineyard.

It is planted at a density of 1 metre by 2.2 metres, with over 4500 vines per hectare, and the trellis is only half a metre high, pruned using the Double Guyot technique. The average yield per vine is between 1.2 and 1.5 kilograms, which translates to around 5–6 tonnes per hectare (2 tonnes per acre). Planting began in 1982 on the poor but well-drained north-facing slopes, and by 1998 12.5 hectares were under vine, with a further 1 acre per year planned, taking the vineyard to its ultimate total capacity of a little under 20 acres.

Olive trees and lavender are also grown, the inspiration for the latter coming from a vintage in the south of France with Mas de Daumas Gassac with founder Aime Guibert. Stephen White is nothing if not eclectic, because before starting Stonyridge he had worked in Tuscany, California and Bordeaux (at Chateaux d'Angludet and Palmer, owned by the late Peter Sichel). His technical grounding for grape growing comes from his Diploma of Horticulture from Lincoln College, Christchurch, while his winemaking expertise has — obviously enough — come from practical experience in many parts of the world.

He is an odd contrast: a night owl who lives in the fast lane, yet one who exercises iron discipline and an almost unbelievable attention to detail when it comes to the vineyard and winery. Thus not only is every bottle of Larose individually numbered, but Stephen White knows exactly who purchased each bottle — with a limit of six bottles per customer. Woe betide the purchaser who succumbs to the lure of reselling the wine to take the undoubted profit he or she would obtain from the auction system (notwithstanding that the wine sells for over $50 en primeur and $85 at the winery restaurant) because that purchaser's name will be forever stricken from the record.

In 1995 and 1997 only 500 cases were made, and in 1996, 800 cases. Even with the increased plantings, Stonyridge Larose is going to remain as scarce as it is marvellous.

(Vintage notes in brackets up to 1996 are from Stephen White, winemaker at Stonyridge.)

First tasted in March 1998, updated, and later vintages added.

◄ Not Ready ＼ Still evolving ▮ Prime of its life ◢ Drink soon ▯ Missed the boat

◄■ **1999 ★★★★★**　　　　　　　　　　　　　　　　　　　*April 2001*

Medium to full red–purple; intense, deep, dark fruits in a blackberry/blueberry spectrum are supported by subtle oak. Eerily similar to the power and length of the 1997 and 1998 wines, notwithstanding a much lower percentage of Cabernet Sauvignon. A wine that is all about structure and length, reflecting the Bordeaux attitude that, if you get this right, everything else will follow. 51 per cent Cabernet Sauvignon, 29 per cent Merlot, 10 per cent Malbec, 8 per cent Cabernet Franc, 2 per cent Petit Verdot.

1998 ★★★★☆　　　　　　　　　　　　　　　　　　　*April 2001*

Medium purple–red; complex, dark berry/blackberry/cassis/spice and a touch of cedar on the bouquet promise more fruit than the palate actually delivers, although it has that Stonyridge hallmark length and structure, sustained by powerful tannins. Runs counter to the general perception of 1998 as a great red wine vintage; 12.2 degrees alcohol tells part of the tale. 72 per cent Cabernet Sauvignon, 14 per cent Merlot, 7 per cent Cabernet Franc, 5 per cent Malbec, 2 per cent Petit Verdot.

1997 ★★★★☆　　　　　　　　　　　　　　　　　　　*April 2001*

Medium red–purple; an aromatic bouquet with a mix of cedar, bramble and blackberry leads into a palate with exceptional structure, and above all else, length, with fine-grained tannins running through the savoury fruit from start to finish. 66 cent Cabernet Sauvignon, 20 per cent Merlot, 7 per cent Malbec, 6 per cent Cabernet Franc, 2 per cent Petit Verdot.

1996 ★★★★★　　　　　　　　　　　　　　　　　　　*March 1998*

Medium to full red–purple; lusciously sweet blackcurrant and cassis aromas flood the bouquet, carrying on seamlessly to the wonderfully concentrated palate. Here cassis, blackberry, chocolate, herb and lavender flavours intermingle joyously. 66 per cent Cabernet Sauvignon, 17 per cent Merlot, 10 per cent Malbec, 6 per cent Cabernet Franc, 1 per cent Petit Verdot. (A classic, problem-free vintage.)

1995 ★★★★★　　　　　　　　　　　　　　　　　　　*March 1998*

Medium to full purple–red; the bouquet is clean and sweet with red and blackcurrant fruit aromas. While less opulent than either the '96 or the '94, the palate has exceptional length and structure, and really is an extraordinary outcome for a vintage with as many problems as '95. 60 per cent Cabernet Sauvignon, 15 per cent Merlot, 18 per cent Malbec, 1 per cent Petit Verdot. (Beautifully dominated by Malbec which was picked before the rains came. Fastidious hand-picking selection at harvest and declassification of 30 per cent of crop.)

1994 ★★★★★　　　　　　　　　　　　　　　　　　　*March 1998*

Medium to full red–purple; the bouquet is exceptionally rich with concentrated, cassis and currant fruit woven through evident but high-quality oak. The palate is a glorious celebration of ripe, concentrated blackberry/cassis cabernet fruit, replete with fine tannins. Really needs another star to do it justice (or a Parker 100 points). 60 per cent Cabernet Sauvignon, 30 per cent Merlot, 4 per cent Malbec, 5 per cent Cabernet Franc, 1 per cent Petit Verdot. (Ripest and earliest harvested wine ever at Stonyridge. Extremely small crop.)

classic wines

★★★★★ Perfect　　★★★★☆ Close to perfect　　★★★★ Very good　　★★★☆ Expected
★★★ Short of standard　　★★☆ Undeserving　　★★ Decayed relic　　NR No rating

1993 ★★★★★ *March 1998*

Strong, full red–purple. The bouquet is clean and powerful with predominantly cassis and berry fruit; a faint whisper of sweet earth underneath. The palate has abundant ripe, sweet fruit with those cassis and dark berry flavours. The tannins are slightly abrasive in comparison with the younger vintages, but should settle down with time. 57 per cent Cabernet Sauvignon, 27 per cent Merlot, 7 per cent Cabernet Franc, 8 per cent Malbec, 1 per cent Petit Verdot. (Hot dry summer, normal crop. First New Zealand wine with Petit Verdot in it.)

1991 ★★★★★ *March 1998*

A distinct colour change into medium red–purple. On the other side, marks the transition point on the bouquet which is lighter and less intense than the younger wines, and shows secondary earthy characters coming up. The palate is elegant and beautifully balanced with fine, sweet cedar flavours and soft, lingering tannins on the finish. Unequivocally at its peak. 74 per cent Cabernet Sauvignon, 17 per cent Merlot, 5 per cent Cabernet Franc and 4 per cent Malbec. (A near-perfect vintage, with many lovely wines made.)

1990 ★★★★☆ *March 1998*

Medium red, with just a touch of purple. The bouquet opens with secondary aromas of earth and cedar, but flows into lingering blackberry. The palate is lively and long, predominantly with cedar and earth flavours and appropriately balanced tannin and acidity. There is just a whisper of slightly green/herbal notes to the fruit. 75 per cent Cabernet Sauvignon, 18 per cent Merlot, 5 per cent Cabernet Franc, 2 per cent Malbec. (Tight powerful pencil lead and cedar Cabernet wine.)

1989 ★★★★★ *March 1998*

Medium purple–red; the bouquet is quite aromatic, with sappy, leafy notes which assume a distinctly sweeter, although sappy, profile on the palate. Elegant but quite mature. 74 per cent Cabernet Sauvignon, 21 per cent Merlot, 3 per cent Cabernet Franc, 2 per cent Malbec. (High alcohol, high pH wine, almost too open.)

1988 ★★★★ *March 1998*

Medium red; the bouquet is clean and of medium intensity, but has developed well into secondary earthy characters. Tannins are starting to grip on the palate as the fruit is starting to fade, with some green, earthy astringency. 87 per cent Cabernet Sauvignon, 7 per cent Merlot and 6 per cent Cabernet Franc. (Cyclone Bola at the end of a good summer. Most of the Merlot and all Malbec declassified.)

1987 NR *March 1998*

Tragically, the bottle was severely corked, but one could see the powerful fruit and structure under the cork taint. For the record, a blend of 79 per cent Cabernet, 15 per cent Merlot, 4 per cent Cabernet Franc and 2 per cent Malbec. (Great summer that did no wrong on a good crop.)

➤ Not Ready   ↘ Still evolving   ▮ Prime of its life   ↗ Drink soon   ▯ Missed the boat

te mata awatea 1982-1999

a watea may yield slightly to Coleraine in terms of price and reputation, but it has an even more distinguished lineage. In 1980 John Buck made a straight Cabernet Sauvignon from a small block of old cabernet on a property he had acquired the previous year. It yielded only 3 or 4 tonnes, and resulted in the 1980 Te Mata Cabernet Sauvignon which won the trophy for the best red at the 1981 National Wine Competition. The following vintage of 1981 won the same trophy at the 1982 Competition, and the reputation of Te Mata was made overnight.

The year 1982 marked the first vintage labelled Awatea; like its precursors, it was made from 100 per cent Cabernet Sauvignon. It, too, was entered in the National Wine Show in 1983, but with a far less happy outcome: it was downgraded from gold to silver medal status because it had too much colour! For this and other reasons Te Mata forthwith ceased entering wine shows, a policy followed to this day.

The 1983 vintage was also made from 100 per cent Cabernet Sauvignon; like the '82, it was and is a marvellous wine. Planting had begun in 1991 on other portions of the Awatea property, and following the 1993 vintage the old, virus-diseased cabernet sauvignon block was removed. Another year was to pass before Awatea was made again (in 1985) this time as a Cabernet Merlot blend (79 per cent/21 per cent).

Since 1989 it, like Coleraine, has ceased to be vineyard-linked, giving John Buck and winemaker Peter Cowley greater scope for refining and defining the style. It is intended to be more immediately appealing in its youth than Coleraine, more fragrant and fruity. The palate is softer and sweeter, with more pronounced ripe berry fruit flavours.

(Vintage notes in brackets from Te Mata.)

First tasted in July 1999, updated, and later vintages added.

1999 ★★★★☆   *April 2001*
Medium purple–red; sweet, spicy cassis/blackberry/plum fruit on the bouquet precedes a palate with abundant character and complexity. Here juicy berry fruit is surrounded by more savoury/spicy characters, and the oak seems far better integrated and balanced than the Coleraine. (Significantly cooler than 1998; as ever, strict discipline in the vineyard was the key to success.)

1998 ★★★★★   *June 2000*
Medium to full red–purple; clean, perfectly ripened red berry fruit intermingles with subtle, cedary/spicy oak. The palate opens with ripe plum, redcurrant and blackberry fruit; what is really surprising is the strength and length of the tannins, which are soft and ripe. (A drought season following a wet winter necessitating extremely careful vineyard management. Those who kept canopies intact and who bunch-thinned achieved outstanding results.)

★★★★★ Perfect   ★★★★☆ Close to perfect   ★★★★ Very good   ★★★☆ Expected
★★★ Short of standard   ★★☆ Undeserving   ★★ Decayed relic   NR No rating

classic wines

1997 ★★★★★   *July 1999*

Excellent bright light to medium red–purple; the bouquet offers masses of sweet blackberry, blackcurrant plum in a silky web. A delicious, perfectly balanced palate; quite intense and ripe cassis/berry fruit finishes with soft tannins. 59 per cent Cabernet Sauvignon, 28 per cent Merlot, 13 per cent Cabernet Franc. (A mixed year, requiring bunch-thinning of an already small crop, with a warm and humid February and March. Another Indian summer produced small crops of high quality.)

1996 ★★★☆   *July 1999*

Light but bright red–purple; herbaceous, gently earthy fruit, albeit with some red berry, lacks the richness and finesse of the best wines. A lighter style which will develop quickly, and already possibly offering as much as it ever will. 55 per cent Cabernet Sauvignon, 29 per cent Merlot, 16 per cent Cabernet Franc. (The growing season in vintage 1996 was a mixture with above-average rainfall and below-average heat.) Te Mata regards the wines as aromatic, soft and appealing, forward and accessible in style, reminiscent of the 1990 vintage. I concur.

1995 ★★★★☆   *July 1999*

Bright and fresh purple–red. There is very attractive fruit on the bouquet offering a mix of redcurrant, blackcurrant and plum, reminiscent of the '91 vintage. The palate is powerful, and still a little distracting. There is a slight element of doubt as to whether the tannins will soften before the fruit disappears. 55 per cent Cabernet Sauvignon, 35 per cent Merlot, 10 per cent Cabernet Franc. (A lovely spring and good weather until late December with Cyclone Fergus producing 85 mm rain on 31 December. January and February were uncharacteristically humid, but then it all came right, with a wonderful harvest period from Easter until the final picking on 6 May.)

1994 ★★★★   *July 1999*

Medium purple–red; the fragrant, clean aromas are very much in the mainstream Awatea style, with red berries, a hint of earth and subtle oak. An elegant wine in the mouth, with good fruit flavour, and milky tannins running through the mid to back palate. Still evolving. 45 per cent Cabernet Sauvignon, 36 per cent Merlot, 19 per cent Cabernet Franc. (The 1994 vintage for Te Mata Estate was of high quality. Although cool weather in November delayed flowering a very warm and dry growing season led to intensely concentrated crops.)

1993 NR

Not tasted. Likewise made with the continuing effects of Mount Pinatubo.
(Was an unusual year, with a harvest at least three weeks later than average. Partially saved by an Indian summer.)

1992 NR

Not tasted. Made in the shadow of Mount Pinatubo, with a Cabernet-dominant blend. (The season started well with very good budbreak, but then cold November and cool December reduced the set at flowering. Thereafter, far cooler than normal, leading to a late harvest.)

1991 ★★★★★ *July 1999*

Medium to full red–purple; the bouquet is ripe, complex, with a mix of mulberry and plum fruit with fractionally gamey overtones. 56 per cent Cabernet Sauvignon, 34 per cent Merlot, 10 per cent Cabernet Franc. (The season was early, with a very hot December and the quickest flowering we have ever experienced, followed by prolonged settled weather, one quite heavy rainfall on 9–10 April and thereafter clear weather until harvest was completed on 27 April. Te Mata considers the year to be the best yet. The wines have very low pHs and quite low acids.)

1990 ★★★☆ *July 1999*

The colour is a healthy red–purple, though slightly less impressive than the '89. Slightly earthy Cabernet varietal characters drive the bouquet, the fruit being less vibrant than in the top wines. A lighter, easy, pleasant drink-now style. 72 per cent Cabernet Sauvignon, 26 per cent Merlot, 2 per cent Cabernet Franc. (Vintage was in mid-season as far as timing went, starting in late March and finishing on 3 May. Te Mata had only 30 mm of rain in April and providentially was missed by the deluges that hit Taranaki and Wanganui.)

1989 ★★★★☆ *July 1999*

Impressive, bright red–purple of medium depth. The bouquet is spotlessly clean and elegant, a masterpiece in restrained understatement, but well balanced and with a faint touch of herbs. An altogether interesting wine, which has power, length and grip not intimidated by the olive and herb flavour components. Finishes with firm tannins. 70 per cent Cabernet Sauvignon, 27 per cent Merlot, 3 per cent Cabernet Franc. (Was a dry year. The total rainfall for the 1 October to 30 April growing season was just over 110 mm. Vintage was almost a month earlier than average and finished on 31 March.)

1988 NR

Awatea made but not tasted. A less intense vintage similar to 1986. 70 per cent Cabernet Sauvignon, 13 per cent Merlot, 8 per cent Cabernet Franc. (Certainly not as bad as made out by media, who dismissed it well before harvest. Fruity, forward wines, with good colours and flavours.)

1987 ★★★ *July 1999*

Light red of medium depth; the bouquet has less sweet fruit than the wines which preceded it, and there is a touch of mint. The palate is clean, light and somewhat bony, and won't improve from here. 84 per cent Cabernet Sauvignon, 14 per cent Merlot, 2 per cent Cabernet Franc. (Very good. Low yields, intense colours and flavours with low pHs. Great cellaring wines with length and breadth of flavour. A year where rain in February enabled fruit to ripen to full maturity without dehydrating.)

1986 NR

Awatea made but not shown; the wine is pretty, but less intense. 75 per cent Cabernet Sauvignon, 25 per cent Merlot. (A year of big crops and very forward, fruity wines, with rich flavours but lacking backbone and length. Higher pHs, especially in Chardonnay. Therefore not so much wines to keep but very good current drinking.)

★★★★★ Perfect　★★★★☆ Close to perfect　★★★★ Very good　★★★☆ Expected
★★★ Short of standard　★★☆ Undeserving　★★ Decayed relic　NR No rating

1985 NR

Not tasted. 79 per cent Cabernet Sauvignon, 21 per cent Merlot. (Very good. Great balance of rain and warmth right through growing season. Wines of good colour, low pH musts and ample phenols. Elegant wines of good keeping qualities.)

1984

No Awatea made.

1983 ★★★★★   July 1999

A truly excellent colour with no browning at all. The bouquet is spotlessly clean, with lovely sweet, red berry fruit and gently sweet oak. An exceptional wine, with powerful Cabernet flavour and texture still there on the palate, and undoubted life in front of it if the cork is good and cellaring conditions likewise. 100 per cent Cabernet Sauvignon; two-thirds French oak, one-third American oak. ('El Niño'. A very dry and windy spring and a dry, dry summer and autumn. Wines of intense flavour and colour that are very slow developers.)

1982 ★★★★   July 1999

The colour is relatively light, but still with an excellent, healthy hue. The fine, fragrant and stylish bouquet has a range of cedary, cigar box and savoury fruit. Structurally holding remarkably well on the palate; although the fruit flavour is well into the secondary phase, it is still totally satisfying. 100 per cent Cabernet Sauvignon. (Very good. Early budburst, a dry spring and warm weather until late March. Heavy rain and strong winds in early April, but very clean crops and wines with good colour, fruit flavours and length.)

◀■ Not Ready   ◥ Still evolving   ▮ Prime of its life   ⌀ Drink soon   ⬭ Missed the boat

te mata coleraine 1982-1999

Standing as it does at the top of the Te Mata Estate portfolio, Coleraine has the bluest blood of all New Zealand's currently made red wines. Between 1982 and 1988 it was made from the 2-hectare Coleraine Vineyard owned by John and Wendy Buck (rather than by Te Mata itself). The vineyard is planted to cabernet sauvignon, merlot and cabernet franc, and these three varieties constitute the wine blend.

Since 1989 it has ceased to be vineyard-linked, instead being made to a style drawn from all of the associated vineyards in the Te Mata stable. That style is intended for medium to long-term cellaring, with powerful, ripe fruit, serious tannins, and cedar/tar/charry oak. It is accorded classic status by all of the leading New Zealand wine journalists, a judgment echoed by their overseas counterparts.

It typically spends between 18 and 19 months in French oak barriques, part new and part several years old, and is racked and fined before bottling, but is not filtered. The contribution of new oak, while far from dominant, is greater than it is in the Awatea — but then so are all of the aroma and flavour components.

From an international perspective, the outstanding feature of the wine is the ripeness of the tannins in all but the coolest vintages. There are none of the mouth-puckering tamarillo flavours which so bedevil many of New Zealand's Cabernet Merlot-based wines. Yet it does not veer to the other extreme: this is a wine which has been made with a gentle hand and a patient mind.

(Vintage notes in brackets from Te Mata.)

First tasted in July 1999, updated, and later vintages added.

1999 ★★★★   *April 2001*

Medium red–purple; savoury blackberry fruit blends with slightly dusty, cedary oak on the bouquet. That oak flexes its muscles throughout the palate, rather assertive and pencilly, and needing time to soften and integrate into the wine. There is good fruit there, and also tannins which should sustain the wine and give it the time it needs. (Significantly cooler than 1998; as ever, strict discipline in the vineyard was the key to success.)

1998 ★★★★★   *June 2000*

Medium to full red–purple; the complex and generous bouquet is swollen with blackcurrant, raspberry, cherry and (unexpectedly) liquorice/game aromas. The palate is richer, deeper, and more powerful than the Awatea; the balance is excellent, the tannins powerful but not overpowering. A great wine with a great future. (A drought season following a wet winter necessitating extremely careful vineyard management. Those who kept canopies intact and who bunch-thinned achieved outstanding results.)

★★★★★ Perfect   ★★★★☆ Close to perfect   ★★★★ Very good   ★★★☆ Expected
★★★ Short of standard   ★★☆ Undeserving   ★★ Decayed relic   NR No rating

381

1997 ★★★★★   *July 1999*

Appealing, bright purple–red; excellent cassis/berry/redcurrant fruit on the bouquet has just the right amount of oak in support. A mouthfilling yet not aggressive or rustic wine, with delectable redcurrant fruit flavours, finishing with soft, fine tannins. 55 per cent Cabernet Sauvignon, 30 per cent Merlot, 15 per cent Cabernet Franc. (A mixed year, requiring bunch-thinning of an already small crop, with a warm and humid February and March. Another Indian summer produced small crops of high quality.)

1996 ★★★☆   *July 1999*

Light to medium red–purple; light, scented red fruit is accompanied by more earthy/herbaceous characters. The palate offers more substance and sweetness than the bouquet would suggest (and certainly more than Awatea), making a nice wine for relatively early drinking. 53 per cent Cabernet Sauvignon, 33 per cent Merlot, 14 per cent Cabernet Franc. (The growing season in vintage 1996 was a mixture with above-average rainfall and below-average heat.) Te Mata regards the wines as aromatic, soft and appealing, forward and accessible in style, reminiscent of the 1990 vintage. I concur.

1995 ★★★★★   *July 1999*

Strong red–purple; complex and concentrated aromas of ripe plum and mulberry fruit with a web of subtle oak introduce a powerful but youthful wine; the tannins are better balanced that those of the Awatea of the same vintage. Still a baby. 59 per cent Cabernet Sauvignon, 34 per cent Merlot, 7 per cent Cabernet Franc. (A lovely spring and good weather until late December with Cyclone Fergus producing 85 mm rain on 31 December. January and February were uncharacteristically humid, but then it all came right, with a wonderful harvest period from Easter until the final picking on 6 May.)

1994 ★★★★   *July 1999*

Medium red–purple; the moderately intense, clean bouquet has attractively ripe fruit with just a touch of earthy cabernet bite. The palate is fresh, clean and lively, although there is a faintly green/earthy touch on the finish and aftertaste. 74 per cent Cabernet Sauvignon, 9 per cent Merlot, 17 per cent Cabernet Franc. (The 1994 vintage for Te Mata Estate was of high quality. Although cool weather in November delayed flowering a very warm and dry growing season led to intensely concentrated crops.)

1993

Not made. (An even later vintage than 1992, thanks to the continuing effect of the Mount Pinatubo eruption. Partially saved by an Indian summer. Coleraine not made; Awatea was.)

1992

Not made. (The first of the Mount Pinatubo vintages, far cooler than normal, leading to a late harvest. No Coleraine made, although Awatea was.)

Not Ready   Still evolving   Prime of its life   Drink soon   Missed the boat

1991 ★★★★★   *July 1999*

Medium to full red–purple; a robust, rich, slightly rustic bouquet with ripe fruit and earthy/charry oak. The palate is rich and full, with masses of ripe blackberry and blackcurrant fruit matched with positive tannins. Good structure, long future. 59 per cent Cabernet Sauvignon, 29 per cent Merlot, 12 per cent Cabernet Franc. (The season was early, with a very hot December and the quickest flowering, followed by prolonged settled weather, one quite heavy rainfall on 9–10 April and thereafter clear weather until harvest was completed on 27 April. Te Mata considers the year to be the best yet.)

1990 ★★★   *July 1999*

Light to medium red–purple; the bouquet is very light and fresh, but tending simple. The palate, likewise, is pleasant but simple; easy drinking, but lacks the distinction of the best wines. 54 per cent Cabernet Sauvignon, 36 per cent Merlot, 10 per cent Cabernet Franc. (Vintage was in mid-season as far as timing went, starting in late March and finishing on 3 May. Te Mata had only 30 mm of rain in April and providentially were missed by the deluges that hit Taranaki and Wanganui.)

1989 ★★★★★   *July 1999*

Medium red–purple; a stylish and elegant bouquet; there is a touch of olive and herb here, but it doesn't detract. A lovely palate, very polished and balanced; gently savoury flavours are rounded off with soft, ripe, fine tannins. 54 per cent Cabernet Sauvignon, 37 per cent Merlot, 9 per cent Cabernet Franc. (Was a dry year. The total rainfall for the 1 October to 30 April growing season was just over 110 mm. Vintage was almost a month earlier than average and finished on 31 March.)

1988 NR

Not tasted, although made. 75 per cent Cabernet Sauvignon, 22 per cent Merlot, 3 per cent Cabernet Franc.

1987 NR

Not tasted, although made. 78 per cent Cabernet Sauvignon, 19 per cent Merlot, 3 per cent Cabernet Franc. (Very good. Low yields, intense colours and flavours with low pHs. Great cellaring wines with length and breadth of flavour. A year where rain in February enabled fruit to ripen to full maturity without dehydrating.)

1986 NR

Not tasted, although made. 73 per cent Cabernet Sauvignon, 24 per cent Merlot, 3 per cent Cabernet Franc. (A year of big crops and very forward, fruity wines, with rich flavours but lacking backbone and length. Higher pHs, especially in Chardonnay. Therefore not so much wines to keep but very good current drinking.)

1985 ★★★   *July 1999*

Medium red–purple; a sweet bouquet with slightly dusty/musty aspects and some slightly coarse caramel aromas probably deriving from the oak. The palate has slightly cooked flavours; all in all, decidedly off the pace, but I feel this was not a typical bottle. Marked as tasted. 72 per cent Cabernet Sauvignon, 25 per cent Merlot, 3 per cent Cabernet Franc. (Very good. Great balance of rain and warmth right through growing season. Wines of good colour, low pH musts and ample phenols. Elegant wines of good keeping qualities.)

★★★★★ Perfect	★★★★☆ Close to perfect	★★★★ Very good	★★★☆ Expected
★★★ Short of standard	★★☆ Undeserving	★★ Decayed relic	NR No rating

classic wines

1984 NR
Not tasted, but made. 83 per cent Cabernet Sauvignon, 15 per cent Merlot, 2 per cent Cabernet Franc. (Cool spring, summer. Late budburst and harvest. Elegant wines, lacking a little weight in Chardonnays and reds but elegant Sauvignon Blancs.)

1983 ★★★★ July 1999
Outstanding colour for a wine of this age, still retaining its bright red–purple hue. The bouquet is likewise youthful, but does seems slightly closed. Powerful, ripe and sweet fruit comes through on the palate, followed by a slightly sharp twist on the finish. There was much debate about the bottle; rated as it presented itself. 75 per cent Cabernet Sauvignon, 22 per cent Merlot, 3 per cent Cabernet Franc. ('El Niño'. A very dry and windy spring and a dry, dry summer and autumn. Wines of intense flavour and colour that are very slow developers.)

1982 ★★★★ July 1999
Light to medium red; the bouquet still retains some freshness, with a mix of light mint and more savoury aromas. A regal old wine on the palate, with well-balanced savoury flavours and fine tannins. Just starting the slide down the other side, but still very attractive, although (surprisingly, perhaps) with less sweet fruit than Awatea of the same vintage. 94 per cent Cabernet Sauvignon, 6 per cent Merlot. (Very good. Early budburst, a dry spring and warm weather until late March. Heavy rain and strong winds in early April, but very clean crops and wines with good colour, fruit flavours and length.) °

◄ Not Ready   ＼ Still evolving   ▮ Prime of its life   ✎ Drink soon   ▯ Missed the boat

villa maria reserve barrique fermented chardonnay 1989-2000

all the New Zealand-based wine writers and commentators have no hesitation in placing Villa Maria Reserve Chardonnay in the classic category. I am more than happy to follow suit, because this wine has always represented — indeed magnified — the core of mainstream Chardonnay style. I do, however, take leave to question whether this wine has the longevity ascribed to it by some wine writers.

Its reflection of style is evident in this tasting: a continuing move towards elegance and away from the heavily oaked, over-the-top wines of the late 1980s and early '90s. The moveable geographic base for the wine is also interesting, emphasising that this is very much the winemaker's choice of the best Chardonnay of the year, irrespective of its origin. While there are many parallels in Australia, this type of approach is relatively uncommon in New Zealand.

First tasted in March 1998, updated, and later vintages added.

2000 Gisborne ★★★★ *May 2001*
Medium to full yellow–green; clean, ripe melon and stonefruit aromas are balanced with controlled oak on the bouquet; at this early stage, the palate is still coming together, the fruit delicate, the oak assertive. Given a year or so, the rating may seem harsh.

1999
Not made.

1998 Gisborne ★★★☆ *January 2000*
Medium yellow–green; extremely spicy/dusty oak utterly overwhelms the fruit on the bouquet, and achieves much the same on the palate, where some fruit can be perceived. The points may seem extreme, particularly given the rating I accorded the '97 vintage, but there really is no halfway point with a wine such as this. You will either love it or hate it.

1997 Marlborough/Hawke's Bay ★★★★★ *March 1998*
Light to medium yellow–green; the bouquet is of medium intensity, with pleasant citrus and melon fruit. The new oak component is a fraction obvious, but should settle down with a year or two in bottle. All of the components are well balanced and well integrated on the palate, featuring citrus, mineral, nectarine and apple fruit. Stylish and elegant.

classic wines

★★★★★ Perfect ★★★★☆ Close to perfect ★★★★ Very good ★★★☆ Expected
★★★ Short of standard ★★☆ Undeserving ★★ Decayed relic NR No rating

385

1996 Hawke's Bay/Gisborne ★★★★★   *March 1998*
Significantly lighter in depth than the earlier vintages. The bouquet is complex, running through nutty malolactic and barrel-ferment fruit aromas underpinned by more mineral characters; on the palate a refreshingly fruit-driven wine with well-above-average intensity and length, and seemingly relatively little malolactic-fermentation characters. At the very end the nectarine fruit moved more towards grapefruit, adding a splash of excitement to the finish.

1995 Gisborne ★★★★   *March 1998*
Medium to full yellow–green, showing the rapid colour shift of so many New Zealand Chardonnays. The bouquet has ripe, smooth peachy fruit, some solids fermentation characters (attractive) and a light coating of vanilla oak. A wine which changed significantly in the glass, with slightly splintery oak evident at first, but the well-weighted, sweet fruit gradually asserted itself, particularly on the relatively long finish.

1994 Gisborne/Hawke's Bay ★★★★☆   *March 1998*
Medium to full yellow–green; the multifaceted bouquet is clean and solid with ripe peach, toasty oak, mineral and citrus components progressively revealing themselves. While not a heavyweight (mercifully) has structure, length and grip on the palate, which is still tight and finishes with sustaining acidity.

1993 Auckland ★★☆   *March 1998*
Full yellow colour, again very advanced for age. The bouquet is complex with an echo of solids fermentation or similar characters; also skin contact/botrytis characters. The palate is entirely at odds with the reputation of the vintage, with rough edges and phenolic break-up. Quite possibly an aberrationally poor bottle.

1992 Gisborne ★★★   *March 1998*
Over-the-top yellow–orange colour for such a relatively young wine. Botrytis-influenced peach and honey aromas have some dusty, maderised aspects; a wine which is hanging on by its fingernails on the palate, still with some honeyed peachy fruit. The oak phenolics are obtrusive, and will become more so as the wine ages.

1991 Gisborne ★★★☆   *March 1998*
Full yellow–orange; the bouquet is of medium to full intensity, with tangy, peachy fruit veering towards marmalade. There is some life still left in the palate, aided by a nice twist of acidity on the finish which does not fully disguise the slightly hollow mid-palate.

1989 Gisborne ★★★   *March 1998*
Deep orange–yellow; the bouquet has strongly modified aromas, part bottle aged and part botrytis, producing jammy marmalade and peach characters. The palate is like a dry botrytis wine, not unpleasant, but with preserved orange peel characters virtually unrecognisable as Chardonnay.

◄■ Not Ready   ◣ Still evolving   ▮ Prime of its life   ◢ Drink soon   ▯ Missed the boat